Islamism in Morocco

ISLAMISM IN MOROCCO

Religion, Authoritarianism, and Electoral Politics

MALIKA ZEGHAL

Translated by George Holoch

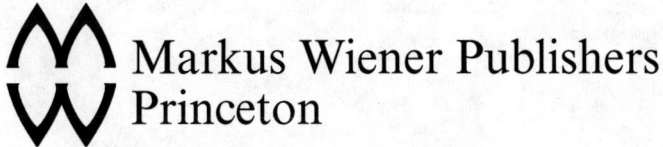

Markus Wiener Publishers
Princeton

The translation of this work was supported by a grant from "French Voices" in partnership with the PEN American Center.

Cet ouvrage, publié dans le cadre d'un programme d'aide à la publication, bénéficie du soutien financier du ministère des Affaires étrangères et du Service culturel de l'ambassade de France aux Etats-Unis.
(This work, published as part of a program providing publication assistance, received financial support from the French Ministry of Foreign Affairs and the Cultural Services of the French Embassy in the United States.)

Copyright © 2008 by Markus Wiener Publishers for the English translation
Copyright © 2008 by Malika Zeghal for the Introduction and Epilogue

Copyright © 2005 by Éditions La Découverte, Paris, for the French edition, entitled *Les Islamistes Marocains: Le Défi à la Monarchie*

All rights reserved. No part of this book may be reproduced or transmitted in any form or by any means, whether electronic or mechanical—including photocopying or recording—or through any information storage or retrieval system, without permission of the copyright owners.

For information, write to Markus Wiener Publishers
231 Nassau Street, Princeton, NJ 08542
www.markuswiener.com

Zeghal, Malika.
 Islamism in Morocco : religion, authoritarianism, and electoral politics / Malika Zeghal.
   p. cm.
 Includes bibliographical references and index.
 ISBN 978-1-55876-442-2 (hardcover : alk. paper)
 ISBN 978-1-55876-443-9 (pbk : alk. paper)
  1. Islam and politics—Morocco. 2. Morocco—Politics and government—1961-1999. 3. Morocco—Politics and government—1999-
I. Title.
BP64.M613Z44 2008
320.964—dc22   2008008335

Markus Wiener Publishers books are printed in the United States of America on acid-free paper and meet the guidelines for permanence and durability of the Committee on Production Guidelines for Book Longevity of the Council on Library Resources.

CONTENTS

Acknowledgments vii
A Note on Transliteration and Spelling ix

Introduction xi

Part I. The Monarchy, the 'Ulama, and Islam 1

Chapter 1. 'Ulama and Power in Independent Morocco 9
Chapter 2. The Monarchy, Mirror of a Fragmented
    Religious Sphere 31
Chapter 3. Conservative Nationalism and Islam 61

Part II. A Rebel Mystic: Abdessalam Yassine 77

Chapter 4. The "Conversion" of Sheikh Yassine 83
Chapter 5. Styles and Figures of Admonition 95
Chapter 6. Justice and Benevolence: Between Mystic
    Community and Political Leadership 119

Part III. The Desacralization of the Monarchy? 143

Chapter 7. The Moroccan Political Regime Confronts
    Islamic Opposition: From Exclusion to Partial Inclusion 155
Chapter 8. Theology and Politics: Differentiated Repertoires 187
Chapter 9. The Commander of the Faithful and
    His Religious Competitors 209
Chapter 10. Redefining the Institution of the Commander
    of the Faithful 231

Epilogue: The Disenchantments of Free Choice 259

Notes 271
Glossary 311
Bibliography 315
Index 329

ACKNOWLEDGMENTS

This book is the revised and updated translation of *Les islamistes marocain: Le défi à la monarchie*, which was published in French by La Découverte in 2005.

Many friends and colleagues have contributed to the various stages of this work. The people I interviewed in Rabat, Casablanca, and Fez were extremely generous with their time and knowledge. I am grateful to them for responding patiently to all my questions.

I am particularly indebted to Mohamed and Yasmina Naciri for their generosity: their friendship has made it possible for this book to come into being in the first place. Scholars and friends have read and generously commented on the earlier versions of the work, and their feedback has been immensely helpful. I would particularly like to mention François Gèze for his rigorous and constructive comments on the French version. I would also like to express my gratitude to John Bowen, Mounia Bennani-Chraïbi, Mark Davis, Philippe Droz-Vincent, Dale Eickelman, Nilüfer Göle, Abdellah Hammoudi, Danièle Hervieu-Léger, Gudrun Krämer, Mary Sue Kranstover, Jean Leca, Rémy Leveau, Khadija Mohsen-Finan, Mohamed Naciri, Enzo Pace, Martin Riesebrodt, Richard Rosengarten, Noah Salomon, Michael Sells, and Lucette Valensi. Students in Paris and Chicago have also played an important role in the development of the ideas presented in this work through our discussions during classes and seminars, first at the Ecole des Hautes Etudes en Sciences Sociales and later at the University of Chicago's Divinity School. I am particularly grateful to Samir Amghar, Amel Boubakeur, Stéphane Lacroix, and Abdellah Tourabi.

My research assistants, Elizabeth Kevern, Lauren Osborne, and Ayse Polat, have also contributed to this book through their first-rate work. I am also grateful to the translator, George Holoch, for such an intellectually rewarding collaborative experience. Janet Stern, from Markus Wiener Publishers, has copyedited the text with great care, and Delphine Ribouchon, from La Découverte, helped this English version come to life through her wise council.

Hédi, Marwan, and Kenz Kallal have patiently accepted my traveling for long periods of time. Without their encouragements and their affection, I could never have written this book.

A NOTE ON TRANSLITERATION AND SPELLING

With the exception of the ' to signify the Arabic letter *'ayn* (as in 'ulama or bay'a) and ' to represent the *hamza* (as in Qur'an), diacritics are not used in this book. The *hamza* itself is only used when it occurs within a word (as in Qur'an) but not when it occurs at the end (hence 'ulama and not 'ulama'). With the notable exception of 'ulama (singular: 'alim), I indicate the plural form by adding an *s* to the word in the singular, as in fatwas.

The spelling of Arabic words and names follows the conventions of the *International Journal of Middle East Studies*, unless words are spelled in their dialect form (such as fqih). The most familiar proper names (for example, Hassan II, Nasser, Boumedienne, Abdessalam Yassine) are spelled following conventional usage.

INTRODUCTION

In recent years, Islamist legal political parties have experienced significant electoral success in the Middle East. These political parties are the offspring of Islamist movements, which developed in the late 1960s and base their political activism and goals on Islamic vocabulary and ideas. This transformation of Islamist movements into political parties has thrust several questions to the fore: should they be excluded from public life or integrated into the functioning of the political regimes of the Middle East? If a pluralistic system of political competition is opened to them, would they use it? And how? If they were to win elections and govern, would they play by the rules of the pluralistic procedures of such a system? Once immersed in *realpolitik*, would they abandon their religious rhetoric? Should governments negotiate with them the conditions of their participation in political competition? This book examines these questions with regard to Morocco by looking at the relationship between the use of religious language in the political domain on the one hand and state design and transformation of political and religious institutions on the other hand.

In the mid 1990s, King Hassan II liberalized the Moroccan political system, which has now stabilized into a regime that combines authoritarianism with electoral competition. It is a multiparty regime in which—contrary to past electoral practices—legislative elections reflect the choices of the citizens but the government still remains under the control of the monarchy.[1] How has this institutional transformation in the domain of politics affected the language, the ideology, and the political programs of Islamists? This question can be answered only if the Islamists are understood within a larger context, historically and politically. Their strategies and discourses are shaped by other major political actors engaged with Islam- mainly the 'ulama (religious scholars) and the monarchy—within the larger framework and constraints of Moroccan religious institutions. As the founder of an authoritarian modern state, the post-colonial Moroccan monarchy has strived to appropriate Islamic language and institutions and has given them a content and a form that have strongly influenced the shape of Islamist movements along with their ideologies.

Therefore, in Morocco as well as in other countries of the Middle East, Islamists do not necessarily define their ideologies and claims against their states by using a language different from that of the state itself. Indeed, Islamists and state elites are not in dissonant states of mind regarding the public presence of Islam: both groups want the religion present in the public space and both seek to define a public Islam. All of them characterize their society as a "community of believers." However, they differ on the issue of who should define public Islam, whether its presence should be circumscribed or enlarged, and, if so, how and in what form. The evolution of the Islamist movements must therefore be analyzed in relation to the mechanisms of appropriation and regulation of religion by the post-colonial authoritarian state, which has not defined itself or the society it governs in secular terms and has made Islam the state religion.[2] Hence, there is no reason why Islamist movements, once integrated into legal politics, should abandon or tone down their religious rhetoric, unless they are coerced to do so. This book demonstrates that when Islamists abandon portions of their religious arguments, they do so under the constraints imposed by the state, and not necessarily because they are led away from religious definitions of politics by their integration into the processes of legal political competition.

More generally, the Moroccan case also shows that the connection between Islam and the state, as well as the delimitation of secular spaces for political activity, is a political construct strategically devised by post-colonial state elites. Authoritarian politics, regime type, and the long history of Islam in Morocco give this overlap a particular institutional shape and specific cultural contents that also have partially determined the idioms used by Islamist groups to articulate their political claims. The overlap between state and religion is also contentious, and different actors may discuss and criticize it whenever they are given the opportunity to do so. Islamism must not, therefore, be deemed as having emerged in opposition to the "secularism" of the state, since the state neither preaches secularism as the norm organizing the state and society nor defines itself in secular terms. Instead, the state insists on its own religious interpretations to articulate its identity and that of its subjects. When the state insists on the necessity of a separation between religion and political activity, it does so in order to ensure its own monopoly on Islam in the sphere of political competition. Islamism, rather than being the ideology of Islamists only, is therefore the product of the accrued competition between Islamists and the state around the understanding of Islam: Islamists question the monopoly of the state over the meaning of the faith and its implementation in the public space. Often, these state definitions have been created and disseminated with the help of the 'ulama, the religious specialists educated in religious institutions of learning who are bearers of Islamic knowledge (*'ilm*). Because the state has co-opted, weakened, and conferred precise institutional roles to the 'ulama, I include the latter in the description of this process of competition for the definition and dissemination of religious meanings. The 'ulama play ambiguous and flexible roles vis-à-vis the monarchy and today take political positions ranging from quietism to more vocal dissent that converges with Islamists. In this sense, the state, as well as the 'ulama and the Islamists, are all actors who participate in the world of political Islam and the debate over its form and content.

The Moroccan King: Prophetic Lineage and Political Sacredness

The Moroccan political system is an authoritarian constitutional monarchy that is tightly linked to Islam. The king, also called "commander of the faithful" (*amir al-mu'minin*), a status inscribed in the Constitution since 1962, claims descent from the prophet (he is, in Arabic, a *sharif*). He has a political function, maintained through his monopoly on the state and on the means of coercion, and a religious function, enhanced by his prophetic lineage: he is the guardian of Moroccan Islam and the political leader of a community of believers. This combination of the guardianship of the religion with the leadership of the community of the faithful implies that the king can legitimately mobilize Islam—and the 'ulama who interpret it—in order to define some of the legal, political, and moral norms that govern the nation.

The King's title denotes proximity among the monarch, his people, and Islam and conjures a fusion between faith, nation, and political sovereignty, as inscribed in the Kingdom's motto: "God, the fatherland, the King." However, this fusion between the sovereign, the people, and religion is a historically constructed political fiction that might become contested, albeit one that has had great mobilizing and legitimizing power.

In the early twentieth century, following the French occupation of Morocco in 1912 and the French colonial elites' appropriation of the reins of government, a clear separation emerged between the person of the Sultan and the government.[3] The Sultan lost *de facto* a political sovereignty that was already highly unstable and did not cover a vast territory. However, the French authorities also gave him religious prerogatives that he then used politically, especially when, at the end of the 1940s, he offered his support to the nationalist cause. It was after 1956, the year of Morocco's independence, that the king progressively activated these dual powers around his person and strove to simultaneously monopolize them. Also after independence, the sacred character of the monarch was inscribed in the Moroccan constitution. To this day, his "person" is constitutionally described as "sacred" (*muqaddas*) and constitutes an inviolable entity (*la tuntahak hurmatuhu*). In the constitution, the inviolability of the person of the king is described in an article separate from the one that hails him as the commander of the faithful. Hence, his sacredness is not characterized exclusively on religious terms: it first and foremost sets the king apart from the ordinary citizens. He is politically sacred and above the law. The use of the word *hurma* imparts to the monarchy an essentially sacred character, which is denoted by the Arab root *h-r-m*. The *haram* is the sacred territory to which access is prohibited. It has a purifying character for those who penetrate it. To penetrate it is also to access a space different from that of ordinary, everyday life. The *haram* is therefore potentially dangerous. It is only approachable in certain conditions, like the *haram* of Mecca or the wives' *harem*. It has to be penetrated with care and with reverence towards the most powerful person who occupies it. To this day, the king is approached by Moroccans with a mix of respect and fear (*hayba* in Arabic).

Since independence, the Moroccan monarchs have situated themselves as the arbiters of the political game, above political actors, whom they have divided in order to rule. They used the same strategy of division with religious actors. Kings Muhammad V and Hassan II divided, under their tight control, the Islamic sphere of religious authorities (and the 'ulama) into fragments that were supposed to support the monarchy, defined as the central religious institution. Both kings structured the monarchy as the most important religious actor, a claim they substantiated by securing the support of institutional networks such as the Ministry of Religious Affairs, mosques put under the surveillance of government agents, and public schools and higher education programs that disseminated authoritatively official religious interpretations. However, within these networks that it regulated, the monarchical state never had total hegemony over the definition of Islam. Thus, the 'ulama, working as mosque imams, interpreters of the doctrine, and educators, negotiated their roles depending on the circumstances. They produced varieties of implicit dissent that also were appropriated and more vocally articulated by Islamists in the 1980s. The analysis of Islamism as a political movement founded on the ideas and vocabulary provided by Islam, therefore, cannot ignore the monarchy and its institutional definition and regulation of Islam. Indeed, the monarchy formed a religious identity for itself and shaped the religious landscape in ways that have impinged on the Islamist movement's ideologies and outlook. This is why Islamist movements present similarities with the monarchy and with official 'ulama in some of their religious interpretations and a degree of proximity to Islamic state institutions.

What Is a Religious Institution?

A religious institution is a set of humanly devised constraints that shape the interaction between this world and the divine, or, in other words, a structure of mediation between this world and the other world, whose members give the interpretation of scriptures to people.[4] Most of the literature on contemporary Islamist movements has neglected the analysis of religious institutions.[5] This book argues that Muslim religious institutions—such as schools of religious learning, offices producing fatwas, ministries of religious affairs and pious endowments—and their religious professionals, the 'ulama, must be considered in order for us to understand the shape and history of these movements.

There is no clergy in the doctrine of Sunni Islam, which gives neither definition of nor prescription for a religious institution.[6] The power to interpret the religious texts may be granted to anyone who is recognized by a given group of people for his piety and knowledge. Theoretically, there is no official authority who can hold a monopoly on religious interpretation. Why, then, do religious institutions exist in the Muslim countries of the Middle East?[7] It is precisely because the Qur'an does not say anything about a religious institution that the embodiment of a religious authority becomes a political stake. The absence of a definition of a religious establishment renders the very notion of religious authority unstable and creates a fierce competition for the acquisition and control of this authority. This instability represents a dangerous threat to any type of political regime, democratic or authoritarian, which can be the object of criticisms by those who can stand up to it on religious grounds.[8] This is why the control of religious interpretation—the devising of state mechanisms of authorization—and, therefore, the building, design, and regulation of a religious institution, are so crucial to a government that needs to secure its control of state and society. "Control" means much more than the authoritarian coercion of religious specialists into following the religious discourse of the regime. It also involves the constant work of reshaping and readjusting the structures of mediation that define the relations between the believers and the religious authorities. This kind of work is done, for instance, when state authorities differentiate between religious functions such as the guidance of the believers regarding rituals, knowledge, or political ideas. More generally, this control involves the authorization or prohibition of religious definitions in particular institutional arrangements: public schools, mosques, and legal courts, but also in electoral politics. This is how an authoritarian government regulates and attempts to keep under its control religious entrepreneurs who, in contrast, would like to defend their independence and autonomy from the state. However, the religious institution is not only a site from which political authority can be imposed. Even if state authorities design it in order to tame potential and real religious opposition, it can also become a contested space. It operates as an intermediate space between state and society for articulating, receiving, and circulating religious ideas, and it provides common as well as competing frames for interpretation and action. Religious institutions are receptacles and transformers of religious ideas, and the ways in which they have been designed have an impact on the meanings that they produce. They lend force and authority to religious interpretations that can compel obedience as well as engender innovation and dissent. They function as part of the state structure, but they also constrain state actions and ideologies and are often used by non-state actors outside of and in opposition to state control.

In post-colonial Morocco, the monarchy has conferred a particular shape to the religious institution, maintaining some of its old features while introducing new ones. The monarchy devised this shape strategically through its relationships with 'ulama, and depending on its own political needs. The mechanism of religious regulation deployed by the monarchy made use of two elements: the centrality of the monarchy and a fragmented set of religious institutions. This hybrid mechanism combining personal charisma and institutional control through fragmentation was not easy to maintain and regulate. Its complexities made it unstable from the start. Once the pressures for political participation emerged from society and in opposition to the authoritarian power of the palace in the 1990s, the fragments of this religious mechanism ceased to support the religious centrality of the monarchy.

To understand the increasing instability of this mechanism of religious regulation by the state at the end of the twentieth century, I intend to examine religious institutions as designed and regulated by post-colonial state elites. Such an in-depth description of the design and functioning of these institutions helps reveal the difficulties the monarchy confronts in acting as the central religious institution, as well as the deep continuity between the state and Islamist movements, a continuity that has been in great part ensured by the mediation of the state-sponsored religious institution itself. I examine the recent history of this institutional structure, which produces official religious discourses that belong not just to the state and do not necessarily always succeed in imposing state hegemony on the definition of a public Islam. As we will see, these discourses circulate widely and are appropriated by non-state actors who relate them to other sources of religious legitimacy and narratives. These discourses might echo and amplify the state-sponsored definitions of Islam or transform and resist them by offering counter-definitions.

Hence, this book is concerned with the interaction between institutions and ideas, the political consequences of post-colonial state regulation of Islam and religious institutions, and, starting in the 1990s, the partial withdrawal of the state from the political sphere of deliberation and from the institutional religious structures created or rearranged by the state after independence. In order to understand Islamism and Islamist politics, it is necessary to include an analysis of the state, its uses and interpretations of Islam, and its shaping and regulation of religious institutions. Islamist movements are often explained as a "revenge of society against the state,"[9] and as the expression of the new strength of "civil society" developing out of and against the realm of the state. In this regard, the existing literature on social movements and political opposition stresses the importance of political mobilization processes against the state in explaining the emergence and the nature of Islamist movements.[10] However, this book underscores the fact that many (but not necessarily all) of these movements must also be understood as by-products of state policies and in conjunction with discourses on Islam disseminated by both the state elites and the 'ulama.

The Legalized Islamist Party, the Islamic State, and Secular Politics

Three types of Islamist movements have developed in Morocco and have built different relationships with the monarchy. First were the Qutbists, who wanted to eliminate secularist intellectuals and destroy the state. The Qutbist movement was harshly repressed, and most of the remainder of its adherents converted to legal political action in the 1990s. Second was Abdessalam Yassine's movement: it employs Sufi and messianic narratives that borrow from the monarchy's vocabulary and structures, as well as from themes from Morocco's long religious history. This Sufi type of opposition recently has been weakened by a third type of Islamism, represented by the Party of Justice and Development (PJD), which finds some of its ideological origins in nineteenth-century Morocco and has emerged in the political arena with new visibility thanks to the strategy of the monarchy.

In the mid 1990s, Hassan II liberalized the functioning of the political regime and allowed the integration into the legal system of political competition a new Islamist political party, the PJD. Like many Islamist parties in the Muslim world, the PJD exhibits innovative features. Its members pragmatically accept the legal system as defined by the monarchy and, by extension, the limits of the process of political liberalization. Its ideology is close to the political discourse of the mainstream Muslim Brothers in other Arab countries such as Egypt and Jordan. However, this *frériste* dimension also deeply resonates with themes developed by Moroccan Salafi and nationalist 'ulama before and after independence.[11] The PJD's leaders want to build a religiously virtuous public through legal political and social activism. According to them, this society, thanks to its piety, will be able to be civically and politically virtuous. However, contrary to the 'ulama, to whom they do not recognize their intellectual debt, the PJD's Islamists want to participate in imperfect political procedures of competition as conceived by the existing system in order to eventually become part of a government. They also articulate demands for these procedures' improvement. They focus on local and associative political work in proximity to their electorate. They show pragmatism and patience in their political endeavors.

Like Palestinian Hamas, the Turkish AKP, or even a quasi-party like the Egyptian Muslim Brothers, the PJD has had important electoral successes. However, even if it accepts the political system, it is not set on a unique interpretation of what "the Islamic state" should be. There are tensions between the different conceptions of political Islam that are deployed by PJD activists and intellectuals in different political spaces. In the legal institutional spaces of deliberation, these Islamists do not put forward the idea of an Islamic state. The parliamentary members of the young PJD act and talk as if the Islamic state had already been established or as if it did not matter, at least for now. What they strive for within the boundaries of parliamentary discussions are experimentation with and respect for democratic procedures by all participants. Having entered into a vertical pact with the monarchy and accepted the rules of the game in exchange for their political participation, these ambitious and pragmatic Islamists have also defined, through a horizontal pact, the possibility of a political debate with other participants in the political society. Unlike older opposition parties, the PJD focuses on the procedures for competition and their implementation: electoral democracy is an instrument that they take seriously.

However, in political spaces outside the institutionalized sphere of political competition, the PJD members forcefully deploy the idea of creating an Islamic State. Thus, their integration into the legal system of competition does not lead them to abandon outside of the parliament the grand narrative of the Islamic state. The fact that they accept the rules dictated by the state in order to participate in political competition does not necessarily distance them from the religious ideas that serve as the foundation for the political community. They take full advantage of the legal procedures of competition and at the same time continue to envision a community of pious citizens and the necessary presence of Islam in the public sphere.

Indeed, these legalized Islamists question the old Qutbist revolutionary Islamic model, but they do not want to appear as being co-opted and domesticated by the monarchy. By taking seriously the democratic procedures in the legal and institutionalized spaces of political deliberation, the Islamist legal party questions the government on its policies, shows its desire to deliberate with its potential allies and competitors (the parties from the left or the right), and does not want to be seen in a position of "servitude" towards the monarchy. As for the monarchy, it defines and imposes on the legalized Islamists secular spaces into which religion cannot be integrated, except by the monarchy itself. These areligious spaces are delimited by the monarchy to circumscribe the usages of religious language by Islamists. In that sense, the Moroccan monarchy is a state that defines itself "Islamically" but uses secularist strategies–the delimitation of specific spaces where religion cannot find its place, be articulated, or be publicly visible—in order to protect and strengthen its own religious and political status.

One can go even further: once political competition opens up, it is precisely because the monarchy is identified in part with Islam that it needs to demarcate the space of legal competition secularly if it wants to protect the religious status it has created for itself. Indeed, the space that the monarchy particularly protects from religious references is that of parliamentary deliberation, where the Islamists' political claims based on religious arguments or lines of reasoning are not authorized. It is in allowing them to penetrate this secular space, in which they have to avoid using religious vocabulary, that the king has attempted to subjugate them. This endeavor has not necessarily succeeded, given the important popular appeal of the PJD and its anchorage in society through its associative and charitable work. However, this state strategy demonstrates that states built explicitly around a religious identity exclude religious actors and ideas from certain public spaces, just as secular liberal democracies do, albeit using different languages.[12] Indeed, like secular democracies, these states are confronted with what they consider a problematic phenomenon: the claim made by religious actors that they be allowed to intervene in the public sphere and their desire to be recognized and to partake in the definition of the "common good."

Religious actors indeed use and reshape religious language and meaning in the political arena: they are often able to reproduce and maintain what Talal Asad has defined as "discursive traditions."[13] In Morocco, however, as in much of the Arab world, the state seems to be the most potent actor in this regard, since it is able to maintain and make use of specific religious discursive traditions. However, the presence and involvement of religious and political state institutions in defining the public place of religion might also cause the dislocations of discursive traditions when the rules determined by these institutions force non-state actors playing their part on the political scene to disseminate religious language as fragments rather than as what is perceived as the continuous line of a discursive tradition.

This book is interested in the production, circulation, and uses of religious ideas when mobilized by state and non-state actors for purposes of political competition, control, dissent, and obedience. It is therefore interested in the supply side of the "religious economy." Religious arguments are deployed and disseminated by state and non-state actors and follow the lines demarcated by the constraints and opportunities provided by history and institutional power. The religious and political competitors of the state share with it a number of religious themes, but they all combine, interpret, and perform them for different purposes, with different styles, and from different locations. This differentiation is in part linked to the fact that the opportunity to produce and disseminate specific interpretations is not given equally to all. The state has been able to define a large Islamic repertoire[14] for itself—probably the most diverse repertoire of all religious actors in Morocco. Therefore, it does not have to pay the cost of "conversion" from one interpretation of Islam to another because it can mobilize a large number of them thanks to its religiously defined history and to its religious institutions. However, while the state's authoritarianism has enabled its religious institutions to impose some of its definitions on the Moroccan public, this process has also been hindered by internal contradictions within state interpretations of Islam and by the utilization and transformation of state formulations of Islam by religious competitors.

Sufism and Salafism: Two Politically Relevant Narratives

In the history of modern Morocco, Sufism and Salafism define two salient and sometimes overlapping elements at play in the political use of Islam by state and non-state actors. They are related to two different conceptions of authority and representation. Indeed, Sufism and Salafism are politically mobilized because they represent two distinct historically and politically meaningful models of authority:[15] the power of genealogical charisma and the power of the community of believers. They involve much more than just political models, as they also touch upon doctrinal matters, rituals, body techniques, and more. However, this book is particularly concerned with the political mobilization of these two paradigms, their interpretation, and their public performances in Morocco.

The debate between Sufism and Salafism as it has played out in Morocco since the nineteenth century is politically relevant because it revolves around the integrated questions of human mediation and political representation. The political mobilization of Sufism has produced a model for obedience as well as one for dissent and rebellion when power relations are molded in the structures of the mystic brotherhood and saintly cult. Sufi collective structures make explicit use of this model, and the monarchy has implicitly reproduced it in regard to its own political and religious sacredness. The master-disciple relationship offers a way (*tariqa*) towards the divine through a relationship of obedience and servitude. Sufi brotherhoods, the 'ulama who belong to them, as well as the monarchy itself employ this paradigm alongside sharifism and genealogical and prophetic charisma.

In the case of the monarchy, an implicit sainthood is at play regarding the king. While he is certainly not a saint, the model of master-disciple shapes the relationships between the king and his subjects, as anthropologist Abdellah Hammoudi has shown, prompting political quietism and even a culture of servitude.[16] The Sufi paradigm might also be used for dissent against the cult of the monarch, as demonstrated by Yassine's rebellion, which I analyze in the second part of this book. In these different mobilizations of Sufism combined with saintly cult, human mediation—and therefore obedience or rebellion vis-à-vis the "mediator"—is the crucial pivot around which the vision of the political community hinges. Personal religious power is at the heart of this model of communal obedience. The combined paradigms of Sufism and sainthood have been successfully used and embodied as a "tradition" by the monarchy.

In contrast, Salafism presents a different model for understanding political authority in relation to religious authority. It is the result of the convergence of two processes: first, the intellectual critique of Sufism and the practices of saintly cult, seen as an "innovation" and an "irrational" contradiction to the principle of the unity of Allah (*tawhid*); second, the desire to rationalize Islam and adapt it to the present time by stipulating that the scriptures—the Qur'an and Sunna—are texts that must be read with no other mediation than the pious and reasoning self. From this perspective, the revealed text is clear and transparent; it directly informs the believer about the original Islamic community and the aim of the revelation.

While different interpretations have emerged within this trend and have evolved historically since the nineteenth century up to the formulations of the recent *Salafiyya jihadiyya*, what remains at the heart of Salafism is the centrality of the revealed text, directly informing the community of believers about the shape and content of their society. No mediating authority, political or religious, may intervene in this process. Pushed to its limits, this principle views politics as defined by the scriptures in a utopian and anti-hermeneutic way;[17] the community must reproduce and therefore reflect the clear meaning of the text. History, as well as culture, is—theoretically—evacuated from the interpreting process: religion is defined purely by its textual foundation and the uncorrupted primeval prophetic moment, not by its historical implementations and cultural manifestations over the ages. These are the principles that define parts of the ideology of Salafism today. However, in reality, the very process of understanding and interpreting the text always remains necessary and must be carried out by specific interpreters, in order for the text's meaning to be reproduced in political, legal, and social embodiments. In this regard, this unmediated mode of understanding the revealed text remains utopian. Therefore, the 'ulama, as specialists in this knowledge, simultaneously participate in and undermine this utopia of religion as "pure text." Indeed, Moroccan nationalist 'ulama who have claimed adherence to Salafism have articulated conceptions of political power. For them, the latter does not come to one person from prophetic descent, but rather from the community of believers who will choose the man who can best ensure the convergence between— even the identity of—the revealed text and the way public norms are organized. In this particular interpretation, knowledge of the revealed text, public piety, and governing power are three closely related principles. The identities of those who govern are determined by the first two principles: the knowledge of scriptures by the 'ulama and the choice made by the pious community, which is given strong political agency.

As we will see, this *Salafiyya*, as used by nationalist 'ulama, as well as by some of the Islamists of the PJD, while central in the political history of Morocco, has experienced dislocation, first because, starting in the 1960s, Moroccan 'ulama were weakened through the state-devised fragmentation of religious institutions and were unable to mobilize this paradigm politically; second because, in the new arrangements devised by the monarchy in the sphere of political competition, the PJD Islamists, since the 1990s, were not allowed to directly borrow from this interpretative tradition. Hence, the models of both Sufism and Salafism are politically present but are not equally authorized to be deployed. They manifest themselves depending on the actors who use them and the institutional channels through which, or outside of and against which, they get mobilized. They also overlap, for they both combine with other narratives, such as nationalism, democracy, and the opposition between Islam and the West.

The Distinction between 'Ulama and Islamists: Religious Ideas vs. Status

Until the 1990s, studies of political Islam and Islamist movements had dismissed the role of the 'ulama in the deployment of religious discourse in the political arena. This book examines the 'ulama's articulation and dissemination of religious arguments that envision an Islamic public domain regulated by the monarchy. Like the Islamists, they deploy the theme of the pious community led by a commander of the faithful who does not draw his power from a religious genealogy but from the people. This common political interpretation results in a convergence of the 'ulama with the Islamists. The literature on Islamism has created a dichotomy between the "new, self-taught, and modern intellectuals" (Islamists) and the "traditional intellectuals" (the 'ulama). Political scientist Olivier Roy has constructed his extensive analysis of contemporary Islam upon these two categories, which need to be revised.[18] For him, the literati (or 'ulama) operate within a closed and circular religious canon, anchored in transcendence. Hence, their discourse is non-reflexive and non-critical. Through their infinite spiral of commentaries upon commentaries, they, like the texts they learn by heart and reproduce unchanged, represent fixity, submission, and repetition—a mental attitude that, for Roy, devalues politics. Their social status stems from their positions in institutional networks of madrasas or in state-sponsored religious institutions.

In contrast, for Roy, the Islamists, who are educated in Westernized universities and in Western fields of knowledge, have no status. In religious matters they are self-taught, since their religious knowledge is acquired outside of religious institutions of learning. Their canon consists of "different matrices": religious texts, scholarly manuals produced by the state, and Western course materials. Their corpus, "immediately accessible," is therefore "fragmented" and individually reinvented and appropriated, without the mediation of a master and "never taken as a whole."[19] "The new intellectual is a *bricoleur* who, depending on his personal agenda, practices the montage of segments of knowledge."[20] His field of reference is therefore "immense and not closed; . . . he can talk about sociology, nuclear physics, economy or theology."[21] Roy describes the Islamists as those new intellectuals who tinker with a fragmented repertoire of references without being disciplined by institutional arrangements, and who therefore challenge the state and its religious partners, the 'ulama.

I agree with Roy's characterization of the unrestricted material the bricoleur works with, but I extend it to the 'ulama, arguing that the Islamists are not the only bricoleurs. I also underline that the difference between Islamists and 'ulama is institutional and not about types of knowledge; therefore, the worlds of ideas they represent do not necessarily coincide with their institutional positions.[22] Moreover, while Roy writes, "There is a clear relation between the configuration of the new intellectual's knowledge and its social fluidity," I show that this fluidity also has become part of many 'ulamas' institutional arrangements, and that ideological and political commonalities between Islamists and 'ulama are widespread. Indeed, the main difference between them lies in the institutional milieu in which they generate—and are perceived to be generating—their ideas. The 'ulama's institutional position allows them to homogenize their discourse so as to be perceived by state and non-state actors as legitimate and acceptable transmitters of a tradition. The Islamists' lack of institutional status makes their interpretations seem more fragmented and illegitimate. This is why Islamists also work at institutionalizing their own social, political, and intellectual positions, and also why 'ulama escape the center of their own institutions, becoming "peripheral 'ulama,"[23] ostensibly demonstrating their affinities with dissenting Islamists. The 'ulama (and their institutional positions) are, therefore, along with the Islamists, important actors defining the relationship between Islam and politics. As historian Muhammad Qasim Zaman has argued in his work on South Asian 'ulama, the ideas articulated by the 'ulama must be taken seriously in order to understand the role in Muslim societies of the Islamic tradition. However, this tradition must also be understood in relation to particular institutional contexts, especially when states define and design them authoritatively, as in the case of Morocco. This book argues that in order to understand Islamist political ideologies and strategies within authoritarian regimes, one has to analyze their emergence and transformation within the historical and institutional context: they can be understood only within the larger context defined by state policies regarding state institutions and the history of the mobilization of religious languages and ideas.

The 'ulama's professional identity is therefore at the crux of the interaction between the available Islamic stock of interpretations and religious institutional structures and change. The 'ulama attempt with great difficulty to inhabit their institutions as their own "territories," from which the state has allowed them to fashion—or prevented them from fashioning—their own access to ideas, power, and influence. I describe this interaction between institutions and ideas by examining the religious narratives worked upon by religious and political actors and by avoiding a strict instrumental perspective on religion in the political sphere.[24]

In this book, I introduce Moroccan Islamism as a set of religious interpretations situated in history as well as deployed and mobilized within particular political structures, and I bring in state actors and institutions in addition to 'ulama. By doing so, I develop a perspective in which the movements referred to as "political Islam" or "Islamism" do not emerge only as an element of "civil society" directed against the state. The political Islamist movements are also related to state policies and institutional arrangements. Hence, Islamist movements must be analyzed in a longer temporal and from a larger institutional perspective. This is why the first part of this book offers a description of the historical context of the early twentieth century within which to read the Islamist trend. The second part analyzes a particular but central character, Abdessalam Yassine, a Sufi scholar who, creating his own stature as a saint, threatens the 1970s-era authoritarian monarchy. The third part focuses on the emergence of new political actors reinstating old and inventing new religious interpretations for purposes of political mobilization in a regime that is in profound transformation. They call into question the master-disciple model based on Sufism and deployed by the monarchy. However, because of institutional constraints, they have difficulty explicitly combining their ideology with the tradition of Salafism. Nonetheless, they invent a new oppositional behavior, a process that leads me in the last two chapters to analyze the consequences of political liberalization and of the eruption of violence on the relationship between state and religion and on the sacred character of the monarchy.

Research Methodology

This work relies on a wide range of sources: ethnographic observation and interviews, archives, and text analysis.

I visited Morocco for several months between 1998 and 2003, during which time I conducted twenty-six interviews with Islamists, 'ulama, and students in graduate and undergraduate religious schools in Rabat (Dar al-Hadith and the Office of Original Education), Casablanca, and, most significantly, Fez, where I met with faculty and students at the University and at the mosque of the Qarawiyyin. Some of those interviewed have requested that their names remain anonymous, which I have respected. I also met and interviewed Nadia Yassine and militants from her father's movement, Justice and Benevolence. I visited the female component of the movement several times. In 2003, I met and interviewed leaders of the Party of Justice and Development and the Movement of Unity and Reform. I also interviewed Moroccan journalists, experts in politics and media, and academics. Among the written sources I used extensively were the Istiqlal party's Arabic journal, *Al-'alam*, and *Da'wat al-haqq*, a publication of the Ministry of Religious Affairs; these sources helped me understand both the 'ulama's points of view in post-colonial Morocco and state policies towards religious institutions. Additional primary sources included books and articles written by 'ulama and Islamists, as well as pamphlets and official publications of the Ministry of Religious Affairs, the PJD, and the MUR.

PART I

The Monarchy, the 'Ulama, and Islam

Many historians of Moroccan nationalism and of the country since independence have pointed to the central importance of the monarchy, describing its slow but certain development beginning in the 1940s as the foundation of the political system, and noting its emphatic symbolic relationship to Islam.[1] This "new" permanence of monarchy and religion and their "superposition" have become commonplace among social scientists writing about Morocco, although Henry Munson in particular has been critical of this view.[2] Shortly after independence, Roger Le Tourneau, for example, noted the importance of the monarch as a unifying figure. "Finally, there is the king, the keystone of Moroccan unity. The monarchical system, as conceived of in Morocco, contains an inherent magnetic force, because the sovereign is not only the descendant of a dynasty that has ruled the country for nearly three centuries and thus enjoys considerable prestige, but he is a descendant of the Prophet, so that he is considered by the Moroccan populace to possess *baraka*, which he bestows on those around him. In addition, the king has for centuries borne the title of 'commander of the faithful,' that is, both religious and political leader. Theoretically, this title designates the head of the entire Muslim community; at the very least, it confers on its holder the quality of spiritual leader of the Muslim community of Morocco. Heir to a dynasty that had not been unworthy, descendant of the Prophet, and leader of Islam in Morocco, Muhammad V was also himself, and after 1953 that was more important than anything else."[3]

Does the legitimacy of the monarchy at the present time now

depend on the religious factor? In the second half of the twentieth century, the king of Morocco was no longer really venerated for his *baraka*. Moroccans identified him rather as the guardian of the country's legitimacy. Then why, at the succession in the summer of 1999, a politically very delicate moment, did men bow down before Muhammad VI, who was not quite yet the king? What role was played by religion and what place did it occupy in this political inauguration? These questions may be answered by referring to the notion of sharifism, the claim of descent from the Prophet through the 'Alawite family. This claim is one of the sources of the legitimacy of a dynastic line that has ruled over parts of the Muslim community of western North Africa since the seventeenth century and over the Moroccan nation since independence in 1956. But the religious element was not the most significant factor. It is especially important to also take into account the authoritarianism of the political system, the existence of the Makhzen (the power structure controlling the army and the administration), the exercise of violence by a powerful coercive apparatus, the subtle opposition between the monarchy and the urban reformist forces that grew out of the nationalist movement, and the alliance of the Makhzen with rural notables, all of which were revealed in the general capacity of the Makhzen—controlled by the post-colonial monarchy—to divide and conquer.[4]

All these religious and secular factors came together to strengthen the power of the monarchy. Focusing on the sphere of political power and distinguishing among the various factors making for the legitimacy of the monarchy, it is possible to identify the role of religion in this edifice. For example, one of the sources of "traditional" legitimacy—the ceremony of *bay'a* (allegiance), creating a convergence of local groups and local interests around the monarchy—has been described as one of the bases for the preservation and continuity of the Moroccan monarchy. In the nineteenth century, the *bay'a* mobilized the 'ulama (religious scholars, plural of *'alim*) and the sharifs (men who claim descent from the Prophet), who held a more important place than they do today. In post-colonial Morocco, members of the government, and more recently heads of parties, have been the ones to sign or adhere to it.[5] In the case of Muhammad VI, military officers and one woman participated in the signature of the *bay'a* to the new monarch. The nature of the political pact had thus become secularized and the group of participants had expanded to meet the needs of the political situation. How can we locate and characterize the religious roots of this changing political structure? While it is quite clear that Islam is today not necessarily the keystone of the Moroccan monarchy's legitimacy, it is just as clear that the regime continues to use Islam strategically. It remains to be seen what methods the monarchy has adopted to establish its relationship to Islam, and how it defines, authorizes, and regulates religion. The first part of this book is therefore devoted to presenting a detailed chronology of the process by which the monarchy shaped the mechanisms through which it endeavors to regulate Islam.

It is therefore necessary not only to call into question the idea that the monarchy and Islam are identified with one another in Morocco, but also to offer a precise description of the way in which they are joined together in a consciously constructed institutional system that is complex and constantly evolving. The emergence of Islamist movements beginning in the 1960s was on the one hand closely connected to this system, for it was in part produced by it while on the other hand profoundly changing it. To understand the most recent changes in the system, a historical detour through the colonial and early postcolonial periods is necessary. This detour also leads to the observation that Moroccan Islamism, as a political or social ideology claiming to represent Islam, finds its roots in part in the religious history of modern Morocco, certain elements of which may be identified here. Organized brotherhoods, sharifism, but also episodes of religious reform between the eighteenth and twentieth centuries, nationalism, the status of Moroccan clerics after independence, and the forms that the monarchy adopted to appropriate and domesticate Islam in the second half of the twentieth century have all shaped a Muslim public sphere which now extends far beyond—and at times threatens—the religious foundations that the monarchy has endeavored to lay for itself. The Islamist movements of the last third of the twentieth century therefore need to be seen in historical continuity, in relation to older intellectual and political genealogies. Some of these currents can be traced back to the world of the 'ulama, but others were produced by the often tense and unequal relations between an increasingly powerful monarchy in the years between 1950 and 1990 and fragmented religious authorities who were attempting to recover a space for public expression.

In Chapter 1, I retrace the history of the Moroccan 'ulama. Fluidity, gradual decline, and the politicization of some towards nationalism from 1930 on were the defining traits of fragmented circles that were nonetheless prepared to join organizations for mass mobilization. These characteristics, which recurred in different forms in the second half of the twentieth century, show that the Moroccan 'ulama were not necessarily political quietists. With regard to ideological and intellectual concerns, the 'ulama participated very thoroughly in the debates arising from the arguments of the *Salafiyya*. The biography of 'Allal al-Fasi between the 1930s and the early years of independence illustrates a trajectory linked to nationalism, Salafism, and a tense but in the end submissive relationship with the monarchy.

Chapter 2 concentrates on the monarchy's post-colonial construction of institutional mechanisms for defining, controlling, and regulating Islam and the 'ulama, particularly through reforms in religious education in the second half of the twentieth century. The monarchy was at the time constructing itself as a central religious institution around which increasingly fragmented institutions for the expression and transmission of religion had to deploy the definitions authorized by the monarchy. These definitions were used to weave tight narratives about the nation, religion, and their language—Arabic—as opposed to the language of the colonizer. The apparatus of religious regulation that the monarchy constructed was a hybrid, bringing together both the person of the king in public demonstrations of his piety and in his lineage, and a strategic institutional complex made up of multiple religious authorities which the monarchy, set in its center, constantly adjusted so as not to lose control over it.

Chapter 3 shows that the 'ulama in the post-colonial period often defined themselves in harmony with many elements present in the later ideologies of Islamist movements. The intellectual questions they raised in the second half of the twentieth century, within the institutional confines authorized by the monarchy, demonstrated deep connections with some of the ideological content that the Islamists produced, particularly on the definition of the Islamic community, its political ethics, and the question of the "other."

CHAPTER 1

'Ulama and Power in Independent Morocco

Authoritarian republics in independent Arab countries appropriated religious institutions, nationalized them, and bureaucratized them by placing them under state control as separate institutions. The post-colonial Moroccan monarchy used a different strategy. Unlike the republics that divided the religious from the political activity under their control, the Moroccan monarchy chose to become itself the central religious institution with control over Islamic affairs. The monarchy used the lineage of the Prophet not only to establish its political legitimacy, but also to justify placing itself at the institutional center in religious terms. The post-colonial monarchy in Morocco thus strove to define itself as the only major religious institution, the body for organized mediation between God and the faithful. Fully conscious of the role the 'ulama might play in limiting its sovereignty, but also in legitimating it, the monarchy, in a historical continuity that would have been difficult to challenge, maintained and institutionalized Islam as the marker of its identity. This was comparatively easy because generally the 'ulama did not deny this aspect of the monarchy.

The decline of the 'ulama after independence, despite their significant representation in the large nationalist party, Istiqlal, was of course due to the modernization of Moroccan education, but also to the novel strategy adopted by the Palace. It domesticated the men of religion by fragmenting their group through the manipulation of the patronage networks and of the institutions under their control, rather than through large-scale systematic reforms of religious institutions. To limit the power of the 'ulama after independence, the monarchy did not offer them any distinctive institution broad enough to serve them as a tribune and a locus for expressing their authority.[1] When men of religion spoke, they did so in controlled and fragmented circumstances: the madrasa, the mosque, Qarawiyyin University, the press, and political parties were at the outset their forums.

The most prominent 'ulama, those who were "well chosen" by the Palace, found themselves within the space delimited by the Makhzen or the monarchy. However, they could not come together to form a professional group united by membership in a homogeneous institution or training in a single school. The policy of the post-colonial regime thereby perpetuated the characteristic fluidity that the historian Edmund Burke noted in the Moroccan 'ulama in the early years of the twentieth century.[2] The essential difference between these two moments was nevertheless demonstrated by the monarchy's grip on this fragmented group.

The "segmentary" model that political scientist John Waterbury used for Moroccan secular political elites thus works just as well for the 'ulama of Morocco.[3] None of them could become too powerful, and internal opposition—in particular divisions between families and/or institutional channels established by the authorities—were used by the regime: if one emerged too powerfully, all that was needed was to support some of its competitors. But the monarchy also needed the support of some 'ulama to have enough prestige to legitimate the government and underpin its sacred character. This prestige was measured by individual access to royal territory, by the services they rendered, and by the favors they received in exchange.

Maintaining a certain distance from the monarchy by avoiding incorporation into the Makhzen was common for the 'ulama, but explicit rebellion remained exceptional because the monarch's response was dangerous for any rebel. The political game that used or rejected clerics individually, however, was not enough to give the monarchy control over them. The institutional structures within which Moroccan religious elites operated and the monarchy's manipulation of these structures were also important factors affecting the relationship between 'ulama and monarchy in Morocco.

The Moroccan 'Ulama at the Dawn of the Twentieth Century: Fluidity and Decline

The Moroccan monarchy had the historical good fortune of being able to maintain patronage relations with the 'ulama because it was not directly confronted in the nineteenth century with a real professional body of men of religion. At the time, in fact, the professional status of doctors of the law, and more generally of religious scholars, was more fluid than in the Ottoman Empire, whether in Istanbul or in the Arab provinces of the empire such as Egypt and Tunisia.

Falling within the category of 'ulama had as much to do with personal and religious charisma as it did with training in scholarship. This religious charisma was most easily appropriated and circulated among the men of the Makhzen, specifically the sultan and the individual religious figures who supported or rejected him.[4] The often fickle 'ulama exhibited some political independence, although they expressed it only intermittently in small groups that established themselves through co-optation: "The Moroccan 'ulama," writes Edmund Burke, "would tend to act less as a corporate group, and more in terms of the conflicting pulls and strains of Moroccan popular Islam."[5]

While the tasks carried out by the 'ulama bore a strong resemblance to those found in other Muslim countries in the legal and educational spheres (*qadis*, *faqihs*—experts in Islamic law—and teachers), within a more or less hierarchical structure, there was, according to Burke, no "separate religious institution" in Moroccan society. Personal ties and local relationships regulated—at the same time as and sometimes in conflict with higher religious authorities—the functions and activities of men of religion. The sultan might thus secure the loyalty of some 'ulama and suffer critical attacks from others. They were as a rule not united in a homogeneous professional body, but they might meet from time to time and forge an ephemeral identity by issuing a fatwa or signing an act of allegiance to the sultan.

In the late nineteenth century, the sultans of Morocco attempted to establish control over these clerics, but they were met with resistance. Roger Le Tourneau explains that, until the middle of the nineteenth century, the chief qadi, or *qadi al-qudat*, himself *qadi* of Fez, appointed the *qadis* of the Makhzen; the sultan put an end to this practice and assumed the right to make those appointments.[6] But the authorities did not always succeed in controlling this protean group, particularly not the teaching 'ulama who declined positions in the judicial system and often remained aloof. Traditionally, as Laroui points out, "the master-teachers of the Qarawiyyin were appointed, after consultation with the sultan, by the *qadi* of Fez, who was one of them; the sultan's opinion tended to become preponderant at the turn of the century . . . so much so that under 'Abd al-'Aziz, the appointment [of teachers] started being made by *dahir* [decree], as for other officials in the Makhzen."[7]

The regime, however, did not establish and institutionalize the "religious" function because it was impossible for the sultan to directly control what the 'ulama transmitted. Their religious authority was enough in itself, insofar as it derived from their ability to interpret the sacred texts. Those who were recognized as 'ulama—because of their knowledge, piety, or charisma—were also able to maintain a degree of independence from the sultan. The administrative reforms in law and education of the last quarter of the nineteenth century eroded this independence only marginally.[8]

Colonial attacks early in the twentieth century, leading to the establishment of the French protectorate in 1912, provided some of the 'ulama with the opportunity to impose themselves in the center of the political arena in the course of several episodes of sporadic opposition to the sultan. These 'ulama were challenging not so much the person of the sultan as his political conduct, which was neglecting the imperative of jihad against the non-Muslim occupier, thereby putting at risk the integrity of the Muslim religion and the community of the faithful. Some 'ulama, grouped around 'Abd al-Kabir al-Kattani, set up at the time a "clerical opposition," and were thus part of the movement responsible for the deposition of Sultan 'Abd al-'Aziz in 1908.[9] But this opposition, which brought together a "chastiser"—founder and leader of a Sufi brotherhood—and some clerics, was of short duration.[10] The 'ulama maintained their characteristic political versatility and experienced the same decline as the Moroccan monarchy in the early twentieth century.

Beginning in the 1930s, when the colonial authorities imposed reforms on them and began to incorporate them into the civil service, the 'ulama returned to the political stage, and many of them participated in the nationalist movement. The reform of the Qarawiyyin in the 1930s, on the initiative of the protectorate and a minority of the 'ulama, was very similar to the reforms undertaken in the second half of the nineteenth century at the Zaytuna in Tunisia[11] and at al-Azhar in Egypt,[12] but it occurred several decades later in Morocco. It involved rationalizing and modernizing the methods and content of teaching: opening the curriculum to scientific subjects and foreign languages, imposing standardized tests, and turning teachers into civil servants. But these changes affected the religious identity of the community. Some religious scholars had difficulty accepting the fact that a minority of reformist 'ulama, in concert with the colonizers, were driving change of their institutions from outside by calling into question the subjects and methods of their teaching.

As in most colonized Muslim countries, the function of the man of religion had become increasingly circumscribed by the emergence of new elites schooled along Western lines. With the establishment in the early years of the protectorate of modernized educational institutions such as the Muslim *collèges* of Fez and Rabat, the Qarawiyyin declined in the face of stiff competition. As had happened in Tunisia when the Collège Sadiki was established forty years earlier, or in Egypt when Dar al-'Ulum was founded in 1872, religious educational institutions began to suffer.[13] But in Morocco, an unusual and essential distinction from the situation in Tunisia and Egypt, the urban 'ulama that had adopted Salafist positions long enjoyed political prominence at the head of the nationalist movement, along with elites educated in secular institutions, and the two groups often spoke with a single voice.

The modernization of religious education, along with other forms of modernization such as urbanization, in fact occurred later in Morocco than it had elsewhere. Religious scholars therefore remained important figures, and they emerged in a symbolically powerful way, for example, at the time of the "Berber *dahir*" (decree) imposed by the authorities of the protectorate on the sultan on May 16, 1930.[14] These scholars provided some of the leaders and ideologues of the Comité d'Action Marocaine,[15] and later of the nationalist Istiqlal Party (founded in 1944). They were able to join modern political movements with other nationalist figures who had received a modern education. When the great nationalist party split in 1959, giving birth on its left to the Union Nationale des Forces Populaires (UNFP, led by Mehdi Ben Barka), some 'ulama and prominent politicians whose education had been in part religious joined the UNFP. Among them were 'Abd Allah Ibrahim and Fqih Basri from the Ibn Yusif Institute[16] and, most important, Sheikh Ibn al-'Arbi al-'Alawi from an older generation. These political choices show that the 'ulama, even though weakened, were involved very early in the new means of mass mobilization, particularly political parties and the press. They did not necessarily divest themselves subsequently of those political commitments.

These two parties—Istiqlal and the UNFP—linked by their history, were not, however, the only places where Moroccan religious scholars were politically educated and mobilized. The 'ulama found other partisan organizations of interest, such as the Parti Démocratique d'Indépendance or PDI (Democratic Independence Party), founded by Muhammad Hasan al-Wazzani in 1946. The PDI attracted the Qarawiyyin scholar 'Abd al-Hadi Shraybi, and some 'ulama of the celebrated Kattani family, which played and continues to play an important role in the history of Morocco. But Istiqlal, through its ideology, continued to embody one strand of Moroccan nationalism linked to *Salafiyya*; and the monarchy in the post-colonial period would have to deal with this major political competitor. The 'ulama thus formed a fluid group, socially weakened but capable of political mobilization. We turn next to the intellectual debates that preoccupied them at the time and the role of the monarchy in those debates.

The First Expressions of Moroccan Salafism: From Wahhabism to Nationalism

The notion of *Salafiyya* refers to a set of religious reforms of Islam, the interpretations of which have varied according to the historical moment and the participants involved. The term refers directly to the Salaf, the "pious ancestors," that is, the first three generations of the history of Islam, among whom were the companions of the Prophet. Salafism thus evokes a reading of Islam at its beginnings and a return to a primeval moment of prophetic revelation and history. It advocates the direct reading of the texts of the Qur'an and the Sunna (collection of words and deeds of the Prophet), without the historical mediation of the many exegeses produced in the course of a history that, as it proceeded, "corrupted" the primeval mythic moment of revelation. Beginning in the eighteenth century, the ideas of a reform that adopted the name *Salafiyya* spread through the Muslim world from various geographic centers: Arabia, India, Syria, and Egypt. In each case, diffusion took place through a process of hybridization, allowing only some elements of a very flexible doctrine to be filtered through local conditions. Sometimes the rationalist aspect was predominant in the spirit of reform, sometimes the conservative and fundamentalist aspect, but in most cases a good deal of room was given to criticism of what were called the "innovative" practices of the Islam of the Sufi brotherhoods.

The Moroccan *Salafiyya* emerged as a religious movement between the late nineteenth and early twentieth centuries, under the joint influence of two centers for the production of religious reforms outside Morocco, each of which, in its own way, claimed to be returning to the "authenticity" of Islam: Arabia and Egypt. Moroccan scholars and pilgrims returning from the Middle East imported the Wahhabi doctrine first and Egyptian reformism thereafter, and one of the most visible signs of the influence of these two doctrines was early on in the fight against the *zawiyas* (religious centers linked to a Sufi brotherhood) and their practices, which were seen as "blameworthy innovations" (*bid'as*).

The brotherhood principle, structured around obedience to a Sufi master, which might serve as a basis for political association and mobilization, was not called into question by the Salafist movement as much as were the practices considered contrary to Muslim orthodoxy: visiting graves, trances, appropriation of animist rituals, and the like. A third element, nationalism, later made it possible to give an ideological and political meaning to Moroccan Salafism, while to some extent moving away from the spirit of introspection and renovation of the first stages of the Middle Eastern movement for religious reform.

The principal agents of this doctrinal evolution were the intellectual elite, mainly the 'ulama and some 'Alawite sultans—who directly associated the monarchy with various episodes and different interpretations of the reform movement. The history of Moroccan Salafism is too complex to be described here in detail, but it is possible to identify, on the basis of secondary sources, some of the questions raised by this diversified movement made up of shifting components at the turn of the nineteenth century, particularly the ways in which it was appropriated by the monarchy and some religious elites. Then, with the aid of primary sources, I will detail one central political journey, that of 'alim 'Allal al-Fasi.

The Salafists of the generation of the great nationalist militant 'Allal al-Fasi (1910-74) traced the roots of Moroccan Salafism back to the Wahhabi reformism of the eighteenth century.[17] In his hagiographic book on the independence movements of North Africa,[18] 'Allal al-Fasi links Salafist nationalism directly to the Wahhabi doctrine, and most 'ulama repeated this genealogy in almost identical terms, emphasizing the fact that the monarchy sometimes agreed with reformist 'ulama returning from abroad who opposed many sheikhs of Sufi brotherhoods.[19] Narratives were usually constructed along the lines of the following example. In 1811, the mufti of Tunis received a letter from King Sa'ud explaining the Wahhabi doctrine and asking Muslims to adhere to it; the mufti passed the letter on to Sultan Sulayman.[20] The sultan was sympathetic to the new reform, but angered many clerics of the time, particularly the 'ulama of Fez: Ibn 'Abd al-Wahhab challenged the cults of the Prophet and of the saints, describing them as polytheism (*shirk*). Mawlay Sulayman denounced aspects of the conduct of some brotherhoods but did not reject Sufism in principle. The doctrine turned out to be politically useful to him because it enabled him to criticize the brotherhoods threatening his authority, such as the Sharqawiyya and the Tayyibiyya—allied to Berber tribes that the Makhzen could not control—and the Darqawiyya, which represented a real challenge to the Sultan. He was himself a follower of the *tariqa* Nasiriyya and received with all due honor the founder of the Tijaniyya, who left Algeria and settled in Fez in 1789.[21]

It was not until the late nineteenth century that the question of religious reform returned to the sultan's court. Having come back from the Middle East with the spirit of reform, 'Abd Allah al-Sannusi of Fez came to see Sultan Mawlay Hasan in 1886 and took part in the circle of his lessons (*durus hadithiyya*) in Fez, but encountered opposition from the 'ulama of the city. This figure of the traveler from the Middle East is only one version of the incursion of *Salafiyya* into Morocco, which gradually took on a Moroccan identity. Shu'ayb al-Dukkali is the most frequently mentioned example of a Salafist Moroccan sheikh; after spending ten years there, he returned from the Middle East in 1907 under the reign of Sultan 'Abd al-Hafiz: he had studied at al-Azhar University in Cairo, had attended the course on Qur'anic exegesis (*tafsir*) given by Muhammad 'Abduh and was apparently influenced by his teaching.[22] Sultan 'Abd al-Hafiz was a scholar, according to Abdallah Laroui: he named Abu Shu'ayb al-Dukkali to head the hadith council that he had reestablished, and he wished to denounce certain religious intermediaries, in particular the heads of some brotherhoods who might be in competition with him. While it was still too soon for the 'ulama of the Maliki school to accept the Salafism of Dukkali, these developments already indicate the establishment of a Salafism of the Makhzen directed against the sheikhs of some *zawiyas*, as well as some *qa'ids*, and by extension, later on, the authorities of the protectorate.[23] But although Sultan 'Abd al-Hafiz criticized the brotherhoods, he joined the Tijaniyya brotherhood after the protectorate replaced him on the throne with Mawlay Yusif in 1912: it was common when a political figure fell out of favor for the sultan to indicate his disgrace by suggesting that he find a Sufi *zawiya* to which he could retreat to pray.[24]

This triangular and temporally discontinuous relationship between the sultan, the reformist 'ulama, and certain brotherhoods was coupled with a complex doctrinal question, the terms of which tended to fluctuate widely. In its call for a return to doctrinal sources, that is, to the Qur'an and the Sunna, Salafism favored recourse to the hadith (the collection of the Prophet's sayings) over the *fiqh* (Muslim jurisprudence). The differences articulated by the *madhhabs* (schools of law) had to be overcome.[25] The followers of the religious reform inspired by the *Salafiyya* considered the treatises of Maliki *fiqh* on which many 'ulama relied to define the norm (*shar'*) as a frozen body of doctrine and ossified casuistry, derived from archaic jurisprudential systems that were out of touch with reality.

This predisposition in favor of a return to the prophetic tradition fit—at that time and still today—with the interests of the monarchy, which focuses on the hadith, the scriptural account of Muhammad's acts and words, that is, the origins from which the 'Alawite monarchy itself claims descent. This is probably why the Moroccan monarchy was deeply interested in Wahhabism at the very beginning of the twentieth century, all the more because an anti-Sufi doctrine could allow it to challenge certain dissident figures. Describing Salafist influence, Abu Bakr al-Qadiri, a cleric who participated in the nationalist movement, confirmed this focus on the hadith rather than on the *fiqh*, which, said the traditionalists, should simply be "followed" (*yutbaʻ*).[26] According to al-Qadiri, the return of Shuʻayb al-Dukkali from the Middle East and his teaching in Morocco made it possible to challenge this method. It was a "cry that awoke those who were in the grave."[27] *Salafiyya* then became the basis for an activist movement.

In his book on the Moroccan independence movement, ʻAllal al-Fasi also noted the importance and the exceptional quality of Dukkali: "He attracted talented young people who distributed Salafist books printed in Egypt and went with him to destroy sacred trees and stones."[28] Dukkali called for a return to the Sunna and giving up innovative and blameworthy practices (*bidʻas*), common in many brotherhoods, while not necessarily condemning the brotherhoods themselves.[29] On the other hand, Muhammad Ibn al-ʻArbi al-ʻAlawi was heavily influenced by the ideas of Ibn Taymiyya (1263-1328), a medieval theologian and legal scholar who lived in Damascus and Cairo and later constituted a central source of Wahhabi doctrine. ʻAlawi was more intransigent than Dukkali, was more hostile to brotherhood organizations and made a number of enemies, later among them ʻAllal al-Fasi himself.[30] These ideas took root in the Qarawiyyin, but also in new modern schools, through the reading of Egyptian journals, the writings of Muhammad ʻAbduh and Rashid Rida, and texts produced by the Association of Algerian ʻulama.

Al-Qadiri's writings show that intellectual discussions of Salafist reform in the first half of the twentieth century were vigorous and much richer than its political expressions.[31] In this theological battle, which was coupled with a clash of political interests, two types of tradition were set in motion. On one hand was the tradition of normative interpretation akin to the *taqlid* (imitation), derived from multiple layers of fixed interpretations in the memorization of legal compendia such as the *Mukhtasar* (treatise of Maliki law) of Khalil Ibn Ishaq. On the other was the prophetic tradition, that of the Sunna and the hadith that described it and presented, as it were, an unmediated vision of the Islam of the origins, or the spirit of a "pure" Islam, because it was seen as "authentic" and made alive by the experience of the original community represented by the deeds of the prophet. In the early twentieth century, the Qarawiyyin was transmitting a frozen *fiqh* characterized by "abstract intellectualism" and an "ideology of preservation."[32] This is why the notion of *fqih*–a contracted form of the word *faqih*—was long used to designate the function of religious teacher and the *'alim*, as well as the jurist (*faqih*). At the time, the Qarawiyyin taught almost exclusively grammar and jurisprudence, and teachers usually did not convey, according to their critics, the spirit of a free and direct exegesis of the Qur'an and the Sunna.

Hence, many figures claimed reliance on the principle of *Salafiyya*, as Abdallah Laroui has shown, pointing out that, while Salafism became the common ideology of a significant number of Moroccan intellectual figures in the early twentieth century, it was invested with different content depending on individual political choices (Makhzen centralization, bourgeois reformism, the 'ulama).[33] This protean Salafism gradually converged in nationalism. The collaboration of many Sufi brotherhoods with the protectorate strengthened in reaction the close relationship between nationalism and Salafist doctrine.[34] In this way, the movement of "free schools" began in the 1920s in a true spirit of educational reform to remedy the failings of the Qarawiyyin and to organize teaching in Arabic. It was aimed at both boys and girls,[35] and became one of the first manifestations of a Salafism with nationalist colors in which students of the Qarawiyyin participated, including 'Allal al-Fasi and Muhammad Ibrahim al-Kattani. They were students of Ibn al-'Arbi al-'Alawi, himself a student of Dukkali, who was very critical of the traditional spirit of the Qarawiyyin, trapped in the pedantry of old treatises of jurisprudence.[36]

This nationalist Salafism was thus created through a detour to the Middle East, a set of individual itineraries that imported reforms from the Mashriq and imprinted their names in what became, starting with the major crisis provoked by the "Berber Decree" of 1930, the great age of national struggle. But Salafism remained fragmented, and it was not always linked to nationalism. It is therefore difficult to speak of a "school." While the movement had ramifications among the educated urban bourgeoisie, it was not specially linked to any particular educational institution. The Qarawiyyin was important, but it was not the only center for the training of educated Salafists and continued to be affected by various currents of thought. Salafism took shape in scattered centers around strong personalities who were dispersed and sometimes mutually antagonistic. The convergence between nationalist 'ulama and the monarchy, which was late in its political arrival, in the 1940s, took shape earlier in religious matters, although some ambiguities and contradictions might continue to trouble it.

Generally representing an urban and bourgeois nationalism, the reformist 'ulama joined the nationalist movement in the 1930s and, in the second half of the 1940s, gradually received the support of the monarchy, which then began to define itself as a nationalist actor. For ten years up to independence, through one faction of Istiqlal, nationalism, monarchism, and Salafism went hand in hand. Salafism at the time was one of the elements of the nationalist matrix, but was not identical to it.

'Allal al-Fasi: The Salafist Nationalist and the Two Kings

The figure of 'Allal al-Fasi illustrates the original union between Salafism, nationalism, and attachment to the monarchy, a union whose intensity fluctuated in the course of his career, sometimes taking the form of latent opposition to the person of the monarch. He clearly represented what nationalist Salafism would become after independence, in the face of an increasingly powerful monarchy that superficially appropriated its principal arguments while weakening its participants. The monarchy co-opted the sacred character of nationalism, which it incorporated into the persons of Kings Muhammad V and Hassan II, while at the same time striving to marginalize one of the most popular representatives of Salafism, 'Allal al-Fasi.

'Allal al-Fasi, born in Fez in 1910, was the son of a cleric. His family was apparently connected to an influential urban *zawiya*, the Darqawiyya, which had been very politically active since the late eighteenth century.³⁷ The family also had connections to the state bureaucracy. 'Allal's father, 'Abd al-Wahid al-Fasi, mufti of Fez and secretary general of the 'ulama council, was also the librarian of the Qarawiyyin and a preacher. Born two years before France set up the protectorate, 'Allal rubbed shoulders with members of the 'ulama who frequented his father's house. He followed his father's example by studying at the Qarawiyyin, beginning at the age of seventeen, where he educated himself about the ideas of Salafism, closely connected to the question of national liberation. His teachers at the time were Abu Shu'ayb al-Dukkali and Muhammad Ibn al-'Arbi al-'Alawi, the most important spokesmen for *Salafiyya*. Unofficially, he obtained the diploma for completion of studies at the Qarawiyyin, the *'alimiyya*, in 1930, but officially only some time later, because his nationalist activism had brought him to the attention of the authorities of the protectorate as one of the most zealous of militants.

'Allal al-Fasi's identity combined religious knowledge, status as a member of the traditional urban bourgeoisie, reformist idealism, and political activism. His courses at the Qarawiyyin were very popular. He helped establish independent schools set up by nationalists to remedy the lack of Moroccan schools and the influence of French culture on young Moroccans. The long history of his persecution (he was in exile in Africa from the mid-1930s on), his charisma, and his talent as a poet made him the most popular representative of Moroccan nationalism, whose importance Clifford Geertz has correctly recognized: "If Morocco had become independent in the 1930s, a sheer impossibility, it would doubtless have done so against the monarchy, and Al-Fasi would have been the Sukarno . . . of Morocco."³⁸

His Salafism represented nationalist reformism more than anything else. For him, defense of the Moroccan nation was closely linked to an internal reform of Islam. But once independence had been achieved in March 1956 and the idea of the nation guaranteed, the questions connected to religious reform changed character. A relationship of subtle opposition developed between al-Fasi and the monarchy, and the concept of religious reform was thereby modified: nationalism had lost its raison d'être as a "struggle" and a combative ideology, and the monarchy was gradually appropriating some elements of Salafism to develop a definition of Moroccan nationalism suiting its purposes.

In order to weaken Istiqlal, King Muhammad V had to deal with Moroccan Salafism and Moroccan nationalism cautiously, appropriating and reinterpreting them in his own way. He was confronting two forces that were each attempting to establish their own dominance: the Moroccan Army of Liberation (the ALM, which had initiated an armed struggle against the colonial troops in 1954) and the Istiqlal Party. Following independence, competition among these three elements intensified, sometimes to the point of involving physical violence. The men of Istiqlal began to be incorporated into the ranks of the administration as early as 1956, a way for the monarchy to neutralize the nationalist party without allowing it to occupy the major positions of power.

This neutralization of the section of Istiqlal inspired and mobilized by 'Allal al-Fasi had a significant symbolic aspect. By the early 1950s, in his *Self-Criticism*, a book that articulated his ideas on intellectual and political reform, al-Fasi was already speaking of the monarch as the "commander of the faithful."[39] In 1953, some 'ulama declared a *bay'a* (allegiance) to Sultan Muhammad Ibn 'Arafa,[40] but 'Allal al-Fasi agitated for the return of the king—a goal associated with that of independence—on the "Voice of the Arabs" radio broadcast from Cairo, a few hours after the deposition: "The king has not been dethroned. He has been removed by enemy force. . . . His majesty the king will soon return to the throne in triumph, and our beloved Morocco will soon recover its independence."[41] Monarchy and nation were joined as one. Some even went so far as to speak of a "Salafist" king: in the very early days of independence, Muhammad Ibrahim al-Kattani, a fervent Salafist and nationalist '*alim*, spoke in *Al-'alam*, the Istiqlal's journal, of the "*Salafiyya* of Muhammad V," in an article that was also broadcast on the radio.[42]

One of the first indications of the king's *Salafiyya*, Kattani asserted, was a symbolic act by which, beginning with his *bay'a*, he prohibited his subjects from prostrating themselves in order to speak to him, explaining that one only prostrates oneself before God; this prohibition, if it was really stated, was in fact never applied. It enabled the ruler to express the principle of the symbolic inversion of the relationship between weak and powerful, which will turn up again later. *Salafiyya* also enabled King Muhammad V to express his support for the 1933 reform of the Qarawiyyin, which meant for Kattani a reformist Salafism, coupled with "political" Salafism. Muhammad V insisted that commentary of the Qur'an become a required subject for examination to become an *'alim*. "This was a revolution. Especially exegesis (*tafsir*) of the Qur'an, which the imitators (*muqallids*) fiercely rejected, saying: 'Certainty is an error, and an error is an impiety.' It was said that if you read a commentary of the Qur'an to the king, he would die! This is why those who read the *tafsir* to the king were accused of wishing for his death."[43]

According to Kattani, exegesis of the Qur'an was no longer taught after the reign of Sultan Sulayman, and was resumed only with Shu'ayb al-Dukkali under 'Abd al-Hafiz. The names of these two sultans evoked periods when *Salafiyya* converged—if only temporarily—with the person of the sultan of Morocco. Kattani reported that he himself read the *tafsir* in utmost secrecy. At the time of the reform of the Qarawiyyin in 1933, the exegesis of the Qur'an by Ibn Kathir, the "student of Ibn Taymiyya," explained Kattani, had been reintroduced, in a version published by Rashid Rida and financed by the "king of *wahhabiyya*, 'Abd al-'Aziz Ibn Sa'ud."[44] Many 'ulama thus saw a convergence between the monarchy of Muhammad V, endowed with great charisma, the Moroccan nation, and Islam in its reformed version.

Despite their place in the nationalist vanguard before independence and their admiration for Muhammad V, the 'ulama had lost their political influence, submitting to the monarchy and agreeing to share with it the enterprise of defining a Moroccan, Muslim, and Arab nation. The nationalist and Salafist 'ulama worked to support the monarchy and to lay the foundations for its future power by constructing the myth of the martyr sultan, which was particularly effective when the king was exiled in 1953. Aware of the opportunity, the

The 'ulama, in allowing themselves to be servants of the monarchy, lose their own voice.

monarchy used this symbolic image and endeavored to control its principal authors, so that by independence, the great majority of 'ulama were snapped up by the regime of Muhammad V. Most of them played the political game according to the rules laid down by the monarchy.

Hence, Muhammad V did not permit the establishment of a constitutional monarchy in the English manner, as 'Allal al-Fasi had wished in 1952: "Moroccan democracy should be based on a parliamentary regime."[45] The monarchy did indeed fear that a single party would be established under the cloak of Istiqlal and therefore encouraged internal divisions in the party. It has already been noted that the 1959 split divided the old independence party into two camps: a leftwing organization, the UNFP, which did not necessarily define the Moroccan nation in religious terms, and Istiqlal, strongly marked by doctrinal orientations connected to Islam, evolving toward a conservatism of the right.

By the end of 1956, Muhammad V was insisting on the Islamic character of the Moroccan nation, defining the regime as one that was both Islamic and democratic: "Thus, there will be established in Morocco an authentically national and constructive democracy, in conformity with the precepts of the Qur'an which commands the faithful to consult one another in matters of common interest and the prophet to take the advice of his companions . . . [even more], this democracy must also conform to our national traditions which have known no political regime but that of imams."[46]

Vaguely defining a political regime in conformity with Islam allowed the monarchy to act on two fronts: on the one hand, to compete with 'Allal al-Fasi on his own territory without attacking him head-on; and on the other, to avoid a liberalization of the political sphere, which could only become disadvantageous to the Palace by giving too much space to parties that had played a significant role in the national struggle.

The monarchy's cautious approach to al-Fasi and his party seemed justified at the time. On his triumphant return from exile on November 16, 1955, Muhammad V had good reasons for seeing 'Allal al-Fasi as a political threat, even though his power was not yet solidly established within Istiqlal.[47] Muhammad V was already endowed with a "religious" identity,[48] and on the eve of independence, only 'Allal al-Fasi could be seen as having a similar status: he was in the vanguard of the nationalist movement, and he was often represented as one of its great charismatic leaders.

His exile, like that of the king, was seen by his supporters as a *hijra*, an analogue to the flight of the Prophet from Mecca to Madina in 622. And his name, just as much as that of Muhammad V, provoked passionate allegiance from crowds, who saw him as playing a political role: "Our political leader (*Za'imuna siyasi*)! Long live 'Allal al-Fasi!"[49] This is why the tensions between al-Fasi and Istiqlal, on the one hand, and the king, on the other, sprang up as soon as the king returned to Morocco in 1955.

It is worth considering the months between the fall of 1955 and the summer of 1956 in greater detail, as this was the period during which Morocco secured its independence. On November 16, 1955, Muhammad V returned from exile, ten days after the signature of the La Celle-Saint-Cloud accords in which France granted Morocco independence "within interdependence" and established Muhammad V as the exclusive representative of the country. 'Allal al-Fasi was still in Cairo. He had accepted only belatedly and unwillingly the Aix-les-Bains agreements (which had begun negotiations between France and Morocco in September), and he had disapproved the protocol of La Celle-Saint-Cloud. He refused to return to Morocco before the country was completely liberated. On March 2, Morocco formally secured its independence. He did not return from his Cairo exile until the summer of 1956, confining himself to the Spanish zone, in Tangiers, where a muffled battle played out between him and the king. "Of course," writes Maati Monjib, "he came to Rabat to see the sultan, but very briefly and with no publicity. On March 18, before a crowd of fifty thousand, he did not fail to show his displeasure at the royal game of swamping Istiqlal by treating it on an equal footing with countless organizations that, in fact, posed the risk of growing uncontrollably in number. In the city of Tangiers, he declared at the time: 'I must not fail to speak to you of the unification of Moroccan patriotism. The Moroccan nation does not need to multiply political tendencies in the current circumstances.'"⁵⁰

Hence, after independence the king strove to weaken the old party, which remained tied to the urban classes, and had difficulty finding adherents in the countryside. The monarchy also neutralized religious leaders through manipulation and by gradually and subtly establishing its control over the men of religion and "religious affairs." Muhammad V did not appoint al-Fasi to a position in the first government he formed.⁵¹ Mukhtar al-Susi,⁵² a respected *'alim* who was a member of Istiqlal, was appointed Minister of *Habus* (pious endowments, or Minister of Religious Affairs).⁵³ The monarch thus chose, in order to represent "official" Islam, a Berber cleric influenced by Salafism, trained by Dukkali, but close to Sufism, who was not the head of a party, and therefore represented a lesser political danger than 'Allal al-Fasi. Al-Fasi, on the other hand, was disappointed but did not call into question his support for the monarchy: the *habus* and education remained for at least a few years in the hands of ministers from Istiqlal.

The king offered al-Fasi the presidency of the committee for the codification of shari'a, satisfying in part a wish that the *'alim* had already expressed in his *Self-Criticism*: "The interests of the country require the establishment of Moroccan public law that would apply in all Moroccan courts of justice, for which the principal source is Islamic shari'a. . . . After the agreement of his majesty, following the judicial proclamation (*ifta'*) of the 'ulama affirming that this law is in accord with the general principles of Islamic law, it will receive the name of 'Moroccan Islamic law.'"⁵⁴

'Allal al-Fasi had to wait for Hassan II to come to power (following the accidental death of his father, Muhammad V, on February 26, 1961, at the age of fifty-two) before being incorporated into the Makhzen. The *za'im* was appointed Minister of Religious Affairs in 1961, when he had been head of Istiqlal for two years. He had thus gotten closer to the monarchy, but this proximity meant that he was overseeing the religious affairs of the kingdom under the surveillance and authority of a king who had restricted him to that ministerial function, in the end a trifling position for a man who wanted to continue to be seen as the great leader of the national struggle and of one of the parties that had originally embodied it. The position offered to al-Fasi did more to enable the king to domesticate this charismatic party leader than to enable al-Fasi to impose his views. He had, in fact, only a very modest budget at his disposal and practically no independence from the Palace.

ʿAllal al-Fasi supported Hassan II from the moment he came to power in 1961, but when the ʿulama offered him their allegiance, the king was not yet constitutionally the "commander of the faithful" (*amir al-muʾminin*). On the initiative of Dr. ʿAbd al-Karim al-Khatib (a major figure in the nationalist movement) and with the support of ʿAllal al-Fasi, the Constitution of 1962 included this title for the king in article 19: "The king, *amir al-muʾminin*, supreme representative of the nation, symbol of its unity, guarantor of the perpetuity and continuity of the state, is responsible for the respect of Islam and the Constitution. He is the protector of the rights and freedoms of citizens, social groups, and communities."

ʿAllal al-Fasi thereby participated in the institutionalization of the sanctification of the king and of his person. The king did not, however, allow al-Fasi, as *ʿalim* and Minister of Religious Affairs, to modify the kingdom's religious policies. The king thus succeeded in restraining the impulses of the minister al-Fasi, whom some, such as Rédha Guédira, saw as too zealous.[55] In the summer of 1962, there was still a muffled competition between the king and Istiqlal concerning a trial of Moroccans who had converted to the Bahaʾi faith. The Ministries of Religious Affairs and Justice, then in the hands of Istiqlal, exerted pressure in favor of severe punishment of these converts, and they secured the death penalty. The king, troubled by the international repercussions of the trial and urged on by Moroccan liberals, commuted the sentences. Less than a year later, a new crisis opposed the monarchy to Istiqlal and led al-Fasi to tell the National Council of his party on April 13, 1963, in fact speaking directly to Hassan II: "I warn his majesty the king of the danger of allowing partisan individuals to pervert the execution of the provisions of the Constitution on the pretext of protecting against organizations alleged to be dangerous. The people could accept anything except contempt for itself and for the achievements for which it fought. I would also like to remind his majesty of the dangers that grew out of the contempt for democracy, first in the Ottoman Empire, and then in Iraq and Egypt."[56]

Following the monarchy's attempts to break Istiqlal and the left by creating its own party, the FDIC (Front for the Defense of Constitutional Institutions), al-Fasi, who had left the government in January 1963 in response to this strategy, thus dared to evoke publicly the possibility of the Moroccan monarchy's coming to an end. Al-Fasi, whose relations with the king had become hostile, did not reproach him for breaches of Islam, but rather for his methods of government.[57] While he had striven, during the eighteen months that he headed the Ministry of Religious Affairs, to create religious periodicals, establish mosques in villages, and develop religious instruction, he was thereafter in latent conflict with the Palace as a head of party. He fluctuated between integration into the Makhzen and joining the opposition *of* His Majesty (as opposed to the opposition *to* His Majesty). Despite all, he therefore continued to accept the monarchical regime until his death in May 1974.

Muhammad al-'Alami has recounted the way in which 'Allal al-Fasi experienced the abortive military coup d'état of Skhirat against the king in 1971, when he was attending a royal reception organized by the Palace.[58] It presents an 'Allal al-Fasi at ease with the realm and the practices of the Makhzen: "Having received as usual from the royal chancellery an invitation to attend the reception of July 10, 1971, on the occasion of the forty-second birthday of His Majesty the king, at the summer residence of Skhirat, 'Allal left his house at nine in the morning in his black Mercedes driven by his chauffeur. Dressed in a fine white djellaba with silk filigree and with slippers on his feet, 'Allal arrived in front of the palace of Skhirat at 9:30. . . . A protocol officer came before 'Allal and deferentially opened a way for him; the reception appeared to be very relaxed and informal: apart from 'ulama clothed in their traditional white dress, all the Moroccan and foreign guests were wearing light sport clothes and some even had beach bags. 'Allal at first joined a group of 'ulama in conversation. . . . Toward half past noon, the guests were directed to the buffet . . . in this carefree atmosphere of a picnic at the sea shore rather than an official reception, and while speakers set around the pool were playing recordings of the latest Moroccan and Middle Eastern hit songs, 'Allal joined 'Abd al-Wahid 'Alawi, adviser to the Supreme Court, and Muhammad al-Fasi, Minister of Cultural Affairs. After a copious meal, Majid Ibn Jallun, Minister of the Royal Cabinet, approached 'Allal and kissed his hand as a sign of respect. 'Allal said lightly: 'May God implant Islam in your heart!' The minister laughed heartily. Then 'Allal asked him to get him a fine Cuban cigar of the kind he likes to smoke sometimes after a good meal. Majid Ibn Jallun disappeared for a few moments and returned with some cigars that he offered to 'Allal and his companions at the table, pointing out that the cigars came from the king's personal supply."

Once the attempt had been thwarted—by means of fierce repression causing hundreds of deaths—the author reports what al-Fasi said: "At about a quarter to six, 'Allal [al-Fasi] heard cries on all sides: 'Long live the king!' 'Allal asked: 'Who is the king?' One of the soldiers answered: 'His Majesty Hassan II.' The leader of Istiqlal then also cried out with all his heart: 'Long live the king!' "[59]

A monarchist without passion, 'Allal thus bowed to the rules of the system instituted by Muhammad V and Hassan II: a monopoly over political power and a subtle transformation of the religious sphere, two policies that I describe in the next chapter.

CHAPTER 2

The Monarchy, Mirror of a Fragmented Religious Sphere

The post-colonial Moroccan monarchy succeeded in imposing its domination over the 'ulama by domesticating them, while simultaneously ensuring that the religious sphere would continue to be porous and fragmented. The regime also gradually institutionalized this fragmentation. Following independence, the monarchy was on the one hand faced with a situation in which the 'ulama were not in its good graces; the regime "forgave" their betrayal, which had taken the form of a collusion of many of them with the *'alim* and sharif 'Abd al-Hayy al-Kattani, who brought Sultan Ibn 'Arafa to the throne in 1953. The monarchy thus took advantage of their weakened state, but it also used them by making them believe that it would be their strongest support in confronting "modernizing" political figures, something it did not really do until the 1970s. On the other hand, the regime managed Islam in a thoroughly paradoxical way because it had simultaneously to divide its representatives to weaken them and also gather them around the throne to control them. In the end, this paradox undermined the religious legitimacy of the monarchy.

After Independence: How the Monarchy Shaped the Religious Sphere

The independent monarchy shaped the religious sphere in a series of steps that largely depended on the political context. The regime adopted a subtle strategy that enabled it to exercise broad control over Islam, while obviating the need for a separate major religious institution. The institution of religion took material form in the monarchy itself, and more specifically in certain characteristics inherent in the king, his family, and the space of the Palace, as well as in the fragmented set of institutions that, under royal control, were charged with defining and regulating Moroccan Islam. This policy deprived the 'ulama of any significant institutional power, but it also deprived the monarchy of any capacity for systematic surveillance of the 'ulama because they were dispersed in fragmented form around the monarchy.

The monarchy's "marking" of its religious territory was therefore a daily and endless task that had to operate in places of religious expression and on their margins. It became difficult as a consequence for the monarchy to create and sustain an "official" Islam based on a well defined set of institutions, as was the case in the Arab republics. Even before being developed doctrinally, this Islam was experienced in the royal person, and it was genealogical above all else: it called on a memory embodied in a living family and on 'ulama who were expected to support this religious construction, although they had no official platform from which to do so.

This was the crux of the Moroccan king's dilemma: how, as a descendant of the Prophet, to control Islam when the social forces that might provide religious legitimacy were fragmented and therefore always likely to contradict one another. It is commonly said that the monarchy was able to control Islam precisely because it used its sharifian lineage. The opposite is just as true: the lineage of the Prophet embodied in the monarchy makes this task of control difficult, laborious, and constraining. In the 1950s and 1960s, in fact, the problem was not only to control Islam from outside, as did Bourguiba in

Tunisia or Nasser in Egypt, who had instituted a division of labor between secular political elites and 'ulama at their service. The monarch's task was also to give life to religion in his conduct and to control the consequences and criticisms of that conduct. Hence, while the Arab republics had secured the services of "muftis of the Republic," a survival of the Ottoman religious hierarchy, the Moroccan monarchy could not count on that official function, which did not exist in the country. This lack later caused crucial problems with respect to the definition of the monarchy's religious authority.

To manage their religious sphere, the independent Arab republics adopted variants of the modernization carried out earlier in Turkey by Mustafa Kamal and generally transformed three areas: the legal system, the pious foundations, and education. The Moroccan monarchy did not reproduce this three-stage model, as it existed in Algeria, Tunisia, and Egypt beginning in the 1950s and 1960s.

After independence, the Palace made no significant reforms in the family code, which remained governed by Muslim law. Promulgated in the text of the *Mudawwana* in 1957 and 1958, it was the product of hasty work by a ten-member codification commission presided over by 'Allal al-Fasi, with the participation of the 'ulama Muhammad Ibn al-'Arbi al-'Alawi and Mukhtar al-Susi.[1] In 297 articles, the text retained and reorganized the provisions of Maliki law. On the status of women, 'Allal al-Fasi refrained from applying the reformist and modernist ideas, such as limitation of the principle of polygamy, which he had developed in his *Self-Criticism* of 1952. Traditional orthodoxy prevailed. The memory of the Berber Decree of 1930, seen as an attempt by the colonial administration to weaken the influence of Muslim law, certainly played a role in this orientation. The spirit of the anti-colonial struggle thus won out over the question of equality of rights, even though al-Fasi had interpreted that equality within the Muslim tradition itself. For al-Fasi and other representatives of the 'ulama, the Islamic character of the law should not, moreover, have been limited to the family code: the 'ulama would constantly demand the Islamization of the entire Moroccan legal system. The text of the *Mudawwana* remained their special preserve, one of the only components of the "territory" of the 'ulama until its reform in 2004.

The *habus*, or religious endowments, were not radically changed either. Their nationalization went back to the protectorate: Lyautey had reformed them beginning in 1915, which enabled the monarchy to avoid making any changes. The spirit of the colonial reform served to rationalize the *habus* and to use them to finance the Moroccan state.[2] The *Mudawwana* of 1957-58 did not mention the religious endowments, and the official Arabic translation of the June 2, 1915, decree that nationalized the *habus* would not be produced until 1967, which meant that the monarchy wanted to avoid open discussions of the question.

The public *habus* were directly managed by the government, whereas the *habus* of the *zawiyas* were managed privately, but under the shared supervision of the Ministries of Religious Affairs and the Interior—the latter supervising local religious activities through the governorates. By the time Muhammad V formed his second government, on October 28, 1956, the Ministry of Religious Affairs[3] was no longer on the list of government appointments, although it continued to exist under the title of "ministry." It thus came under direct control of the Palace—it is still supervised by the Interior Ministry, following the practice of the protectorate—and became a part of the monarchy's reserved domain. It publishes journals, such as *Da'wat al-haqq* ("The Call of Truth"), and manages religious endowments, but it also, in theory, controls mosques and preachers.

The Qarawiyyin: Marginalization and Fragmentation

With regard to the religious university, the Qarawiyyin and its provincial branches, the monarchy again appeared to act very subtly. The only way it had to channel the 'ulama that had come out of the institution and the nationalist youth connected to it, particularly in traditionally rebellious Fez that had been in the nationalist camp, was to neglect the university and to leave it open to attacks from secular institutions of learning. The regime could not in fact afford to reform the institutions of religious education through a major substantive law because this would mean fully introducing the 'ulama into debates about education in Morocco, and thereby offering them a basis for political mobilization. But this lack of a response to the 'ulama who demanded reforms could also be interpreted as the consequence of the regime's political hesitation: on the one hand, in the first stage of independence, until the early 1960s, the monarchy had not yet established its absolute power; and on the other, it probably preferred to leave the question up to the government, even if it meant getting involved later.

Controversies over the Modernization of Education

The swift marginalization of the 'ulama, in any event, indicated that the monarchy was counting primarily on its own religious legitimacy to ensure its survival in independent Morocco. But there is no doubt that the regime was committed from the outset to the intention to modernize education.[4] In December 1955, Muhammad al-Fasi was appointed Minister of Education. A graduate of the *collège* Moulay-Idriss[5] and a cousin of 'Allal al-Fasi, he served as rector of the Qarawiyyin after 1941 and as the teacher of Prince Hassan.[6] Previously run by the Ministry of Religious Affairs, the Qarawiyyin came under the control of the Ministry of Education in 1956, which set up a specific department for religious education within the Ministry, the "Office of Original Education" (*ta'lim asli*).

Political figures and intellectuals agreed at the time on the general program for unification and diffusion of education. The intellectual and political elites were aware of the role that religious institutions and the Qarawiyyin had played in the national struggle and raised the question of their role in the future.[7] But not everyone saw the process of reform in the same way. Modernist segments wanted to minimize the place of religious education and modernize education as a whole. Within Istiqlal, on the other hand, modernizing religious education meant not necessarily marginalizing it but integrating modern subjects into it, along the lines of the reform that took place at al-Azhar in 1961, whose principles, known to the Moroccan elite, had already been under discussion in Egypt in the mid-1950s.[8] But in practice, the university of Qarawiyyin and the other primary and secondary institutes for religious education were much less reformed than neglected and nearly forgotten, to the point that the 'ulama lived in fear that religious education would disappear, and they endeavored to secure recognition for their role and their educational institutions.

The modern University of Rabat was established between 1957 and 1959.[9] The new generations of students chose to enter the modern university rather than undertaking religious studies that no longer offered any prospects on the job market. Much more than the transformation of the religious system itself, the prospect of the creation of a modern university frightened the 'ulama and the students of the Qarawiyyin as early as 1956. They could clearly see the different treatment accorded to diplomas awarded by the institutes that were the kernels of the modern faculties of the future.

That very year, the *tolbas* (religious students) of Fez went on strike several times, to lay claim to the same opportunities on the job market as graduates of modern universities.[10] In January 1956, these students called for the convening of a congress of 'ulama to demand reforms. In particular, they asked that teaching methods be modernized and that equivalence be established between their diplomas and those of the modern system.[11] Seeing no prospect of reform, male and female students of the religious university again went on strike in March 1956, and the movement spread to all institutions of religious education.

Criticism of the teaching methods of the Qarawiyyin increased.[12] The Istiqlal Party paper, *Al-'alam*, covered all these controversies and offered a platform for the striking students. One of them, who was in favor of the unification and Arabization of education, declared: "The creation of a Moroccan university is the only way to unify education. . . . I think that this Moroccan university should be named the Qarawiyyin University, because it was the Qarawiyyin that stood up to the colonizer and thereby had the honor of preserving the language and religion."[13] 'Abd al-Hadi Tazi, professor at the Qarawiyyin and secretary general of the association of 'ulama, was himself interviewed by a reporter from *Al-'alam*. He proposed to integrate, at both primary and secondary levels, religious education with modern education as an alternate track. The solution he advocated was in the end partially adopted, but it did not force the *'alim* Tazi to continue working in the religious sector, since he moved into modern education and had a successful academic and diplomatic career.

But one student described the extent of the problems that the young students of the Qarawiyyin were then facing: "No one can be unaware that the Ministry of Education has carried out reforms, just as one cannot fail to see that these reforms are superficial and incomplete. The curriculum has not changed. We are still studying sitting on mats, exams are conducted in disorder, and we live on very little. No one recognizes the value of this extraordinary diploma that requires such prolonged effort. The graduate ends up unemployed, or turns to teaching like someone with a certificate of primary education and with the same salary. A child of twelve studies side by side with a man of fifty, old enough to be his grandfather."[14]

The Ministry of Education came out the victor of this close-fought battle with the Qarawiyyin, particularly thanks to the subtle game (or was it merely indecisiveness?) of the monarchy. Between the middle and the end of 1956, King Muhammad V, an *homme-fétiche*[15] at the center of a veritable "royal cult"—spontaneous at first and then consciously organized to support the regime—offered tokens of reassurance to the 'ulama. In July 1956, following prolonged strikes by Qarawiyyin students, Muhammad V addressed the nation from the pulpit of the Qarawiyyin mosque in Fez.[16] He evoked the need to "close ranks" and to engage in the construction of the Moroccan nation. The speech also dwelled on the Qarawiyyin. It spoke vaguely of a needed reform that would modernize the Qarawiyyin without changing its identity and ought to mobilize the 'ulama of the ancient institution.

In the fall of 1956, then, a new secondary school was opened at the Qarawiyyin in Fez that allowed students to change from sitting cross-legged to seats in modern classrooms provided with tables, chairs, blackboards, and chalk. But for the 'ulama, the situation was still far behind that of al-Azhar, where three large "modern" buildings had been built for the religious faculties in the 1930s under the leadership of Sheikh Maraghi. The students' problems were numerous: they were dissatisfied with the curriculum, which offered them subjects they considered "useless." Qarawiyyin students from the youth wing of the Istiqlal therefore demanded a new curriculum. Discussions commenced with the Ministry of Education, which responded only with symbolic letters.[17]

The Association of 'Ulama of Morocco (jam'iyyat 'ulama al-maghrib) came to the aid of the students by demanding a revision of the curriculum and the establishment of equivalence between diplomas, as well as modernization of teaching methods, a separation between primary and university classes, sending teachers abroad for training, a reform of the bureaucracy, and the establishment of university residence halls for the students.[18] There was strong pressure from religious educators for quick reform, but they were already no longer part of the intellectual elite. The regime in fact had to train its own "cadres" to develop a modern administration, and disillusion spread among the 'ulama, who were widely criticized.

On August 23, 1956, for example, Al-'alam published an article that raised the question of the future of the 'ulama: "When Will the 'Ulama Do Their Duty?" The author describes his disappointment with the Association of 'Ulama. They are incapable, he says, of producing more than three communiqués a year, and do nothing but express their nostalgia for the past. The comparison with Egypt once again springs to mind. While the sheikh of al-Azhar had called for jihad during the 1956 Suez crisis, the Moroccan 'ulama had not come out of their slumber, according to the author: "The 'ulama must come down from their ivory tower, if they have one," he goes on to say. In practice, the Moroccan 'ulama were as marginalized at the time as the Egyptian 'ulama, but the questioning of the very existence of a place of refuge for them (an "ivory tower") clearly shows that the Moroccan 'ulama, unlike their Egyptian counterparts, had no institutional locus for mutual recognition and assembly. The monarchy, aware of this fact, was careful not to offer them one.

The Recommendations of Mehdi Ben Barka

One of the modernist leaders of Istiqlal in 1957, Mehdi Ben Barka, although held in contempt by many conservative 'ulama, did not think that the Qarawiyyin was condemned to disappear as an institution after independence, but he clearly set out the broad outlines of opposition to the conservative 'ulama over the reform of religious education. Ben Barka's position showed that in addressing the religious elite, the political leaders of the Moroccan left were not as aggressive as their counterparts in the Arab republics, which were at the time partly under the sway of socialist ideology:

> The Moroccan university ... is the heir of two systems of education: a national system embodied in the centers for Islamic studies of Qarawiyyin, Ibn Yusif, Meknes, and Tetouan. They have a real and symbolic value that we ought to preserve to the extent that that preservation enriches us, but we ought to reform them in drawing inspiration precisely from the second system of education that exists in our country. ...
>
> At the time we [Istiqlal] approached this problem of the university, opinions were divided. There were two tendencies in the commission [of education of Istiqlal]: one wanted to make the old Islamic university centers, Qarawiyyin and Ibn Yusif, into faculties of theology and shari'a completely separate from the modern system of education; in contrast, another tendency wanted to see these old systems of education disappear, always in the name of effectiveness, but effectiveness seen from too narrow a point of view, and to establish in Morocco only modern faculties of science, law, and letters.
>
> In the first solution, we risked having our students, for example, in legal disciplines, sometimes educated in the [faculty] of shari'a at Qarawiyyin, sometimes in the faculty of law in Rabat or Casablanca, which would be a divided

education for our youth harmful to the national unity that must exist. Some diversity is acceptable, but not so much as to train judges in the future belonging to two totally different disciplines. And on this subject, our education commission had some very instructive sessions, perhaps a little stormy, but at their conclusion we managed to see more clearly in this area, which is really very delicate and where you can't venture forth lightly, especially since we have in front of us the ongoing Egyptian experience.[19]

Mehdi Ben Barka's speech gave voice to a nagging question that was emerging at the time in the independent Arab countries: how to define the foundations of the country in a non-contradictory way, particularly through education, without challenging Islam and its traditional representatives, the 'ulama, and simultaneously satisfying modernist demands.

The solution advocated by Mehdi Ben Barka in the summer of 1957 consisted of abandoning primary and secondary education in the Qarawiyyin, as well as the first level of higher education in the religious university. The institution would continue only as a center for specialized graduate studies that students could enter after getting a *licence* from the modern university.

> You will ask me where will the 'ulama be educated? Well, the 'ulama now coming out of the Qarawiyyin don't have the same quality as their predecessors; and this is a judgment that I would not allow myself to make if it had not been pronounced by leading figures from Ibn Yusif and Qarawiyyin on the education commission. . . . So, we who want to see Moroccan science promoted, we who want to restore value to the title *'alim*, the value it had in the enlightened centuries of our country, we want the education of 'ulama to come after the education of graduates in law and letters. The centers of Qarawiyyin and Ibn Yusif will recover all their value when they serve as centers for higher education issuing degrees of higher education. At that

point, they will give our country true researchers, true scholars, that is, true 'ulama. And thus we will have preserved them, but in the dynamism that we want to instill in our country, which must always look toward the future with the same concern for effectiveness.[20]

The approach the government adopted toward religious education was an ambiguous compromise compared with this program. On the one hand, in fact, beginning in the second half of the 1950s, religious education was introduced into public secondary schools as a specialized and distinct course of study given entirely in Arabic, unlike the rest of secondary education still given in French. It did not bear the name "Qarawiyyin," but was called *asli* (original) or *taqlidi* (traditional) education. This new policy encountered resistance from the 'ulama and students of the Qarawiyyin, who wanted to be independent from a government and a school that they considered too close to French rather than Islamic education. On the other hand, religious higher education remained endowed with the specific identity of the Qarawiyyin, but at this point was only one specialization among others, losing prestige because it was slow in reforming, despite the demands on the part of its members.

Attempts at Independence: The Associations of 'Ulama

Immediately following independence, the 'ulama, who had voluntarily come together in regional associations—notable among them the association of 'ulama of Sus—[21] tried to join forces to create a general association of 'ulama. In May 1957, the members of the various associations, in a meeting in Fez in the home of Abu Shu'ayb al-Dukkali, hosted by one of his descendants, Major Dukkali—official *'alim* of the Royal Armed Forces—and chaired by Mukhtar al-Susi, discussed ways of implementing this unification: "Defining our plan of action for a Salafist revolution [*thawra*] which will engender reform of our society and the education of Salafist youth deeply attached to religion."[22]

On January 21, 1956, in the midst of a strike by the students of the Qarawiyyin, the 'ulama had attempted to set up the Association of 'Ulama of Morocco and asked Muhammad V to appoint his heir, the future Hassan II, honorary chairman of the association. This was one of the first attempts to establish a pressure group to defend the interests of the 'ulama. But this preliminary attempt at creating an organization to defend the interests of the men of religion was not realized, and the 'ulama still had no platform for political expression.

In 1960, the 'ulama of the Qarawiyyin were preparing to celebrate the eleven hundredth anniversary of the institution's existence. They took the opportunity to establish the League of 'Ulama of Morocco. But the atmosphere was tense because of a rumor circulating among 'ulama that the regime would try to prevent their establishing an association.[23] Sheikh 'Abd Allah Kannun wrote a blunt article for *Da'wat al-haqq*, the journal of the Ministry of Religious Affairs, in which he deplored the intellectual decline and institutional marginalization of the Qarawiyyin: "The Qarawiyyin used to be described as a university, and the expression 'Moroccan universities' is still used.[24] But it is no longer a faculty among the faculties of Rabat, and if I wanted to be more precise, I would say that it has become an annex of the faculty of law."[25] For Sheikh Kannun the Qarawiyyin, moreover, no longer had any connection with religious education, which was under the control of elites with a secular education. "How can Qarawiyyin University remain a university whose role remains up in the air, that has no idea about its future, and that constantly gets contradictory orders concerning its supreme goals and its eternal mission?"

The League of 'Ulama of Morocco also deplored the state of religious education and presented to the Ministry of Education a *Project . . . for the Development of Education and the Establishment of Qarawiyyin University.*[26]

> At the dawn of independence, this education was expected to receive the aid it deserved, but the opposite happened. It is sometimes neglected, at other times interfered with, so that it no longer has the same name that it bears in the rest

of the Islamic world. Sometimes it is called traditional education, whereas it is the worst enemy of the imitative tradition. Sometimes it is called original education, based on the claim that it is the origin of all knowledge and that all sciences derive from its branches. . . . When the preceding government presented the principle of the unification of education bringing together religious and modern (*'asri*) education, it became clear that this alleged origin of all knowledge was nothing but a mockery and that the two names had been chosen only to avoid the words 'religion' and 'Islam'.

The document continued ironically, criticizing what it represented as a secularization of public education: "For we are, without boasting, a modern nation that considers religion as a bond [*'alaqa*] between the individual and his God that has no role to play in matters of education."[27] In the eyes of the 'ulama, by pursuing its program to secularize Moroccan education, the Ministry of Education was denying their very legitimacy.

The 'ulama of the League therefore demanded a "recognition of the Qarawiyyin and its independence . . . of course under the supervision of the government"—a statement indicating their contradictory wishes as well as the difficulties they experienced in radically opposing government policy.[28]

These corporatist reactions were not accompanied by attempts to reform the content of what was taught by the Qarawiyyin. Already convinced of the futility of this demand, the 'ulama chose to devote their efforts to preserving the status quo.

The False Reform of the Qarawiyyin in 1963

When Hassan II mounted the 'Alawite throne in 1961, it was his duty to uphold the symbols of continuity between the monarchy and Islam, all the more because the political circumstances and some religious figures gave him the opportunity to do so. Article 6 of the

Constitution adopted by referendum on December 7, 1962, made Islam the "religion of the state, which guarantees freedom of worship to all," in a kingdom with the motto, "God, the Fatherland, the King." In a press conference in Rabat on December 13, 1962, the king declared:

> It is certain that Jewish worship may be carried on in compete freedom. These are religions of the Book. These religions are accepted by Islam. They are not only accepted, but it is recommended that we believe in their prophets. This does not mean that in the future, in maintaining public order, Morocco will allow someone to worship the sun or a fetish in public. It does not mean that it will accept the Baha'i sect or others that are veritable heresies. Morocco is a Muslim state, which is tolerant of the religions of the Book and accepts the unity and the singleness of God, that is, the eternal and universal religions, the Jewish religion and the Christian religion.[29]

Establishing the Islamic identity of the state (by excluding heresies) was thus for Hassan II a way of ensuring that his authority as a monarch was established over the definition of Moroccan Islam.

"All Sciences Are Islamic"

When the new Constitution was being drafted in 1962, as we have seen, 'Allal al-Fasi and Dr. 'Abd al-Karim Khatib proposed including the official status of "commander of the faithful" (*amir al-mu'minin*) attributed to the king. 'Allal al-Fasi was thereby offering the king an institutionalized religious stature, strengthening the sacred status conferred by belonging to the sharifian lineage. At the same time, however, the cleric Muhammad Ibn al-'Arbi al-'Alawi, in agreement with the UNFP, vehemently criticized the proposed Constitution. Two years earlier, Sheikh al-'Alawi, one of the most celebrated founders of nationalist Salafism, had resigned from the purely honorific position of Minister of the Crown Council to protest against the way the monarchy had treated the government of 'Abd Allah Ibrahim of the UNFP, which was summarily dismissed in May 1960. In 1962, the sheikh, at the age of eighty-two, sided with the political opposition, in contrast to his former student al-Fasi, whose Istiqlal Party was then in government. He was as deeply shocked by the principle of hereditary monarchy through primogeniture as he was by the power of legislating attributed to the monarch.[30] The opposition between the two 'ulama was violent and gave rise to bitter accusations on both sides.[31] The break between the two was complete, and Hassan II had managed to briefly establish an alliance with 'Allal al-Fasi.

One year later, with his standing as "commander of the faithful" firmly established, after seven years of agitation by the 'ulama over their status, Hassan II responded by offering them a few slender symbolic gestures regarding their status. The law of February 6, 1963, regulating the operations of the Qarawiyyin, merely recognized the existence of the university, along with its name, and confirmed its control by the Moroccan state.[32]

While the Qarawiyyin was the subject of a law in 1963, its identity was not destroyed as was that of the Zaytuna in Tunisia.[33] It kept its name but found itself geographically dispersed among the faculties of Fez, Tetouan, and Meknes. Officially, it did not include primary and secondary education, and was reduced to undergraduate higher education with no doctoral program, that is, with no possibility for its students to obtain the celebrated *'alimiyya*, the degree that granted the title of *'alim*, or religious scholar. The ambitions of the Qarawiyyin were thus radically restricted, and the statutory identity of the 'ulama was abolished at a stroke by the nullification of their title. And yet, the 1963 law was not preserved in the memory of the Moroccan 'ulama as a traumatic experience, as was the Egyptian law of 1961 or Bourguiba's reform of the Zaytuna in 1958-59.[34] The Moroccan 'ulama today display some degree of indifference toward the transformation of the Qarawiyyin at that time because, rather than focusing on that issue, it had become more urgent for them to concentrate on the struggle for Arabization and to establish a presence in other arenas.[35]

Hence, there was no transformation of the Qarawiyyin in the sense of internal *islah* (reform) or *tahdith* (modernization): the monarchy did not attack the 'ulama on that front and never sought to impose on them a reform of their educational institution, probably for fear that it would turn into a political platform. The shaping of the religious institution by the monarchy was thus less systematic than in Tunisia and Egypt. The Moroccan monarchy did not really "touch" or profane the system of religious education represented by the Qarawiyyin: it simply allowed it to wither, whereas in Egypt Nasser broadened and modernized it, and in Tunisia Bourguiba reduced it to a minimal expression. Broadening and modernizing the Qarawiyyin along the lines of al-Azhar in Egypt would have provided a political platform for the Moroccan 'ulama. Explicitly reducing its ambitions from one day to the next, following the model of the Tunisian Zaytuna, would have provoked resistance,[36] and for this reason the "reform" in Morocco was not really a reform.

Thus, the Qarawiyyin was not recognized officially until 1963, although no change was made to the content and methods of teaching. The 1963 law made it possible to institutionalize and officially recognize it as a Moroccan university after the long trial of strength between the 'ulama and the Ministry of Education. Paths were thereby opened between religious education and the civil service. For instance, the Ministries of Justice, Education, Religious Affairs, and even Interior selected some Qarawiyyin graduates for their own schools of administration. The marginalization of the 'ulama was attenuated by this legal recognition, which allowed them to be integrated into the sphere of the administration.

Reacting to the reform, 'Allal al-Fasi wrote in 1967:

> A few years ago, the state celebrated the one thousandth anniversary of the Qarawiyyin,[37] the oldest university in the world. Various representatives of sister universities attended the celebration. But the state tried to prevent the 'ulama from celebrating the event, even though they had the right to, because it thought that the celebration would be an

homage to the Qarawiyyin, to their conduct, and to their support of the nationalist movement. We succeeded in securing a decree that restored to the Qarawiyyin its name as Qarawiyyin University. . . . We agreed to have the faculties of the university scattered between Tetouan, Marrakesh, and Fez. Hence, the university is now made up of three faculties—theology in Tetouan, Arabic language in Marrakesh, and Islamic law in Fez.[38]

Despite the problems associated with the application of the 1963 law, he was pleased that the graduates of Qarawiyyin could obtain equivalence with the graduates of the modern university: "None of us wants the Qarawiyyin to become a non-religious university, but we want it to keep the role of the university that preserves the Arabic language and Islamic culture, and at the same time gradually opens itself to the faculties that the country needs."[39] This did not deter 'Allal al-Fasi from holding a position as professor of law at Muhammad V University. This institutional ambiguity was echoed in his representation of Islamic education: al-Fasi, although fiercely opposed to the marginalization of the Qarawiyyin, at times legitimized the dichotomy between secular and religious education by simply stating that the whole educational system was in fact Islamic, echoing the concept of a comprehensive Islam that defined all types of knowledge.

> The cultural future of our country will be created by many universities. It is certain that the Qarawiyyin is one of the most important. But right now, it is not in its interest to enter into competition with Muhammad V University, which covers various faculties, because if it did, it would lose its primary mission, which is to preserve the language and culture of Islam. But there must not be a strict boundary between the two universities. *All sciences are Islamic. And Muhammad V University is Islamic as well.*[40]

Al-Fasi against the Fragmentation
of the Sphere of Religious Teaching

The very same year, on the occasion of the eighth congress of Istiqlal in Casablanca in November 1967, 'Allal al-Fasi directly accused the Ministry of Education of having conspired with the "colonizers" to destroy religious education.[41] He deplored the decline in the number of students in the primary and secondary institutes of the Qarawiyyin as well as in the Qarawiyyin undergraduate level, and directly associated the government's lack of interest in the religious institution with foreign control over Moroccan culture. The weakness of religious education, like the presence of foreign experts in the administration, was in his view the result of a neocolonial and imperialist conspiracy. This is why, according to al-Fasi, Qarawiyyin graduates were not accepted in the labor market, whereas legally they ought to have been.[42] In particular, those with a degree in shari'a could not become members of the bar. They were often rejected by administrative agencies because they did not speak French. 'Allal al-Fasi then challenged the legitimacy of the Ministry of Education to control religious education.[43]

Comparing the modern Muhammad V University with the Qarawiyyin, 'Allal al-Fasi showed how much the latter had been neglected. Instead of creating a new university, why not develop the Qarawiyyin into a modern Islamic university, as had been done with al-Azhar in Egypt?[44] He made the strange suggestion that a university be situated in the center of old Fez (which would be renovated) near the mosque and the old student residences. This is how he presented this renewal of the old, a kind of perfect blend of old and new:

> The renovation of the water system in Fez is continuing, which will make it easier for cars to enter the old city at several points, in particular Saffarin square, which is very near the gates of the Qarawiyyin mosque. It is possible to build student housing in the Saffarin . . . as well as classrooms for existing and future faculties, and to build a hospital and a general library [khizana] and various institutes. Old Fez,

the capital of traditional learning, and this area in particular, which harbors the Qarawiyyin mosque where the reformist spirit and then nationalism flourished earlier in the century, could thus become the beacon of learning and religion, alongside the Qarawiyyin mosque which would continue to exist for prayer, religious instruction, and general education (which takes place within the mosque).[45]

This utopian and rather unrealistic vision is surprising coming from al-Fasi, particularly considering the limited space actually available in old Fez. But the picture, however utopian, expressed a deep desire to "recenter" religious education and more generally the place of Islam in Moroccan society. It was articulated in radical opposition to the monarchy's effort to fragment the sphere of religious education. Indeed, after the 1963 reform of the Qarawiyyin, which divided it geographically, the establishment in 1964 of Dar al-Hadith al-Hassaniyya ("Hassan's House of Hadith") aggravated that fragmentation: this higher institute for religious studies, which specialized in the study of the prophetic traditions and depended on a training program within the Ministry of Education, was nonetheless directly financed by the monarchy.

Dar al-Hadith was located in the well-to-do neighborhood of Agdal, just outside Rabat, and was bequeathed as a pious foundation by a rich Rabat bourgeois. The gardens surrounding it and the zellige and decorations ornamenting it made it a more pleasant place to work than the soulless architecture of the faculties of Fez, which were isolated on the outskirts of the city and hard to reach by public transportation. The establishment of Dar al-Hadith enabled the king, by reference to the hadith, to bring forward royal descent from the Prophet: its graduates would in fact be called on to participate in Hassan's lessons, which brought together every year during the month of Ramadan, in the sanctuary of the royal palace, Moroccan and foreign 'ulama hand-picked by the Ministry of Religious Affairs. During this month of fasting, some of them habitually presented a religious lesson in front of the monarch, surrounded by invited 'ulama, dignitaries, and politicians chosen by the Palace. The 1964 creation of Dar al-Hadith and the 1967 establishment of an association of graduates of Dar al-Hadith also meant the establishment of an arena in competition with the Qarawiyyin, as well as with the League of 'Ulama.[46] The Institute welcomed teachers from Syria and Egypt, who were often influenced by the doctrine of the Muslim Brotherhood, such as Faruq Nabhan.[47]

The king thus gradually institutionalized the fragmentation of state-controlled religious education. He multiplied arenas in competition with the Qarawiyyin, and constructed them in close connection with his sharifian identity: Islam controlled by the monarchy was deployed around it as a scattered collection of fragments manipulated so as to reflect and reproduce, as in a mirror, the religious dimension of the king.

Islam, Nation, and Arabization

The question of religious education must be linked more broadly to educational policies and to the internal contradictions of the Arabization and Islamization policies. By 1956, the issue of the unification and extension of education was on the table: the principle adopted offered all Moroccans a unified national education. The cultural criteria upon which it would be based and the place of religious education were the issues at hand. The 'ulama showed unwavering determination to participate in the debates about the definition of the Moroccan nation and the position that Islam should hold within it.

At that time, the Qarawiyyin served as one of the symbols of the drive for Arabization. For many 'ulama, reforming the Qarawiyyin and making it into a major university would have meant recognizing the predominant status of the Arabic language and Islam in guaranteeing the permanence of Moroccan identity.[48] Aware of the regime's modernizing line, the 'ulama played an obstructive role against attempts to narrow the domain occupied by religious learning in the educational system and acted as a pressure group promoting the Arabization of education as a replacement for French-Arabic bilingual education.[49] This was in accordance with the ideology of Istiqlal, which had always supported education in Arabic, as far back as the establishment of free schools in the 1920s, which were a lever against colonialism. The first governments of independent Morocco, when the Ministry of Education was in the hands of Istiqlal, seemed to be moving in this direction, although they lacked resources.[50] In the aftermath of independence, there was a game of musical chairs among ministers in the area of education and a series of contradictory reforms; but despite this confusion, the line of controlled and limited Arabization gradually gained ground. The process was always symbolically and officially in place, but it remained very slow. The monarchy, as a result, offered compensations for this slowness and tried to satisfy the leading figures of Istiqlal and more broadly those who expressed support for Arabization, in particular the League of 'Ulama.

Hassan II had received a bilingual education, in the royal palace, in the *collège royal* created by his father in 1942. 'Abd al-Hadi bu Talib, a graduate of the Qarawiyyin and a scholar close to the king, was one of his teachers. Proficient in Arabic, the future king also had a solid French education—he studied law in France. And he was always a fervent supporter of bilingualism, even if he had to make concessions to the demands for Arabization.

In April 1964, one year after the symbolic recognition of Qarawiyyin University by the regime, the "Oak Camp" conference organized by the Conseil Supérieur de l'Éducation Nationale in the forest of Maamora officially raised the question of traditional education by bringing 'ulama into the debate.[51] At the same time, the students of the Qarawiyyin were again on strike to demonstrate against the lack of openings on the job market. The conference came up with recommendations for a speedier and more thorough Arabization, against the views of the king and of Yusif Ibn al-'Abbas, then Minister of Education. But the continuing increase in access to education raised difficult problems of management: early in 1965, the new Minister of Education, Muhammad Ibn Hima, restricted admission to secondary schools, a reform that led to riots in Casablanca in March of that year, their violent repression, and the declaration of a state of emergency. On April 6, 1966, the Minister of Education ordered a pause in Arabization, provoking a general uproar in circles favoring that path. Arabization was thus continued only in primary schools when the session began that fall. In May 1967, 'Abd al-Hadi bu Talib was appointed Minister of Education. But this appointment appeased supporters of Arabization only briefly because of the continuing suspension of the program.

In the same year, Istiqlal published a memorandum titled *For Reform and Arabization of Education*, in which the party reiterated its commitment to complete Arabization and also mentioned the role the 'ulama should play in this reform.[52] Through the League, the 'ulama had in fact begun by the mid-1960s to play the role of a veritable pressure group, which led to the development of a virtually independent system of original education (*ta'lim asli*). A break was thus established between students in the modern system and those in the "original" system, producing a real cultural dichotomy. Original education had become for its critics an "apparatus in the hands of a traditional intellectual elite that strongly defended its interests."[53] In the late 1970s, Islamic education also became a required subject in the modern public educational system. Similarly, departments of Islamic Studies were set up in universities beginning in the 1970s, a step that created further fragmentation in the organization of religious education. The addition of more official channels to an already fragmented system of religious education was also the sign of a new push by the monarchy to adopt symbols of identity and religion that it associated with its genealogy and put back at the heart of its political territory.

The Spirit and the Language of the King

It was in fact through a direct relationship with his subjects that the king, beginning in the late 1960s, attempted to strengthen the religious arrangements of the monarchy around the Muslim identity of his person, his family, and the nation. This did not keep student protest in the spring of 1968 from reaching the Qarawiyyin, where students' material conditions had become increasingly difficult.[54] Demands for unification and Arabization were expressed at the time as much by the conservatives of Istiqlal (who advocated education in accordance with the Arab-Muslim personality) as by the left (who invoked education for the people). The Islamism that arose in the late 1960s was a blend of these demands, appealing to populist religious feeling and to justice.

Although Arabization and Islamization owed more to the 'ulama and Istiqlal than to the king, he tried to co-opt them for his own purposes, at a time when official memory was once again adopting the language of Islam to establish a visible and public correspondence between royal and religious rituals, notably in the festival of the *mawlid* (birthday) of the Prophet and the various *mawsims* (local festivals with a religious dimension), particularly that of Mawlay Idriss.[55] In 1968, Hassan II launched a "Qur'anic schools" program and, in a speech on October 10, emphasized the need to preserve and develop bilingualism.[56] However, "We must not go against the Islamic current," he explained.

> As a father . . . I said to myself: if my children are educated in one way and my citizens in another, is it reasonable for them to live in this country as foreigners in relation to all their citizens who will grow up in the future? Or will we rather make the future generations into generations that get the same education as we do?
>
> From which generations did independence come? From the generations who were educated in the *kuttabs* [Qur'anic elementary schools]. Which generations built independence? The generations who sat cross-legged in front of the *fqih*. Which are the generations who are now growing weary? Those who know the active and passive forms, the five daily prayers, what fasting is, and the rules of pilgrimage to Mecca. Have the generations who doubt, who go astray, who hesitate between being drawn to the East or to the West, the North or the South, contributed anything?[57]

The *kuttabs* would prepare children to learn to read and write before primary school, along with a little math and a part of the Qur'an. For the monarch, it was necessary to return to the space of the mosque and form new generations there. Children would all go to a *kuttab* between the ages of five and seven, and those who had done so would have priority in admission to primary school. The *fqih* would take the children to the mosque every Friday for the sermon. He would be a kind of modern Qur'an teacher, who would have to follow a syllabus, using a textbook published by the Ministry of Education.

> I hereby impress on our Minister of Primary Education our firm directive that as of today no one will be accepted, no matter who his father may be, if he has not spent a year or two in the *kuttab*. I know many people of the upper classes, from the social and political point of view, whose children are in the [French] Mission.[58] It is up to us to show an example. My children will not go to the Mission schools and in ten days, Allah willing, they will enter the *kuttab* with all the Moroccans.

He inaugurated the "Qur'anic schools" program at the royal palace on October 22, 1968, in a religious ceremony with his children and his nephew, in the presence of the Prime Minister, many 'ulama, and young students who had memorized the Qur'an. The Ifrane conference, held from March 11 to March 15, 1970, marked a break with the "Ibn Hima doctrine" and heralded the Arabization of secondary education. A few weeks later in May, a manifesto by 'ulama and intellectuals, signed by five hundred key figures, protested against bilingualism and demanded the complete Arabization of Moroccan education to remedy "linguistic mongrelization," preserving national unity and the national "personality" while at the same time opening this education to the secular world and to foreign countries.[59]

As a result, in continuity with the entirely symbolic program of the *msids*,[60] Hassan II began to direct renewed and intense attention to religious education. Its growth in public primary and secondary schools—along with that of a broad sector of private bilingual education—helped to relieve public education from new population pressures and to respond to the problem of illiteracy, which would have been difficult to resolve through an elitist educational policy. But it also gave the king the opportunity to launch into a sanctification of his territory, while at the same time finding a way to more effectively weaken the left, which was still very powerful in the university sphere. As was true everywhere else in the Arab and Muslim world, Hassan II was hoping to mobilize religious conservatism to restrain leftist student agitation.

The supporters of Arabization and the 'ulama joined in the operation because they had never tired of criticizing socialism. As early as 1960, 'Abd al-Salam Harras, an *'alim* of Fez, had written:

> The socialist movement has banished religion everywhere. . . . It believes in matter and matter alone. Every argument of its well ordered thought, its scientific style, as long as socialist thought draws breath, are attractive and profound. Empty pockets and hungry stomachs await it, and it nourishes the tendencies of the young toward rebellion, their idealistic dreams of permanent happiness, of paradise. . . . All of that is only reinforced by the accomplishments of the state that is the leader of this current of thought [the Soviet Union], taking the form of incredible scientific, economic, and technical achievements, not to mention the extraordinary Chinese experiment. . . . But as for us, have we fortified ourselves in the face of these or other ideas? . . . Have we chosen with sincerity the path that we must follow? Have we defined our objective, our goals?[61]

In Harras's view, it was necessary to return to the idea of a "pious citizen," "that is, believing." "We expect the leaders to renew the *mithaq* [covenant] with God."[62]

The Moroccan 'ulama were clearly aware of leftist thinking, since they had encountered it in schools, on campuses, and in the political arena. What is more, it fascinated them, as it was to fascinate

Abdessalam Yassine, a teacher of Arabic who became an inspector in the educational system, and who will be discussed at length in Part II. Suffice it to say here that, beginning in the 1970s, the king used the anti-socialist sentiments of the 'ulama in responding positively to their calls for the Arabization and Islamization of education.

On June 11, 1971, the king received representatives of the League of 'Ulama of Morocco; the deans of the shari'a, Arabic language, and theology faculties; and the dean of Dar al-Hadith, along with the Prime Minister, the Minister of State in charge of religious education, and the Minister of Religious Affairs. He expressed his interest in religious education and initiated a movement opposing the one that had marginalized traditional education and had restricted its representatives from the 1950s on.[63] In late 1972, a cabinet committee was established to study the question of traditional education. The king chose at that time to replace the term *asli* (original) with *asil* (authentic). This change in terminology was designed to emphasize the character of authenticity contained in this education. The attempt was to strengthen original education by introducing a scientific section at the beginning of the new term in October 1973. Holders of a bachelors degree in original education could thus continue their studies at the Qarawiyyin or in modern universities. The budget for original education was increased to 65 million dirhams for the five-year plan 1973-77.[64] And more traditional secondary schools were built in many Moroccan cities in the 1970s.

Beginning in 1973, while Arabization was rapidly progressing, the government offered teaching positions in public schools to graduates from institutions of religious education. Later on, university students who had been educated in schools by many of these graduates moved into the leadership of student protest, slowly marginalizing leftist agitation and producing a new form of protest based on the language of Islam.

Beginning in 1977, a member of Istiqlal, 'Izz al-din al-'Araki, led the process of Arabization as Minister of Education. He joined the government in a break from his own party, thereby allowing the king to make concessions to Istiqlal, notably by authorizing the establishment of departments of Islamic Studies in the faculties of letters that would later educate many Islamists. At the time, national unity was formed around the cause of Western Sahara, a strategy undertaken by the monarchy to neutralize opposition forces. Al-'Araki, who remained Minister of Education for nine years, was Prime Minister from September 1986 to August 1992. By then the Arabization of secondary education was complete. Al-'Araki was not an unconditional supporter of Arabization—he declared that Morocco was "doomed to Arabization"—but he was a member of Istiqlal, and this was a way for Hassan II to integrate the opposition party into the management of the country's affairs.[65]

Control and Reversal: The Lesson of Hassan II

It can be said in summary that in the 1960s the monarchy allowed the 'ulama to maintain their educational institution, modifying it only marginally, and delegated to them the interpretation of family law, but very subtly manipulated the remainder of the religious sphere by fragmenting it. It kept control over the pious foundations, diversified training programs for 'ulama or producers of religious meaning, and co-opted individual members of the 'ulama by attaching them directly to the Makhzen. The monarchy also weakened Istiqlal, one of the original political organizations of the 'ulama. Oversight of the religious sphere was conducted both through its fragmentation associated with strict control of the political sphere and through the buttressing and daily management of the religious aspect of the monarchy.

While Islam, in its fragmented reality, was gradually brought under the authoritarian control of the monarchy, it remained divided among diverse training networks and individual 'ulama who pledged allegiance to the monarchy, as in the highly symbolic moments of the *bay'a* (a rare occurrence) or "Hassanian lessons" repeated annually in the month of Ramadan. In the early years of independence, the relationship of the monarchy with individual 'ulama was also expressed in the movement of Qarawiyyin graduates into secular fields, for instance, by entering politics. The case of 'Allal al-Fasi, distinctive because of his stature and his political role, is worth recalling, but other younger men also entered the ranks of the upper administration—for example, 'Abd al-Hadi bu Talib, Ahmad Ibn Suda, and 'Abd al-Hadi Tazi. They entered government service, but they also functioned as advisers to the king, members of the Royal Academy, or members of the diplomatic corps, which made it possible to domesticate them. They were admitted into the king's court but they were unable to act in a truly autonomous way in the religious sphere. This generation often successfully moved into the secular sphere but seems to have been the last generation of Qarawiyyin graduates that has managed to assume high positions in the Makhzen, in contrast to the younger generation of graduates of the religious educational system of today, which will be considered later.[66]

The only institution controlling this fragmented complex of diverse institutional channels and individuals was the monarchy itself which, unlike other Arab regimes, had not created a genuinely homogeneous, separate, and mediating institution to bring the 'ulama together and establish them as a professional body. In Morocco, the 'ulama thus expressed themselves in institutional arenas that did not belong to them. A Moroccan religious scholar could therefore not occupy the intermediary space offered elsewhere in the Arab world by religious institutions that function as a protective and relatively autonomous sphere in relation to the political authorities. Deprived of a platform of expression independent from the regime, or one that might provide them with a precise identity, the Moroccan 'ulama could really express themselves only within the Makhzen, as long as the political sphere remained under the control of an authoritarian regime that did not permit its liberalization. This is why, from the second half of the twentieth century up to the 1990s, no religious figure can be found who expressed himself totally outside that sphere, on pain of censorship. Even those clerics who were boldest in their approach to the monarchy were included in the system in one way or another, like Sheikh 'Abd Allah Kannun, who found a sphere of expression in the Ministry of Religious Affairs, even though it was controlled by the monarchy. Lacking a genuine religious institution, the 'ulama remained at the mercy of the Makhzen and, if they did venture to speak, found themselves in direct confrontation with the sovereign.

Hassan II's lessons in the month of Ramadan made it possible for the king to "mark," once a year, the extent of his religious territory by including the 'ulama within it and extending it to the borders of the Muslim *umma*, thereby recalling the royal lineage of descent from the Prophet. In December 1968, when he had just launched the *msid* program, Hassan II, in a highly unusual step, presented his own commentary on a verse of the Qur'an. He spoke directly to the 'ulama and explained to them that he had established Dar al-Hadith to strengthen hadith studies.[67] He offered a reading of a difficult verse that was explicitly very personal, exemplifying the figure of the *mujtahid* (the one who makes the effort of interpretation): "I prefer this meaning over that one," he said in substance, interpreting Surat 33, verse 72, the interpretation of which may vary according to the meaning attributed to the word *amana*. The scholarly king leaned toward an exegesis pointing to man's responsibility on earth: "We did indeed offer the Trust [*amana*] to the Heavens and the Earth and the Mountains; but they refused to undertake it, being afraid thereof: but man undertook it—he was indeed unjust and foolish."[68]

The king declared to the 'ulama: "This is not my field of specialization, I do not wish to produce blameworthy innovations." He nonetheless explained the rhythm with which the verse should be read and also raised questions that were articulated as interpretative challenges posed to the 'ulama that made him into a "scholarly" king (*malik 'alim*).[69]

The lesson, given by the 'ulama and commented on by the king, established a reciprocal relationship between the monarch and the clerics, a relationship that was gradually systematized and publicized. This year, 1968, was in fact the first time that the Ministry of Religious Affairs published the collection of lessons of the month of Ramadan, and they were also broadcast on radio and television. According to the Minister of Religious Affairs at the time, the intent was to reproduce Hassan's lesson throughout the kingdom, producing a kind of unification of the physical territory through the sacred.[70] The king, flanked by his two sons and facing his 'ulama, gave the example, and the scholarly circle had to reproduce itself, as though in a mirror, by imitating the lesson given by the clerics to the commander of the faithful.

That same year as well, the old festival of the "sultan of the *tolbas*" in Fez disappeared on orders of the monarchy.[71] Sultan Mawlay Rashid was said to have established this festival in the late seventeenth century "in homage to his student comrades in Fez who, according to legend, helped him seize power."[72] In a carnivalesque reversal of political roles for the space of a week, a *taleb* from the Qarawiyyin would play the part of the king. In the company of an imitation government, he was visited by the real sultan, who joined in a masquerade of the encounter of two rulers on horseback, the sultan and his mirror image embodied by the *taleb*.[73] The post-colonial authoritarian monarchy put an end to this annual ritual of reversal. Along with Hassan II's lessons, the content of which was reviewed in advance, reversals became controllable by the king, because they were conducted within the Palace itself, in the territory of royal sacredness, and lasted for only a few hours.

I next consider how the 'ulama, although domesticated by the monarchy, at the same time propagated their interpretations of Islam among the Moroccan public and continued to play an important role in the definitions of the Islamic tradition.

CHAPTER 3

Conservative Nationalism and Islam

The 'Ulama's Anti-Western Vision

The 'ulama's battle for Arabization was fought against the secular segments of Moroccan society who had assimilated French influences, but also, more symbolically, against an enemy that had a shadowy existence as a foreign element—the West, which was still, implicitly and subtly, the colonial power. The 'ulama created an autonomous sphere of activity in formulating the question of the cultural confrontation between Islam and the West, which included intense arguments over the definition of ethical and social norms and, for a small minority, political demands.

Salafism versus Marxism

With regard to its historical roots, the language of the 'ulama in the 1960s and 1970s took the concept of opposition to the West from the Salafism of the early part of the twentieth century and relegated domestic political matters to the margins. With regard to later developments, I will show how the legalist Islamists of the 1990s reiterated this focus on cultural and moral questions that brought the opposition between Islam and the West to the fore, while they simultaneously entered into political considerations and political activity. In this sense, the language used by the 'ulama between the 1960s and the 1980s is central, because it set forth a religious discourse focused on questions of cultural identity, which was later reappropriated by the Islamists.

As the preceding chapter showed, after independence many 'ulama became involved at all levels of modern public education, including the university. They transmitted this language in classrooms, became one of its most significant public voices, and educated in part—particularly in the *lycées*—the younger generation of Islamists who emerged politically in the 1990s. In 1957, Hasan al-Sa'ih, a cleric who wrote often for religious magazines after independence, described Salafism in the second issue of *Da'wat al-haqq*. In his view, *Salafiyya* had

> created a new generation that knows Islam *as it is* and knows at the same time how eager the West is to capture Islam and Muslims in its nets, deprive them of their ability to resist, and alienate them from their civilization. . . . This was the task of the Salafist movement before independence: the struggle against the occupier, the purification of thought, and the return of Islam to its pure sources. But today the Salafist movement is facing different problems. And I think they are more difficult than those it faced before independence. Yesterday, its enemies acted in the light of day. But today, they are acting against it in the dark. . . . There is no doubt that young Moroccans have read Western philosophers, their materialist philosophy. . . . These young people represent a danger for our rebirth, because they are alienated from Moroccan ways of thinking.[1]

This Salafism later evolved into a form of fundamentalism attached to the monarchic principle (that of al-Fasi, for example, and more generally of the Ministry of Religious Affairs) or into a radical position that was primarily opposed to everything that was not Islamic, within and outside the borders of the country.

'Allal al-Fasi also linked the question of national identity to the influence of the West and the revitalization of shari'a. But his notion of Qur'anic law had undergone significant change between writing his first work on the subject, *The Intentions of Shari'a*, and his *Defense of Shari'a*. In the first work, written during his exile in Cairo between 1949 and 1952, al-Fasi centered his attention on the internal reform of Islam. But in his *Defense of Shari'a* of 1966, he developed an argument in favor of the application of shari'a in conjunction with a rejection of Western culture, which he interpreted as cultural, economic, and political neocolonialism. He presented a harsh diagnosis of the shift of Moroccan identity toward that of a "mutant" or a "schizophrenic." Al-Fasi was at the time in a defensive position and represented Islam as the victim of a more powerful "other." While before independence the concern had been to rethink religion in order to reform it, it was now more important to protect it and to preserve it from outside attack. The idea of reform, of interpreting the text to harmonize it with the cultural developments of Moroccan society, was thus abandoned. Rather than reinterpreting the text, it was necessary to see to its immediate application.

When Hassan II came to power, the 1960s were apparently manifesting the triumph of socialist ideology in the Arab world. Boumediene took power in its name in Algeria in 1965; Tunisia also followed a socialist path, with Bourguiba adopting a very anticlerical attitude; and in Egypt, Nasserism was in full swing. The Moroccan revolutionary left was strongly influenced by and attracted to these experiences.

By the 1970s, most 'ulama, who had been institutionally domesticated by the monarchy, were participating in the government-orchestrated and government-encouraged mobilization against socialist ideas, including a meeting of Muslim heads of state in Rabat in September 1969, which gave birth to the Organization of the Islamic Conference (OIC), on the initiative of King Faysal of Saudi Arabia and with the energetic support of Hassan II. 'Allal al-Fasi had already been one of the founding members of the World Muslim League (WML), set up by King Faysal in 1962 as a weapon against Nasserism.² I have already pointed out that the Moroccan 'ulama showed some familiarity with left-wing thinking at the time, which, because it was so prevalent and powerful in the 1960s, they encountered in *lycées* and at university. From the 1970s on, the official journal of the Ministry of Religious Affairs, *Da'wat al-haqq*, used the 'ulama to refine and spread anti-leftist thinking. They entered into the enterprise wholeheartedly, much more than their Egyptian colleagues did in the columns of the official Islamic press in the 1970s, because the Egyptian 'ulama had lived under Nasser's authoritarian socialist regime for fifteen years. The mobilization in support of "Moroccan" Sahara (Western Sahara), initiated by the "green march" of November 1975, also used Islam and the preachers of the Ministry of Religious Affairs,³ who contrasted "atheist" Algeria with "Muslim" Morocco.⁴ In the spring of 1978, *Da'wat al-haqq* published an editorial entitled "The Fable of Scientific Thought," in which the ideologies of the left were reduced to the rank of mere ideas with no relationship to science: "Marxism is not a science and never will be, there is no scientific socialism and there never will be."⁵ Yes to the true scientific spirit, said the article, no to ideology and revolution.

Islamism Unsettles the 'Ulama

A year later, on the occasion of their seventh conference, held in Oujda from May 18 to May 20, 1979, the members of the Moroccan League of 'Ulama began to speak publicly about these questions, carefully defining the identity of an "enemy" and the way to oppose it. The conference proceedings provide a clear summary of these clerics' favorite themes, beginning with global Islam in the face of its enemies, in particular Zionism. Morocco had just established that year the al-Quds Committee—over which Hassan II presided as long as he lived—which represented the position of the OIC on the status of Jerusalem. Next came the question of the family, and particularly the norms that ought to regulate it. One of the points that the conference proceedings particularly emphasized was the separation of sexes in public life, in the administration, in education, and in public transportation. There was also discussion of the rebirth of religion through the revitalization of pious endowments, the role of religious propaganda and the mosques, and the Islamic institution of the *hisba* (an institution responsible for overseeing the proper functioning of economic activity and the legality of contracts, but also, more recently, in the interpretation of many Islamists, a morals police). The prohibition of usury (*riba*), of gambling, and of alcohol occupied a prominent place among their demands. The 'ulama also asked that prayer be required in public places, and that the royal decree imposing prayer in schools be applied. They offered the vision of an art in harmony with Islam and devoted an entire paragraph to Arabization.

Their list was eclectic, to say the least, mixing strictly religious demands with social questions (improvements in hospital conditions, concern for the treatment of the disabled). It clearly showed that these 'ulama were out of step with the regime—which they were trying to drive into an "Islamic" corner—but primarily that they were now being confronted with new religious figures who shared their language without having been educated in religious schools: the Islamists. The Islamists were in fact beginning to appropriate the themes connected to major social problems and were making progress in direct confrontation with the left on university campuses. The 'ulama thus attempted to make up for lost time against these two protagonists by adopting the broad outlines of the Islamists' religious themes and the left's social demands. The themes of the legalist Islamism of the late 1990s and the early years of the following decade would reflect these same preoccupations.

This new scope of the expression of opinions adopted by the 'ulama of the League in the late 1970s, in conjunction with the growth of Islamism, incited the monarchy to invent a new way of organizing and overseeing its institutional mechanisms of religious regulation. In 1980, Hassan II announced the establishment of "scientific councils" of the 'ulama, an organization for oversight presided over by the monarch and made up of regional organizations. Having worked toward the fragmentation of the world of the 'ulama, the monarchy had to find an instrument of control that it lacked, in order to attempt to pacify a League that was beginning to become too active.

The Ministry of Religious Affairs and the 'ulama were in fact gradually converging. I have already noted that the Ministry of Religious Affairs published material by the 'ulama of the League in its magazine. In the 1970s, some writers outlined there the image of a victimized *umma* that had become the prey of a threefold enemy: socialism, Zionism, and Christendom.[6] This was true for the Minister of Religious Affairs, Ahmad Ramzi,[7] but it was also true for the League of 'Ulama, which, under the firm guidance of its secretary general, Sheikh 'Abd Allah Kannun, submitted to the political rules defined by the monarchy, but also spoke of Islam as the solution to the ills that troubled Morocco.

Born into a great 'ulama family of Fez around 1908, Sheikh Kannun, often celebrated as one of the last great scholars of his age, studied religious sciences with his father, then with his paternal uncle and the 'ulama of Tangiers.[8] Tied to the nationalism of the Salafist 'ulama, after independence he participated in the establishment of the League of 'Ulama and the publication of its newspaper, *Al-mithaq*. He was a member of the prestigious Arabic Language Academy in Cairo, as well as of the Academy of Islamic Studies of al-Azhar. An independent figure—and admired by his peers for that reason—'Abd Allah Kannun worked with other 'ulama to lay the basis for a veritable state fundamentalism, which, incidentally, the monarchy encouraged: Hassan II, like his 'ulama, denounced the tendency of Muslims to imitate the West.[9]

In his opening speech at the seventh conference of the League of 'Ulama in Oujda in May 1979, Sheikh Kannun declared: "There can be no rebirth without a return to Islam," and opposed those who were living "in Western culture." "If they persist in their imitation of the West, if they continue to shift Muslims from the position of leadership where God has placed them to that of servile imitators, they may be certain that a volcano will erupt and that the power of faith will surround them regardless of their own power. The example of Iran has given them the most overwhelming proof of that."[10] The League of 'Ulama thus gave its blessing to the very recent Iranian revolution; and the messianic tone recalled, practically word for word, that used a few years earlier by Abdessalam Yassine: "You are sitting on a volcano that is about to erupt," he said to Hassan II in 1973. But rather than apostrophizing the king, the 'ulama were addressing "Westernized" Moroccan Muslims. Reading between the lines, one can also interpret their words as a warning to the Moroccan monarchy that it might one day suffer the fate of the Shah of Iran.[11]

'Abd Allah Kannun did not stop with this indirect critique. In the same issue of *Da'wat al-haqq*, official organ of the Ministry of Religious Affairs, he wrote a long article on the "system of government in Islam."[12] Remaining vague about the identity of the regimes he was discussing, he presented a vision of contemporary political regimes that owed a good deal to the ideologues of the Iranian revolution and was close to that of the mystic Islamist, Abdessalam Yassine. In Sheikh Kannun's view, the world was divided between the powerful and the deprived (*mustadh'afun*), the Arabic term used to translate Frantz Fanon's *The Wretched of the Earth* and deployed by the Iranian revolution's rhetoric:

> People have begun to believe in brute force [*quwwa*]. It has now become the very goal of civilization. How wonderful it would be if that force were used to put an end to injustice.... But it is used to humiliate the deprived, to impose its power on other peoples, to exploit their natural resources and their poor in order to enrich the powerful nations.... Politics is the prerogative of great nations who determine the future of the world. They have placed the United Nations under their control. They have assumed the right to oppose any decision that does not suit them. They are delaying the progress of humanity toward mutual understanding and fraternity.

He went on to ask how these great powers could legitimately claim to be socialist or democratic when "humanity was constantly suffering," "was living in fear ... and anguish."[13]

For the *'alim* Kannun, Islam was the solution. He spoke of Muslim heads of state in these terms:

> There is no doubt that the heartbreaks ... experienced by Muslim peoples are the result of this blind imitation [of Western life], of this subordination into which they are driven by leaders and heads of state who have filled their hearts with faith in foreigners and imported doctrines. They have constructed these doctrines for themselves, failing to recognize that they were not suitable for their people, failing to understand the dislocation it would cause for their people, and the mistrust it would breed among them toward their political guides. They did not think of the gulf that was widening day after day between peoples and their governments, which had become strange, or even alien.[14]

Kannun went on to describe the institution of the caliphate and the person of the caliph, the lieutenant of the Prophet, elected by Muslims and governing by relying on consultation with "experts in politics, war, society, and the economy," not with the majority, which may be mistaken. Kannun did not use the word *bay'a* (allegiance), as it was symbolically used by the monarchy. Shifting from "caliph" to "king," he explained that the king had to reign and govern as a caliph who ensured that divine law was properly applied. This passage contained a reassurance for the Moroccan monarchy, unlike the preceding denunciation of leaders who did not meet the conditions of the caliphate as Kannun had set them forth.

Kannun was certainly a cleric in a class of his own, as much in the quality and subtlety of his writing as in the boldness of his political positions and the distance he took from the Moroccan monarchy. In the late 1970s, this freedom of tone was adopted by one of the most official centers of Islam, the Ministry of Religious Affairs, within which this unusual cleric was able to speak. During the 1970s, other signs of distance from the regime came from this same location under the supervision and control of the monarchy, expressed, for example, by frequent publication in the pages of *Da'wat al-haqq* of articles by one of the founders of contemporary Islamism, the Pakistani Abu al-'Ala al-Mawdudi.[15]

This Islam of the clerics, until then domesticated by the monarchy and used to combat the left, was now in a position to increase the stakes. The clerics' demands were, however, never directed expressly to the king, who remained, in the language used by the League of 'Ulama, in an external position. They addressed Moroccans, Muslims, or else socialists, missionaries, and Zionists—three groups considered enemies of a victimized Islam.

This oblique relationship of the 'ulama to the monarchy was also seen in the figure of 'Allal al-Fasi, who, as a politician, produced a thoroughgoing critique of the postcolonial Moroccan regime. His thinking, however, was far from unified, and he left a heterogeneous legacy of articles, books, and speeches from which no clear ideology can be drawn. His analyses were, in fact, also a reflection of political circumstances, in particular his relations with the regime; but a clearer view can be had by examining some of his writings on the religious question.

What Is a Religious Power?

In the view of 'Allal al-Fasi, the 'ulama as such had no power because there is no such thing as "religious power" in Islam. For him, the first task of the 'ulama was not to act politically but to admonish the prince and Muslims, when that was necessary. Their *da'wa* (preaching) was not to be organized by the state; it was consubstantial with their learning. Although he sometimes considered challenging the power of the king, he never really did so as a cleric, but only as the head of a political party, a position he did not reach until 1959. The dual identity of 'Allal al-Fasi as *'alim* and head of Istiqlal made it easier for the Makhzen to deal with a figure at first seen as a political threat. As an *'alim*, he was co-opted by the king's sacred territory, but he was marginalized as a party leader.

His simultaneous presence in these two territories placed him in a position that was both ambiguous and full of tension. Within the area where he expressed rebellion—politics—he was in fact easily undermined by the king who held power. 'Allal al-Fasi never connected his own activity of political critique to his presence as a cleric in the religious sphere, in contrast to the strategy of the monarchy, which strove to bring religion and political power together. 'Allal al-Fasi did not use his status as an *'alim* to challenge the monarchy's policies because, in his view, power could not come from the 'ulama, whose status derived from learning rather than power. While they articulated the norm, they did not play the role of enforcing it. Clerics did not have the power of the sultan, and the sultan himself was not a cleric, in the sense that he was not a doctor of the law.

By saying that effective political power could not be religious in its nature, 'Allal al-Fasi was challenging a tradition that had been heavily exploited and stabilized by the 'Alawite kings of Morocco: the convergence of genealogical, prophetic, and spiritual charisma in the monarchic institution.[16] For 'Allal al-Fasi, the relationship between religion and politics was defined ideally as a partnership of independent functions, in a balance of power. The monarch was obliged to consult the 'ulama and see to the application of Islamic legality defined through their learning. Islam thus encompassed the regime, but the opposite was not the case. Similarly, the king's power was not "religious." If a religious power did exist, it was in each one of the faithful, recalling the political mysticism of Sayyid Qutb.[17] This is why, in al-Fasi's view, the foundation of politics remained the people. This conception of Islam and its relationship to politics was also the basis for his populism and that of his party, Istiqlal. The West "got rid of its religion," al-Fasi explained,

> because it was under the control of the clergy and the feudal power with which the clergy was allied. . . . But we Muslims have no clergy and we are laymen by the very nature of our religion. For each of us is connected to Allah, who is closer to us than our own jugular vein. We don't need a pontiff or a monk to permit or prohibit, or to pardon sins that we might confess to them. Our 'ulama are not monks. They are specialists in one field of knowledge among others, the shari'a, as others have specialized in sci-

ence or engineering. We consult them to profit from their knowledge when we are unable to answer ourselves the questions we ask.... Everyone of us can be a *mujtahid*, if he has the ability.... The clergy is not responsible for the path religion follows. Each Muslim man and Muslim woman is responsible for the state of Islam and must combat its enemies.[18]

Political power and religious learning were thus functionally separated, even though in terms of principle and norm, the fusion of the two had to be perfect since the only legitimate power was the one who upheld the principles of shari'a. 'Allal al-Fasi thus rejected the idea of a religious authority in the sense of an institution, as he also rejected, while obscuring this position in his writings, the religious power of the king. Al-Fasi was thus implicitly targeting the very process by which the monarchy of Hassan II was constructing its religious territory. If a religious authority existed, it had to operate on the basis of accepted norms, as well as on the basis of knowledge and interpretative ability, as exercised by men of religious learning, and not be grounded in the power conferred by the monopoly on the legitimate use of force. This is why the one particular religious institution he emphasized was of course that involved in the formulation and the transmission of legal knowledge, much more than the institution of the monarchy, which was in the end only the guardian of the norms of shari'a and the will of the people, the two of which could only coincide.

He thus implicitly upended the hierarchy originally outlined by Moroccan Salafism, which favored the tradition of the Prophet (Sunna) over the work of jurisprudence (*fiqh*), and he reemphasized the need to work on law to produce the norm. But he drew no political conclusions from this conceptual reversal. In his *Defense of Shari'a*, published one year after the 1965 state of emergency, he merely asked for the establishment of a genuine institute for Islamic studies (even though the king himself had established Dar al-Hadith in 1964) and expressed distress at students' lack of interest in shari'a studies: "This is the result of neglect by the state and the authorities of the Ministry of Education of the greatest [*a'zam*] Islamic university and the oldest university in the world."[19]

He also wrote: "Kings and heads of state do not have power or rights that come to them from heaven." And he explained: "This power and these rights belong to the people who, by virtue of the status of its individual members, vice-regents of God on earth, is the source of *siyada* (sovereignty), the source of power. Whoever is born from this source is a *wali* [master], otherwise there is no *wali*."[20]

The principles for the definition of religion as of power were thus found in each believer, and they could not fail to converge. For 'Allal al-Fasi, a true democracy could show only that the people wanted shari'a to be applied: because they were perfect, the divine norms stood on their own through the agreement they found in the heart of each believer. This is why, for al-Fasi, knowledge of the norm was so important, and it is why, in his view, the 'ulama had to guarantee the transmission and dynamism of this learning. The only role of the political regime was to ensure the conformity of society with those norms as interpreted through that learning.

His vision was that of a democratic society made up of believing citizens. Like Hasan al-Banna, the Egyptian founder of the Muslim Brotherhood in 1928, he saw a society informed by *din* (religion) in which democracy, no matter what form it took, could bring forth only a political structure whose acts would be in conformity with Islam. After 1969, in fact, he had Istiqlal publish books by the Egyptian Islamist Sayyid Qutb, who had been executed by Nasser's regime in 1966.[21]

'Allal al-Fasi: A Monarchist Rebel?

Al-Fasi's political vision did not immediately manage to find a place in Moroccan society, although some of his ideas recovered vitality in the public realm in the 1990s. His time in the Ministry of Religious Affairs from June 1961 to January 1963 was the only period he was in government. From 1965 on, the state of emergency froze political discussion between parties that were too weakened by the monarchy to launch a public debate on the forms of political activity. But in 1971 and 1972, two failed army coups d'état shook the monarchy and impelled it to turn back to the political parties: it was time to reestablish its legitimacy.

On September 23, 1972, Hassan II sent a message to the executive committee of Istiqlal and to the other political parties asking them to participate in the government that he intended to establish on October 16. Determining that some of the bases for the legitimacy of the political regime were lacking, 'Allal al-Fasi wrote a strong letter of rejection to the king. And in a document published in the name of Istiqlal, entitled *Evaluation of the Political Situation*, he drew up a severe diagnosis and formulated the conditions under which his party would accede to the royal request: a national government that expressed the popular will. "National independence can be established only through the liberation of the citizen from all forms of political, economic, and social servitude [he used the Arabic term *'ubudiyya*, which had been used by Mawdudi and Qutb]. It can be accomplished only by closing the door to the imperialist countries that are conspiring against the sovereignty of Morocco."[22]

He also criticized the manner of governing, particularly the electoral frauds that had taken place since 1963. He called for free elections and criticized the parliament that had been deprived of its functions of government oversight and representation of the popular will. 'Allal al-Fasi thus drew up a balance sheet covering ten years of political life. In 1962, a year after Hassan II came to power, Istiqlal had participated in the drafting of the new Constitution, but the elections in the following year had not been transparent, and the results had been falsified. It had been a difficult moment for Istiqlal and for the other political parties. The 1965 state of emergency, which followed the Casablanca riots and their repression by the army, had given unchecked power to the monarchy.

The diagnosis, supported by the shock of the 1971 and 1972 coups d'état, was harsh: political institutions had been emptied of meaning, and the state had been privatized for the benefit of the Makhzen, which had led to corruption and the creation of new baronial powers with networks of clients benefiting from land redistribution. Al-Fasi also pointed out violations of human rights, the lack of freedom of the press, and major problems in education, particularly the lack of attention to the Qarawiyyin and other religious institutions. And he evoked the decline (*tadahwir*) of Islamic culture.

For 'Allal al-Fasi and the party he led, the root of the problem lay in the first place in the regime's mode of political operation. He did not directly address the king (except in his polite but strong letter of refusal) and never directly criticized the monarchy. Democracy, liberty, and justice were the key words of this program that brought together the vocabulary of liberal democracy and vague arguments about social justice taken from both leftist ideologies and the early works of Sayyid Qutb. In this document with populist overtones, alongside the idea of agrarian reform he spoke of a "classless" society, echoing the ideology of the National Liberation Front of Algeria.[23]

This long document was also a way of recalling his nationalist past and bringing the party's program to the fore: constitutional monarchy, democracy, the land belonging to those who worked it, social justice through the equitable redistribution of national income and application of an agrarian reform, and Arabization of the administration and the educational system.[24]

'Allal al-Fasi was not the only one to answer the king with a rejection. 'Abd al-Karim Khatib, the head of the People's Movement—which had become the MPDC (Mouvement Populaire Démocratique et Constitutionnel, People's Democratic and Constitutional Movement)—refused to participate in a system that he blamed for the crisis Morocco was going through, crystallized by the two failed coups d'état. But the texts by al-Fasi and Khatib, the two men who had decided to introduce the idea of commander of the faithful into the text of the 1962 Constitution, were very different from one another. Al-Fasi reacted as the head of a political party, a function that had taken priority over that of traditional cleric, and coolly analyzed the political situation by using essentially political categories: he demanded a true democracy—a legitimate government founded on the sovereignty of law, responsible before its citizens and elected by them. Khatib, for his part, put as much emphasis on shari'a as on democracy, and dwelled on the legitimate conditions of the *bay'a*.

Istiqlal, in the voice of its leader, a graduate of the Qarawiyyin who had been Minister of Religious Affairs, had finally secularized its political arguments. Khatib, for his part, demonstrated more sustained attention to Islam. A year later in 1973, Abdessalam Yassine developed a discourse and a religious posture that he linked closely to politics, starting from an entirely different register, that of sharifism, and in a relationship to the government very different from that of Al-Fasi and Khatib, that is, outside any institutional position.

As political leaders, Al-Fasi and Khatib in fact began their lean years after 1971 and 1972. Brief and inconclusive for 'Allal al-Fasi, who died in 1974, they lasted longer for Khatib, ending in the mid-1990s when he formed an alliance with the legalist Islamists. They, incidentally, obliterated the memory of al-Fasi and of his writings, which are rarely mentioned by the new ideologues of legalist Islamism.

But in the early 1970s, as these two representatives of the old nationalism were becoming marginal in the political realm, a new figure emerged who had passed through neither nationalism nor salafism: Abdessalam Yassine. Yassine established a new political opposition that held itself apart from the partisan system, criticized the regime from an outside position, and made Islam not merely an ideological reference but the symbolic foundation of its political posture. Abdessalam Yassine based his rebellion on holiness and attempted to establish in himself a new prophetic line, whose prospects for survival are still uncertain.

Demands for the Islamicization of society from the 'ulama revolved around the establishment of and respect for Islamic norms. The 'ulama never tied those demands to the person and the Islamic nature of the king. On the other hand, as the following chapters show, Abdessalam Yassine directly addressed the sovereign and fully entered the king's domain to question his Islamic identity even before raising the question of the Islamic character of Moroccan society. In this sense, he profaned a sacred sphere, that of the monarchy. He dislocated the royal territory and disconnected Islam from the monarchy, crowning an undertaking that had begun in the aftermath of independence: the gradual separation of individual royal power from genealogical charisma.

PART II

A Rebel Mystic: Abdessalam Yassine

Early in 1974, in the wake of the two failed military coups of 1971 and 1972, Sheikh Abdessalam Yassine addressed a written admonition to the king of Morocco, with the title *Islam or the Deluge*. This letter changed the tone of the political challenge. The armed force of the military had not worked, and religion had become a political resource that gave coherent form to this new rebellion.

Yassine made sure that his message was made public even before he sent it to the monarch. Rather than Hassan II, his primary audience was the Moroccan people. He asked them to take note of the relationship he was establishing with the commander of the faithful and to act as witnesses to this relationship between the man of learning and the prince. Traditionally, the *nasihat al-muluk*'s genre—advice to rulers or mirror for princes—was primarily a treatise on the art of governing (*tadbir al-muluk*), on the way a ruler was to behave toward both God and his subjects.[1] But Yassine's letters to the monarchy—he repeated the gesture in 2000—were not abstract messages about what the standards of behavior of the head of the nation ought to be. Yassine's admonition publicly mirrored and reflected on the prince's errors. The letter described a triangular power relation that was unequal in two respects: Yassine contrasted the monarch's omnipotence to his own weakness, but also suggested the underlying warning that the power of the people might exceed that of the prince.

The position Yassine adopted in 1974 evoked an ancient and recurring theme in the history of Morocco: the pious man who becomes a rebel through mystical experience and the manifestation of a messianism derived from the religious and political tradition of the

Maghreb, which oscillated between apocalyptic visions tied to the utopia of a radical restoration of the golden age and a speculative orientation linked to a more inward mysticism. Other figures had played the role of holy chastiser long before he did, and they had succeeded in seizing power, at least locally.

At the end of the first millennium of the Hegira, Ibn Abi Mahalli (1560?-1613) adopted the figure of the Mahdi, the "rightly guided one," "brought forth by God's command," and became king of Marrakesh.[2] In a different way, Hasan al-Yusi (b. 1631) was later, as the nation state was beginning to develop, an "ethical regulator," who dealt with the authorities through admonition but did not mobilize the people on the political level. Closer in time and more present in Moroccan collective memory is Ibn 'Abd al-Kabir al-Kattani (1873-1909), whom Abdessalam Yassine has invoked as a model.[3]

Yassine is thus rooted in the religious and political history of Morocco and its diversified traditions, but he also poses questions pertaining to the contemporary production and experience of what he himself dubs "modernity" and its traumatic consequences.[4] His interventions respond to a crisis situation which appears, as in the time of Ibn Abi Mahalli, to call for the advent of a reformer: "Trouble has become unbearable in every area . . . deterioration is growing, the nation is falling into decay. Darkness is spreading. Impiety is deepening. . . . Every scholar follows his whims, every saint his own illusion, every prince his ambition."[5] The difference is that, in the second half of the twentieth century, the monarchy has assumed unchecked dominion over the nation.

By the mid-1960s, Morocco was experiencing numerous economic and social difficulties. In 1970, John Waterbury pointed out the system's inability to integrate the new generation of school and university students into the administrative elites of the Makhzen or of the private sector, which remained quite small.[6] The gap between the Arabic-speaking population and graduates of French schools had widened. The great volatility of the agricultural sector, dependent as it was on the climate; the rapid growth of the rural population (which remained above 50 percent until the 1990s); and the spread of education and mechanization in the countryside were all factors driving thousands of rural inhabitants to seek opportunities in the cities. Gradually, a new population of young college graduates in search of a job that would correspond to their level of education, or rural migrants searching for work that would bring in a basic income, saw their future blocked.

Although demographic indicators have improved since then, the younger generation still sees a system that is unable to provide social and economic integration.[7] But rather than relying on a strong policy of economic development, beginning in the mid-1960s the monarchy chose to satisfy the elites in power by reinforcing the authoritarian features of the regime, leaving the field open for an often inefficient economic system based on patronage. Those excluded by the system were thus not only the traditional opposition parties but also an entire new generation of university graduates whom these partisan organizations had not always managed to accommodate. The tension between the democratization of education and the educational system's inadequate adaptation to the labor market has only deepened since then, swelling the ranks of the discontented, who were thus made available for mobilization to challenge the regime.[8]

By articulating his individual political rebellion through mysticism and messianism, even before establishing an organized political framework, Yassine emphasized the individual and subjective nature of the suffering induced by the distortions of a society undergoing rapid change. At the same time, his movement, Justice and Benevolence, transcended him as an individual and gradually became a totalizing if not totalitarian movement: individual suffering was identified with communal injury and pathos, which he treated by creating a community that disciplined individuals and restored their shattered existence through the fostering of the illusion of religious intensity and completeness.

The success of the movement can be attributed to the conjunction of these two domains, concern for both individual and community structure. Its current numerical strength is not known precisely, but its capacity for mobilization at least until the mid-1990s was clear:

"They took care of me in every way. They pay attention to everything, everything!" exclaimed a female militant to explain to me her adherence to the Yassine movement.

To understand the link between the subjective and communal domains, we need to return to the founding moment of the admonition: Abdessalam Yassine individually questioned the religious position of the monarchy and profaned its sacred status. With the pretext of reconnecting the monarch to religion, the pious man alerted the public to the monarchy's secularization and also made himself, paradoxically, one of its most active agents of change.

CHAPTER 4

The "Conversion" of Sheikh Yassine

The details of Sheikh Yassine's life are hard to uncover. In fact, only very recently, in 2004, were his official biography and genealogy made public by being included on his website, Yassine Online (www.yassineonline.net). His path, now made official in a medium with a worldwide audience, took more than thirty years to forge. Far from being a "finished product," his ongoing status is the result of an unstable identity, which is still in process. Still alive and open to change, Yassine's image has not yet entered collective memory and the long-term history that would foster the creation of a saint's stabilized hagiography. While some see him as a living saint, this saintly status might disappear upon his death.

His career has been marked by contradictions that he himself has no hesitation in bringing forward. Born, educated, and having made his career in the city, he exalts his rural origins. Born poor, as he likes to recall, his life has been one of upward social mobility. Educated in Arabic, he has been known to refer to his Berber origins, but he also occasionally writes in French,[1] a language to which he came late. Commenting ironically on the king's genealogical tracing back to the Prophet, he reminds the king that he, too, is a descendant of the

Prophet, and of Idrissid rather than 'Alawite ancestry.[2] Identifying himself with mystical experience, he has attempted to obscure his scholarly background, with which he maintains an ambiguous relationship.

To build up the personal charisma necessary for his political success, Yassine appropriated the figure of the great chastising saint, relying on two principal elements to endow him with some stature: sharifism, on the one hand, attesting to descent from the Prophet; and the figure of the mystic, on the other, who, moving from initiation to clairvoyance, can address the person of the prince with no intermediary. But Yassine received an academic religious education: he went through a scriptural and institutional Islamic education. Before being able to attain the esoteric sphere, he went through exoteric learning, which he put together with the former, but above which he was able to rise once he had established his position as a mystic.

The combination of these two steps has often been ignored in accounts of his career. Yassine has also attempted to obscure them from his listeners and readers: he is said, in fact, to have entered into Islamism without troubling himself with any academic preparation—except that provided by the revealed texts—or with institutional religious structures. Sheikh Yassine has attempted to show that he truly entered the path of religion through mystical Islam and his relationship with the Sufi master. Mystical Islam and the principle of companionship, he has said, opened the way for him to politics and enabled him to build up the charisma he needed to turn himself into the figure of a hero and martyr.

A Sussi Official in the Capital

His family came originally from the village of Haha in the Suss region, although Abdessalam Yassine was born in 1928 in Marrakesh, where his father had come at a very young age.[3] His official genealogy tells us that he is part of an old family named "Ait-Bihi," "Idrissid descendants of the Prophet" from the Suss region of Morocco.[4] His first schooling was in a *ma'had dini*, a religious institute founded by Mukhtar al-Susi.[5] The time was in the years following the great Berber *dahir* (decree) crisis of 1930 which gave rise to the first major wave of Moroccan nationalism. In 1943, he entered the Ibn Yusif Institute for Arabic and Islamic Studies in Marrakesh for secondary education.

The Ibn Yusif madrasa, or Yusufiyya, an old institution for religious education, had been reformed and authorized, beginning in 1939, like the Qarawiyyin in 1931, to train *qadis* (judges).[6] Abu Shu'ayb al-Dukkali had taught there between 1918 and 1923, dispensing reformist Salafist teachings, and Mukhtar al-Susi had been a teacher there in the 1930s. But it did not have the prestige and the cosmopolitan standing of the Qarawiyyin. Describing the capital of Suss in the early twentieth century, Gaston Deverdun wrote in 1959: "Islam in Fez, the cradle of art and law, was expressed primarily by the illustrious doctors of the Qarawiyyin mosque, whereas Marrakesh was principally known as the 'tomb of the saints.'" Abdessalam Yassine completed his schooling in the madrasa in 1947, and entered the teacher training school in Rabat where, he reports, he began learning French at the age of nineteen.[7] His career thus began in Marrakesh, the southern capital of the Berber region, the country of saints and the stronghold of al-Glawi,[8] and continued in Rabat, the modern administrative center, without going through the city of Fez and the major nationalist 'ulama associated with the Qarawiyyin.

Sheikh Yassine thus came out of a local religious institution—but one that had been reformed and modernized—where he learned Arabic and studied the major religious texts. He was not drawn to the monarchy's program for political conquest of the rural world, nor was he accepted by the bourgeois circles of the Istiqlal and their learned representatives such as 'Allal al-Fasi. He was not an autodidact in religion like most of the young Islamists who appeared on the political and ideological stage in the 1980s. He did not, however, fully belong to the religious 'ulama scholarly world, but was located on the border between it and one more connected to the spread of modern learning.[9] He took courses given by Mukhtar al-Susi and appreciated them,[10] but did not intend to become an *'alim*, a doctor of the law, in the classic sense of the word. He became a teacher of Arabic in 1948 and moved up through the hierarchy of the public education system until being appointed supervisor of the teaching of Arabic in Casablanca in 1955. He retired in the summer of 1967 for health reasons. Yassine thus seems to have followed the conventional career of a civil servant. He later wrote in his celebrated 1974 pamphlet, *Islam or the Deluge*, that his experience inside the Moroccan bureaucracy had opened his eyes to the corruption of the administration.[11]

> No, I was not cut off from religion. I had learned the Qur'an when I was a young child. I studied in the traditional Ibn Yusif madrasa in Marrakesh, and my education was primarily traditional: Qur'an, *fiqh*. . . But this traditional education meant that I lived my Islam very quietly; that is, I was observant, I said my prayers, I sometimes recited the Qur'an so that I wouldn't entirely forget it, having learned it by heart. And I was known in the circles I frequented as a reserved man. . . . All this time, my Islam was very sweet, very nice, you see, an Islam that didn't raise any questions.[12]

Yassine's Islam was practiced as a routine, "very quietly," he says, and remained personal. He had not yet objectified it. Yassine establishes a parallel between the teaching of religious knowledge in "traditional" institutions and the practice of an Islam without "expectations," which is observed day by day without its definition giving rise to "questions" or provoking self-examination.

Yassine was thus not trained in the mold of the great "school of Fez," but in that of an institution that was perceived to be just as "traditional," but provincial. As early as the 1930s, the Yusufiyya madrasa, like its more renowned counterpart in Fez, the Qarawiyyin, began to lose prestige: students came from increasingly rural backgrounds, and hopes for social mobility were embodied in the *collèges* established by the protectorate in 1914 (Collège Moulay-Idriss in Fez) and 1916 (Collège Moulay-Youssef in Rabat). These new educational establishments attracted the sons of major families of notables who deserted the institutions for the propagation of religious knowledge.[13] When Yassine entered the Yusufiyya in 1943, the few 'ulama in the vanguard of the movement joining nationalism to Salafism against French occupation, such as 'Allal al-Fasi, belonged to an older generation that seemed to hold sway much more in Fez and Rabat than in Marrakesh. In his book on the independence movements in the Maghreb, 'Allal al-Fasi never mentions Marrakesh much less the Yussufiyya, an omission that may reveal some contempt on his part.

In any event, Yassine perhaps had no great teacher of nationalism, whereas many students at the Ibn Yusif madrasa in the 1940s were drawn to the Istiqlal. In the 1930s and 1940s, major reformers and well known nationalists—Mukhtar al-Susi, the *fqih* Basri, and Muhammad Ibn 'Uthman, for example—studied or taught at the Yusufiyya. Far from being troubling for Yassine, his lack of connection with nationalist circles was later recast by a "rebellious" Yassine and used as part of a strategy of opposition to the model of the nationalist and Salafist man of learning that was co-opted by the monarchy of Muhammad V and that of his successor.[14] For this reason, Yassine's absence from the Moroccan nationalist movement against French occupation is extremely significant, particularly for a younger generation that did not experience the nationalist struggle. By his very silence on the subject, he has skipped a generation and established a connection with the young Islamists—whom he has lured away from nationalist language and drawn to the language of a universalist Islamism. Furthermore, the figure of the *'alim* that Yassine has adopted is not that of the nationalist man of learning, but that of the holy chastiser. He has thereby bridged a generation gap by allying with young Islamists, as well as an intellectual gap by bringing together mysticism and politics in an alliance that is exceptional in the world of Islamism today.

The Mystical Connection

The only true master that Abdessalam Yassine mentions as a direct influence is 'Abbas al-Qadiri, sheikh of the Budshishiyya Sufi brotherhood, a branch of the Qadiriyya established in the Beni-Snassen region in the seventeenth century, in Madagh, a village overlooking Oujda in northeastern Morocco. Sidi 'Ali al-Qadiri founded the *zawiya* in Madagh. It is said that he served people in times of famine a soup made of cracked wheat, *dshisha*, which led to his being called Budshishi. His descendant, Sidi al-Mukhtar, was famous for fomenting revolts against the protectorate by taking up arms against the French occupation of Oujda in 1907. He was succeeded by his cousin Sidi Bu Madyan, and he in turn initiated Sidi al-Haj 'Abbas (son of Sidi al-Mukhtar) as well as his son, now sheikh of the brotherhood, Sidi Hamza. Sidi Bu Madyan, who is said to have revived the teaching of Sidi al-Mukhtar, died in 1957.

After Moroccan independence, the brotherhood, over which Haj 'Abbas did not officially take control until 1962, grew significantly, particularly in the major cities and in scholarly circles, and the social origins of its membership became more diverse.[15] Sidi al-Haj 'Abbas did in fact "lighten" the Sufi ritual of the Budshishiyya,[16] a change made explicit and put into practice by his son, Sheikh Hamza, beginning in 1972. Sidi al-Haj 'Abbas wrote little, since his relationship with his disciples was essentially based on oral transmission. Among the few documents that have been mentioned is his spiritual testament designating his son as his successor at the head of the *tariqa*. To understand the role Yassine later played in his own group, we need to look at al-Haj al-'Abbas' conception of the role of the *sheikh al-tarbiyya* or "spiritual educator": "For Sidi al-Haj al-'Abbas, an important characteristic [of the spiritual educator] is to hold authority (*idhn*) from the Supreme Name. . . . The spiritual educator is also known as the 'master of the present time' (*mul al-waqt*)."[17]

> Sidi al-Haj 'Abbas himself explains:
> It should be said that I am neither a preacher nor a learned man who lays claim to legal knowledge, nor a reporter of traditions who instructs the public through exegesis of the Qur'an and the hadith. This is the task of scholars specialized in the study, analysis, and authentica-

tion of texts. My relationship with you is rather a spiritual one, educational and ethical, whose foundations are Companionship (*suhba*), love of God, meeting in order to invoke His name, reception of His divine breath, hunger for divine knowledge, acceptance of the constant help of His Prophet, aspiration toward purification of the heart, purity of conscience, strengthening of inwardness, as well as its illumination by the light of faith.[18]

Some of these mystical elements were later appropriated by Yassine, in particular the concept of companionship, but others were ignored with the aim of politicizing his approach.

The brotherhood, which is now very active—it is said to have about 15 thousand members—recruits primarily among notables, who may also have important responsibilities in the Makhzen. It is extremely visible both nationally and internationally because its members include Arabic-speaking and French-speaking intellectuals who write texts of high quality and are linked to Moroccan and foreign academic networks. The lightening up of Sufi ritual and its flexibility make it attractive for intellectuals seeking inspiration in Muslim tradition: Sheikh Hamza explicitly shifted his Sufism from a ritual of often physical ordeals to the experience of spirituality.

Karim Ben Driss, a disciple of the Budshishiyya, quotes Sheikh Hamza explaining why "Sufism has changed":

> In the old days, masters tested their disciples. They enabled them through these ordeals to conquer their souls and in the end to win. Like Sidi 'Ali Jamal who asked his disciple Mawlay al-'Arbi al-Darqawi to put a basket of figs on his fine white djellaba. If they did not do so, their soul would not surrender.[19]

This test, which Sheikh Hamza cites as being difficult, is so only metaphorically, because of the stain it makes on the "fine white" cloth. It calls for self-analysis and metaphorical impoverishment suitable for a bourgeois audience. Sheikh Hamza therefore eliminates the test and replaces it with the *dhikr*, the invocation of the name of God, an eminently spiritual practice. He inverts the order of the traditional ritual: instead of fostering "impoverishment," he suggests spiritual "embellishment" as a response to the "excess of materiality" one finds in the world.[20]

For Muslims who want to "rediscover" the aesthetic and intellectual manifestations of religion while simultaneously avoiding expressions of Islamism or political Islam, the Budshishiyya brotherhood provides an ideal vehicle. It in fact rejects the posture of political opposition and remains politically quietist. Yassine's early approach to the Budshishiyya was not a political one. Before his discovery of mysticism, he was a great admirer of European classical music and he wore Western suits and ties. When he decided to become a disciple of Sheikh 'Abbas, he gave away the things that pointed to his attachments to the Western material world, such as his collection of issues of *Time* magazine.

His daughter Nadia recounts the "conversion" of her father, emphasizing the duration of a process that began with a mystical crisis followed by a long spiritual "search," leading to the discovery of Sheikh 'Abbas:

> He needed a spiritual master. He went to see men whom he had been told were pious. But he always came back disappointed.... My father was very drawn to culture and poetry, and he had a critical attitude toward Sufism. In the late 1960s, he moved into politics, but before that came a spiritual awakening ... in the early 1960s. He was in search of something. Nothing made it possible to foretell his choice.[21]

From Mystical Experience to Political Commitment

When Yassine joined the Budshishiyya brotherhood, his associates were surprised. Between 1965 and 1972, he became a disciple of Sheikh 'Abbas, whose lessons he was listening to at the time. There was no master providing knowledge through books: the initiation was between individuals, only by means of the master-disciple relationship. "I found the truth with the Sufis," he explains,

> as al-Ghazali did. . . . When God enabled me to free myself from ignorance and from an inherited and badly understood Islam and to place myself on the pathway of truth and life, He drove me to seek to know Him. . . . God gave me a Sufi sheikh, to whom I attached myself and whom I loved.[22]

Yassine sets at the center of his mysticism the importance of the education transmitted by the master more than by texts: an education supposed to be that of the heart that cannot be carried on by the intellect alone.[23]

This explains the importance of the concept and practice of companionship (*suhba*). '*Ilm*, or formal religious knowledge, does not operate as the primary basis for defining his religious legitimacy, which Yassine bases on his mystical experience much more than on a fund of knowledge. Unlike most 'ulama, Yassine does not lard his writings with biographies of his masters: the intellectual genealogies found in major Moroccan scholars' works are absent from Yassine's writings. Far from connecting himself to an intellectual generation, Yassine has explicitly isolated himself from those he might have included in a circle of influences or fellow students. In this way, Yassine has individualized his relationship to Islam, a relationship which, notably at the time of the "mystical crisis," moved through the internalization of Islam and the obliteration of the outside world, represented in particular by impoverishment and the renunciation of material things.

In his 1974 admonition, *Islam or the Deluge*, Yassine reports his "conversion" in these terms:

> I met . . . a man . . . who had me sit down in the midst of a group of Muslims among whom were an artisan and an unemployed man. He had me sit in a group of poor men, when I was living in a mansion and I was one of the princes

> of the administration. I called on the name of Allah along with the poor.
>
> This was a spiritual crisis that those who knew me mistook for a mental illness, and when God sent me a mystical sheikh, whom I loved and followed, they spread the news that I had become a mystic and crazy. But I was going through an ordeal.[24]

The encounter with his sheikh is thus the prelude to a "mystical sleep, which lasted for six years, in the course of which I reread the noble Qur'an and the prophetic tradition with a new heart."[25]

Three moments thus come together to forge the sheikh's path: religious education based on the essential texts—which he barely mentions; the mystical crisis which is revealed in the encounter with the master and individual internalization; and the movement into politics, which takes shape in the objectification of religious norms and direct opposition to the monarch. These three moments are not mutually exclusive; they come together to construct the meaning of a path that begins with a turn inward and then transcends that inwardness by becoming public through political action.

The death of the Budshishiyya's sheikh in 1972 seems to have awakened him from his "sleep," and enabled him to enter politics. But while his master was still alive, Yassine already had a battle to fight within the brotherhood, some of whose members dubbed him Mister Shari'a because he criticized the withdrawal from politics.[26] After his master's death, Yassine entered into conflict with the sheikh's family because, according to his critics, his ambition was to accede to power in place of the descendants of the brotherhood's leader. There is obviously no mention of this episode in the hagiographic writings of the brotherhood. On the other hand, the Budshishiyya now emphasizes the spiritual testament of Sidi al-Haj al-'Abbas, which granted his son Sidi Hamza the role of "spiritual educator." But Yassine explains his break with the brotherhood as caused by his rejection of the deviations he encountered in its "innovative" (bid'as) practices. The brotherhood became for him a "site of consumption" instead of remaining a "refuge for the poor." "I saw furniture introduced into the *zawiya* and how it was invaded by gifts," he says to explain his having left. The break with the brotherhood served later in the creation of the figure of the saint.

Yassine's move into politics was not a clear break from his mystical experience. Quite the contrary, it occurred within the very realm of the mystical. According to his daughter, Yassine decided to send his letter before the death of his master.[27] The move into politics thus did not date from the sending of *Islam or the Deluge* to the monarch, but it was ripening in the disciple's attitude and was revealed even in his writings preceding the famous 1974 letter.

Once outside the circle of the Budshishiyya brotherhood, adopting the classic moment of secession as a necessary preliminary condition for the construction of charisma,[28] Yassine did not cast off his connection to mysticism. Although, with the death of his master in mysticism, he lost his status as a disciple, and thereby the link he might have maintained with a chain of initiation, a *silsila*, he constructed his image as a charismatic leader and attempted to build the foundations of a new genealogy elsewhere. The loss of the spiritual master coincided with the abandonment of the foundation of a mystical transmission that he had to reestablish by creating a sacred space that took elements both from his mystical experience and from political Islamism.

In 1972 and 1973, he took up a position on the public stage by publishing two books,[29] whose most important themes foreshadow some of the content of the 1974 letter. The admonition of the prince—and its political consequences—later provided him with material to become a master himself by establishing in the early 1980s his own religious organization with multiple facets; while it may not have had the name, it had a structure that resembled that of a Sufi brotherhood, and that structure served as a basis for recruiting an opposition political movement that shifted back and forth between the underground and public visibility.

By following this mystical path, Yassine has confirmed his distance from the Salafist ideology represented by the 'ulama who are more focused on juridical studies and theology than on mystical initiation, which they openly criticize for what they see as deviations. Yassine has rejected this figure of the man of learning that he perceives as having been domesticated by the monarchy. This is why he returned to an older version of the learned man, embodied by Muhammad Ibn 'Abd al-Kabir al-Kattani (d. 1909), well versed in both the science of shari'a and the mystical path, who also practiced the admonition of the monarch. Episodes of rebellion by the devout have punctuated the history of Muslim Morocco, and, as we will see in the next chapter, through the model of al-Kattani, Yassine has associated himself with the most recent of its manifestations.

Sanctity, individuality, and censure of politicians are the three components explicitly associating Yassine with al-Kattani, whose descendants are still present on the religious scene in Morocco, as we will see in Chapter 9. His position as a mystic is ideal for what Yassine has in mind. The model that he has proposed to the prince is in fact that of self-examination and impoverishment. At least in his letter, it is much more strongly emphasized than the idea of building an "Islamic state," a principle already contained in the text of the Moroccan constitution.

Since his accession to the throne in 1961, Hassan II has gradually built and constantly restructured the religious component of his realm of power, a protected realm in which Yassine, the entrepreneur in salvation, has no foothold. The king, as we have seen, has surrounded himself with diversified and fragmented religious institutions, directed by 'ulama whose function is to control the faithful and to legitimate the activities of the Makhzen. Yassine, rather than attacking the foundations of this realm, has therefore invited the king to follow more mysterious and "inward" paths. Since the realm controlled by the monarchy has been mapped out, is religiously occupied, and is institutionally too fragmented to become a base for mobilization, Yassine has attacked the king's inwardness, his very individuality. Indeed, as the next chapter shows, the 1974 letter does not put the emphasis on the application of religious standards to Moroccan society, but on the religiosity and religious sincerity of the person of the king himself.

CHAPTER 5

Styles and Figures of Admonition

Let us consider Sheikh Yassine's intervention in the context of the religious organization established by the post-colonial monarchy. He began his professional career as a young man in the 1950s, just as the social function of clerics was losing legitimacy. It ended in the mid-1960s, when the 'ulama began to adopt a new identity as a pressure group for the Arabization of education and the Islamization of public life. Himself a teacher of Arabic, Yassine joined the bureaucratic apparatus managed and controlled by the Makhzen and gradually came into conflict with it. Similarly, he rejected the nationalist Salafism that had been partially adopted by the monarchy, while agreeing with many of the ideas produced by the 'ulama of the League in the 1970s.

In considering the way in which Yassine articulates the relationship between religion and politics, it is unquestionably his first book, published in 1972, that presents the fullest picture of the foundations and the ambiguities of his position. He affirms the necessity of bringing together religion (*din*) and the state (*dawla*) because their separation is a practice derived from *jahiliyya*, or non-Muslim, society. It is up to the state to take on the roles of preaching (*da'wa*) and jihad.[1] But while state and religion must be joined together, the latter must also be protected from the former. This is why Yassine proposes a functional separation between the two entities by establishing a division of labor between statesmen (*rijal al-dawla*) and preachers (*rijal al-da'wa*), guaranteeing that the state cannot use religion for despotic purposes. Rather than politicizing religion, Yassine thereby proposes to Islamize politics.

Denouncing the materialist views of leftist parties, he writes: "The politician speaks to the destitute about their alienation and their status as victims . . . but he does not speak to them about the hereafter because he is unfamiliar with it or because, even if he is a Muslim, his Islam is incomplete, cut off from the arena of action, individual, isolated." On the other hand, the "Islamic activist" strives to "build an Islamic state that follows the law of Allah in the lives of its individuals, its families, and its social groups, as well as in their economy, their production, and their culture."[2]

In this sense, the man of religion has a superior position to that of the politician. In his first two books, of 1971 and 1972, Yassine did not differentiate himself from the Islamism already at play in the writings of the Muslim Brotherhood in the Middle East or those reflecting their influence in the Maghreb. But in 1974, he crossed a threshold by putting this division of labor into active practice. Hence, Yassine adopted the monarchic model of the proximity of religion and politics, but reversed the roles: it is not up to the commander of the faithful and the 'ulama subject to him to monopolize religious interpretation in the service of their interests. The man of religion must play the supreme role of arbitration and supervision. To challenge the Moroccan pattern of the distribution of religious and political functions, which he criticized as a utilization of religion by the throne, Yassine did not directly oppose the concept of the sharifian monarchy. He proposed that the monarch adopt new standards of conduct, and focused his most direct institutional criticism on the role and the character of the 'ulama who submitted to the monarchy.

In the fiction created by his letter, Yassine entered fully into the heart of the realm of the monarchy by speaking directly to the king.

Far from simply and abstractly reversing the roles of religion and politics, he applied this reversal in his personal conduct.

Yassine and Hassan II: The Admonition of the Monarch

The letter Yassine composed in 1973 is the most original of his writings. It established the sheikh's renown and directly incorporated him into the realm of politics. In a violent critique of King Hassan II, Yassine thus set himself against the monarch and called him to repentance (*tawba*), using the language of submission along with mordant irony.

In the letter, Yassine presents himself as a heroic man who dares to defy the monarchy unaided. He was, however, not the first to directly oppose the king, since military figures, whom he mentions, had twice tried to overthrow the monarchy. The left had also made attempts, and the repression against both sectors had been and still was extremely harsh when Yassine sent his letter to Hassan II. Yassine adopted an innovative tone compared to the one ordinarily used by opponents of the monarchy. He used a messianic style, centered on the relationship and the structure of master and disciple, while at the same time reiterating the demands expressed by the left as well as by the Istiqlal party: the fight against economic inequality, corruption, and authoritarian power. Yassine pointed to the ineffectiveness and weakness of partisan opposition and emphasized the failure of the military. Because of his asserted proximity to the divine, he presented himself as the "savior" of the king and the nation.

Abdessalam Yassine drafted his letter to the king in Marrakesh in 1973 with two friends, Muhammad al-'Alawi al-Sulaymani and Ahmad Mallakh. The letter was sent by mail along with Yassine's business card in early 1974 in approximately two thousand envelopes addressed to professional people (doctors, teachers, lawyers) whose names were taken from the phone book. A week later, he sent it to Hassan II through the governor of Marrakesh. As Mohamed Tozy has pointed out, Yassine took pains to present the essential elements of his career as an introduction to his letter: he reminded his reader that he was of sharifian descent, and hence on the same footing as his addressee.[3] But he brought to the fore the fact that he belonged to a branch different from the king's—as we have seen, he claims descent from the Idrissid—as well as his peasant and Berber origins, and his experience as a mystic.[4]

Proclaiming his right to chastise the prince, to address an exhortation (*nasiha*) to him, he does not wish to present himself as a political opponent, but as a religious cleric, a simple scholar who is exercising his critique of the politician. Yassine stages his reprimand of the king: he is acting, just as much as the monarch, as a vital participant in the admonition scene. The first parts of the letter have the primary purpose of exhibiting—as on stage, but also in the sense of "exposing to danger"—the person of the king, while pointing out that Yassine himself can also be defined by a religious lineage and a relationship to Islam.

Hassan II's reaction to Yassine's letter was brutal: arrested in September 1974, he remained in detention in a psychiatric hospital for three and a half years without trial.[5] Muhammad al-'Alawi al-Sulaymani and Ahmad Mallakh were interned for fifteen months in a secret prison in Casablanca. Yassine was imprisoned not so much for formulating a general critique of the monarchy as for having desanctified the realm of the Makhzen by addressing and "exposing" to the public its central occupant: the king.

The Staging of the Admonition

Yassine organizes his *mise en scène* by putting himself on stage: Yassine is a man alone, and he addresses the king in the first person, without preliminaries. After the invocation of Allah, the letter to the king begins directly as follows: "To His Highness al-Hasan Ibn Muhammad Ibn Yusif, descendant of the messenger of God (may God's blessing and grace be upon him), tired from occupying the 'throne of his ancestors' in the difficult circumstances experienced by Morocco, and particularly by its king."[6] The figure of Yassine appears in the fourth line as the author of the letter and the king's direct interlocutor: "my letter" and "my beloved" are the two expressions that first introduce Yassine to the king. Then the sheikh makes the introductions: "I am a slave of God (*'abd Allah*) and a sinner, son of a Berber peasant raised in poverty and material deprivation."[7] Again: "I am merely a student in search of knowledge (*talib al-'ilm*) who recognizes every day the limits his ignorance imposes on him."[8] He presents himself as a "man alone, who speaks the truth by relying on God,"[9] and, unconcerned about the contradiction,[10] "an Idrissid Berber, an educated man, who is between two ages (*mukhadhram*), a Sufi whom his brothers have deserted. . . . These are three forms of exile on the path to truth."[11]

But Yassine's solitude can be understood only in contrast to his relationship to the divine. Although he is alone, he is, as he himself emphasizes, a believer (*mu'min*).[12] Hence, he does not present himself as a political competitor of the king, but as the chastiser who puts him back on the right path. In the French version, *L'Islam ou le déluge*, written in 1983:

> Allow me to heap reproaches upon you. I am not unaware of the crushing burden you bear, I am not the dreamer outside time and free of gravity that I might appear to be. I have the immense advantage of having the necessary distance to judge the course of events. I have the divine blessing of having a cause to defend. The truth may very well spring from a heart that loves God and men, whereas it shuns self-interested men and fragments into contradictory truths in the hands of politicians. I am naïve to be sure, but in a particular way: naïve through faith.[13]

Yassine has distanced himself from men, he has "neither weapons nor group (*jama'a*),"[14] because, he says, he has come close to God: "I have sold my self to Allah, and have thereby agreed to cut myself off from my brothers and those dear to me. . . . I have chosen to be in the company of God, with the chastisers, while others have chosen silence."[15]

The Person of the King: The Junction of Good and Evil

While Yassine presents himself in the mode of pure simplicity, he blurs the image of the king by projecting him into the realm of ambiguity. The figure of the monarch is included in a series of dichotomies in which he appears to represent the two contradictory terms simultaneously: the king is alone, but surrounded by false friends and evil advisers; he is strong, but weak and in danger; he is hardened by holding power, but softened by the pleasures of the court; he is tyrannical, but able to weep. He instills fear in his subjects, but appears "frightened," disoriented (*ha'ir*), and trembling with fear (*madh'ur*) before the army that betrayed him. These ambiguities running through the letter serve not merely to produce a negative image of the sovereign, but also to delineate a sacred space in which Yassine may detect, describe, and bring forward the elements of impurity. They thereby make it possible to criticize the monarch by exposing elements not in conformity with the ideal of a Muslim ruler in order to present the possibility of a royal conversion to the public. The king therefore still dwells in a realm imbued with the quality of the sacred, from which Yassine can lead him to repentance.

The letter recognizes that its recipient is a descendant of the Prophet (*hafidh al-rasul*) and a "Sufi" king. Although bestowed with irony, these two characteristics are essential for Yassine to be able to challenge the position of power occupied by the king. The two attributes are never called into question in the letter because they are the two indications of proximity and thereby of the possibility of exchange between Yassine and the ruler. On the other hand, the king's strength and the unshakable and permanent nature of his power are mentioned only to be immediately called into question.

Yassine simultaneously points to the king's solitude and the fact that he is surrounded by courtiers: "Abu Bakr gave his neighbors milk and continued to do the same when he became caliph and until he died. You are unable to do that, not because you do not know how to milk cattle, but because you have no neighbors. Your palace is a city that stands in solitude."[16] The king lives in a densely populated space, but one that is isolated from the real city of men. Similarly, while the letter on several occasions calls Hassan II weak (*miskin*), this is not to call for compassion toward him, but rather to emphasize his power because he is also the man who has destroyed all virility in his own subjects: "Did you never realize that they each have their own virility? That the man you force to prostrate himself in the eyes of the entire *umma* on television has cursed you in his heart because you have killed his virility and despised him?"[17] And: "You make yourself and those who are blind believe that you are the unshakable sovereign, whereas you are, by Allah, only a weak man whose fate has already been decided."

Yassine presents the two unsuccessful coups d'état of 1971 and 1972 as harbingers of possible perdition, but the historic failure is also a sign of divine intervention: "Men bore arms against you and God delivered you."[18] "Two signals came to you from God. When he saved you, you continued to disobey and you intensified your despotism."[19] He then insists on the king's unstable state, which is due to fear, as the following passage shows: "A frightened king, who has lost his balance, who is receiving my letter at the same time as the people. A king who nevertheless remains attached to the throne of his ancestors, as he calls it.... The king is sitting on a volcano that is about to erupt."[20] What better time to repent than this moment of instability, fear, and fragility, which Yassine describes in the weeping of the man who holds power? The admonition is aimed at making the sovereign weep and return to God. It must provoke fear followed immediately by repentance, so that tears will relieve the tension created by terror. Yassine suggests that the king humiliate himself before men through his repentance and his acceptance of the impertinence of the one giving the *nasiha*, but he also suggests that by this very act he will raise himself in the eyes of God. Once he has demonstrated his humility he will also recover his glory among men.

He later returns to the king's ability to approach God to move on to the possibility of repentance. He mixes a touch of pity for the monarch with recognition of what is "good" in him and with an underlying threat: "I believe in the king's faith. I know that his prayer beads are not only a lie, as most people believe. I know that he sometimes fears God and that he weeps." He immediately goes on to say: "But I believe that his tears do not excuse his ignorance of Islam."[21]

Yassine's king thus oscillates between omnipotence and weakness, and, surrounded as he is by false friends, he is as alone as Yassine himself. For this reason, he proposes the model of companionship of the "true" 'ulama, such as Ziyad Ibn Abi Ziyad, who addressed questions to the caliph 'Umar that ultimately made his tears flow.[22] The king's solitude is in a way replicated in that of Yassine, allowing him, as a mirror image of the prince, to speak to the monarch in personal terms.

Yassine's construction of this face-to-face encounter can be related to the royal strategy after the 1971 attempted coup. The king spoke to the people after July 10, 1971, using both the language of threat and that of fear. In his speech, he presented the monarchy as the best shield against political chaos. Addressing the opposition, he drove the point home: "You are digging your own graves. . . . This is why we say to you, you who shape Moroccan public opinion either directly in the press or by circulating rumors: take care, if you sow the wind you will reap the whirlwind."[23] The threat was matched by a description of a frightened political elite: "For example, among the wounded yesterday was Mr. Hasan al-Wazzani, one of whose arms was torn off, and among those who were roughed up was Mr. 'Allal al-Fasi and Dr. Miswak, whose opinions are well known. The latter was seen lying on the ground and trembling."

Hassan II thus attributed the feeling of fear to politicians and recalled—still addressing his "dear people"—that he and his family both enjoyed divine protection:

> We remember . . . that on July 8 when we spoke to you on the occasion of the youth festival, we implored the Most High to protect our life and to preserve our family and our offspring. We then took God as our witness to the extent of our love for you, a love that approaches idolatry. We asked God, the All Powerful, to spare neither our life nor our

dynasty if this love was only a simulation. . . . God provided us the concrete proof of the sincerity of our feeling barely one day later. It was thus that He spared us, our little family, and our great family from the misfortune and annihilation that threatened us.[24]

By evoking *baraka*, or divine grace, the king excluded the politicians and established closeness, alone with his family, to the people, his subjects.

How to Penetrate into the Royal Sphere: Proximity and Profanation

In his letter, Yassine is simultaneously a subject in two senses, as a man subjected to the power of the king and as an acting subject, actively confronting the royal power. Yassine's address is direct, not softened by polite formulas. He uses the familiar form of the second person pronoun in speaking to Hassan II. The sheikh's erasure of any mediating device between himself and the sovereign is reinforced by his style of direct address to the king.

In the last part of the twentieth century, Islamist ideologues have generally written impersonal texts demonstrating the supposed "impiety" of the prince, of whom they speak in the third person and often in abstract terms. These texts are given to militants to read, then to wider circles, to identify and make public this deviation from Islamic standards. In contrast, Yassine deviates from this model. He establishes a direct and unmediated encounter with the king through a message written for the latter and given to the public to read. Yassine thereby enters into the king's domain, seeking proximity to the sovereign. He does not integrate himself into the official religious space that the king has established—the mosque controlled by the ministry of religious affairs or Hassan II's religious lessons—but into the personal space of the king. He thereby penetrates from the outset into monarchic space, not to bow before the sovereign but to place himself in the center, facing the king, creating a mirror effect depriving the prince of the attributes that usually give him his power. As

Houari Touati has said, "The prince is the saint's other whom he has renounced. Just as the saint is the 'almost nothing' who reminds the prince that, despite his omnipotence, he is 'nothing.'"[25]

This is why Yassine's long apostrophe simultaneously evokes closeness to and distance from the king. It alternates between loving and critical formulations: Yassine speaks of the king as his "beloved" (*habibi*), his brother (*akhi*); calls him My Lord (*sayyidi*); includes him in the category of "Sufi king" and "believer"; and recognizes his prophetic ancestry. "Good Sufis taught me reciprocal friendship (*mahabba*) and they taught me compassion (*rifq*). I am a companion for you (*rafiq*), and I love you as God has ordered me to love the people of the house of the Prophet."[26] Yassine thus acts out the scene of master and disciple, in which the king plays the role of Sufi master, and then immediately turns it around so that Yassine is the companion and indeed the master leading the disciple to repentance. Yassine offers the sovereign a kind of temporary utopian companionship: "Allow me to direct you toward God."[27] And: "If you thought for a moment, you would discover that I am your only friend."[28] But he simultaneously reformulates the relationship. The reversal recurs throughout the letter, in sentences that at first reflect an affectionate relationship, which then changes into one in which Yassine directs the king, finally coming to a head with a threat: "My beloved, grandson of the Prophet, you believe in God and in judgment day. Allow me to tell you the truth and advise you so that you do not throw yourself into the flames. . . . You will die as your fathers died, not having repented before God. The disobedience of ordinary mortals to God cannot be compared to the treachery of a king."[29] Sometimes the address moves in the opposite direction, beginning with an injunction and ending with Yassine recognizing the king's attributes: "And by Allah, I am not afraid of you, while I wish to testify in the way of God. But I am horrified that my enemy in the hands of God is a descendant of the Prophet."[30] The accumulation of contradictory sentiments is intended to "stir" the person of the king, place him in a position of instability, "awaken" him, bring him to tears and to repentance: "May God make my letter a shock (*sadma*) that awakens you."[31]

Rather than being punctuated by verses from the Qur'an, Yassine's text presents a series of exempla, scenes inserted into a hall of mirrors. We see Sulayman Ibn ʿAbd al-Malik in Madina listening to Abu Hazm: "I hope that you will accept my *nasiha* from his mouth."[32] And: "Listen from my mouth to the *nasiha* of the people of God, the people of the Qur'an, those who are like Abu Hazm." Yassine quotes the dialogue between the caliph and the scholar, while blending this exchange with his address to the king.[33] He fuses the present and the distant past and increases the intensity of his own intervention with Hassan II. The reader may thus imagine two scenes echoing one another: the one Yassine presents to the king and also the one in which the king listens to Yassine.

The King and the Figure of the Saint

Yassine suggests that the king attain saintly status through destitution. Sufi voluntary piety functions as a model:

> As a hero, you are in service to yourself, you are the idol and the priest of your own cult, you attach yourself to illusory values that will fall into ruin and be scattered in ashes that historians will sift through. As a hero, you pose for history, you tend to your public image, you put the resources that God has bestowed on you at the service of your vanity. But as a saint, you cease to belong to yourself and to history so that you may belong to God. You escape from the empty vanity of earthly values so that you may participate in eternal values. ʿUmar the Second took that step. He was a man, a true man.[34]

"Return Your Possessions to Morocco!"

During the lessons of the month of Ramadan, noble ʿulama are sent to the king. The king occupies the place of honor, he sits facing them as tyrants do. But if he had in his heart only a little mercy for the good, he would sit facing them in the position of a pupil, in the position of one who is learning, who occupies a position of compassion and sincerity.[35]

Yassine criticizes the exploitation of the 'ulama by the monarchy. He suggests that the king move from the status of master to that of disciple, thereby agreeing—on the model of the mythical caliph 'Umar Ibn 'Abd al-'Aziz—to join in a reconstituted form of companionship. Here Yassine is interpreting the institution of the lesson delivered by Hassan II as a reproduction of the structure of authority, and he proposes a reversal of roles.

It may be said of Hassan II's lesson, however, that on an essentially symbolic level it provides an inversion of the king-'ulama relationship for the duration of the month of Ramadan. The relationship that it exhibits is in fact more subtle than Yassine's description would lead one to believe. During the lesson, the king adopts the physical posture of a pupil, alone or accompanied by his two sons, sitting cross-legged facing his guests and on a lower level than the *'alim* who delivers his message to the king from a pulpit, in the company of Moroccan and foreign religious dignitaries. The Sufi posture is obvious here, but the message flowing from it is subtle. Hassan II's lesson makes it possible to institutionally revive for an evening a considerably softened version, and one controlled by the prince, of the cleric's address to the king. The roles are falsely reversed. The posture of the chastiser is physically offered to the cleric, but in a domesticated political context in which admonition is not possible.

To reverse the hierarchy emphasized by Hassan II's lesson, Yassine devotes a large part of his letter to criticizing those he presents as the king's disciples, that is, not only the 'ulama, but also the king's entourage, which both live in a constant "exchange" relationship with the palace. It is the notion of "market," or *suq*, that allows Yassine to describe this relationship of reciprocity between the king and his subjects. By designating the bond between the sovereign and his subjects as being characterized by trade, Yassine eliminates any description of religious or political institutions and focuses on the heart of the individual exchange relationship—an unequal one—between the king and those who obey him.

First of all, in considering the 'ulama, Yassine's approach is not very original: he merely demonstrates his contempt for them. He calls them "corrupt readers" (*didan al-qurra*) on several occasions. "Some of them play the role of hypocrites and liars in public life. In their company, the king learns how to use Islam as a subterfuge to win over the trust of the *umma*. They produce fatwas saying that Hassan is the reformer of Islam. They are lying and they know they are lying."[36] "They are absorbed by the accumulation of wealth. Some are in the transportation business, others in construction, and still others speak lies and devour illicit money."[37] "If he speaks, it is to defend his possessions, if he creates an association, it is nothing but a syndicate that defends his rights and does not mention his duties. In the houses of the 'ulama there emerges the degeneracy that follows the model of any house. And our poor *'alim* does not know how to escape from the situation."[38]

It is not criticism of the 'ulama, however, that turns out to be most threatening to the king, but rather the criticism directed at the exchanges he carries on with the Moroccan political elites:

> You are a market in which nothing can be seen but consciences at bargain prices.... You are a market, my brother, my beloved. And in your market we see only half men, semblances of men. In your market we see only sycophants and swindlers, and behind them their helpers, conscious or unconscious, who are the technicians thanks to whom you seal the gaps and whom you force to prostrate themselves before you and whom you force into servility.[39]

In asking him to give up this "market," Yassine suggests that the monarch move closer to God, become *wali li'l-lah*, a quintessentially Sufi term designating one who is close to God, hence a saint. This step is to bring the king back to God via an individual movement toward the divine, by having him at the same time lose his status of master imposing servitude on others. Yassine thus speaks of a pact (*'ahd*) between Hassan II and God.[40]

Moving closer to the figure of sanctity presupposes not only a change in companions but also giving up the things of this world. Yassine's introduction of the Sufi posture enables him to present a violent economic critique of the sovereign. The chastiser thus asks the king to give his fortune to the Moroccans, or rather to "return" it to them. This is the third of the seven proposals made at the end of the letter to the king: "Return your possessions to Morocco. Sell your palaces. Return all the possessions and the palaces in the hands of your friends and your family to the treasury of the Muslims."[41]

The myth of Caliph 'Umar Ibn 'Abd al-'Aziz, who, tradition says, returned his goods once he had repented, is obviously opportune for Yassine:

> 'Umar Ibn 'Abd al-'Aziz grew up as a prince amusing himself in the palaces of Bani Umayya with those we have seen dancing, taking off their clothes, falling down, and going to bed intoxicated and waking up drunk. He grew up in the shadow of a state that ignored Islam, which made itself into an object of adoration for Muslims and imposed on them the power of tyrannical pharaohs . . . who loved money and killed people. 'Umar grew up among female servants. He was handsome, vigorous, and richly dressed. He was famous for his arrogant stance. . . . Like his Umayyad forebears, he was proud. But I do not need to describe to the king the affairs of the sovereigns of that princely line, and all the pleasures and diversions they had the opportunity to engage in.[42]

Figures of the Feminine and the Masculine

For the Yassine of *Islam or the Deluge*, political change cannot be accomplished through replacement of the men at the head of the state, but rather through their *conversion*. The religious legitimacy constructed by the Moroccan monarchy requires that Yassine accept—even fictionally—the royal institution, while demanding its change from within. The text of the letter is punctuated by appeals to repentance (*tub ila allah*), appeals set within the framework of dichotomies between hell and paradise, disorder and order, violence and peace: "Turn toward God, fear his punishment, be repentant." Yassine does not present himself as a political competitor of the monarch. He proposes the institution of a second caliphate, a reconnection of the present time to a mythical, primeval, uncorrupted time.

The notion of virility (*rujula*), contrasted with femininity, appears on several occasions to characterize the converted prince, the king who has become a saint, through the ideas of *rujula* and *fahula* (vigor). They are preconditions for destitution: moving into the status of *wali* of God requires courage. "This, Hassan my brother, is *how one becomes a man*, how one enters into goodness instead of violence." The relation of master to disciple, the basis of a "cultural scheme" that the anthropologist Abdellah Hammoudi has set at the center of Moroccan authoritarianism, is thus reiterated at several levels in the rebel's text.[43] The movement into sainthood involves a symbolic passage from feminine weakness to masculine strength. Yassine calls the servitude experienced by the subjects of the king into question and urges him to enter into a superior type of servitude, one which would bind him, in his repentance, to God.

The Threat of Punishment: The Punishment of God or of Men?

"I made sure that [this letter] would fall into the hands of the nation [*umma*] before it reached you."[44] Yassine is protecting himself against the punishment the king might choose, but also makes his staging more effective by giving it a public. If the prince is to be criticized for his faults, this is to be done not somewhere sheltered from view, but before the faithful. Yassine demonstrates his audacity primarily in the eyes of the Moroccans: "It is your right, and the right of Muslims, to know who is writing to you."[45] Yassine asks the sovereign himself to turn toward the public to inform it of his repentance: "You have no choice but the true one of turning toward [God] and making your repentance public."[46]

The title of the letter is clear: if Islam is not applied, there will be a "deluge," a catastrophe. The function of the scholar, which Yassine seeks to represent, has several different versions, from the simple *nasiha* to the *qawma*, the Islamic uprising, if the prince does not follow the path of repentance.[47] As early as the 1974 letter, Yassine displays a constant back and forth between the two options, reformist (*nasiha*) and revolutionary (*qawma*). Their primary and common aim is to restore an order defined by the religious norm, oscillating between inner mysticism and messianism, expressed in the figure of the Mahdi, the "rightly guided one" or the "envoy," who arises to reestablish the purity of the early days and to put an end to oppression and injustice.[48] But through the paradigm of *nasiha*, Yassine also calls the monarch to conversion, to repentance, and to a radical break with the present in order to institute a second caliphate.

Yassine then goes so far as to offer the image of the repentant king: "And here is poor Hassan, the believer, slave of God, who touches divine mercy and declares the past impious."[49] This ideal of the repentant caliph—which, by the ironic tone of his description, Yassine clearly intends as a fiction—echoes that of an Islamic society united by a shared faith, which Yassine proposes as a model to be attained. He adopts the notion of *nasiha* as a clarification of the Qur'an and the Sunna, with the function of bringing the Muslim community together. He returns to the etymology of *nasiha* to find the image of needle and thread attaching and uniting pieces that at first were scattered.[50]

"Can we resolve our problems in Morocco without recourse to violence? The answer is up to the king and to his choice."[51] "I am waiting . . . for you to tremble from fear of God before the earth swallows you or a star falls from heaven on your head."[52] "It is eternity in hell or eternity in paradise."[53] "It is a path I advise you to take. Otherwise, prepare yourself for violence around you."[54]

Yassine's letter is written in a way designed to provoke a reply, even though Yassine does not really expect the prince to repent. Hassan II never replied in words to the letter. To defuse its effects, he publicly ignored it, while repressing the troublemaker. By his silence, he made the proximity that Yassine had attempted to establish with him impossible. The historical schema of the successful admonition, however, operated as an implicit foil for the real situation.

The Mythical Figures of Challenge and Admonition

By taking as his inspiration the figure of the cleric who challenges authority, Yassine in fact sets himself up as a direct descendant of three activists whom he presents to the king as a trio of 'ulama and of whom he claims to be the heir and successor. First is the Moroccan Muhammad Ibn 'Abd al-Kabir al-Kattani, and the two others are the Egyptians Hasan al-Banna and Sayyid Qutb, major figures in the Muslim Brotherhood: three men who challenged the political authorities, all three of whom had tragic ends, killed by the governments they had criticized. They are presented by Yassine as martyrs of tyrannical governments.

Yassine puts forth al-Banna and Qutb, whose political roles and ideas were very different,to celebrate the figure of two martyrs for the Islamist cause and for the theoretical apparatus that they produced.[55] But they do not represent the essential for Yassine. He reiterates the concepts developed by al-Banna and the more radical form given them by Qutb: Islam as a global way of life, as *din/dunya/dawla*, the chronological and logical concept of *jahiliyya*, the figure of the despotic pharaoh who is an enemy of religion. But these references function primarily as a way of anchoring the figure of Yassine to the Moroccan and international networks of Islamism and to give him political legitimacy in the eyes of outside observers. Sheikh Yassine knows these "classics" of Middle Eastern Islamist ideology, which does not prevent him from inserting them into a mystical conception: he heavily emphasizes the mystical origins of al-Banna, and transforms Qutb into *sidi* Sayyid Qutb, a title often given to Sufi masters.[56]

While Yassine may have been influenced by Mawdudi, Qutb, and al-Banna, the principal bases of his ideological approach are not to be found among them. For that we must look to the figure of Muhammad al-Kattani, who died in Fez in 1909, in the prisons of Sultan 'Abd al-Hafiz. He makes it possible for Yassine to integrate himself into a mystical and militant tradition and to adopt a critical stance that involves both messianism and admonition of the prince.[57]

Muhammad al-Kattani: A Sufi Chastiser

Kattani was, like Yassine, of Idrissid origin. The history of his relations with the monarch also has interesting parallels with those between Yassine and Hassan II. Mohamed Tozy has described his career in detail.[58] Born in Fez in 1873, he entered the Qarawiyyin at a very young age; he thus belonged to the world of clerics, but was not influenced by the *Salafiyya* movement that reached Morocco in the period between the late nineteenth century and the first quarter of the twentieth. He was a member of a brotherhood, the Kattaniyya, then quite recently established, that was to experience extraordinary growth and incorporate perhaps thousands of disciples. This expansion troubled the Makhzen, which suspected the young *'alim* of planning an Idrissid restoration.

In 1895, the sultan ordered some 'ulama to challenge the young scholar, who had not hesitated to openly criticize the sultan's policy regarding the protected status enjoyed by the European powers.[59] Saved from condemnation in 1896 by *'alim* Ma al-'Aynayn, he tried to stay out of the limelight, while his brotherhood continued to expand. From 1902 or 1903 on, he was allied with Sultan 'Abd al-'Aziz in his war against the tribes. The sultan, whose interests at the time coincided with those of the Kattaniyya brotherhood, "showered him with favors."[60] But the sheikh finally joined the clerical opposition, which wanted to depose Mawlay 'Abd al-'Aziz as sultan. Kattani rebelled again against Sultan 'Abd al-Hafiz, inaugurated on January 4, 1908: he disputed the text of the *bay'a* (act of allegiance) drafted by the 'ulama of Fez. He proposed a new *bay'a* accompanied by conditions, a demand that ruined relations between Kattani and the new sultan and finally sealed the sheikh's fate.[61] 'Abd al-Hafiz considered himself a scholar of Islam; he opposed the practices of the brotherhoods and entered into a cycle of *munadharat* (controversies) with Kattani, in which Kattani sometimes adopted a fierce tone—not too distant from that of Yassine addressing the sultan as an ordinary mortal and placing himself at the same hierarchical level as his ruler. Kattani became a mythical political figure, and we will later find some of his descendants in contemporary Moroccan Islamist circles, once more firmly establishing their distance from the 'Alawite monarchy.

It must, however, be emphasized that, in the early twentieth century, Kattani was not a figure entirely defined by the challenge he posed to the prince. He would speak to, oppose, or submit to the government, which itself actively participated in exchanges with the rebel, through 'ulama that supported or contradicted him. His positions were characterized by nuances and ambiguities: he gave way, kept silent, and then resumed speaking against the monarch.

Conversely, in the last quarter of the twentieth century, the monarchy responded to Yassine with repression and remained silent about his rebellion. Times had changed, and the monarchy, no longer in a position of weakness as with Kattani, severed relations with those who rebelled against it; it adopted the position of ignoring and marginalizing them in order to neutralize their power.

Hasan al-Yusi: The Model of Admonition

Although Yassine does not mention him, he has also been compared to Hasan al-Yusi (1631-91).[62] In his lifetime al-Yusi witnessed the regression of the Sa'di monarchy and the rise of its 'Alawite rival.[63] As Jacques Berque has pointed out, Morocco was then going through a period of great agitation and political instability: "The overthrow of the declining dynasty liberated almost everywhere men of God who were also eager for territorial lordship: the marabouts, some of whom established durable principalities."[64]

Around 1684, armed with a moral position and his reputation as "reformer of the century" (*mujaddid al-qarn*), he wrote an admonition to the 'Alawite Sultan Mawlay Isma'il (1672-1727). This sultan showed little respect for the ʻulama and sought to isolate the counterforce that they might represent. In Fez, the clerics had led a campaign against the sultan's establishment of an army of *ʻabids* (black slaves) which, according to the ʻulama, should have been dealt with as free Muslims. Al-Yusi's relationship with Mawlay Ismaʻil was ambiguous. Along with Sheikh ʻAbd al-Qadir al-Fasi, he presided over the monarch's *bayʻa*; and some of his *Rasaʼil* (letters) contain fatwas ordered by the prince.[65] But on two occasions al-Yusi took the initiative of addressing an admonition to the prince: a "short letter" and an "exhortation to kings to render justice."[66] The first was the more direct and audacious of the two.

Ahmad Ibn Khalid al-Nasiri (1835-97), great chronicler of Moroccan history, presents its content in these terms:

> Greetings, may the mercy and blessing of God be upon Our Lord! All that remains is for me to express my affection, my respect, and my boundless veneration for Our Lord and to address him my wishes for his prosperity: this is a very small part of what I owe to his hand always open to me for benevolence and generosity, to his virtue, to his energy, to his kindness and his largesse; it is also very little in comparison to what we all owe to his imperial dignity and to his powerful rank as a descendant of Fatima.
>
> I am writing you this letter because it is no longer possible for me to keep silent. For a long time I have seen that Our Lord has been seeking exhortations and advice, and that he has wished to see the gates of prosperity and success swing open. I have therefore decided to write a letter to Our Lord which, if he can take heed of it, will allow me to hope that the benefits of this world and those of eternity will be his, and that he will rise to the most glorious heights; and if I am not worthy to address exhortations, I hope that Our Lord will be worthy of receiving them and will refrain from reproaches.
>
> Let Our Lord be told, then, that the Earth with all that

it contains is the kingdom of the Most High God who has no companion, and that living creatures are the slaves of God and his servants. Our Lord is one of those slaves, to whom God has granted power over his slaves to test him and to make him suffer. If he rules them with justice, with mercy, with equity, and with integrity, he is the lieutenant of God on Earth and the shadow of God on his slaves: he holds a high rank next to God. But if he governs them with tyranny, with harshness, with arrogance, with injustice, and with oppression, he rebels against His Master in his kingdom, he is nothing but an insolent usurper, and he exposes himself to the most terrible punishment from His Master and to his anger. Our Lord knows what is reserved for one who decides to tyrannize his subjects without the consent of the Master and to make slaves of them, and the fate that awaits him on the day when he is in His Master's hands.

I say next that many obligations weigh upon the sultan that I cannot fully describe in this letter. I will mention only three of them, which are the basis for all the others. The first is to collect taxes and to distribute the revenue justly. The second is to organize holy war to bring about the triumph of the word of God and, with this aim, to supply military posts with all they need in the way of arms and men. The third consists of causing justice to be rendered to the oppressed against the oppressor and, with this aim, to bring denials of justice to an end.

These three obligations have remained a dead letter under the reign of Our Lord, and I am therefore obliged to point this situation out to him so that he may not later excuse himself because he was not informed and he did not know. If he takes heed of this advice and makes the most of it, it is salvation for him; it will also safeguard the interests of the moment, the interests of all, it will provide well-being and prosperity. Otherwise, I will have the satisfaction of having done my duty.[67]

Al-Yusi deployed his art of *nasiha* regarding Mawlay Isma'il in full awareness of the rules as well as the consequences. In his *Muhadharat*, he had himself written about this kind of relationship with the sovereign.[68] And in his *Rasa'il*, he cited as an example the repentance and the tears of Caliph 'Umar Ibn 'Abd al-'Aziz.[69] The sultan did not react to al-Yusi's admonition, and the latter left shortly thereafter on a pilgrimage with the king's son, al-Mu'tasim.

It is possible that Yassine does not call on the figure of Yusi because he did not end his life as a martyr to the authorities and because he was not tied as explicitly as Kattani to a *zawiya*. In addition, Yusi's period in the history of Morocco is too distant for Yassine's disciples to relate to. Jacques Berque, however, describes Yusi as a "hero of the periphery," a formulation that could be applied to Yassine.[70] He frequented the Qarawiyyin only rarely and accidentally; he had Berber and rustic origins: he was born south of the sources of the Moulouya. He was subject to the cabals of his colleagues in the school of Fez: "Beyond personal grudges, what he held against them was that they were in the process of establishing an academicism, more than half tied to a modus vivendi with the bourgeoisie of Fez and the monarchy, whereas he remained a man of untamed culture."[71]

Shattering Sacred Space

Like al-Yusi and al-Kattani, Yassine loses—for the time of the *nasiha*, and despite the customary formulas used to address the sovereign—any sense of *hayba*, a feeling of veneration mixed with fear. These three clerics remain silent about the catastrophic consequences of the prince's failure to repent: they would possibly involve their own martyrdom. The *nasiha* seems to make its author lose his footing, and to take him outside reasonable discourse into a moment of unreason, of great impudence and imprudence, as evidenced by the last sentence of al-Yusi's admonition: "I will have the satisfaction of having done my duty." It is this moment of unreason that makes possible the individual confrontation with the sovereign. The *'alim* Kannun is himself said to have advised Hassan II to intern Yassine in a psychiatric hospital, which is what he did, because only a madman could address the king in that tone.[72] Yassine thus did not suffer the fate of the military rebels of 1971 and 1972.

The king did not respond directly to Yassine. Through this silence he was rejecting the reverse model of master and disciple. He mobilized the Makhzen, particularly the Ministry of the Interior, to defuse the effects of Yassine's letter, but remained—as an individual—absent from the confrontation. The staging put in place by Yassine was thus reversed in turn by the king: he did not become the sheikh's disciple and refused to follow the model of destitution. For becoming the disciple of a master—as Yassine made himself a disciple in order to become a master and founder in his turn—means losing everything and accepting a violent internal transformation. This is in fact how Yassine defines the concept of *suhba*: "That luminous force that one borrows[73] from one's companion, the one you follow, which disturbs the reason of the disciple (*murid*) and companion (*sahib*) and disorients him."[74]

The idea of a political organization supporting Yassine's action appeared in neither of the two letters to the king, even after his political group was established. The institution of the monarchy itself is targeted only through the *person* of the king. Yassine de-institutionalizes and individualizes the relationship to the monarch in the establishment of an interpersonal connection. He demonstrates the insertion of the monarch into the worldly sphere, sanctifies the relationship that he constructs with (or against) him through his mystical posture, and offers him a passage toward the divine. But at the same time, he "publicizes" the offer, and makes it visible to all. He inserts this individual relationship into the public sphere, normally debarred by the authorities.

This paradoxical insertion of an individual relationship into the public sphere shows that the sway of the sacred in this play of relationships is very important, while the sway of the religious is much less so. By touching the person of the king, the center of the Makhzen, Yassine penetrates a space that he desanctifies. This space is in fact sacred, in the sense established by Marcel Mauss: the sacred is the forbidden, "from which effective force derives," the separate, that some individuals may nevertheless enter into.[75] This space has boundaries, but they are porous. The sacredness of the space of the Makhzen is not constituted so much by reference to religion, but rather primarily by the establishment of extreme distance between that space and the rest of society, a distance supported by the force of physical coercion, which constitutes the power of the monarchy. Yassine's purpose, much more than to make the prince give way, is to reduce that distance by profaning the circle of the Makhzen and to commit sacrilege by attempting to abolish the space that surrounds the king and maintains the distance.

Yassine's letter thus reveals the eminently ambivalent character of the sacredness of the Makhzen: a sacredness that is to be desanctified, through the dangerous operation of coming together in a face-to-face confrontation, rather than in servitude. This is why Yassine's strategy remains primarily an effort at desanctification much more than a strategy of "overthrow" along the lines of the military.

Hence, if Yassine is "mad," as indicated by the stigma of the psychiatric asylum where he was confined, he is not the "king's buffoon": he does not reverse the order of things with a purely cathartic purpose. Wanting to bring the king back to himself, he transgresses in order to undo, not to legitimate. He does not establish a disorder that will legitimate order, but he "restores order" (an "Islamic" order) for the time of his letter. The sacrilege carried out by Yassine does not derive from the fact that the monarchy is "religious." Hence, his critique of the 'ulama, whose function is essentially religious, is not a sacrilege. The moment of profanation flows from the close scrutiny of a machinery that functions more or less continuously to situate the monarchy in a space governed simultaneously by fear and attraction.

CHAPTER 6

Justice and Benevolence: Between Mystic Community and Political Leadership

Although Yassine is most often associated with the 1973-74 letter, his political writings in fact go back to 1972, the year in which he articulated his doctrine in two essays, *Islam between Preaching and State* and *Islam Tomorrow*. The official journal *Da'wat al-haqq*—published by the Ministry of Religious Affairs—gave a very favorable notice to Yassine's "valuable" book in 1972, devoting a full paragraph to it in the general news section, just before a brief review of a book by Sheikh 'Abd Allah Kannun. The principal elements of the book are reproduced in *The Prophetic Way* (*Al-minhaj al-nabawi*), which served as a practical and political guide for Yassine's disciples.

He was, in fact, no longer an isolated scholar. After the death of his sheikh, he had left the Budshishiyya and had gathered his own followers around himself. Having left one communal religious organization, he created another a few years later, with a paradoxical political emphasis: it was a group with affinities to a mystic brotherhood (*zawiya*), while at the same time having a strong Islamist and political identity. Yassine, who had become a master commanding great authority in the wide circle of his disciples, also declared himself to be a "messiah," or messenger of God.

He constructed his movement, eventually called Justice and Benevolence, between 1970 and 1987. Yassine regained his freedom in March 1978, after three and a half years in a psychiatric hospital. The task ahead of him was to extend his surrounding circle of activists, and especially to cast a wide net over Moroccan Islamist groups. In February 1979, he published the first issue of the magazine *Al-jama'a*, in which he set forth the principal elements of his doctrine. Sixteen issues were published up until July 1985, when the magazine was suppressed.

This periodical called on all Moroccan Islamist groups to unite around Yassine, an attempt that met with failure. In September 1981, Yassine launched the association *Usrat al-jama'a*, registered its by-laws, and asked that it be legally recognized. Hassan II's government refused to recognize the group, and thereupon began a power struggle between Yassine's followers and the authorities. On March 29, a new name, *Jam'iyyat al-jama'a*, was adopted. In November 1983, came a new publication with the title *Al-subh* (Morning), of which only two issues were published, since it was promptly suppressed by the government. On December 27, 1983, Yassine—who had just sent another letter to the king, written in French this time—was again jailed (until December 1985). Finally, in September 1987, the association became *al-'adl wa'l-ihsan*, Justice and Benevolence.

From December 30, 1989, on, Yassine was placed under restrictions and thereafter members of his association were frequently arrested by the police. In January 1990, the association was formally prohibited, an event that inaugurated a period of very strained relations with the government, which lasted until the end of the decade.[1]

The "Prophetic Way": Soldiers, Disciples, and Believers

The Prophetic Way functions as a manual that explains to the disciple "what is to be done." Its publication began in August 1981, in the columns of the magazine *Al-jama'a*. The book is long and often obscure, making it a difficult task to work through its 500 pages. But it is the ultimate reference for the movement's members, and its difficult or muddled passages—which disciples endeavor to read and reread—are a way of maintaining Sheikh Yassine's exceptional status for his followers, who draw from it interpretations that are "final," because they have been stated by the guide, or *murshid*. Yassine publishes very frequently, which lends continuity to his role as guide and allows him to endure.

Just as the monarchy is related to prophecy, Yassine connects himself with the prophetic figure not directly through his lineage and his person—at least in this book—but rather by setting forth the exemplary nature of prophetic conduct. He once again takes one of his basic references from the king and, much like him, uses the prophetic figure as a political resource, but for a different purpose. While it is inherited by the king, Yassine constructs it as a model of conduct, and he prefers not to emphasize—as his 1974 letter shows—the concept of hereditary charisma.

The introduction to the book presents in minute detail the proposed structure of the organization that was to become Justice and Benevolence. As the author himself has admitted, this description does not really correspond to the present nature of the movement. It presents a curious construction mixing together the real internal organizing principles of the movement (organization in cells, uses of the mosque, patterns of ritual—in particular of prayers and the *dhikr*, or recitation of the divine names) and the general theoretical principles establishing the political and religious legitimacy of the movement.

Defining the Enemy, Preparing the Struggle

The Prophetic Way outlines a strategy for conducting war against the external enemy ("crusaders" and "Zionists"),[2] but also the internal enemy (the *kafirs* or impious). The demands and arguments Yassine sets forth are not very different from those presented by the 'ulama of the League, but the tone is much harsher: "This *umma* has long lived under the yoke of the crusaders and colonialists. It is now living through the nightmare of the worldwide Zionist conspiracy."[3]

From the outset, the reader encounters a militant and warlike vocabulary, with the evocation of the *junud Allah* (soldiers of Allah) who must respond to a "war set in motion against us."[4] "Inner jihad and jihad against enemies make it necessary to come into close contact with others, to conspire, plot, and oppose them with the means imposed by circumstances. We must not neglect the realm of plots and combat (*qital*)."[5] The questions of revolution and the use of violence, along with the political question, are addressed from the outset: "We must learn the rules of political warfare."[6] The themes of suffering, of following the "difficult way" (*iqtiham al-'aqaba*, a term from the Qur'an) are fully developed: "A time will come when the believer will understand that life was not created for the comfort of the believers. It is a bitter struggle (*jihad shaqq*)."[7]

At the same time, Yassine refers to the individual and his feelings: "The Islamic commitment to faith and benevolence (*ihsan*) is not like political commitment, which does not require an education of one's thinking. Entering into the world of the believers requires an emotional, intellectual, and active fusion (*indimaj*) with the body (*jism*) of the community (*jama'a*). A fusion that does not end with the end of life, but extends to eternal life."[8] He thereby emphasizes the idea of a continuity between individuals and their relationship to the divine and the mysterious on the one hand, and political combat on the other. He presents the mystic paradigm of nearness to God, along with the vocabulary of sovereignty (*hakimiyya*) of the divine law borrowed from the ideology of Mawdudi and the entire Middle Eastern tradition of political Islamism derived from Sayyid Qutb, all articulated in the form of a mystic messianism taken from the tradition of the greatest saintly Moroccan clerics.[9]

Living a Life That Prepares One for Death

In *The Way*, the theme of suffering in this world is linked to that of struggle. It is also directly tied to the notion of the promise of victory in this world: "Victory is promised to the faithful."[10] One must love death more than life and prepare oneself for the beyond, Yassine advises his disciples. For Yassine, the assertion "We are afraid of death and love life" needs to be reversed.[11] Referring to death, he goes on to say that we also have to "make history."[12] For the sheikh then, to love death means simultaneously informing the present and the future: it means giving one's life to shape the future and thinking about establishing an "Islamic state"—which is, however, he hastens to add, not an end in itself, but merely the "means" that make it possible to get closer to God.

The mystical posture here once again tempers political goals. *The Way* exhibits a constant oscillation between the believer's inner faith and his political aims, and a parallel back and forth between this life and the beyond. The political and hierarchical organization of the movement as this manual presents it is in fact bound up together with the depth of its members' faith and their capacity for jihad,[13] with no explicit statement of the classic distinction between the two meanings of the word jihad (individual or collective effort to achieve personal improvement, and war). Men must therefore all wish to become imams on earth, but each one also has "his place" to occupy.[14]

While *The Way* opens with the day-to-day organization and the political structure of the movement, it also sets out the sheikh's intent to make the movement widely visible, which means putting it into action in the public realm. But the public spaces that are to be penetrated are defined outside of those traditionally occupied by political actors, obscuring the important place held by parties in the Moroccan political sphere.[15] Sheikh Yassine's refusal to enter the legal sphere of political life was understood in the 1980s and 1990s as an opposition to the very operating mechanisms of Moroccan political life under its authoritarian regime. In this sense, at the time *The Way* was published, he had still located himself in a utopian realm, except if the movement were to use violence.

The opening of politics to democratic participation after 1997 and 1998 legalized a segment of the Islamist movement and thereby marginalized the role of Justice and Benevolence in the public realm. Not that this weakened its base—which seems to have remained very strong—but it denied the movement guaranteed public visibility by offering the opportunity for significant participation to its Islamist competitors, whose religious and political style diminished the relevance of the sharifian and mystical registers.

The Way and Revolution

Earlier, in the 1980s, Sheikh Yassine developed his messianic vision of political change: "When the gigantic wave rears up, the faithful may stop corruption by total disobedience, a general strike, taking to the streets, so that Allah may cover with shame the wastrels, evildoers on earth who do not mend their ways."[16]

Sheikh Yassine's ideology is not indifferent to movements of the left, but he emphasizes the difference between *qawma* (uprising), a noun derived from the verb *qama* (get up), and *thawra* (revolution). He makes a further distinction between force (*quwwa*) and violence (*'unf*). In this context, force is violence channeled and informed by faith and divine rules, and cannot be identified with brute force: "We use the word *qawma* so as not to use the word *thawra*. For in *thawra* there is violence (*'unf*), and we want force (*quwwa*). Force acts on the basis of legality (*mawadhi' shar'iyya*), whereas violence (*'unf*) follows the criteria of desire and anger."[17] Yassine expresses his disagreement with the idea of revolution advocated by secular revolutionary movements, which were still legion on university campuses: "We will not dirty ourselves with the traditions of the impious."[18]

The assertion of this divergence is, however, merely symbolic and enables Yassine to temper any inclination toward violence that might overwhelm him from inside the movement. His doctrine in fact remains very ambiguous concerning violence; he openly evokes the use of force, but at the same time develops the idea of a struggle that must be based on the education of the faithful—they may "change the world" later on.[19]

The Organization's Principles

The Way speaks of the need to transform a world subjected to a modernity that has escaped human mastery, and sets forth a highly organized political structure based on a strict hierarchical principle, which is to govern the activity of the militant-disciple. The guide, Yassine, wishes to reintroduce the Islamic tradition into current history primarily so that Islam may be experienced: As a comprehensive religion, it must be lived by the members of the movement, here and now. Discipline of mind and body—which finds intense expression in collective *dhikr* or the recitation of *wirds* –litanies made of sequences of Qur'anic texts- composed by Yassine, sometimes conducted throughout the night—permits the stabilization and channeling of inner feelings. The individual may thus construct himself and rediscover what he experiences as fullness within the communal framework of mystical experience.

The advisory board sits atop a structure that is made up of several levels. Beneath itself, the board appoints chiefs (*naqibs*), who meet in cells (*shu'bas*) located in the regions, and are the heads of "families" (*usras*). The "families" take charge of believers, whom they are to educate and introduce into the movement. But how is the believer to be recognized? Sheikh Yassine answers: "There remain the believers. They must have certain traits that make them recognizable. And an education that prepares them for taking upon themselves the responsibility for bringing about Allah's order. And an organization that makes them soldiers able to accomplish that, and a law (*qanun*) leading to their progression in jihad."[20]

The disciple's days and nights are in fact organized like those of a well supervised soldier. *The Way* explains what books the disciple should read and how many times and at what time of day he must recite the *dhikr*. Supplementary prayers are also provided in this minutely detailed schedule. In what Yassine demands from his disciples, there are simultaneously elements of asceticism, spirituality, and political commitment. He also requires unfailing submission to the sheikh, the group's spiritual guide, whose function is defined in these terms: "The general guide appoints the heads of cells and makes all educational and organizational decisions. . . . He has the right to make urgent executive decisions without consulting the advisory board."[21]

The book categorically rejects, at least for the disciple, the development of an "intellectualized" Islam. Religion must not be objectified, something to be gazed upon and thus made external to the lives of believers. Rather one must "live Islam," and instead of contemplating it from a distance, give it subjective content through a close relationship with the religion, and give it objective form in political struggle: "What is Islam for me as an individual located in a particular time and place, who has a place and a function in society, desires, reason, ambitions, and a coming death? Then, what is the meaning of Islam, of faith and benevolence in relation to the future history of humanity, for the present and future of Muslims?"[22] Subjective experience is articulated by the recitation of the "seventy-seven branches of faith and the ten merits," which concern the individual disciples.

The construction of this typology is odd, but is intended to correspond exactly to the text of the prophetic tradition and to bear the mark of the sheikh, like the recitations composed by each different Sufi master in the *zawiya* he founds.[23] All this is given objective form in the structure of the organization, in the movement to preaching and then into political action. Between these two levels, the manifestation of inner faith and the expression of political activism, there are no theological arguments or jurisprudential bridges.

Yassine reiterates the principle of obedience to the chief in obedience to Allah.[24] This principle of obedience must always be accompanied by that of *nasiha* and *shura* (admonition and consultation). These very general considerations, which repeat the broad notions of classical Islam, enable him to politicize the master-disciple relationship, while maintaining its character as a relationship that has been internalized primarily through the heart and comparing it to the relationship that links the believer with the person of the Prophet: "It is not necessary," he writes, "for relations between the sovereign and the community to be expressed in legal and administrative form. Codification in law of the principle of obedience . . . is only a means, not an end. The end is the satisfaction of Allah, the satisfaction of Allah through the effort that is made to bring forth his word. There must be in this effort (*jihad*) a chief and one who submits. . . . The obedience of Muslims to the chief is not a simple copy of revolutionary discipline. It is an adoration (*'ibada*) that comes from the heart. The chief is loved (*mahbub*), feared with respect (*muhabb*), looked upon as great, and venerated."[25]

The relationship between chief and militants is thus presented in the terms that define the bond between master and disciples: unfailing obedience is simply a variant of the nearness of friendship felt for the one who expresses—through his mystic posture—his proximity to God. In this sense, Sheikh Yassine perpetuates one of the founding principles of the Moroccan monarchy. This is why he endeavors to distance himself from it, at least in his use of vocabulary: he refuses, for example, to adopt the notion of *bayʿa* (pact of allegiance) because it is one of the symbolic bases for monarchical legitimacy. He prefers the word *mithaq* or *ʿahd*, meaning contract.

Justice and Benevolence thus has two faces. The first is that of a religious organization that exists in a very tense relationship with its environment, shown by its resemblance to a sectarian group, entry into which is difficult and subject to conditions and the commitment to which is very strong. The second is of a kind of organization that allows the few charismatic figures in the group to speak publicly and to echo a large segment of public opinion or the community in the broad sense. Nadia Yassine, the daughter of the spiritual guide, plays an important role in the connection between these two aspects: the role of bringing the community together (based at the outset on a mystic relationship), but also a wider ideological function focusing all its attention on the major social, cultural, and political problems of the day.

While Yassine's group refuses to participate in the political arena defined by the government, it carries the expression of its political struggle beyond the group, into the public sphere, through a variety of channels that carefully avoid the realm of partisan politics. It is within these public networks—consisting of the university, street demonstrations, and traditional and new media, such as the letters to the monarchy and the internet—that the movement expresses itself in the public sphere. When the group thus speaks publicly, a certain aspect of Yassine's ideology is discernible, conveyed particularly by his daughter Nadia. With a French educational background and extensive knowledge about Islam and Islamism, she can speak to the outside world, particularly to international media, especially in France and the rest of Europe.

In the 1990s, these various kinds of networks were used by the movement to make it more visible in Moroccan public life—particularly in the university, where clashes with the left and with the police were frequent, as were arrests of students, large numbers of whom had been recruited by Yassine.[26] These incursions into public life were brief, but they demonstrated a great capacity for mobilization.

The strength of the movement could be observed during large street demonstrations, when it sometimes participated with other Islamist movements demonstrating in defense of Muslims in other countries. One example was the December 7, 1989, demonstration commemorating the first Palestinian Intifada. Another was the demonstration of June 5, 1990, organized by the national committee of support for the struggle of the Palestinian people. Yet another was the February 3, 1991, demonstration for the Iraqi people, joined by Moroccans of diverse political tendencies, during which demonstrators burned French, American, and Israeli flags.

After a break in the mid-1990s, large street demonstrations began to proliferate late in the decade. They were encouraged by the process of democratic opening that Hassan II undertook very slowly beginning in 1992 and by the failure of the attempt by the Ministry of Religious Affairs to resolve negotiations—begun in 1990—with Yassine's movement, which persisted in not recognizing the principle of the king as commander of the faithful. The large march in the spring of 2000 against the reform of the family code (*Mudawwana*) was the most powerful demonstration of the strength of Justice and Benevolence and its objective alliance with the other Moroccan Islamist movements.

The Mystic Leader and His Disciples

In these public "sorties" by Sheikh Yassine's organization, he himself remained invisible. It is true that he was under house arrest in the

1990s, a situation that was, of course, criticized by militants, but also skillfully used by the guide. Disciples said, for example, that their sheikh was ubiquitous, that he was seen praying in a mosque while he was confined to his house in Salé. "Saint Yassine" (*al-wali Yassine*), it was said, works miracles through his uninterrupted connection to God. He knows, as a gnostic, how to pierce the Mystery.

Among both male and female disciples, the cult of the guide is important. During the Sunday morning "conferences," when Yassine speaks in his house in Salé, marks of veneration are displayed in the same way that disciples venerate their Sufi sheikhs. As in the royal palace, they all kiss the chief's hand. The movement's members are so eager to attend these meetings that a system of "tickets" has been set up, whereby each cell, in each region, is entitled to one entry ticket.

Oral accounts that I have heard from female disciples show that the sheikh has a definite aura of holiness (shared by his daughter Nadia —some militants call her "noble," in the expression *sharifa Nadia*). One of these militants, a member of Nadia Yassine's women's group, in telling me of her joining Justice and Benevolence, reiterated the visions that often recur about Yassine and his family: "Mother had a vision at that time. Yassine was in prison and we were reading his books. . . . There was an attachment . . . then the day before we met him [during a prison visit], she saw Abdessalam Yassine. She saw his face in the moon. In the heavens was written *la ilah illa Allah wa Muhammad rasul Allah* [There is no God but Allah and Muhammad is his Prophet]."[27] The evocation of these visions recalls those that were told about Mohamed V, whose features were said to have appeared to Moroccans in the moon's halo during his exile in Madagascar. "Nadia also had a vision when she was young, when she was thirteen in 1973. The letter [sent to King Hassan II] was secret, but she saw herself in dreams four times facing Hassan II. . . . Nadia is our mother and our father."

Muhammad Bashiri, long second in command of the movement, was excluded in 1998 for criticizing this mystic posture and rejecting the absolute power of the spiritual guide, who was considered by many disciples to be infallible.[28] For example, Bashiri called Yassine a

"Sufi, an extremist, and an inveterate liar,"[29] who has "transformed a militant movement into a *zawiya* in every sense of the word."[30]

The person of Yassine remains the means by which disciples may accomplish the movement into politics. In fact, in his last book, *Justice*, published after the death of Hassan II, Yassine explicitly designates himself as God's envoy (*mab'uth*). He finally brings together publicly, after Hassan's death, spiritual and political aspects in his very person. Speaking of the state, he writes: "It is a single machine (*alah*), the same machine that carries off the oppressed (*mustadh'afs*) with its tyranny and strikes them with its violence. . . . I have power over it only as an envoy (*mab'uth*) and transmitter, whom the Almighty has ordered to prepare his strength and to whom he has promised victory."[31]

In these images, the man of God becomes the political leader and combines the attributes of saint, imam, and messiah, uniting the role of leader of the community with that of producer of redemption and salvation. This use of messianic imagery, similar to that of Khomeini in both vocabulary and political concept, enables him to last politically by proclaiming the *inqilab*, or the overthrow.[32] He enacts this position on occasion on campuses or in street demonstrations, as well as in the operation of the religious cleaning up of beaches (made "Islamic" in the summer of 1998 by separating men and women and imposing Islamic dress), while refraining from revolutionary violence, and at the same time maintaining and managing his continued charisma. However, in the course of the 1990s, the danger represented by Yassine's group began to fade, thanks to a new strategy set in motion by Hassan II himself: the opening of the political arena to a relative pluralism.

Beginning in the summer of 1996, Hassan II mentioned the possible political integration of moderate Moroccan Islamists, "as long as they have not manifested a schism or a heresy and they conform to the laws and regulations of the state."[33] Many possible explanations may be found for this new strategy, and I will come back to the subject. One of them is certainly to domesticate some of the Islamists to create competition with more radical movements such as Yassine's, thereby taking away some of his clientele, real or potential. This redefinition of the rules of political competition, which introduced an element of risk for all participants, profoundly changed Yassine's strategy, and these transformations became particularly apparent after the death of Hassan II.

Surviving the Death of the King: New Forms of Opposition

King Hassan II died on July 23, 1999, after a reign of thirty-eight years. His son, who became Muhammad VI, inherited the throne of Morocco at the age of thirty-six. On the very night his father died, the young king received the allegiance of civilian and military figures, who made obeisance to him in the royal palace. The ceremony of the *bay'a* took place in four stages, involving each of four circles in turn: the royal family (the crown prince, brother of the new king, and his cousins Mawlay Hisham and Mawlay Isma'il); members of the government—among whom must be noted the presence of two women who were signatories of the pact of allegiance; followed by the 'ulama, who discussed the details of the funeral, but who formerly enjoyed a better position; and finally the military. These elite figures, repeating in turn their allegiance, made possible the formal continuity of the 'Alawite dynasty (the 'ulama had recognized Muhammad as crown prince in 1984), as they had done for Hassan II in 1961.[34]

Outside the palace, the new monarchical regime was not challenged at the outset. At first, Moroccans in general expressed their hopes and concretely articulated their expectations, however diverse they might be.[35] This was all the more the case because at the beginning of his reign the young king gave indications of a possible modernization of the monarchy. One of the strongest symbols of a break with the past was the dismissal, on November 9, 1999, of the Minister of the Interior, Driss Basri, who had for nearly twenty years symbolized the regime's authoritarianism and its dark side.

A few days later, on November 14, Abdessalem Yassine composed a *Memorandum to Whom it May Concern* addressed to the new monarch. Written in French to ironically demonstrate that Yassine adapted to the language spoken by the Gallicized Moroccan elites, it was not made public until several weeks had passed, in late January 2000 (on the internet site Yassine Online). As will be apparent, this memorandum extended, and also qualified, the admonition sent in 1974, which, written in Arabic, had long circulated clandestinely.

On the one hand, the *bay'a* was renewed by official religious figures; on the other hand, the admonition was reiterated by a leader of the Islamist opposition. In the summer of 1999, the terms of the political pact seemed to be repeated to ensure—despite the implicit hostility toward Muhammad VI in the new letter—the continuity of a political regime. Without compelling these political actors, the monarchy found itself reinvested, as though through the will of those actors alone, with the power that it might have lost with the death of the man who embodied it and tightly controlled its operations. The king was dead, and his most humble servants along with his opponents could immediately shout "Long live the king!" Submission and opposition to the monarchy continued to exist because there was no question of the king's physical death bringing about his political death. By the very actions of those gravitating around it, the monarchy thus remained at the heart of the political arena and of political rankings and changes in rank.

When the new king inherited the title of "commander of the faithful" from his father, the *bay'a* renewed the terms of the pact that symbolically united Hassan II and the Moroccans. Signed on the night of July 23, 1999, and read aloud in front of the signatories and the king by the Minister of Religious Affairs, 'Abd al-Kabir 'Alawi Mdaghri, it mentioned the supreme imam, the *bay'a* as pact (*mithaq*), and obedience to those in power, the will of God. Muhammad VI was thus political leader (*amir*), religious leader (*imam*), and commander of the faithful (*amir al-mu'minin*).

The Second Admonition: A Secular Opposition?

But early in 2000, Yassine once again disturbed the alliance between the king and his people, and produced an anti-pact with his new letter addressed to the young King Muhammad VI. With Hassan II gone, the 1974 letter had in fact lost its political significance. The opposition expressed by the first letter was kept alive only by the presence of the king. With his death, the concrete admonition and the political and religious standards it expressed had lost their meaning.

While the 'ulama close to the palace offered Muhammad VI the *bay'a*, Yassine reiterated, on new grounds, his admonition. He perhaps hoped his *nasiha* would enable him to survive politically, but it was considerably different from the one he had addressed to the new king's father: less virulent in tone and less dramatic, it was shorter and aimed at reproducing the terms of the conflict in virtually identical form. This time, however, it contained something that might shake the foundations of power: his most secular critique.

The Context of the New Letter

Yassine again established a connection with the monarchy, one which he would continue to elaborate in personal terms, although one of the protagonists had changed identity. The new king was young, had not yet established his power over the Makhzen, and had no particular relationship with Yassine. His image was that of a king sensitive to poverty—he was called the "king of the poor," recalling his grandfather Muhammad V. In his new letter, Sheikh Yassine presents a nuanced picture of the new monarch, as a young man who has not yet had the opportunity to really exercise power, even though his father had placed him at the head of the military services, but who has the ability to reform the institution of the monarchy to deliver Morocco from all its evils.

Yassine and his group also began behaving in more moderate ways. They were prepared to make some concessions to show that Justice and Benevolence could behave reasonably in the public sphere. In December 1999, for example, group leaders Fathallah Arslane, 'Abd al-Wahid al-Mutawakkil, and 'Abd Allah Shibani requested authorization for a march in favor of the Chechen people. The Ministry of the Interior denied permission. A year earlier, the movement had ignored the banning of a demonstration in favor of Iraq. This time, the movement's leaders acceded to the government's decision.

The letter "to whom it may concern" was, as we have seen, written a few days after Driss Basri had been dismissed as Interior Minister. This new political situation, a sign of opening on the part of Muhammad VI, allowed the sheikh to feel that he could renegotiate his status without taking too many political risks: "The young King Muhammad VI enjoys an obvious degree of sympathy among Moroccan youth, who seem to see in him a friend, a symbol of deliverance, and a fresh promise of a better future.... Everything leads us to believe that after a long nightmare a glimmer of sunlight can finally be seen on the horizon. The dark shadows of an age of lead seem to be drifting off and giving way to the sunlight of an approaching dawn."[36] But the letter was not made public until later, on the tenth anniversary of the beginning of Yassine's house arrest, January 28, 2000, in order to coincide with a press conference organized by Justice and Benevolence. The letter was then posted on the movement's website, hence, on this occasion, not sent to the king. According to Nadia Yassine, important members of the movement had asked to see Hasan Awrid, the king's spokesman, to give him a copy. He had refused to meet with them, but this time, publicly distributing the message meant going "over the head" of the monarchy.

The style and tone of the 2000 memorandum are different from those of the 1974 letter. The recipient, of course, had changed; he was in a sense "unknown" in comparison to his father, unlike Yassine himself. Much shorter and less polished, it is written in French and is practically devoid of religious content and symbolism. Its tone is "youthful," using an up-to-date vocabulary in which it is possible to recognize something of the style of Yassine's daughter Nadia. The situation had changed from that of mimeographed letter to one sent through the internet, made available for everyone to read in an open public forum: "We are in a more open world. My father has taken advantage of this for the memorandum," Nadia Yassine explained. "In 1973, it circulated slowly. Long live technology! Long live the internet!"[37]

Yassine also wished to renew his legitimacy and restore his presence on the public stage, while testing what the monarchy had become after the death of Hassan II. But the second admonition was less secret than the first, and thereby more banal, in a society which had seen a proliferation of political discussion since the mid-1990s and in which religion might be appropriated or left aside according to the preferences of participants in politics.

The Secular Critique of the Government and the Routinization of Charisma

The admonition to Muhammad VI thus expressed the beginnings of a kind of normalization. It contained no call for a caliphate. Yassine's demands had become close to those of other parties, except with respect to the king's fortune: "Redeem your poor father from torment by restoring to the people the goods that rightfully belong to the people. Redeem yourself! Repent! Fear the King of Kings!"[38]

The text hews closely to the subjects of human rights—through the description of the king's "secret garden" and of tragedies such as Tazmamart—[39] justice, and major economic problems, particularly in a sketchy discussion of globalization and its destructive effects. "Let's talk. Let's discuss figures and households, let's speak concretely and clearly!. . . From bad to worse, the Morocco of the *tontons macoutes* has deteriorated in the area of human rights. . . . The machine excelled in producing poverty for all and insolent wealth for the favorites. . . . The underlying situation that the attractive sovereign has inherited (who should not be taken in by the euphoria of the moment) is one of widespread waste, poverty for many, flashy comfort for a few, corruption as a means of administration and government, and institutional and practical manipulation of democratic elections: in short, the stew of the Makhzen."[40]

While the letter put Yassine back on the public stage, it also showed how he had moderated his language, not only because the unequal balance of power with the monarchy was ongoing, but also because the political scene had considerably changed. Yassine was no longer the only one to speak politically and publicly from a religious standpoint, and he was now practically a part of the routine operations of Moroccan politics. For example, nearly two years previously, on November 15, 1998, he had been able to display his books officially at a book fair.[41]

The letter to Muhammad VI was not the only text Yassine made public in the period following the death of Hassan II. A much longer document was published in Casablanca in 2000, in the form of a book entitled *Justice* (*Al-'adl*). It deals with the major subjects discussed in the letter, but focuses primarily on questions of political strategy, which include the existence of multiple parties and the opening granted by Hassan II in the 1990s, notably the plurality of Islamist voices, the question of violence, and the future of Islamism in the world. The answers to the questions raised by Yassine remain very vague—which is probably what impelled his detractors to criticize the obscurity of his style. But this lack of clarity of expression is not without its reasons.

Yassine, in fact, oscillates constantly between two subjects. The first is the diagnosis of present evils: the "nightmare" and the "sickness" afflicting Islam, which is not limited to the existence of despotic regimes, but is also explained by the unjust effects of globalization, pollution, and other catastrophes linked to modernity. From this follows the description of the despair of Moroccan youth demonstrated in clandestine migration to Europe, the *hrig* (from the Arabic verb "to burn"), during which many young men who set sail on *pateras* (makeshift craft) die in the Straits of Gibraltar.

The second subject is the necessity of continuing political struggle, for which each disciple should prepare himself, since Yassine still asserts that catastrophe is near. At the same time, he emphasizes the need for nonviolence and the importance of dialogue with democrats and secular figures, even though he attributes to them all kinds of negative characteristics. He points to the central importance of the political question and uses military and militant vocabulary, but finally puts the work of preaching before that of overthrowing the political order.

These ambiguities obviously arose from the relative democratization introduced in the late 1990s. It was hardly possible to maintain radical discourse against the monarchy when it offered to some the chance to participate in the political debate and even in power. I will later consider how Yassine's movement took on a routine character in the radically new political context of the late 1990s.

On May 19, 2000, Muhammad VI released Yassine from the house arrest to which he had been confined since 1989. While continuing the recognition of the legalized—and tamed—wing of moderate Islamism that had begun in 1997, the king freed a man who had vehemently criticized the political power of Hassan II. By freeing Yassine, Muhammad VI disrupted the relationship of opposition between his father and Yassine, and thereby weakened Justice and Benevolence. The movement of the *murshid* (guide) was neutralized in the organizational structure of the *zawiya*. The original moment of dissidence in 1974 had grown distant, and the 2000 letter did not have the same effects.

Since 1998, Yassine's movement had aspired to become a political party whose embryonic form was established in an internal organization called a "political circle," which meant losing the radical "distance" created by the path the opposition had taken to set itself up as a mirror of the sharifian monarchy. Two identities were superimposed on one another: Yassine himself and the organizational structure, which, while now mutually dependent, might become distinct in the future and bring one or the other into political prominence.

The routinization of Yassine's charisma in an organized group had spread beyond the borders of Morocco, since his movement had followers in France and elsewhere in Europe (particularly in Belgium and Holland), and had also begun to establish a presence in the United States. Nadia Yassine had recovered significant freedom of movement and frequently gave lectures in Europe. France was the first foreign country in which Justice and Benevolence established a foothold: the association Muslim Participation and Spirituality (PSM), set up in a mosque in the Paris suburb of Stains, discreetly represented Sheikh Yassine's movement.

PSM was established in the 1990s by Moroccan students. The association now attracts a clientele similar to that drawn to the Union of Islamic Organizations of France (UOIF): young students and French Muslim professionals. The UOIF, present in France since 1983, but also really active only since the 1990s, leaves little room in its governing apparatus for newcomers, whose rise through the hierarchy is now blocked. Unlike the UOIF, PSM cultivates discretion: it makes no direct reference to Sheikh Yassine or to the situation in Morocco because it wishes to adapt itself directly to the French context and does not want to be tarred with a reputation for political radicalism. The UOIF sees Yassine's followers as serious competitors, and in 2003, PSM had to fight to get a booth at the large meeting of Muslim associations held in Bourget.

For the uninitiated, the culture of Sufism was watered down and the organic bond with Justice and Benevolence was minimized. But the texts of Sheikh Yassine were the direct reference for the initiates, and they were expected to work tirelessly to penetrate their secrets by assiduously studying *The Way* and other works by the guide. As in Morocco, disciples follow the practice of *Qiyam al-lil*, in which disciples meet at night. The women's section devotes itself to prayers and spiritual exercises, but also undertakes "relaxation" sessions.

While French youth in the Paris suburbs are patiently deciphering his writings, in his house in Salé, the frail and white-bearded figure of Yassine delivers his lessons in Sunday morning meetings, surrounded by disciples when he is not too weakened by his advanced age and illness. If one wants to participate from a distance, it is possible to attend live on his website and to e-mail questions to him. The technological tools connected to the globalization of the circulation of ideas and images have thus been skillfully used by Yassine's group to establish footholds in Europe, Canada, and the United States. This has not prevented the organization from taking an interest in the antiglobalization movement as it seeks new bases for mobilization in harmony with its primary activity and its continued refusal to recognize the political legitimacy of the Moroccan monarchy.

By becoming transnational, Yassine's movement secured greater freedom to maneuver, allowing the group and its ideas to become part of everyday life in the Moroccan political landscape. It should be pointed out that this relative normalization has been authorized by the monarchy itself, which thereby hopes to neutralize the movement's capacity, and that of its competitors, for political troublemaking, following a pattern of political fragmentation that has recurred throughout the history of the modern monarchy and its relationship with Islam. In 2004, the few plainclothes police maintaining surveillance over people entering and leaving Sheikh Yassine's house in Salé and the other houses in the neighborhood where the movement held meetings, including the women's section *insaf* (equity) led by Nadia and the "political circle," were known to everyone, and visitors were greeted by a relaxed atmosphere. This did not prevent the police from often arresting excessively zealous militants, particularly on university campuses: there have been dozens of trials of members of the movement in Rabat, Fez, Taroudant, and Tinghir.

This paradoxical situation can be seen as an indication that the movement has taken root in Moroccan society, but also as one of a simultaneous process of normalization and preservation of dissidence: continuing, but low-intensity repression has not caused the movement to collapse and in fact constitutes an implicit authorization for its existence, which has never been legally recognized.

The Changing Relations between Islam and the Monarchy

The evolution of relations between the regime and Justice and Benevolence indicates that the relationship between Islam and the monarchy has undergone important changes since the 1970s and then a major transformation in the 1990s. The monarchy did in fact become more deeply involved with Islam in the 1970s and 1980s. But this process was not one which, more than in the past, involved an identification making Islam the very foundation of the regime. On the contrary, the involvement was an indication of difficulty and tension, indeed of a deficit that the monarchy constantly strove to overcome, deriving from the perception on the part of a segment of the Islamist opposition that the monarchy had grown increasingly disconnected from Islam.

However, this disconnection did not mean, on the other hand, that the two had ever been indissolubly joined together. Their relations in fact have to be analyzed in terms of representations and perceptions: the production, appropriation, and management of religious signs and religious language enable the monarchy to "signal" its bonds with Islam to the public. Yassine's interventions beginning in 1974 publicly contradicted these religious signs. The importance of his first letter to Hassan II lies in the disjunction it carried out between the monarchy and Islam, which no longer appeared as two spheres naturally joined together, but rather as two domains intersecting thanks to a constructed convergence built by the authoritarian regime.

In the early 1980s, the creation of 'ulama councils presided over by the king or, a few years later, of an annual summer university of the "Islamic renaissance" by the Ministry of Religious Affairs indicated an attempt by Hassan II to bring under his control the elements of the religious sphere that, starting in the 1960s, he had been carefully working to fragment as they were exerting pressure to increase their autonomy. But these new signals, constantly sent out by the government, were too scattered and could not operate as a system of control over a religious realm that was extremely fragmented.

The king then adopted a new strategy, instituting some degree of pluralism, and accepting, from 1997-98 on, the integration of legalist Islamists into political activity. From then on, Islam began to penetrate more deeply into public deliberations, which gained a wider circulation, and was frequently discussed. At the time, at least, the monarchy agreed to structurally disconnect itself from monopolizing Islam, not in the sense of giving up any religious definition of itself, but rather by agreeing to become a religious actor among others, which it had in fact traditionally been.

Analyzing the sharifian dynasties of the seventeenth century, and distinguishing between political function and "religious sign," Jacques Berque has written: "It was normal that a power *under a religious sign* acceded to royalty. It did not in fact exercise power as a religious entity. These shorfas [Arabic plural of sharif] were neither marabouts nor saints, nor propagators of a brotherhood, nor religious reformers. *They acted primarily as political agents*, founders of a state."[42] The postcolonial period, during which the 'Alawite monarchy secured the monopoly of political violence within national boundaries, also provided it with the opportunity to attempt to identify its realm of political sacredness with the realm of Islam. The attempt, however, turned out to be futile, coming up against an older persistent phenomenon whereby religion might also function—through the intermediary of men of religion—as an opposition force.

In fact, the emergence of the Islamist challenge beginning in the 1970s coincided with the royal attempt to control the religious sphere on its own. And, beginning in the 1990s, it probably became too costly for the regime to continue to maintain the monopoly while managing and controlling its fragments. It was at this point that the regime agreed to not necessarily confine religious actors to proclaiming the monarchy's own existence and legitimacy. The monarchy disconnected religious voices with a political dimension from its own sphere, and allowed them to circulate outside the king's domain, provided that such discourses not call into question the political legitimacy of the monarchy. At the same time, to ensure that independent religious authorities not unite against the monarchy, Hassan II included a segment of the Islamist opposition within the field of legal political activity, in a classic strategy aimed at disciplining potential challengers. This strategy also served to maintain a religious continuum between the monarchy and religious dissidence. The palace thereby made sure that there were intermediaries subject to control located between the Makhzen, the center of political power, and the more radical religious opposition located in the periphery, such as the one Yassine defined.

This was the strategy that provoked an important change in the relations between the monarchy's political authority and religion: the emergence of political pluralism, however modest, in a society of believers could not fail to lead to religious pluralism, to the diversification of cultural, social, and political manifestations of Islam. The religious organizations that secured increased autonomy established new areas for mobilizing and controlling the faithful and channeled their demands, in a manner that was more or less free from control by the monarchy.

Democratic opening thus tended to bring new religious spheres to light, like so many public spaces, and to disconnect them from state control. On the other hand, if these new areas for religious mobilization wished to enter political competition through participation in the legal political system—illustrated by the example of the Party of Justice and Development—they had to gradually give up their religious claims so that they might fully enter the political sphere.

The public sphere thus retained its religious signs, which were diverse, fragmented, and very vibrant in Morocco. On the other hand, the newly pluralistic legal political sphere was forced to give them up. The religious element established a vital and deep presence in social life and on the fringes of "authorized" political competition. It was also prevalent in the imagery and the official religious representations of court society. But it grew attenuated in the sphere of legal political competition, even though the questions—related to that attenuation—that were raised by various political actors were often discussed with great virulence.

The monarchy thus found itself in a paradoxical position that made it more solitary in religious terms: it remained, through the maintenance of its prophetic lineage that was in part responsible for its sacred status, "above" the sphere of political debate (and this was even truer because of its position of political dominance), but it also exhibited a certain resemblance to its most determined religious adversaries, who, like Yassine, imitated the religious posture of the monarchy.

PART III

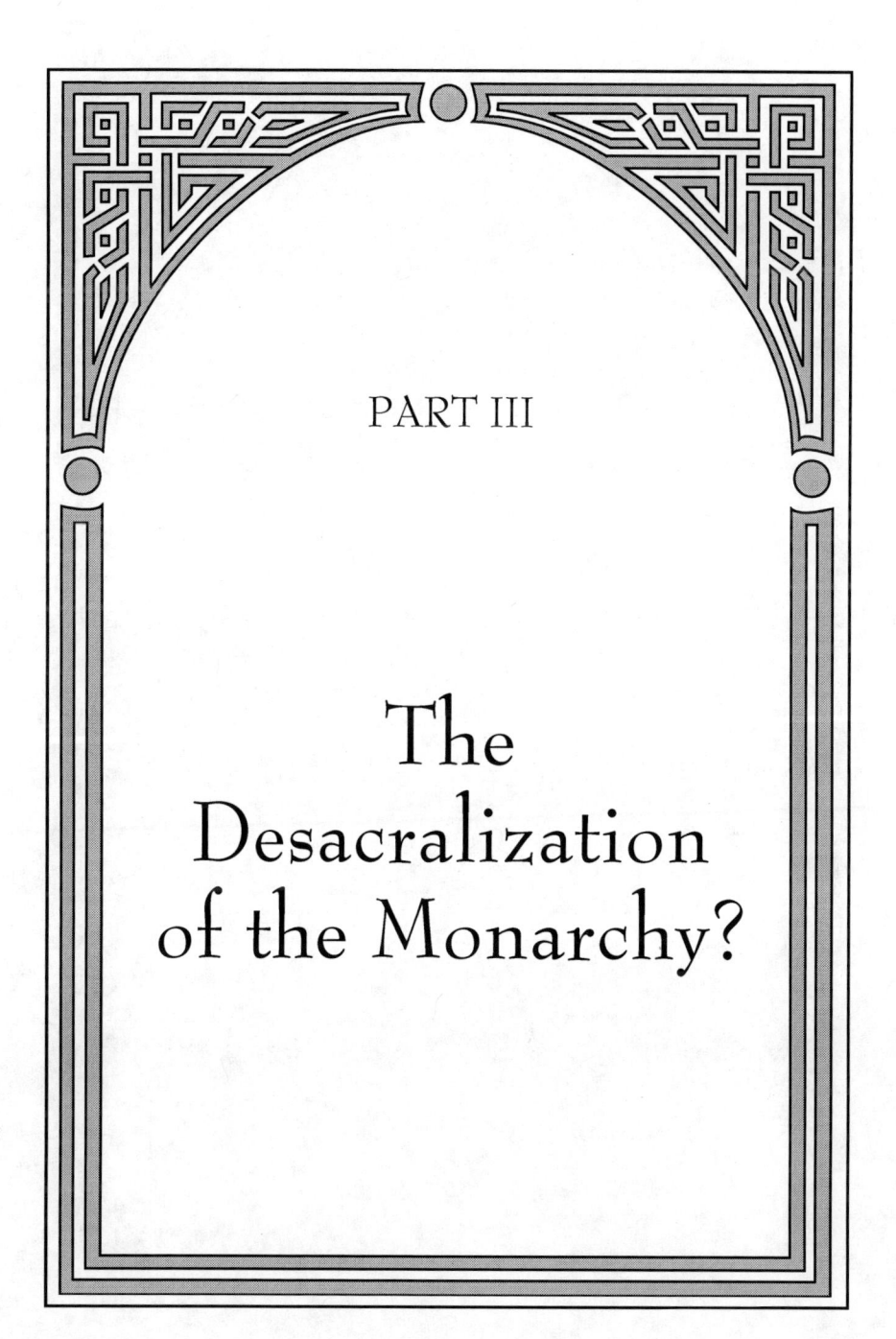

The Desacralization of the Monarchy?

Sheikh Abdessalam Yassine and his followers use a repertoire that blends messianism and mysticism with political resistance. His movement has resisted any integration into the operations of the legal political system. Refusing to recognize the monarchy's legitimacy, it constitutes an opposition at the margin of legal institutions and has put a counter-society in place, an "anti-political" politics, which bases the social bond on a mystical Islam. In addition, a paradox runs through Yassine's program: although he rejects the monarchy's legitimacy, he reproduces many of its mechanisms. His rebellion is based on an antagonistic mimesis of the monarchy, and the relationship oscillates between peaceful coexistence and violent confrontation. But Moroccan Islamism is not homogeneous: other movements, rooted in religious and political terms of reference different from those of Yassine give Islamism in Morocco a pluralistic and fragmented character.[1]

This third part begins with a description of the Justice and Development Party (PJD). I analyze this new Islamist party through its relations with the monarchy and the operations of the political system in order to understand the transformation of Moroccan authoritarianism and the tensions now pervading the foundations of the sacred character of the monarchy. The PJD is a political movement that contrasts sharply with Yassine's, and it defines a new type of relationship between Moroccan Islamism and the monarchy. Indeed, in contrast with Yassine's construction of an antagonistic mimesis of the monarchy, this new Islamist party bases its opposition on the principle of rapprochement and inclusion in the structures authorized by the monarchy. Whereas relations between the monarchy and Yassine are based on reciprocal exclusion and the confrontation of two antagonistic entities that are in reality mirror images of each other, relations between the PJD and the monarchy are based on principles of inclusion and integration. They allow the use of strategies of reciprocal domestication of a competitor different from oneself. This relationship, unprecedented in Moroccan Islamism, is based on the establishment of a *pact* between the monarchy and the opposition Islamist party, a pact that has established a certain number of new political rules. This pact provides a new structure of political and discursive opportunities and constraints for Moroccan Islamism.

I therefore focus more particularly on the period beginning in the 1990s, during the course of which the monarchy initiated a profound transformation in the functioning of the Moroccan political system by making two decisions which it implemented in swift succession. First, beginning in 1992, Hassan II opened up the political system to some degree of competition, the terms of which he negotiated with the major opposition parties and which were made concrete by a reform of the Moroccan constitution. Then, between 1996 and 1998, he legalized an Islamist movement which adopted the name Justice and Development Party (PJD), some of whose members participated in the 1997 election. This election brought the socialist party to power, a significant event in the annals of Moroccan politics. The regime had thus made the decision to open the political system to more political competition and transparency at the very time when the presence of Islamist movements and their demands on the regime were becoming increasingly visible to the public and the subject of intense debates in Moroccan society. The inclusion of an Islamist party in the operations of the Moroccan political regime is considered here on the one hand because it contrasts sharply with the example of the Justice and Benevolence movement treated in the second part, and on the other hand because the PJD represents an unprecedented and atypical actor on the Moroccan political stage. The integration of the PJD transformed this stage by producing a new kind of relationship between the state and the Islamist opposition and also by profoundly changing the relationship between the monarchy and Islam.

This section, however, does not dwell on the causes of the liberalization of the functioning of the political system. Rather, it describes the process and its consequences in detail. Most researchers today agree that a social and economic crisis in the Middle East and North Africa is continuing to call into question the implicit contracts between societies and governments that had exchanged the distribution of state subsidies for the guarantee of a certain degree of political peace. To stave off the political tensions created by this crisis, most Arab regimes have put in place new pacts encouraging some political actors formerly excluded from legal politics and government affairs to have hope of participating in them. This paradigm stipulates that in order to last, the regimes that have lost the capacity to distribute subsidies have had to compensate by allowing some of the opposition to participate in legal political competition.[2] The example of Morocco also shows that monarchies, accustomed to managing a diversity of constituents, are better equipped than republics to carry out this political transition, as Jordan showed in the late 1980s. Morocco thus corresponds to the paradigm of a transition through pact negotiation.[3] This process of transition is initiated by the regime and is not necessarily a process of democratization. It has become stabilized for now in the form of a regime of competitive authoritarianism.[4] I thus use the notion of the "opening" of the political system rather than that of "democratization." This "opening" is not a process in which the regime is heading toward a democracy of the liberal kind. I do not compare and contrast an incomplete or imperfect democracy with an external model located in the West. I intend rather to analyze here the mechanisms and the participants involved in this process of opening.

First, the process was initiated by the regime, which increased the number of participants in legal competition while continuing to exclude some of them. In this respect, the regime is continuing to follow one of the underlying principles of the Moroccan political system: division of opposition forces. It "divides to conquer" while simultaneously becoming more inclusive. Second, the rules of operation of political competition and of relations between government and opposition were modified by a reform of the constitution, which to some extent widened the limits of the government's responsibility to parliament. A space for communication between government and opposition was thus opened up, making criticism and public exchanges between the two bodies possible. In addition, and this was novel and important, both the conduct and the public reporting of results of elections became more transparent. But the role of elections is not necessarily to periodically change the identity of the members of the government and to redefine successive government policies by reflecting election results. Moroccan governments are today still under the control of the monarchy, which reigns and governs in the last resort. Elections do on the other hand publicly reveal the relative political strength of each party. This information, now known by the Moroccan public, may become the central variable in pre- and post-election bargaining between the monarchy and the different components of the political opposition. Because the information is public, it cannot be seriously and flagrantly manipulated by the state, unless the process of opening, itself, were to be called into question. Both the Moroccan monarchy and Moroccan society thus show constant concern for voter mobilization and the results of elections. Political actors and the public read in them a reflection of the major tendencies in public opinion, as though elections were playing the role of opinion polls. A press that is freer than in the past has reported on the situation and thereby broken many political taboos. Political opening has thus been defined on the one hand by an enlargement of the space for negotiations between regime and opposition, and on the other by increased transparency, which has modified the expectations of participants. However, this opening has taken on shifting dimensions. The rules underlying the Moroccan political system have been defined so that the monarchy never loses control of the government. The transformations of the Moroccan political regime have thus fallen far below the expectations of Moroccan citizens.[5]

With respect to the causes of political opening, the case of Morocco confirms the paradigm developed by the "contingency school" founded by Dankwart Rustow in the 1970s and reinterpreted in the 1990s by political scientists.[6] Against the idea that to promote democracy it is first necessary to create democratic minds, Rustow writes: "Instead, we should allow for the possibility that circumstances may force, trick, lure, or cajole non-democrats into democratic behavior and that their beliefs may adjust in due course by some process of rationalization or adaptation."[7] The transition, the by-product of fortuitous circumstances, thus produces a democratic political culture: "A distasteful decision, once made, is likely to seem more palatable as one is forced to live with it. . . . Democracy is by definition a competitive process and this competition gives an edge to those who sincerely believe in it."[8] Over time, opposition actors, like the government, become democrats, realizing through processes of "habituation" that it is in their interest to adhere to that political norm.[9]

This argument has been applied in particular to Islamist movements to explain the transformation of their ideologies: thanks to political liberalization, they have entered into the operations of political competition and they have become fluent in the language of democracy. The Moroccan case shows that this is indeed the case for the Party of Justice and Development. However, this line of reasoning has been elaborated further by recognizing in the integration of Islamists into the electoral arena the initiation of a process of "dilution" of Islamism in democracy and the beginnings of a general process of separation between Islam and politics. For instance, Olivier Roy writes that Islamists have given up "a key element: the demand for a monopoly of the representation of religion in politics, replaced by the acceptance of a political sphere independent from religion."[10] Meticulous observation of the development of religious ideologies by Islamists in the political realm has led me to strongly modify this assertion.

This third part, therefore, is concerned principally with the effects of the recent political opening in Morocco, focusing on the combination of two simultaneous processes: changes in political procedures and institutions on the one hand and, on the other, the transformation of the use and content of specific religious repertoires in the political sphere. Rather than considering when and under what conditions political opening may occur, I answer the following question: toward what forms of political functioning is this transition leading? More specifically, what are the consequences of this opening, itself limited, for a very particular domain, that of religion and its interactions with politics? Does a process of political liberalization necessitate the depoliticization of Islam, as many writers have claimed?[11] I answer this question in the negative by showing the connection between changes in the functioning of legal political competition and the production and use of religious repertoires by the monarchy and its Islamist opponents.

The formation, development, and ideology of the PJD show that Islamism, in a liberalized political context, profoundly changes its political practices and its use of religious references.[12] However, this transformation is far from uniform, differing depending on the areas in which it operates. By focusing simultaneously on the institutional context and discursive contents, it can be shown how Islamist activists use religious references in different ways in different contexts. In the sphere of political society, the constraints imposed by the palace and by a great number of political actors generate an increased tension between Islam and politics in the discourse of Islamist parliamentary representatives, particularly in the parliament itself and in relations between parties. In a system that is in the process of liberalization, political society is defined as a domain "in which the polity specifically arranges itself to contest the legitimate right to exercise control over public power and the state apparatus."[13] The institutions located at the center of political society are political parties, elections, electoral rules, party alliances, and legislatures.[14] In this particular political situation, the politicization of Islamist discourse and the confrontation with its political competitors marginalize the use of Islam though never completely eliminating it. PJD deputies speak of Islam implicitly, as a frame of reference, and in a distanced way, but it is always present in the background. In the Moroccan political society open to electoral competition, the monarchy, as well as an important number of political parties, defines political competition as necessarily secular. Constrained by this definition, PJD Islamists in parliament then change the definition of Islam into an ethics of political conduct. On the other hand, that is true neither for the monarchical state, which is making a vain attempt to recover a crumbling religious monopoly, nor for social and religious movements acting in close cooperation with the PJD on the margins of political society. Outside political society and within the network of Islamist associations, the theological thinking of some PJD Islamists represents an Islam with flexible and adaptable terms, which does not necessarily develop a notion of the Islamic state but makes Islam the standard of reference for defining a community of believing citizens, a community that is the stage for their political activity.[15]

In the case of Morocco, new tensions have surfaced between the realms of religion and politics, but far from leading to their separation into autonomous spheres, these tensions have had the effect of reshaping relations between the two, depending on the context: the definitions and the uses of Islam therefore change from one area of political activity to another, according to the strategies of the actors and the constraints under which they are operating.[16] I offer, then, a differentiated interpretation of the relations between religious and political repertoires depending on particular spheres of political activity. In the electoral arena, Islamists disconnect religion and politics, whereas the monarchy, with regard to the state and religious institutions, like the Islamists in civil society, strives to bring them together.

To reveal the operation of these two contradictory processes, the analysis of state policies with regard to the forms of political competition must be supplemented with an understanding of the monarchy's policies with regard to Islam.

Indeed, the first part of this book showed how, beginning with independence, the monarchical state had domesticated the form and content of Moroccan Islam through institutional fragmentation. However, this mechanism for the definition and control of Islam, already unstable because of its fragmented nature, was relentlessly challenged in the 1990s when new religious authorities emerged, diversified, and became more difficult for the monarchy to co-opt or suppress. The mechanism for the regulation of Islam was therefore reconsidered: the monarchy urged that Islamic references be absent from the sphere of political deliberation. In addition, early in the new century, the system of state regulation of religion was transformed into a more organized and bureaucratic apparatus centered in the Ministry of Religious Affairs. This was an institutional change that established an apparatus for the regulation of Islam well beyond the religious authority of the monarch, even though he theoretically controls the religious apparatus. The relations between monarchy and Islam have thus been radically changed, because the person of the king is no longer the central religious institution. In this sense, the forms of regulation of Islam by the monarchy—despite the prophetic lineage of the 'Alawite king—have begun to resemble those in the Arab republics, where they are based on the control of Islam in a separate institution.

The proliferation of religious authorities beginning in the 1980s had induced competition among them and constituted a threat to the monarchy.[17] In the 1990s, political opening came about to protect the monarchy against that threat by co-opting a segment of Islamism. The temporal coincidence of the emergence of religious authorities outside monarchic control and the opening up of political competition shows that the development and the circulation in the public sphere of ideological repertoires linked to Islam, produced by the monarchy as well as by the opposition, can accompany political opening. The diversification and competition of these religious repertoires are thus in step with an increasingly pluralist political society and the establishment of political pacts between government and opposition, contrary to the idea that "where the scriptures are both holy and explicit, as in the case of Islam, pragmatic compromise will be very difficult."[18]

Political liberalization therefore does not necessarily require a depoliticization of Islam (that is, an Islam defined without political activism and devoid of political theology) or its withdrawal from all public space. But that political activism and those political theologies threaten the religious foundations of the monarchy. For this reason, the monarchy prevents Islamist discourse from penetrating one particular part of public space: the parliament, the site of open political competition institutionalized by the monarchy. The monarchy, which has constructed itself as Islamic, thereby imposes a principle of secularism in the sphere of political competition to protect itself from the effects of the integration of religion into party politics. The repertoires of Islamists are therefore differentiated according to the arenas they enter. At the same time, the transition to more political pluralism has been carried on simultaneously with the crumbling of the state monopoly on Islam, whereas Islam has remained the normative frame of reference shared by all actors, but interpreted differently by each one, and articulated in the public sphere within the limits set by the monarchy. The monarchy thus finds itself in a profound contradiction: opening the space of politics to increased competition to ensure its own survival, while at the same time finding its religious foundations threatened by the effects of that competition, which impel it to remove Islam from the sphere of political competition and to attempt to regulate it—unsuccessfully—in an authoritarian way.

To underline the tensions among authoritarianism, electoral politics, and the Islamic identity of the monarchy and its opponents, Chapter 7 presents a narrative of the reshaping of Moroccan authoritarianism and the transformation of Moroccan political society, simultaneous with the transformation of the monarchy's relationship with Islam and the change in its strategy toward Islamism. It shows how the Justice and Development Party was integrated into the operation of the political system through elections. Chapter 8 describes the effects of that integration on the political ideology of legalist Islamism. In particular, it brings out the ambivalence of the Islamists' ideological shifts prompted by the definition of parliament as a secular space. One of these shifts focused the ideology of the PJD on the representation of an internal and external split between Islam and the West, which echoed the language of certain 'ulama. Chapter 9 shows how the monarchy continues to attempt to exercise its control over Islam even within a context in which religious authorities have proliferated, differentiated themselves, and been appropriated by opposition figures who have become credible for many Moroccans. Criticism of Moroccan foreign policy is again expressed, by the participants in the debate I present, in terms of a split between Islam and the West. Echoing this split, the effects of the violent attacks of May 2003 are analyzed in Chapter 10. They demonstrate the tensions haunting the Moroccan monarchy in its relations with Islam and the way in which it has changed its own position within the mechanism for the institutional control of Islam—in the process creating profound contradictions between the reaffirmation of its religious role and the political opening that it has initiated.

CHAPTER 7

The Moroccan Political Regime Confronts Islamic Opposition: From Exclusion to Partial Inclusion

The Transformation of Moroccan Authoritarianism

The transformation of the Moroccan political system between the late twentieth and early twenty-first century did not turn it into a "liberal democracy." The countervailing powers characteristic of most Western democracies do not exist in Morocco. The monarchy remains the dominant and most powerful actor in the political system. It controls the course of political life and can exclude opposition parties at will through the use of force, ad hoc legal decisions, or fixing elections. The forms of Moroccan authoritarianism, however, have been radically changed. The press is relatively freer than in the past and, compared to the rest of the Arab world, elections are more frequent, and candidates contest them vigorously. Even more significant, it has become possible for opposition parties to join the government and thus secure control of the administration, as evidenced, for example, by the Moroccan Socialist Party's time in government from 1997-98 to 2002.

The Moroccan political system defined after independence in 1956 was organized under the principle of a multiparty system broadly held in check by an authoritarian monarchy that limited its scope depending on the particular political context. In 1958, the legal framework regulating the activities of associations established the multiparty principle,[1] confirmed by Article 3 of the 1962 Constitution: "If political parties participate in the organization and representation of citizens, a one-party system cannot exist in Morocco." This principle was established in practice by the second half of the 1950s, in keeping with a strategy initiated by the Palace of taking advantage of pluralism in the political sphere by using major divisions for its own benefit. Hassan II, in turn, used partisan divisions to define himself as an arbiter exercising his power above the parties, to which he granted only limited room for maneuver, leaving them with a certain feeling of frustration.

As John Waterbury has shown, the monarchy strove to regulate the balance of power among political parties so that it would never feel threatened by a single one, in contrast to the Arab republics, which based their authoritarian power on a single party that mobilized and controlled the population (the Algerian FLN, the Destour Party in Tunisia, or Nasser's Rally in Egypt). Political actors in Morocco who submitted to the regime received the monarch's favor in return; material or symbolic advantages and political appointments integrated them into royal territory. And to round out this strategy of fragmentation and patronage, Hassan II also made broad use of state violence, symbolic and physical, particularly against the Marxist extreme left, but also against military figures involved in coups.

Weakened by the two attempted coups d'état, the king revived the question of Western Sahara with the Green March in 1974, and brandished external danger to unite Moroccans around the theme of national unity. He was thereby able to integrate political parties into a culture of compromise and stave off, following the two attempted coups, any further political ambitions the army might harbor. Political representation was defined from above, through a simulated democracy. Partisan political life was carried on within the system of "administration" parties: "The representative character of parties was discussed from above, was negotiated and granted according to *pre-established quotas* which guaranteed the government the unshakeable support of a parliamentary majority by orienting the 'choice' of the voters toward candidates or ad hoc groups, initiated by the administration and supported by the regime."[2] The parliament was thus merely a "recording chamber." The conception of the Moroccan multi-party system was from the outset tied to the logic of authoritarianism. This logic was not defined by competitive and transparent procedures allowing candidates to win votes from the electorate. Rather, it was an instrumental conception intended to neutralize, through competition, parties that might become too powerful, as Istiqlal might have right after independence.

The year 1992 saw the inauguration of a major change with a reform of the Constitution, increasing the prerogatives of parliament in its relations with the government. According to the new constitution, any government appointed by the king was subject to a vote of confidence by parliament, to which the government was therefore answerable. Parliament debated the new prime minister's program and could dismiss his government if the program was rejected. Public availability of assembly debates opened a space for political deliberation that overcame many taboos. A 1996 amendment provided for direct election of members of parliament by Moroccan citizens, but imposed a second chamber elected indirectly.[3] The monarchy negotiated these new rules at length with the political opposition. As a culmination of these discussions, the legislative elections of 1997 brought one of the major figures of the socialist opposition, Abderrahman Youssoufi, into leadership of the Moroccan government. In response, whereas Islamism had previously been excluded from any legal political competition, the Palace then authorized the entry of a segment of Moroccan Islamism into partisan politics in order to counterbalance this entry of the left into the government from the late 1990s on. The Justice and Development Party (PJD) elected a small number of deputies in 1997, a number that gradually increased to 13 percent in 2002 and has been predicted to reach 47 percent in the legislative elections of September 2007.[4] This entry of an Islamist party into the electoral arena represents a major change for all political actors, not only because this is a party of a new kind, but also because it has had significant electoral success.

To understand the change of logic beginning in the 1990s, one must consider several factors. The collapse of the Soviet bloc at the close of the 1980s heralded the decline of leftist parties around the world, and Arab socialist and leftist parties were no exception. The first Gulf War demonstrated the strength of the Islamists through their vigorous reaction to the pro-American alliance. The Algerian crisis following the cancellation of the 1991 elections again revealed the ability of the Islamists of North Africa to mobilize while at the same time demonstrating the risks of destabilization connected with too sudden a political opening that had been prepared without reaching a transition pact with the Islamist opposition. Domestically, after working as a uniting force, the regime's stance on the Western Sahara question and the need to recover the "Sahara provinces" ran out of steam. The image of Morocco in the rest of the world was tarnished by its handling of human rights. In 1995, a devastating World Bank report on the state of the Moroccan economy, prepared at the request of Hassan II, finally persuaded him that it was necessary to include elites in political competition and to offer them the possibility of eventually sharing control of the government in order to reduce the tension arising from the major economic problems that the extensive riots of the 1980s had brought to the fore. The king thus chose the path of political opening with a view to his political survival.

The regime followed a dual strategy in implementing this transformation. On the one hand, it liberalized the political arena within certain limits. On the other, it relied on an already well tested strategy in organizing opposition movements, which it replicated with regard to the Islamist opposition: Yassine's movement remained excluded from legal competition, while the regime granted recognition to the Justice and Development Party by legalizing it as a political party. This distinction made by the monarchy between opposition forces, leading to the division of the structure of contention between "radicals" and "moderates," incited the PJD, the recognized Islamist party, to adopt a moderate stance for fear of being excluded like Justice and Benevolence. At first, this dynamic stabilized the system of political competition around the two major Islamic movements: Justice and Benevolence, the radicals, which relied on threats of popular mobilization outside political society, and the PJD, the moderates, which relied on mobilization for elections.[5] The PJD generally avoided assembling its activists to perform the repertoire of street demonstrations for fear of provoking a de facto alliance with more radical groups and a repression of all of them, which would end up damaging it and excluding it from the system. But in the first decade of the new century, the monarchy's strategy of segmenting Islamism between "radicals" and "moderates" was no longer enough to stabilize the political system.[6]

Indeed, the current electoral success of the PJD contradicts the effects of the monarchy's long-standing practice of this strategy vis-à-vis the opposition. It has allowed the legalized Islamist party to develop its political strategies without considering the relations between the excluded opposition and the monarchy. Moreover, when election results that are favorable for the PJD are announced, it further marginalizes the excluded movement (Abdessalam Yassine's movement), by drawing to the winning party (the PJD) the attention of voters who are ideologically close to Islamism. It has become more difficult for the regime to exclude the PJD—even when it uses popular mobilization outside the legal system of political competition—since it has become a dominant party in the eyes of the public because of its electoral success. Electoral success thus makes the way in which the opposition is structured by the regime's policies of inclusion and exclusion less central in explaining the stability or instability of a process of political liberalization.

Hence, the monarchy's old strategy of segmenting the Islamist opposition has now become more difficult for the regime to use effectively. In addition to the segmentation of the Islamist opposition and its having been thrown off balance by the PJD's success at the polls, a new element has to be taken into account in order to describe the transformation of Moroccan authoritarianism: the transparency of the electoral process and the publication of election results. This has profoundly changed the functioning of the political system, because it has become more difficult for the monarchy to manipulate elections after the fact and thereby to contradict the recognized and public success of a legalized party. Free circulation of news implies that it would become costly for the regime to undermine the political openings it has undertaken so far, because it would risk losing credibility both domestically and abroad.

The regime has at the same time attempted to thwart possible successes of the legalist Islamist opposition by alternating repression and tolerance, an alternation whose rules it is impossible for the opposition to discern. Transparency thus exists in some areas and not in others: it now dominates the electoral realm—which was not the case before the 1990s—by means of the regular holding of legislative and municipal elections whose final results are announced, as well as by the repeated publication of polls by the press and NGOs. But transparency is not the rule when it comes to the practices of the monarchy, which can intervene to exclude some members of the opposition or the press when it pleases and in ways that its targets cannot predict. While the "red lines" established by the monarchy were once well known to the opposition, it is no longer able to read or recognize them. This reversal in the areas of transparency is also characteristic of the transformation of Moroccan authoritarianism.[7]

To understand the conjunction between political opening and the inclusion of an Islamist party in the functioning of this new kind of political regime, it is necessary to consider the recent history of the relations between monarchy and Islamism.

Islamism and the Regulation of Islam by the Monarchy

As in the rest of the Arab and Muslim world, the first manifestations of Moroccan Islamism emerged in the late 1960s. The Islamic youth group Shabiba drew the government's attention at the time because its members were challenging the ideologies of the left, which were still very popular and which they considered "atheistic." They also expressed their aversion to a state that they saw as secularizing and secularized, and that they described as "ungodly." The movement was comparable to the radical organizations that were then beginning to emerge in the Middle East, particularly in Egypt, but it was weaker and more isolated since the religious structure of the monarchy had made the "ungodly" label more difficult to apply to the regime. For this reason, at least in its early stages, Islamism in Morocco was less troubling and less massive than in other countries, particularly those under republican regimes that had not developed a close relationship with Islam.

The Birth of Radical Islamism

A movement with a murky history, the Shabiba was established by 'Abd al-Karim Muti', born in 1936, a former member of the UNFP and an inspector of primary schools in the Ministry of Education. When he became an Islamist, he took as his manifesto *Milestones*, the book published by the Egyptian Sayyid Qutb in 1964. The Shabiba had two wings: a clandestine group established in 1969 (the Shabiba Islamiyya movement) and an association (the Shabiba Islamiyya association), which was authorized in the fall of 1972.[8]

The division of the movement into two parts was the result of a political tactic that was repeated by later incarnations of the Shabiba: on the one hand, showing an acceptable face to the regime through the association, which concentrated on the religious education of its members and presented itself as politically quietist; on the other, recruiting young members, particularly students, into a clandestine movement that emphasized the ideas derived from Qutb. Current society was plunged into *jahiliyya* (the "barbarism" of the pre-Islamic period) and "atheist" Marxist movements were anathemized. The clandestine wing of the Shabiba was organized by professions into a pyramid structure and had a paramilitary wing.

Between 1972 and 1975, the movement was active primarily in the university, especially because the National Union of Moroccan

Students (UNEM), which attracted mostly leftist students, had been banned by the regime in 1973, leaving a considerable political vacuum. The student movement of the left had in fact been radicalized in the late 1960s. The UNEM, which was affiliated with the UNFP, had been infiltrated in 1972 by two clandestine organizations claiming affinity with Marxism-Leninism, the March 23 Movement and Ila'l-amam (Forward), which had been established two years earlier and both of which attacked the wait-and-see political attitude and reformist stance of the traditional parties of the left. The Shabiba emerged as a competitor to these groups, which also benefited the regime.

The development of the small Islamist group on campuses, coinciding as it did with the severe repression of organizations of the extreme left, suggests that there was an objective short-term alliance —the elements of which are still obscure—between the Shabiba and the regime. This period of shared interests came to an end in 1975 with the assassination of the union leader, 'Umar Ibn Jallun, by elements of the Shabiba. Muti', given a life sentence in 1980 in absentia for the murder, subsequently fled Morocco and his movement for foreign exile. He left behind a network of Islamist militants, some of whom at that time gave up the "revolutionary" aspect of the movement in anticipation of joining more organized movements.

The Impact of the Iranian Revolution

At the same time, the evolution of Islamism on the international stage was not without influence in Morocco. The Iranian revolution of 1979 had significant repercussions on young Moroccan Islamists, for whom the overthrow of a powerful monarchy by groups representing Islam became conceivable. Sheikh Abdessalam Yassine expressed in his writings the influence on him of Khomeini and his notion of *Vileyet-i-faqih* (which ascribes the role of head of state to a specialist in religious law).[9] His magazine, *Al-jama'a*, transmitted this influence and showed Yassine's admiration for the principles of the Iranian revolution. That same year, Hassan II described the mistake that the Iranian ruler had made. He considered that the shah had not been capable of using Islam, although the Iranian mullahs, organized in a hierarchical structure, could have been mobilized and exploited: "The shah wanted to rule by the sword but without, and even against, the clergy. ... If the shah had agreed not to play exclusively the card of secularism, the imams, almost in their entirety, would have followed him."[10] On August 5, 1980, the Minister of Religious Affairs presented a letter to the king from the president of the Council of 'Ulama, which, after a long silence, confirmed Hassan II's critique of the Iranian revolution.[11] Hassan II thus channeled domestically any political expression of Islam by his 'ulama, while at the same time presenting himself both at home and abroad as the strongest defender of the *umma*, who had become president of the Al-Quds Committee in 1979, and by multiplying interventions in support of the Palestinian cause.

Hassan II Mobilizes the 'Ulama

But Hassan II was fully aware that domestically these gestures were no longer enough to consolidate his power, which had been shaken by the Islamist challenge. The very structure of his relations with the religious authorities had to be overhauled. The 'ulama were considered the instruments of this recovery of control, which was intended to reach even those Moroccans who had emigrated.

Hence, at the very beginning of 1980, the monarchy redefined its way of dealing with Islam and changed its original strategy of fragmenting the religious sphere. In fact, it needed to control these scattered fragments that it had itself preserved and reshaped between the coming of independence and the late 1970s and bring them together under the control of a homogeneous and more centralized structure. Domestic and foreign events, signs of the dilution of the king's religious territory, made it clear to him that management and control of the religious sphere were gradually slipping from his grasp.

In a speech to the 'ulama in his palace in Marrakesh on February 1, 1980, Hassan II made the "observation" that they were absent from social life, an absence that he had himself deliberately organized starting in the 1960s. He wanted to revitalize the doctrinal role of the 'ulama meeting in council against "subversive movements":

> I do not know, and I do not want to know, noble 'ulama, to whom or to what . . . should be attributed your absence from everyday Moroccan life. I can even say that you have become strangers. . . . Gentlemen, together we are paying . . . the price for this phenomenon, because in universities and secondary schools, when it comes to the teaching of Islam, all that is discussed are the causes of interrupting ablutions and of the invalidity of prayer, and there is scarcely any analysis of the truly socialist economic and social system of Islam. University and school students are no longer learning that religion is primarily a matter of relations among men.[12]

In the king's view, the 'ulama were not to be the righters of wrongs or the moralizers—he was referring to the propositions they published after every meeting of the congress of the League in the areas of the Arabization of education, the Islamization of law and society, and the moralization of public behavior.[13]

> The role of the 'alim cannot be limited to denouncing evil. One cannot show him a film poster showing, for example, a woman in a bathing suit and say: that is evil. By doing that one would assimilate his role to that of a neighborhood *muqaddam* [agent of the Ministry of Interior] in charge of posters. Your interventions should not be those of 'ulama confronting the government, because the fact is that *the government and the 'ulama are one and the same family*.[14] Religion and this world are intertwined. The day when a Muslim state separates religion and world (*din wa dunya*), that day—if it ever comes—would justify celebrating that state's funeral in advance.[15]

The king was thereby directly rebuking the 'ulama and confirming that they were merely an extension of his own territory, that their separation from the royal domain meant a separation between religion and politics, and that they could therefore not perform the function of admonishing the representatives of political authority. Speaking to them in their own language—that of the union of *din* (religion) and the *dunya* (world)—Hassan II criticized the men of religion, forcing them to abandon their posture of submissive distance and to clearly adopt the objectives of the regime, particularly in its fight against anti-monarchical Islamism. Establishing a convergence between the idea of state control over Islam (the secular world of state power controlling religion) and that of Islam defining political life (religion as the foundation of all secular life), that is, respectively, the language of monarchical authoritarianism and the language of Islamism, he defined the bases of a paradoxical and difficult-to-sustain partnership between the king and the 'ulama. The purpose of this unequal alliance was in fact both to revitalize the language of Islam in defining public life and to impose monarchical control over the authors of those definitions. The 'ulama were thus encouraged to intervene in public life, but only according to the terms authorized by the monarchy.

From the platform of the eighth congress of the League of 'Ulama in Nador in June 1981, Ahmad Ibn Suda, an adviser to the king, confirmed the law that had restored the old councils of 'ulama. The king inserted them into a hierarchy over which he presided in a Supreme Council of 'Ulama organized both nationally and regionally, the better to control, supervise, and use the men of religion and the mosques.16 These councils were charged with assisting the governors in controlling all forms of religious expression.17 The Rabat-Salé council was offered to Sheikh Makki Nasiri, who came from a line of sharifs in Dra'. An unconditional supporter of the monarchy and a strong adversary of Istiqlal, he had been Minister of Religious Affairs between November 1972 and April 1974. In the last years of his life he helped the monarchy in its enterprise of restructuring Islam. When 'Abd Allah Kannun died in October 1989, Makki Nasiri succeeded him as secretary-general of the League of 'Ulama. At his death, he was one of the few 'ulama to receive public homage from

Hassan II, an event that was broadcast on television. The monarchy co-opted religious authorities, supervised public displays of religion, and restructured the mechanism for control of the religious phenomenon.

In addition, the Ministry of the Interior also kept a careful watch on the mosques, and it recruited from graduates of the shari'a faculties some of the students for the Kenitra training school for Interior Ministry officials. Once graduating, their task would be to regulate religious affairs in their provinces.[18] In the 1980s, there were about sixty qadis who had followed this course of training. Then, they had to establish relations with the new councils, which had been restored after 1980.[19] The preachers bowed to the directives of the Ministry of Religious Affairs on the content of Friday sermons. "We are obliged to call for divine blessing of the king. We don't like it, but we live with it.... The reality of relations between religion and the state has a bitter taste. While Morocco is in a much better position than many Muslim countries, is that enough?" asserted a Qarawiyyin graduate, member of a regional council of 'ulama, university teacher, director of an Islamic association dedicated to literacy in Casablanca, and preacher certified by the Ministry of Religious Affairs.[20] The 'ulama's attitude was then a patient wait-and-see policy. Supervision of mosques was received badly: "The regime has no respect for the religious spaces that belong to it. The colonizer had more respect for religion than the king. It is the *muqaddam* who oversees the mosque. He is the lowest-ranking man in the Ministry of the Interior!" indignantly remarked an Islamist jurist.[21]

Demands for Recognition by Islamism

This belated and hasty attempt by the monarchy to reassemble the fragments of the religious sphere in the royal territory developed in parallel with, and as though in imitation of, the strategy initiated by Sheikh Yassine in the 1980s of unifying Moroccan Islamism—most notably including former members of the Shabiba—around his person. Some joined him, but others did not necessarily accept the mystical aspect of Justice and Benevolence. In the face of the monarchy's reassertion of control, the two major currents of Moroccan Islamism remained distinct: on the one hand, Yassine's movement, based on a central figure and on a radical rejection of the legitimacy of the monarchy; and on the other, a loose network of members of a younger generation prepared to make concessions to participate in political life and organized at first following the model of an association.[22] This network of associations formed the basis of a movement that became central in the Moroccan political arena beginning in the late 1990s. Transformed into a political party, the PJD, this movement provided a model that was very different from the mystical and revolutionary model of Yassine.

Among these activists was Abdellilah Ben Kirane, a former member of the Shabiba who had joined in 1976, one year after the assassination of Ibn Jallun. Whereas 'Abd al-Karim Muti' launched a radical journal titled *Al-mujahid* (The Combatant) from abroad in March 1981, in the 1980s Ben Kirane began publicly denouncing the underground action and the ideology of the Shabiba's founder. In 1983, he established the Association of the Islamic Group (*jam'iyyat al-jam'a al-islamiyya*) with a legalist perspective. The association renounced any challenge to the Islamic nature of the Moroccan state, as Ben Kirane explained to me: "I realized very early on that what people were thinking of doing was practically impossible. We had no chance if we stayed outside society. . . . We had to support and reform from within. We had understood that we were lucky enough to have an Islamic state."[23] These Islamist militants were hungry for power and therefore, in order to normalize their relations with the monarchy, sought to make the Moroccan elite, who were deeply shaken by the assassination of Ibn Jallun in 1975, forget the very sectarian Shabiba. But they did not succeed in their enterprise until the late 1990s.

In the 1980s, the regime harshly repressed Islamist movements and the left, without bothering with human rights. The Casablanca riots in 1981, followed in 1984 by those in Nador and Marrakesh, which resulted from austerity policies, were interpreted by the regime as the demonstration of an Islamist "danger" and led to a policy of repressing Islamist associations, including those that, like *Jama'at al-tabligh* (Faith and Practice), adhered to a genuine political quietism.[24] During this period, Ben Kirane and his associates on several occasions asked the authorities to legalize their association. Despite letters to the Ministry of the Interior and the royal cabinet attempting to persuade the authorities of the sincerity of the former members of the Shabiba, these requests met with no response in the 1980s.

The Turning Point of the First Gulf War

As the decade of the 1990s opened, the repressive stance no longer seemed effective for the monarchy, which was beginning to show signs of vulnerability. Hassan II then became the principal agent in an enterprise of political opening that mobilized participants in the realm of partisan politics, who engaged in long negotiations over the terms of a new political pact redefining the relations between the legislature and the executive. The economic context was unfavorable, and the regime accepted the risk of disengaging the state in social and economic matters, liberalizing the economy, and imposing austerity. In the late 1980s, the society was troubled by general and sectorial strikes, and Islamist challenges were growing in the university.

Morocco's sending troops to Saudi Arabia during the First Gulf War in 1991-1992 provoked demonstrations against the American coalition defending Kuwait and stirred up street protests in favor of Saddam Hussein against the Gulf monarchies that were traditional allies of the Moroccan monarchy.[25] The war also demonstrated to the king that segments of the society—in particular young unemployed graduates—could be easily mobilized by the Islamists using the argument of an insurmountable opposition between the Islamic *umma* and the West. Some Islamists gradually integrated this division into their representation of Moroccan society, which they described as deeply divided between two antagonistic blocs. Some of the 'ulama had laid the groundwork for the emergence of these ideas, in conjunction with Islamist associations. It is not surprising then that the first dissident voices coming from the Moroccan 'ulama focused on questions of international politics.

In 1991, some 'ulama did in fact join in opposition to the Gulf War. They were thus becoming involved on this occasion in major political issues, in marked opposition to the monarchy. One group of clerics, for example, publicly stated its opposition to the fatwas of Ibn Baz in Saudi Arabia and Sheikh Gad al-Haqq of al-Azhar, which authorized armed intervention by the Western alliance on the Arabian Peninsula. Among the eleven signatories were the names of Driss al-Kattani, 'Abd Allah Muhammad Ibn Siddiq, 'Abd al-'Aziz Ibn Siddiq, the great scholar Muhammad al-Mannuni, and Ahmad Raysuni. They denounced any participation by Morocco in the American coalition.[26] The Minister of Religious Affairs, 'Abd al-Kabir 'Alawi al-Mdaghri, reacted by having some 'ulama sign a "counter-fatwa," which was circulated from hand to hand and signed by everyone to whom it was presented, with the exception of the *fqih* Muhammad al-Mannuni, who loftily dismissed it. This direct pressure from the Makhzen did not prevent the association of Dar al-Hadith graduates from denouncing the alliance of "crusaders and Zionists," in the same vein as the fatwa issued by the dissenting 'ulama.[27]

Some 'ulama were thus beginning to show their opposition in a public forum, in alliance with preachers and Islamists, making up a religious opposition that was still latent but that might challenge, if only temporarily, the foreign policy of the Makhzen. While the debate might seem to have concerned only international questions, it in fact had deep domestic repercussions. On the one hand, it indicated that the debates beginning to emerge in the Gulf on the legitimacy of the ruling families might also surface in Morocco, a dangerous implication for the 'Alawite monarchy. On the other hand, by reiterating the division between Islam and the West, it might serve to describe a Moroccan society split between Muslims and unbelievers.

Official Islam Attempts to Control and Co-opt Islamism

Other international events also influenced the Moroccan political scene. In January 1992, the sudden interruption by the army leadership of the electoral process in Algeria—which was about to produce a victory for the Islamic Salvation Front (FIS)—provoked the outbreak of a bloody civil war between the Islamists and the military; in Morocco, both a large number of Islamists and the inner circles of the regime feared that it would spread across the border. More generally, the end of the cold war and the collapse of the Soviet bloc foreshadowed the weakening of left-wing parties and opened new political opportunities for Islamists, in the West as well as in their own country. Moreover, beginning in the late 1980s, Justice and Benevolence demonstrated its ability to mobilize on university campuses, where Islamists seized control of the UNEM (National Union of Moroccan Students). Islam thus entered into politics, not by means of a partisan vehicle but in a public sphere that these new religious actors were themselves creating and informing, giving it a new visibility, sometimes outside the religious and political spaces controlled by Hassan II, sometimes fully fitting within them. The absence of a sharp boundary between official Islam and some manifestations of Islamism and the Ministry of Religious Affairs' dual commitment to control and co-opt Islamism were clearly illustrated by the policies of this Ministry in the 1980s and 1990s. This duality showed a relationship between Islamism and the Islam of official institutions and suggested a certain level of continuity between them.

During this period, the Ministry of Religious Affairs, headed by 'Abd al-Kabir 'Alawi al-Mdaghri from February 1984 to December 2002, used the supervisory structures set up in 1980-81 in the councils of 'ulama in order to co-opt them along with the preachers. He took office during the second phase of the reassertion of control over the religious sphere; a 1984 decree provided for controlling of mosques by closing them outside of prayer times and for regulating their construction. Preachers and imams were appointed by the ministry, "after advice from the governor of the prefecture or the province and consultation with the regional council of 'ulama concerned."[28] A veritable policy of state control of Islam, these new directives could never really be applied. So-called free preachers were already flourishing. To revitalize official Islam outside the networks constructed by departments of Islamic studies and the faculties of the Qarawiyyin established between 1963 and 1979, the policy of the ministry looked back to the original center of religious teaching; the minister established "scholarly chairs" in mosques, first in 1984 in the mosque of the Qarawiyyin in Fez and then gradually in other mosques controlled by the Ministry of Religious Affairs. In addition, advanced religious studies were reinstituted in the mosque of the Qarawiyyin in 1988 for the first time since they had been abolished following independence.[29] Under the umbrella of the Ministry of Religious Affairs, it admitted students—200 when I visited in 1998—from a rural background who knew the text of the Qur'an by heart, and it aimed at bringing religious education closer to the sacred space of the mosque, while even further fragmenting the networks of religious training.

Born in 1942 and a graduate of Dar al-Hadith, al-Mdaghri was a product of the religious policies of the monarchy in the 1960s. He remained clearly submissive to the king, on whom he depended directly, as demonstrated by his Hassanian lesson of 1990, in which he defined the sultan as the "shadow of Allah on earth," a description that created a sensation and provoked an outraged reaction from many political figures on both left and right.[30] The concept was strongly criticized by an *'alim* of Tangiers, Sheikh 'Abd al-'Aziz Ibn Siddiq, who had already had a brush with the security services of the Interior Ministry in 1979 over his statements in favor of the Iranian revolution.[31]

At the same time, with great dynamism and with a good deal of political maneuvering, al-Mdaghri gave impetus to the co-optation of Islamists—for which he was to be severely criticized after the 2003 Casablanca bombings. On February 20, 1990, he received at the Ministry of Religious Affairs the leaders of the Association of the Islamic Group of Ben Kirane, along with members of the councils of 'ulama. The exchanges between the minister and Ben Kirane were reported by the latter, who, in front of the invited 'ulama, recognized the status of commander of the faithful and announced his intention of working hand in hand with the official 'ulama: "We are in the country of the commander of the faithful, and its Constitution affirms that the official religion of the state is Islam. And here, too, the Islamic caliphate is passed down from father to son, and it is not suitable that it be said of us that we are opposed to the 'ulama and to those who call on Islam."[32] Sheikh Ma al-'Aynayn, chairman of the council of 'ulama of La'yun, addressed Ben Kirane: "[If] you really match your appearance, which would make us rejoice . . . you can collaborate with the 'ulama. But if the opposite is true, then the 'ulama will be the first to fight you."[33]

Beginning in 1989, the Ministry of Religious Affairs organized summer universities of the "Islamic awakening," which brought together well known figures in Moroccan and foreign Islamism. In the summer of 1991, under the patronage of the king, the minister invited the participants in these meetings to a reception at the Palace of Skhirat. A diverse group of religious, intellectual, and political figures were among the invitees: Sheikh Makki Nasiri and Abdellilah Ben Kirane in person, but also the South African Sheikh Ahmad Didat; the Syrian Muhammad Sa'id Ramadan al-Buti; the Egyptian intellectual Tariq al-Bishri; Rashid Ghannushi, one of the leaders of Tunisian Islamism; and Mahfuz Nahnah, the Algerian representative of the Muslim Brotherhood.

By sponsoring these dialogues, which had gained official status through the Ministry of Religious Affairs, the monarchy was seeking to neutralize the effects of the emergence of this new space of opposition formed by interpretations of Islam expressed by Islamists outside its control but also by certain 'ulama on the fringes of its own territory. Dismissed from office by Muhammad VI in December 2002, al-Mdaghri explained his role in the fall of 2004. He admitted having "harmonized points of view" between the PJD and the Palace and having attempted a first step toward conciliation—which failed—with Justice and Benevolence: "Abdessalam Yassine was under house arrest. The king gave me a green light. A commission was set up for the purpose, we took Yassine with us, and we went to the prison of Salé. . . . We reached some concrete results . . . *al-'Adl* was on the point of becoming a political party and participating in the 1992 elections."

More generally, he explained, "I have always been convinced that the Islamist movement in Morocco deserves to be treated like all other political and ideological tendencies, with the same tools that democracy provides us . . . violence against the Islamists will lead nowhere. Worse, it might precipitate their recourse to underground work and the undermining of security. . . . I have therefore always supported and contributed to dialogue with them."[34] The ideological and religious differences between Yassine and the PJD hardly mattered; in the view of the former Minister of Religious Affairs, they had to be brought together and co-opted under the slogan "Islamic rebirth," whose precise foundations he did not define, but whose ultimate purpose was to support the principle of the commander of the faithful.

But this policy of opportunistic co-optation, or domestication through inclusion of independent religious authorities in the patronage networks, was no longer enough to enable the monarchy to control the religious sphere. Hence, rather than allowing the Islamists to enter political debate outside supervision by the monarchy, which had become unable to co-opt them or exclude them through constant adjustment of its relations with various religious networks, Hassan II chose to insert them into the partisan realm that he hoped to be able to continue to control. He therefore radically modified his strategy for Islamism by transforming the functioning of the political regime. He announced the revision of the Constitution of 1992, without, however, directly mentioning the Islamists, who were still not organized into authorized partisan entities. In his speech from the throne on March 3, 1992, he declared:

> We have always thought that, whatever their merits, institutions could not remain unchangeable and untouchable. . . . Our domestic elections [must] be conducted with the most complete transparency and without any ambiguity. . . . Partisan battles, legitimate in every democratic system, sometimes have the effect of casting shadows over social life. [We] wish precisely to remove those areas of darkness and have a photograph of [our] people as close as possible to reality. Only free, fair, and credible elections can provide [us] with that photograph.[35]

The Integration of Legitimist Islamism into the Electoral Arena

The revision of the Constitution provided an opportunity to hold more transparent elections, and following the November 1997 elections, in which some Islamists participated without a partisan apparatus—a first test—the socialists of the USFP (Socialist Union of Popular Forces) joined the government in 1998, thereby accepting the principle of participating in power. This royal strategy of accepting the participation of the USFP, which had long been in opposition, brought about a split in Islamist circles between those who agreed to be drawn into the territory of the monarchy by integration into the sphere of partisan politics and those who, like Sheikh Yassine, did not. This rearrangement formed a continuum of ideological positions in which political Islam was now spread out from the monarchical center to the periphery. In this spectrum of positions, the center of gravity was moving away from monarchical Islam. Indeed, the PJD's legalization by the monarchy brought Islam and the debates around its definitions into the very sphere of the newly opened legal and partisan competition, outside of the religious territory of the monarchy.

The PJD, an Islamist Mosaic

The history of the Justice and Development Party unfolded differently from that of Sheikh Yassine's group. The PJD was established in 1998, coming out of the dissolution and reconstitution of old groups, rather complex splits and rearrangements which were the consequence of the methods of political regulation authorized by the monarchy. Yassine's group was organized around a person, the spiritual guide, and never (at least explicitly) accepted state regulation. The conflicts that might arise in the Justice and Benevolence movement were often masked from outside observers (the only clearly visible conflict was the external one of its direct opposition to the regime). For its part, the PJD arose from the alliance of diverse individuals who had followed various religious and political career paths and now came together in a "mosaic" structure; internal conflicts were in the open and competition among members was an accepted part of its procedures.

Instead of a single, central figure, the party contained strong and ambitious personalities who were eager for social and political mobility—often a cause of internal conflict that threatened the unity of a party subject to numerous centrifugal forces. Yassine's group demonstrated a religious and political zeal tied to the expression of social and religious anxiety and took a stance outside the political system controlled by the monarchy. The men of the PJD, on the other hand, exhibited a more enthusiastic and optimistic style and participated untroubled in all areas of the political system, although they did not hesitate to criticize some of its aspects.

But the process of integrating these "legitimist" Islamists into the legal political sphere was different from what had occurred immediately following independence to domesticate political parties. Now armed with a representative status arising from a relatively transparent electoral process, the Islamists of the PJD, as we shall see, sometimes attempted to impose some of their conditions. Young men of the generation that had been educated in Arabized schools and universities, the PJD leaders in their forties were not frightened by the culture of political compromise and threw themselves wholeheartedly into the adventure of party politics and elections. This new political generation will repay more careful scrutiny.

The "Palace Islamist," Abdellilah Ben Kirane

Born in 1954 in a family with Istiqlal connections, Abdellilah Ben Kirane, who wears an elegantly trimmed beard and speaks both French and Arabic with great ease, represents a generation that has moved from radical Islamism to participation in the existing political system. Trained as an engineer, he had been a member of *Shabiba islamiyya* and in the early 1980s founded the Association of the Islamic Group, which officially became Reform and Renewal (*Islah wa tajdid*) in February 1992.[36] At that time, Ben Kirane's association abandoned the term "Islamic": questioning the Islamic nature of the society and the regime was no longer on the agenda. In that year of 1992, the Algerian civil war terrified the regime and the Moroccan elites, including the younger generation of Islamists. It therefore decided to adopt the tactic of "entryism" into political institutions, while maintaining a low profile to avoid producing counterparts to the Algerian "eradicators" within the regime.

In the 1990s, Ben Kirane's association publicly minimized its role, making certain not to frighten Moroccans and not to create the image of a group that wanted to monopolize Islam. This "legitimist" branch of Islamism thereby recognized that it was not the possessor of religious truth and that it could not act like a clerical group.[37] Ben Kirane and his associates entered into political action in 1992 by asking the regime for authorization to establish a political party called the Party of National Renewal (*hizb al-tajdid al-watani*), again avoiding religious vocabulary and making a distinction between the work of preaching (*da'wa*) and political activity.[38] This caution turned out to be futile, however, because the regime denied the authorization. The men of Reform and Renewal patiently looked elsewhere for a way to have themselves recognized politically. If they were not authorized to define their autonomous political space, they would find a way of intervening in already existing partisan structures.

Ideologically, the organization closest to the group by virtue of its references to Islam and its conservatism was the old Istiqlal party. The leaders of Reform and Renewal approached its secretary general, who agreed to allow them to join the party provided they made no claim to become part of its leadership. In this way, they were relegated to a marginal role. However, the Islamist leaders were certain that they could do better, because they offered to the party that would accept them the hundreds of members of Islamist associations that were operating in their wake. Ben Kirane and his friends then turned to another party, and to an older figure than the current leaders of Istiqlal: Dr. 'Abd al-Karim Khatib, "who had never stopped speaking of Islam," according to Ben Kirane.[39] Dr. Khatib, who began his political career in Istiqlal, had established the Popular Movement in 1957. When it excluded him in 1967, he created, along with Ben 'Abd

Allah Ugati, his own party, the Popular Democratic and Constitutional Movement (MPDC), which then remained inactive during the long period of repression following the coups d'état of 1971 and 1972. 'Abd al-Karim Khatib was an enigmatic and long-standing presence in Moroccan political life. He was the first Moroccan surgeon trained in France and had been Muhammad V's official doctor. He was connected to the Palace by family ties, but his political activity had been greatly reduced since the 1970s.

For the octogenarian Khatib, having the Islamists join his party provided an opportunity to play a new political role by operating as a liaison between the Islamists and the Palace, which probably enabled him to establish closer relations with the king. Khatib had in fact needed a green light from the king before he could accept the request of the Islamists gathered around Ben Kirane, who had himself aggregated various Islamist associations that he attached to the MPDC.[40] The merger of the Islamists with the MPDC was accomplished in the course of the year 1996, in two steps.

First, Ben Kirane brought together a network of Islamist associations. In 1996, three Islamist associations merged: the Islamic Association of Ksar Kabir (created in 1976 by Ahmad Raysuni), the *al-Shuruq* Association of Rabat (which had come out of a split in the Shabiba in 1986), and the *Al-da'wa* Islamic Association of Fez (created in 1976 by an *'alim* of the Qarawiyyin, 'Abd al-Salam Harras).[41] The group adopted the name League of the Islamic Future (*Rabitat al-mustaqbal al-islami*) under the leadership of Ahmad Raysuni. This League joined the Reform and Renewal Association, which then became the Movement of Unity and Reform (*Harakat al-tawhid wa-l islah*), which then grouped together more than two hundred Islamist associations. The new name (MUR) signified the unification of one strand of Moroccan Islamism but also introduced a more explicitly religious term, *tawhid*, which directly referred to the unity of the divine in Islam.

Then, at the special congress of the MPDC in 1996, Ben Kirane was elected assistant secretary general of the party, second in command after 'Abd al-Karim Khatib. The Islamist groups that agreed to participate in the party system were thus gathered around an old party, the MPDC, and a network of associations attached to it to provide its members with great structural flexibility.

The MPDC and its leader thus domesticated on behalf of the monarchy the turbulent and ambitious Islamists. The opportunity the Islamists were granted to participate in legal political competition was in fact accompanied by stringent conditions, limiting the room for maneuver of the two generations that had formed the coalition. Recognition of the concept of commander of the faithful, renunciation of violence, recognition of the Maliki religious school, and the legitimacy of Moroccan territorial integrity—all were conditions accepted by the participants in an informal agreement that defined a pact between the monarchy and the Islamists of the MPDC.

PJD and MUR, a Twofold Movement

The coming together of this heterogeneous group, which mixed conservative 'ulama with new graduates in religion, former members of the Shabiba, and heads of charitable associations, made it possible to broaden the formerly very narrow base of Khatib's old party and to give it powerful tools for the political mobilization of future Islamist militants and potential voters. At its fourth congress in 1998, the MPDC became the Party "of Justice and Development," again avoiding the word "Islam" in the political group's title. Sa'd al-Din 'Uthmani, another conciliatory figure, succeeded Ben Kirane as assistant secretary general in 1998, and replaced 'Abd al-Karim Khatib as head of the party in April 2004.

In 1996, the unification of associations that gave birth to the MUR was given little media attention, and the press was primarily interested in the entry of Islamists into the MPDC. The MUR was, however, the keystone of the construction fostering the political integration of the Islamists and the basis for recruiting party members, while remaining separate from the party itself.

In 2003, most leaders of the PJD also belonged to the MUR: out of seventeen members of the general secretariat, only six were former members of the MPDC. The MUR had thus infiltrated the PJD and was recruiting its future militants in secondary schools, notably through associations of teachers of traditional learning, mosques, and charitable associations. The MUR might also serve as a fallback base: if the monarchy's slogan had always been "divide and rule," the slogan of the two-headed organization MUR/PJD might be "divide oneself to survive." This political duo enabled the same individuals to belong to two organizations with different functions. The PJD, which had about four thousand members, played a role in support of the Makhzen, whereas the MUR demonstrated a centrifugal tendency with reference to the regime and served as an ideological sounding board for the PJD by circulating its ideas through preaching, the media, and the activity of associations.

This duo established two "places," one of which could serve as a fallback position, but also made it possible to cast their nets wide for political recruitment and mobilization. The leaders could be present on the stage of the establishment while remaining close to their base, and could thus speak in different registers, which led a number of their critics to accuse them of using a "dual language." This diversity of attachments and individual career paths also pointed to future splits in the party, which, despite appearances, maintained a polyphonic identity that could be useful for its survival, but that also might turn out to be immobilizing.

The Islamists' Apprenticeship in Parliamentary Life

The 1997 municipal election provided the future PJD with its first test, after the 1996 takeover, in its apprenticeship in party politics. Worried about being outflanked on his right, however, 'Abd al-Karim Khatib, the leader of the MPDC, decided to boycott the election without securing the agreement of the members of the MUR.[42] As a result, the leaders of the MUR lost access to the channel of the MPDC, which they had hoped to use to participate in the election. This did not keep them from taking part in the electoral process under a non-party label, presenting nearly two thousand Islamist candidates of the MUR and winning one hundred seats as municipal councilors and three mayoralties.[43]

1997: The Entry into Parliament

In the legislative election that followed, on November 14, 1997, the MPDC campaigned on the theme: "For a complete renaissance: authenticity (*asala*), justice, development." To respect the principle of a political endeavor "in stages," it presented one hundred forty candidates, although it could have contested three hundred twenty-five seats.[44] At the 1998 Congress, 'Abd al-Karim Khatib reconsidered this decision to participate and explained it to the PJD militants. To do so, he turned back to the long period of abstention that the MPDC had observed since the 1970s: "Despite our faith in political participation, this party refused to participate in elections for a long time, because of significant falsification of the will of the people. . . . By deciding to boycott [the election] we wanted to express our refusal to participate in this political scourge."[45]

In Khatib's view, participation in the election in the fall of 1997 was not the result of a false calculation:

> The decision to participate was made because there had been commitments to turn over a new political leaf. We therefore decided to respond positively to these invitations, with not too many illusions, and to play our role in setting in motion the wheel of change by making contact with citizens and presenting our program.[46]

The legislative election of the fall of 1997 thus marked the entry of the Islamists into the parliamentary sphere when they won nine seats, five in Casablanca, one in Tangiers, one in Tetouan, one in the countryside near Fez, and one in Agadir.[47] They had won one third the number of votes of the USFP, established by these elections as the largest party in Morocco. The secretary of the USFP, Abderrahman Youssoufi, was appointed prime minister after extended bargaining in March 1998. A former nationalist militant who had become one of the principal figures in opposition to the regime, he had been sentenced to death and then pardoned and returned from exile in 1980. As the USFP was ending its long history of opposition to the regime, a new type of party was entering the parliament and normalizing, slowly but surely, the existence of Islamism in the sphere of debate and political competition legalized by the state. The by-elections of April 1999 secured a new parliamentary seat for Abdellilah Ben Kirane in the district of Salé. On August 31, 2000, new by-elections won it two more seats, and the PJD ended the fifth Moroccan legislature with fourteen deputies.

What exactly did this Islamist parliamentary membership represent? Although the real power of the parliament in relation to the government was in practice marginal, as it was for the government in relation to the Palace, the existence of Islamist deputies represented an important turning point in parliamentary life. The parliament was long known as a simple "recording chamber," but it started to play a role as a public forum for deliberation. At first, the PJD expressed itself on the principle of "critical support" for the government: it entered into the sphere of the majority, while criticizing the government on certain points, notably on questions of the family code (the *Mudawwana*) and of micro-credit. This ambiguous support provided the PJD deputies with a comfortable solution that allowed them to situate themselves as non-"disruptive" elements while reserving the right to speak when religious questions were at issue. But criticism of the socialist government was already being voiced, most notably because of the lack of religious references in government declarations and because of its neglect of traditional and official religious institutions in its campaign against illiteracy and in its battle against corruption.[48]

The death of Hassan II on July 23, 1999, did not put into question the presence of the PJD in parliament or its participation in political life. For the first Ramadan of King Muhammad VI, the head of the MUR, Ahmad Raysuni, was invited to deliver a lesson whose theme was the purposes of the prophetic mission. There was nothing particularly striking in the content of the lesson, if not for the identity of its author, who fit very well into the mold of the Hassanian lesson. This symbolic integration into royal territory, widely noted by political commentators, encouraged the legalist Islamists to participate fully in political debate in parliament and to carefully prepare for the legislative elections of 2002.

From October 2000 on, the PJD moved more explicitly into the anti-government camp, declaring that it had joined the "loyal opposition." This change in terminology was connected to a more vigorous critique of the measures of the Youssoufi government that began in the summer of 2000.[49] There was, however, no unity in the ranks of the PJD about this decision, and Ben Kirane came out against this move into the opposition.[50] "We made false steps, politically. After moving into the opposition, we found ourselves isolated. Then [there was the mistake] of not having agreed to participate in the government after 2002. I was for participating. For the others, participating meant declining in popularity. You can't stay in the opposition all your life!"[51] The PJD also came to recognize the difficulties hampering its expression in parliament, which weakened the effectiveness of its position of support for the government: the bicameral system, the government's use of article 51 of the Constitution,[52] the government's failure to respond to questions from the PJD, the absenteeism of deputies, and also the hardening and the opposition of other parties in general in the face of the assertion of the religious question.[53] The PJD's critique of the USFP inaugurated a recurrent conflict between the two organizations, which gradually grew more inflamed. The media gave wide coverage to this ever clearer split on the religious question between the legalist Islamists and the left-wing government.

The Legislative Election of September 27, 2002: The Breakthrough of the PJD

The legislative election of September 27, 2002, demonstrated major advances in the transparency of electoral procedures.[54] They were conducted without the presence of the former Minister of the Interior, Driss Basri, who had been dismissed by the young king.

The PJD won forty-two of the three hundred twenty-five seats.

Once again, the party had not offered candidates in all districts (fifty-seven out of ninety-one), but it won some from both the USFP and Istiqlal. In particular, it made a real show of force in a city as important as Casablanca, where it was able to elect eleven deputies. And it also showed its ability to mobilize the electorate in districts in the city of Rabat—Rabat-Océan and Rabat-Chellah. The PJD, which recruited a large number of its voters in major urban centers, as well as among the young and the educated, thus found itself at the same level of votes as the three major parties, which had an approximately equal number of seats (USFP, Istiqlal, and National Assembly of Independents). The proportional voting had favored this fragmentation, which the regime had intended in order not to have to confront a single dominant party.

While the elections were organized in a nearly transparent manner, however, there was a certain amount of continuity with the undemocratic practices of the regime of Hassan II. Following the elections, unofficial sources leaked word of negotiations between the palace and 'Abd al-Karim Khatib, who was said to have urged the PJD to accept a score of forty-two seats, fifteen fewer than it had actually won. If the parliament had accurately reflected the vote, the PJD would have been the largest party, and the government could theoretically have been headed by an Islamist prime minister. These secret negotiations obviously introduced a distortion into the process of selecting representatives of the nation and revealed the inception of a negotiating mechanism, which was apparently peaceful, controlled, and accepted, between the monarchy and the first legalist Islamist party.

Between the elections of 1997 and 2002, then, unlike the other parties, the PJD lost no seats. Moreover, it retained an image of probity, which derived not only from its moralizing language but also from the fact that the party was still young. The other parties were losing momentum: the USFP won the most votes, but its members were generally disappointed by the massive defection of members from its youth organization, the resignation from the party of a group of intellectuals (called "Loyalty to Democracy"), and a split in its union branch. The Youssoufi government had accomplished little. The

USFP had finally been domesticated by the monarchy and had not had the legal and constitutional tools that would have enabled it to implement its program. 'Uthmani attributed this failure to the left's inability to talk about religion: "We were told: no religion to identify parties. We answered: but use it!"[55] Although there were 'ulama allied with the left and although the left rarely thought of itself as secular, the various elements of the Moroccan left did not really develop the religious theme in close connection with its popular base but rather made an abstract analysis of it, aimed chiefly at making Islam compatible with socialism.[56]

Following the announcement of the results of the 2002 election, the PJD considered participating in the new government. It could make an alliance with Istiqlal and accept a government headed by a prime minister from Istiqlal, as Ben Kirane thought at the time. But this coalition turned out to be difficult for Khatib. A former member of the Popular Movement who had adopted a position in opposition to Istiqlal, he had trouble accepting a coalition with his old rival.[57] As for relations with the USFP, we have already seen the level of conflict that had been realized in the course of the years 1998 to 2002, and there was no question of the PJD participating in a government alongside socialist ministers.[58] Istiqlal called for a prime minister from its party, arguing that it had come in only slightly behind the USFP, and that a coalition was possible between the two major victorious parties, the National Assembly of Independents (RNI) and the PJD.[59]

On October 8, 2002, Istiqlal and the PJD published a joint communiqué announcing their coalition. Even before knowing the makeup of the government, some leaders of the Islamist party agreed to support the government if it included in its program "a few points," such as the "introduction of no-interest loans in banks."[60] Some party leaders thus thought they had won the first round in the battle for Islamization by using the strategy of entryism. After the elections, Muhammad VI received representatives of the major parties in his palace in Marrakesh, including Sa'd al-Din 'Uthmani from the PJD. The political class as a whole expected the Palace to appoint a prime minister from the USFP or Istiqlal, but the king put an end to the intense competition between the two parties by appointing a technocrat close to the Palace, Driss Jettou.

The premiership thus became again a "sovereign ministry,"[61] which was a step backward from Hassan II's appointment of Youssoufi as head of government after the 1997 elections. Public opinion reflected surprise and disappointment in a decision that did not represent the election results, and that completed the defeat of the party system and the alternation between parties in power that had been inaugurated in 1998.[62] Although, following the appointment of Driss Jettou as prime minister on October 9, 2002, the leadership of the PJD as a whole, including Ben Kirane and 'Uthmani, agreed to possible participation in the government, there were also some dissident voices among the "hardliners" in the party, such as Mustafa Ramid and Lahsan al-Daoudi, who spoke in favor of the PJD's remaining in the opposition.[63]

In the end, the PJD did not join the government.[64] The minor ministries offered by the palace did not satisfy the party, which chose the strategy of mobilizing voters and staying out of government. It appeared, in fact, certain to maintain some degree of popularity as long as it did not participate in government. As Khatib put it: "What do you expect one or two ministers to do in a heterogeneous government? I had that experience under Muhammad V. The PJD rejected it: we were offered one ministry."[65] The PJD thus remained in an intermediate position: through its presence in the parliament, it was close to the Makhzen, whose periphery it had finally penetrated, but it allowed itself to be excluded for the moment from governmental affairs. At the same time, in order to avoid frightening the elites in power, it was working patiently, and it limited the number of candidates it ran at the national level in order to occupy the political terrain at the local level. In the local elections of September 2003, the PJD managed to take control of seventeen localities over which it presided, and it began political penetration in major cities, for example in Meknès, Beni Mellal, and Tetouan. Locally elected officials insisted that their towns were not being governed along Islamist lines and worked particularly hard to demonstrate their political competence in managing their responsibilities. They wanted to set themselves apart from the old parties that were often subject to corruption, struggles for influence, and internal dissension. Their success would depend on their results, often positively evaluated for the more efficient management of towns that they introduced, but also because the regime tended to accept these successes. On this point, the PJD modeled itself largely on the example of the Justice and Development Party in Turkey, by making apprenticeship in the management of local affairs the first step toward participation in a national government. Armed with its electoral successes, the PJD is now an atypical party; it is establishing closer relations with the regime, not because it has been domesticated by the regime, but because it has succeeded in becoming one of the central actors in Moroccan political society. I turn next to its ideological output.

CHAPTER 8

Theology and Politics: Differentiated Repertoires

The integration of the PJD into the operations of the Moroccan political system provided the legalist Islamists with room for political mobilization, which included new opportunities for and new limitations on their public discourse, partially changing the content of what they actually said. By analyzing the writings and speeches of some of the leaders of the PJD it is possible to distinguish three levels of political discourse. First are theological texts, exemplified by the writings of Ahmad Raysuni, who reinvents Islamist political activism by adopting procedural definitions of democracy and by focusing on the community of "pious" citizens, which he sees as the foundation of politics. Second are political programs, represented by the charter of the MUR, which, unlike Raysuni, continues to be expressed in terms of the Islamic state. And third is the language used in the arena of political deliberation—represented by PJD interventions in parliament—which uses religious repertoires while maintaining a distance from religion itself. The simultaneous existence of these three kinds of repertoires shows that the duo of the MUR and the PJD uses religious references contextually, and that, although the PJD as a whole has been integrated into the operations of the regime, it has not given up its religious language, but rather has adapted it to a context that the monarchy and many political participants want to define as areligious: the parliament.

The Political Theology of Ahmad Raysuni: Democracy as a Means

Ahmad Raysuni, head of the MUR until the spring of 2003, is one of the few outstanding intellectuals associated with the MUR and the PJD. Born in 1953 near Larache, he received a degree in Shari'a from the Qarawiyyin in Fez in 1978, and then in 1992 a *doctorat d'état* in Theology from Muhammad V University in Rabat. Until recently, he was a professor of Shari'a in the Department of Islamic Studies of the Faculty of Letters and Human Sciences of Rabat. He is thus a typical product of the fragmentation of the networks of religious education. In his youth, Raysuni was drawn to an apolitical Islamism and, while still a lycée student, joined the *tabligh wa da'wa* association, which prohibited its members from engaging in any political action or speech. In 1976, at the age of twenty-three, he broke with apolitical Islam and created his own organization, the *jam'iyya islamiyya* (Islamic Association) of Ksar al-Kabir. It took him two decades from that point to enter an organization connected directly to a recognized political party, the PJD.

Raysuni's ideas are worth detailed consideration, in part because of their sharp contrast with the Islamism of Yassine. In the tradition of the Middle Eastern reformism of Muhammad 'Abduh of the late nineteenth century and that of 'Allal al-Fasi and the Tunisian Sheikh Al-Tahar Ibn 'Ashur in the early twentieth, they are based on the concept of the "intentions" (*maqasid*) of shari'a. Raysuni wrote one of his university theses on the thought of Abu Ishaq al-Shatibi (d. 1388) and published it in 1990.[1] Imam al-Shatibi, an Andalusian scholar, had reformed the Maliki school by using the notions of the common good (*maslaha*) and the intentions (*maqasid*) of the revealed text as flexible principles for interpreting the law. Al-Shatibi's ideas had been widely appropriated by the first reformist Arab intellectuals of the

Salafiyya, but rarely drawn on by political Islamism in the second half of the twentieth century.[2] Raysuni's thesis restores al-Shatibi to a central place in an Islamist model for the elaboration of Muslim law. Informed largely by al-Shatibi's thought, Raysuni's works present a peaceful aspect of Islam, more bourgeois than that offered by Abdessalam Yassine, for whom suffering on earth and the thought of death are constantly present. In Raysuni, one detects, in contrast, a humanist theology, recalling this quotation from al-Shatibi: "While it is certain that the truth is to be grasped beyond mankind, truth cannot be known without human mediation. Further, truth is reached through human beings. They are evidence on the way."[3] In Raysuni's view, therefore, religious truth is reached by men only through the interpretations they produce. Determining the meaning of shari'a through exegesis rather than describing a reified Islamic law makes the law malleable. This is why this law is able to correspond to the intentions of the revelation and helps mankind flourish in society. While man is subject to the law, he is simultaneously its first object *and* its interpreter. The common good (*maslaha*) is the principal intention of shari'a in both moral and material realms. Shari'a thus consists of rules, each of which has its own *raison d'être*, and is informed by God. But the faithful have to discover those reasons through an unending search, knowing that the most important among these reasons is to ensure human happiness on earth. Raysuni is opposed to the idea that it is impossible to discover the reasons for the '*ibadat*, the modes of adoring God. From this point of view, the *mu'amalat*, relations among men, and the '*ibadat*, relations of man with God, both have precise goals that are organized by divine authority. For example, to pray is to remind oneself of God: "Remembering all-powerful God is one of the greatest things in this life. Is the highest thing that people desire in their life, the thing they seek night and day, not happiness? And is happiness not the feeling of comfort, contentment, serenity, and pleasure (*mut'a*)?"[4]

And again: "The highest degree of pleasure in this world and its most sublime point (*maqamat*) is the one reached by those who pronounce the name of God and place themselves humbly beneath his protection...."⁵ For Raysuni, it is a veritable "state of the heart" and the soul that affects the entire person. Despite many mystical touches in Raysuni's vocabulary, this is very different from Yassine, who encourages a way of life in preparation for the beyond and defines the world as the messianic theater of a long and bitter political struggle.

Raysuni, on the other hand, makes religion more present and alive. He situates it *in the world*. The purpose of fasting is not to protect oneself against hell, but rather a way of testing oneself and devoting oneself to study. One of the goals of pilgrimage, in addition to the adoration of God, is to bring men together and involve them in all kinds of trade, including economic exchange.⁶ Similarly, democracy is only a way of reaching one of the goals of shari'a, the absence of political and social discord.⁷ Connecting the method of the *maqasid* to the question of political procedures legitimate in Islam, he writes: "There are those who reject democracy in whole or in part on the pretext that it is linked to a secularist philosophy and an areligious vocation (*la diniyya*)."⁸ Raysuni answers this objection in this way: "The principle of consultation (*shura*), like democracy, is a means of action and not an end in itself. Evaluating them means evaluating what they include, what they use, and what they lead to.... Democracy is not a mechanical device with a manual of required instructions. It is neither a religion nor a doctrine. It is not necessarily liberal or capitalist."⁹ He goes on: "If a predetermined content is imposed on democracy... it is no longer democracy.... The foundation and the essence of democracy are for groups and peoples freedom of choice and procedure. ... In Muslim societies, democracy can only be at the service of Islam and will necessarily lead to Islamic choices."¹⁰ Starting from a procedural and instrumental definition of democracy, Raysuni intends to show that in a Muslim society, democracy necessarily takes on Islamic content and that it therefore cannot be rejected. It is because it is only a procedure, defined by freedom (*hurriyya*), that in its ultimate content it cannot fail to coincide with the religious identity of Muslim voters. Democracy, Raysuni wrote in 2004, "is not a religion, has no religion, and is not against religion."¹¹ Democracy, he tells us, is an "experiment,"¹² and one "cannot impose conditions on the use of democracy."[13] This position on democracy allows Raysuni to respond to the Islamist movements that advocate an Islamic state operating directly by application of divine law and that reject the principles of electoral democracy. Countering those who define democracy as government by human law, and hence reject democracy because they see it as contrary to divine law, Raysuni writes:

> Are elections Islamic, European, or non-religious? Elections are a way . . . of expressing opinions. . . . Within the MUR we practice democracy and we do not say that it contradicts Islam. It is only an organizational device that we have taken on, explained, adapted, and now use. . . . We do not claim to have extracted it from books of jurisprudence or theology. And it is impossible for anyone to claim that we have westernized or secularized ourselves because of this democracy that we practice. . . . I say yes to unlimited democracy, even if it is possible that one day democracy will lead to a kind of exit from Islam. That would be good, because democracy would then make us realize the state of real dysfunction that we could not see in society.[14]

Raysuni here refers to the possibility that citizens of a democracy might pass legislation contradicting the divine laws, a central argument made by Islamists opposed to democracy. He answers that democracy plays the role of revealing public opinion and enables citizens to recognize the evolution of the level and quality of their piety. The legitimation of parliamentary democracy is also a way of justifying the strategy chosen by the PJD, which uses a vocabulary in conformity with the cultural code of the Islamists, although Raysuni subjects it to a significant modification. In Raysuni's view, the proposal for an Islamic state is in fact a mistake:

> As for the question of the Islamic state, regardless of what Hasan al-Banna had in mind and regardless of his program, I say personally that thinking through the prism of the Islamic state is a mistake. . . . Imagining an Islamic state

and giving it functions to fulfill is all a mistake. . . . The state is a means among others, nothing more. I believe in the activism of society (*mujtama'*) and not in the activism of the state. We have to rely on the *umma*, not on the state . . . and I would be happy if the idea of an Islamic state were to fade. Those who have accomplished it have begun to discover the truth, as in Iran or Sudan. They are discovering that the state is not a strike force that does everything it wishes and changes people as it wishes. There is something other than the state that must be in control.[15]

The Islamic movement must therefore detach itself from the question of the state: "We do not need to turn to the state but to the community of the faithful," he wrote in 2000.[16] Raysuni in fact sees the state as weak in the face of Islam and unable to guarantee the function of *da'wa*. Power is coercive and has nothing to do with ideals. To guarantee the religious continuity of society, it is therefore better to remain out of the purview of the state. In Raysuni's view, Islam should be restored to the community of the faithful and not defined and appropriated by the elite in power. The head of the community derives his power from the *umma* or its representatives, not from Allah: "It is impossible," writes Raysuni, echoing 'Allal al-Fasi, "for a leader to say in any way that he holds his power from Allah."[17] The *umma* thus precedes the state, religiously and politically: religiously because the community, given its duty to maintain Islam, must remain "alive, alert, and participatory";[18] politically because the community manages its own affairs on the basis of institutional arrangements of its choosing. He therefore denounces a dominating state that would monopolize the definition of the common good. While he contemplates the prospect of a pious society made up of citizens, it seems to Raysuni impossible to imagine a pious state. His political theology therefore concentrates on the community, the source of the choice of its own leaders and of the definition of the common good.

Like the 'ulama gravitating around the monarchy in the 1970s and 1980s, Raysuni thinks of the state as an entity that is not to be confronted directly. But that does not prevent him from working out an idea of political activism, which must be built upon a pluralistic political foundation and seek in a pragmatic and progressive manner the ideal of a community of religiously and politically virtuous citizens: "Experience has taught me not to ask for the impossible."[19] More pragmatic than most theoreticians of political Islamism, Raysuni abstains from theoretical analysis of the state. Unlike many Moroccan 'ulama, however, Raysuni gives his theology a political aspect in order to legitimate democracy. He also maintains that authoritarianism, linked to the "state's savagery,"[20] explains many failings in Islamic political thought.[21] Raysuni thus represents a new type of 'alim: trained in religious institutions controlled and fragmented by the monarchy, he remains distant from the state—he does not confront it, but he does not abstain from criticizing its authoritarianism. He thus offers an optimistic view of a Moroccan society that has, according to him, been re-Islamized after finding itself an "orphan of its Islam."[22] He writes: "And then, beginning in the 1960s, many people sensed the danger. They sensed that the danger facing them was more important than the one that had threatened them when Spain and France invaded Morocco." 'Ulama such as 'Allal al-Fasi, he explains, "had lost hope."[23] It was difficult for Raysuni to understand the 'ulama's inability to ensure the continuity of Islam in Morocco:

> I was among those who felt a certain apprehension about the 'ulama and perhaps up to a certain point I condemned them. The fact was that we didn't understand how the marginalization of the 'ulama had come about. Nor did we understand that they could have any excuse. . . . But this state of affairs quickly dissipated and pious youth began to understand the situation of the 'ulama, their efforts, and their condition. . . . The Islamic movements . . . began to train their own 'ulama or to attract 'ulama. Their influence was transmitted to traditional 'ulama, who became more dynamic, as in Iraq and to a lesser extent in Egypt.[24]

Raysuni's thinking and activism particularly reflect that convergence between Islamist intellectuals and 'ulama, a convergence that was accomplished through state institutions of religious learning, as his own educational experience demonstrates.

I turn next to the relationship between this procedural redefinition of democracy by Raysuni, an Islamist *'alim*, and the ideological positions adopted by the PJD and the MUR, which are more concerned with political mobilization than with the theological definition of their political practices and ideals.

The Movement of Unity and Reform: A Rhetoric of Identity

Unlike Raysuni's works of theological and political reflection, which endeavor to establish continuity between theological discourse and a theory of political practice, the ideology of the Movement of Unity and Reform did not come from major intellectual figures or arise from a homogeneous line of thinking. The movement's ideology arose pragmatically from individual political careers, representing diverse political families and many Islamist ideological traditions. The ideology remains flexible and appears to anyone attempting to understand it as a disparate set of statements articulated in the media (particularly the movement's press organs[25]), a few documents published by the movement, and sometimes contradictory speeches by its representatives in parliament and elsewhere.

The press connected to the movement is also heterogeneous in its content. It includes articles by Driss al-Kattani, a scholar who will be considered later. It often publishes communiqués from Yassine's Justice and Benevolence movement, as well as controversial sermons by independent preachers. From time to time, speeches by the Minister of Religious Affairs, al-Mdaghri, and ideas circulating in the summer universities he has organized since 1989 are subjects of discussion. Islamist experiences elsewhere in the Muslim world are important for the movement, and its press constantly considers them. The major document of reference produced by the MUR is its charter, a 97-page pamphlet. It explains in accessible language the movement's program, supporting its positions with verses from the Qur'an and prophetic traditions and excluding any other sources. There is no reference to any Muslim author in the text, implicitly making the argument of a return to the "essentials," that is, to the direct and unmediated interpretation of the sacred texts. The key element of the charter is its intention to "establish" religion (*iqamat al-din*) in state and nation, and to work toward the application of shari'a. The text offers as a political model an "electoral caliphate" (*khilafa intikhabiyya*), a way of asking for free political participation while recognizing the concept of commander of the faithful on an abstract level and making no direct judgment on the person occupying that position. This explanatory text points to the meaning of the movement's name: unity, referring not only to Allah but also to the unity of the Moroccan people; reform, namely, the one that must be set into motion in Morocco, toward which the movement intends to work, using the fundamental and unchangeable basis of the Qur'an and the Sunna.

The MUR charter emphasizes the concept of freedom of worship, which helps to reassure the public about the movement's spirit of tolerance, but also to justify the political rights of the Islamist movement.[26] The pamphlet entitled *Political Vision*, published by the MUR in September 1998, sets up the main principles of political action.[27] This brief document places the rule of law, democracy, and the rights of man in an "Islamic" perspective, through the models of the prophet and the caliphate.

While the PJD is publicly monarchist, the MUR is more ambiguous on this point: "Morocco today is in many ways in contradiction with Islam in political, legal, constitutional, and social matters." Further on: "The Moroccan Constitution states explicitly that the person of the king is sacred and that it is not permitted (to the nation or its representatives) to criticize the content of what he says."[28] Denouncing the lack of a true *bay'a*, the text explicitly attacks article 19 of the Constitution: "Whereas, historically, it was thought that criticism or deposition of the king was the result of an infraction of the terms of the *bay'a*, this rule is not part of the conception of the constitution after independence."[29]

But the political representation of the king that the MUR develops does not go beyond this preliminary negative observation. With pragmatism, the principle of the constitutional monarchy is in fact recognized by the movement as "one of the constitutive elements of political reality, and the most important."[30] The political work of reform will therefore be carried out within the framework defined by the constitutional monarchy. The king in fact has a "religious quality," set out in the Constitution, which guarantees the preservation of religion and its values . . . with no acceptance of secularism supported from outside."[31] The religious quality of the king is to be respected because it is present in the text of the constitution, and because the state respects religion and citizen rights. In a few lines and in a subtle way, the conditions for a legitimate *bay'a* are set out:[32] implicitly the *bay'a* is presented as the key element, the sine qua non, for the sacredness of the monarch, and not, conversely, the king's sacredness as the basis for the pact of allegiance.

When Muhammad VI succeeded his father, the MUR drafted a communiqué in support of the *bay'a* of the new king, which was published on the front page of the daily *Al-tajdid* and signed by Ahmad Raysuni.[33] The MUR communiqué recognized that the late king had built the political institutions of Morocco, had achieved territorial integrity, and had broadened the range of public freedom, which had enabled the Islamic movement to participate in the enterprise of reform. But it then turned to his son and recommended that he develop the Islamic identity of the country and restore legitimacy to shari'a.

The movement thereby declared its complete support for the principle of the Islamic identity of the Moroccan state, "a historic fact and a constitutional advantage. It is a principle that cannot be challenged."[34] Note the subtlety of the reference to the Islamic identity of the state and not to the sacred nature of the king: if there is an Islamic identity, it belongs first to the state with no explicit relationship to the person of the 'Alawite sovereign.

The movement's intention to work for reform starting from the few surviving bastions of Islam makes it all the more necessary to recognize an Islamic identity for the Moroccan state. Hence, both the state and the *Mudawwana* (the family code) are examples of domains that have already been stamped with the seal of Islam, and they must be expanded. The principle of the Islamic identity of the state is in fact "superior to all the articles of the Constitution. It is on this basis that judgment is made on the constitutionality of the laws and decisions that the legislative, judicial, and executive institutions produce."[35] Further on: "The affirmation of the Islamic identity of the state necessitates making shari'a the supreme source of all the laws, which also means . . . giving up all laws, rulings, and policies that contradict Islamic shari'a."[36] In this political program, the principles of interpretation of shari'a and the concepts of *maslaha* and *maqasid*, even though they had been developed by Raysuni, are not mentioned. Similarly, his criticism of excessive attention to the question of the Islamic state is not taken into account.

Respect for democracy in the sense of respect for popular sovereignty is one of the key words of the MUR's political program: the people must have the right of "choice" and of "censure" of the government, and the right to hold leaders responsible. Political pluralism and the multiparty system are respected.[37] There is no question of "leaving" the community of the faithful and establishing a sectarian group that would consider the rest of Moroccan society impious, following the model of the old *Shabiba islamiyya*, the first organization to which many members of the MUR had belonged.[38]

The MUR, like many opposition movements and political parties, thus calls for democratization of institutions, while remaining opposed to "Western democracy," which authorizes "liberalism" and "materialism."[39] The preferred model of the MUR is the *shura*, or consultation, although it is not clear precisely what that means in practice, compared with the concept of liberal democracy. In this sense, unlike in the case of Raysuni, the programmatic writings of the MUR do not delve into defining the meaning of democracy and explicitly support the dichotomy between Western democracy and

Islamic *shura*. While political pluralism is a principle accepted in practice, resistance to neocolonialism bars expressing it in terms borrowed from the West.

Islam and the West: The Representation of a Split

Products of the Arabized educational system, the elites of the PJD, like its members, are in direct competition with their cohorts coming out of French schools or study abroad. The replication of French-trained elites in the highest positions of the state hierarchy is difficult for today's younger generation to accept. The emergence of the PJD and the MUR on the political stage also reflects a demand for recognition of and participation by new elites that are often marginalized by the state. According to the MUR ideology, the colonization of Morocco was an essential element in the decline of Islam: among its long-term effects, it has in particular compelled Moroccans to adopt "Western" styles of consumption and behavior and to de-Islamize the way in which the economy operates.[40] Colonization also changed the status of the law, aside from family matters where shari'a is still applied. Emphasis is placed on the negative effects of "cultural penetration" following independence, which has "created a Moroccan elite that defends the values of the colonizer, fights for his language, and thinks as he does."[41] Postcolonial policies have therefore merely followed the Western model in the areas of law, education, and cultural values in general. This split has produced a dichotomy in Moroccan life, recalling the letter that Khatib addressed to the king in 1972, as well as many documents published by the 'ulama after independence in favor of Arabization.[42]

This document detailing the political vision of the MUR also dwells on individual conduct, the norms governing it, and its visibility in the public domain:

> The ruling elites that have been imbued with the cultural values of the colonizer have diffused new kinds of values, meanings, and conduct, such as excessive consumption,

challenges to prohibitions such as the consumption of wine and cigarettes, for men and women, the use of *riba* (interest charges), indecent nudity, the reprehensible mixing of the sexes, the practice of corruption, and the rejection of the Arabic language.[43]

Educational policies have been particularly erroneous because they have weakened the link between education and morality. The political elites' neglect of original education and their emphasis on modern education, like the importance given to the French Mission schools, have also reinforced the dichotomy running through society between its Westernized elites and the rest of the population. The Moroccan nation must now redefine itself as a body of Muslim citizens and not as an entity that has been fragmented and dislocated by the impact of the West.

This political vision has also been generalized to the world scene: the great powers—which "obey the Zionist forces" and organize "international pillage"[44]—have undermined Moroccan political and economic independence. They have declared their opposition to Islamist movements. Without explicitly identifying the United States, the movement focuses on Israel and its allies, rooting its argument in a description of the signs of the suffering of a Muslim community that is the victim of wars in Palestine, Afghanistan, Chechnya, Bosnia, and Iraq.[45]

Since the end of the cold war, Islamist movements everywhere have indeed extensively mobilized their adherents around the theme of religious wars against "external enemies." The PJD and the MUR are no exceptions. But in the commander of the faithful's Morocco, it is difficult to incorporate this theme into the debate on national identity, because, as I have shown, the duo of the MUR and the PJD cannot allow itself to mention, within Morocco as a Muslim country, differences in "Islamic identity"—the MUR/PJD would then appear as a sectarian entity. This is why, while not challenging the Muslim identity of Moroccans and their state, the PJD and the MUR have developed, as one of the distinctive traits of their ideological set of references, a harsh critique of the "duality" of Moroccan society and its state. By repeating these criticisms in parliament, the PJD has cloaked the state, the government, and the society in an image of "immorality," rather than characterizing them as non-Muslim or "impious." The ideology of the PJD, which is the public, legal, and monarchist face of the MUR network, is thus crystallized in the question of morality, transforming its reference to Islam into a social and political "ethics."

Religion or Ethics?
The PJD in Parliament

The ideas of the PJD reveal an ultimate lack of clarity, arising as much from political constraints as from the diverse political backgrounds and political thinking of those who came together in the party. As a high-ranking member of the party explained to me, "We do our own tinkering. We have thinkers, but they don't write."[46] The only exception to the lack of clarity in the language of the leadership of the PJD is their demand that shari'a be applied on specific points and in limited areas. Pragmatism and negotiation predominate over the delineation of a clear ideology covering every area, and for this they have in fact been criticized by radical Islamists.

Following the 2002 legislative elections, Abu Hafs, a radical preacher, wrote a speech addressed to "our Islamists in parliament."[47] He criticized the bargaining and negotiations conducted by the PJD and its lack of clarity on the question of the application of shari'a. Referring to the costume worn by deputies for the opening session of parliament, he wrote ironically of the presence of these Islamists in parliament, fearful that their white robes would "get soiled . . . the ones they wear on that famous Friday in honor of the opening of the [parliamentary] season, presenting their offerings to receive in exchange the *baraka* of that place, and I wonder if they have made their Friday prayers. . . . I say that I fear that their clothing may be stained by the mud [of that place], by the sale of their identity, the filth of their concessions, and the falsification of the constant principles of shariʿa." "What then," he adds, "is the difference between you and the secular parties?" And yet the PJD speaks in and out of parliament in favor of the moralization of public and private life, targeting specifically "places of debauchery," the youth who listen to hard rock, and Morocco's participation in the Miss World contest. But for the radicals, this is a futile battle; they would rather directly attack the "root of the evil," that is the state and political society, which they see as secular. The PJD is thus caught in the crossfire between the critiques from more radical Islamists and those from non-Islamist figures.

For example, the issue of the production and sale of alcoholic beverages was introduced in parliament by PJD representatives between June 1998 and November 1999, but the government did not discuss the question.[48] Morality in public life was further addressed in August 2000, this time on the question of beaches. Referring to the mixing of the sexes and the wearing of bathing suits, the PJD spoke of practices "in defiance of morality and customary behavior and in contradiction to Islamic religion and its values."[49] This moralization of public behavior, one key issue for the PJD, allowed it to express an Islamist ideology its public could recognize while refraining from contesting the very functioning of the political system. The PJD tried at all costs to remain within the field of the morality of public behavior and to solve the issue, which it considered pressing, of everyday conduct and the public norms that should determine it. On the other hand, the PJD's competitors in political society and the government characterized the PJD's demands for the establishment of Islamic norms in public behavior as an "exploitation of religion for political purposes," to which the PJD replied that it was concerned with moralizing the public realm, a moralization defined on the basis of a "religious reference." The PJD's response to the Minister of the Interior on the matter of beaches shows this clearly: "The minister has discussed problems that had nothing to do with the question posed. . . . He has avoided what is really at stake in the issue and started to discuss the problem of the relationship between religion and politics, and has said that religion ought not to be exploited for political purposes, that he would not allow it."[50] The PJD insisted that the question of public morality had nothing to do with the issues related to "religion and politics." As a comprehensive frame of reference, Islam was kept at a distance by the PJD's deputies, because the government made it difficult for them to explicitly articulate a religious discourse in the parliamentary sphere.[51] This distancing was the direct result both of parliamentary deliberations on the question of Islamic norms and of the coercive power of the government's defining the parliament as a secular space.

The PJD thus claimed that it wanted to apply shari'a, but did not demand the application of legal penalties (*hudud*). And it certainly did not undertake deep analysis of the subject: "We never proclaimed that the veil should be imposed on women, nor that all citizens should be required to pray. That requires faith. Without faith, one can impose nothing. On the other hand, some measures that are part of shari'a, such as taxes, can be applied. As for the application of penalties, this is not on the agenda in our program."[52]

The elections in the fall of 2002 revealed internal conflicts in the party, notably between Mustafa Ramid, one of the "hard-liners" of the PJD, and Ben Kirane, who offered a broad definition of shari'a: "We understand shari'a in a broad sense. Shari'a in Morocco today is the battle against immorality and corruption, it means finding work for people, educating citizens, reforming their conduct. Shari'a as *hudud* has not existed in the nation for quite some time."[53] For Ben Kirane, religious questions had to be addressed first on the cultural level, before moving on to direct application of a text that had not been codified: "Moroccans did not vote for us so we would cut off the thieves' hands or stone adulterers. Moroccans voted for us because they placed their trust in our honesty and think that that is sufficient to entrust their affairs to us and to resolve their problems."[54]

What Is a Religious Party?

For the PJD, as for its political rivals, calling itself a "religious" party implicitly means that the other parties are areligious, which would amount to denying them the right to call themselves "Muslim." This is why the PJD has evinced a constant concern to demonstrate publicly that it does not want to appropriate and exclude others from religion, which is given to all. The duo of the PJD and the MUR, unlike radical Islamism, therefore accepts competition from the state and from other groups in the religious sphere, while operating as a transmitter for many religious actors who can compete or ally themselves with the PJD and the MUR: conservative 'ulama, preachers, teachers in the system of original education, but also members of official institutions such as the Minister of Religious Affairs, 'Abd al-Kabir 'Alawi Mdaghri. The MUR's "preparatory program" states the following: "We are not the 'society of Muslims' (*jama'at al-muslimin*) but a movement of a call to Islam among others."[55] Hence, because Islam is not the monopoly of any single body, it can be a frame of reference for all and thus become universal. For the same reason, it becomes difficult to define Islam as a norm governing the public realm, beyond definitions authorized by (and negotiated with) the state. On the question of the relationship between politics and religion, Sa'd al-Din 'Uthmani, the leader of the PJD, replied:

> We have always said that the PJD is not an *Islamist party*, but a *political party with an Islamic frame of reference*, which is fully a part of the national project for a modern and democratic society. The Islamic frame of reference, like the values of modernity, is not the exclusive possession of any party. Some parties adhere to a liberal frame of reference, others to a socialist or Marxist frame. It is because Islam belongs to us all that no one party can prohibit any other from drawing inspiration from it for its programs. Otherwise, one should not speak of *zakat* [charity], nor of *waqf* [pious endowments], nor of moralization in the conduct of public affairs mentioned so frequently by several political parties in their programs. In other words, should we cloister Islam within the confines of the mosque?[56]

The reasoning is subtle, and while arguing that because there is no monopoly there is freedom, it also enables the party to appropriate Islam as a frame of reference. It thus becomes possible to posit the principle of the universality of Islam, and to demonstrate the legitimacy of the political work undertaken by the legalist Islamists. The monarchy would endeavor to reverse this reasoning: it is because Islam ought to be shared by all that no political party can lay claim to it. For the Palace, the only actor who can legitimately appropriate Islam is still the monarchy, which is both the guardian of Islam and the ultimate political arbiter.

For the PJD's elites, their flexible position on religious discourse implies not an "exit" from religion or a social and political weakening of Islam, but on the contrary the legitimation of an appropriation of Islam by all, notably by political actors—a legitimation that gives shape to the ideal of an ethical civil society based on an interpretation of norms derived from Islam.[57] In a context in which the monarch is the commander of the faithful, the appropriation by a legally recognized Islamist party of the theme of Islam as the basis for the norms of public conduct engenders some adjustments in the religious sacredness of the monarchy. By appropriating a discourse on Islam while not restricting its use by others, and incidentally recalling that it *also* belongs to the state, the PJD in fact exemplifies the decentralization of the legitimacy of religious discourse. Free preachers and opposition Islamists not participating in partisan politics had already done so before the PJD, and more effectively, because of their position outside the system of political competition. But precisely what has changed with the Justice and Development Party is the fact that it has appropriated Islam while being incorporated into the functioning of the political system and playing the game of political competition as regulated by the monarchy. Further, by differentiating itself from the representative of official Islam—the Ministry of Religious Affairs—through its status as a political party and its popular base, the PJD occupies a unique position in the functioning of the Moroccan political system: it shapes a discourse on Islam in a sphere authorized by the monarchy, but it can also, on occasion, divert that discourse to contest the religious legitimacy of the regime.

To give only one example: by publishing a proposal for constitutional reform in the Arabic-language weekly *Al-sahifa*, on the eve of the Fifth Congress of the PJD, Mustafa Ramid redefined the role of the commander of the faithful, who would be an arbiter with essentially religious and not absolute power, and would delegate executive power to elected majorities that would be chosen democratically and would be accountable to the people and the voters.[58] This declaration recalls the one made by Raysuni in the spring of 2003, when in a brief interview with *Aujourd'hui le Maroc*, he declared that the commander of the faithful could be represented by a king or a prime minister, and that King Muhammad VI did not have the required qualifications.[59] The affair caused an uproar, coming at a time when a journalist, 'Ali al-Mrabit, who did not belong to the Islamist movement, was also accused of having challenged royal sacredness by publishing drawings and photomontages in the paper he edited. While the affair of 'Ali al-Mrabit, who was imprisoned, stirred up a storm in Morocco and in France, that of Raysuni remained strictly within national confines and merely led Raysuni to resign as president of the MUR. The contrast is instructive: it shows that while it is often easy for the monarchy to exclude political actors who call its sacred nature into question, it is more difficult for it to do so when those actors define themselves as legitimate authors of a religious discourse and it has itself decided to integrate them into the arena of legal competition.

Can a Religious Party Participate in Politics?

The PJD's way of thinking about the relations between Islam and politics is the direct result of the paradoxical situation of the legalist Islamists in the Moroccan political arena. The PJD has often been accused by its enemies of being unable to participate in politics because it is "drowned" in religious issues. Its nature as a religious movement is said to set it apart from the play of party politics. The PJD elites reply that they have put together a primarily political movement, as Ben Kirane explains: "Our leaders are steeped in religion [or *mutadayyinun*, practicing believers], but they are concerned with political affairs."[60] And Saʻd al-Din ʻUthmani had this to say: "The other parties made a mistake, a false diagnosis [by calling us a religious party], then they were surprised. They tried to get at us from the religious side. But we responded politically. We did not enter into a religious debate."[61]

The men of the PJD are thus compelled to take their stand directly in the political sphere, and this is probably what explains the small space devoted to religious and theological arguments in their discussions with the rest of political society. They have distanced themselves from Islam by calling it a "frame of reference," and refrain from using it as a defining characteristic of their party. Their various critics place them outside the utopian pairing, traditionally invoked by Islamists, of *din* (religion) and *dunya* (world) and set them on one side or the other while denying that they have any ability or any legitimacy to bring the two together. Hence, they have been constantly driven to reconfigure this pairing—which is always in tension—in new ways. This is why they have not found it possible to bring theology and politics together in the sphere of parliamentary political activity. For the same reason, other political parties have also often accused them of formulating an ideology that is shallow, vague, and inconsistent. But it also explains their ability to create connections or alliances with non-Islamist parties on particular political issues: with the small liberal party Citizen Forces, for example, by organizing a joint conference in May 2004 on the free trade agreement reached that year between Morocco and the United States. The president of Citizen Forces stated on that occasion:

> I noted with great interest how close the PJD experts often came to our concerns. Most participants responded to the expectations arising from economic and social imperatives. . . . [They] unequivocally confirm their backing and support for economic liberalism in solidarity with others and private initiative, which our party holds dear. Moreover, with all their strength, they are calling for the establishment of mechanisms capable of fostering the integration of our economy into the international economy.[62]

It is thus precisely because the PJD has agreed to participate in the political system and to establish relations with its direct political competitors that it has ended up developing a distanced, strained, but ever-present relationship with the Islamic frame of reference. Parliament has also become a battlefield on which the PJD intensely—and often in vain—"watches over" the democratic procedures of control of government by parliament. In parliament, its competitors have given it the image of a religious party that has no place in political society, which they wish to be secular, except for parliamentary interventions by the commander of the faithful. But outside local and national political society and its rules, the Islamists of the PJD, through the connections they maintain with the MUR, the party's associative base in urban centers, and its Islamic intellectuals, have kept up a discourse that is more deeply rooted in political theology. This spectrum of positions enables it to act, in relation to the monarchy and the political society, in both proximity and dissent, through the use of repertoires whose contents depend on the areas of politics involved. The PJD has thus not allowed itself to be domesticated by the monarchy's program of transition towards "democracy." Beyond the mechanisms of co-optation of the Islamist opposition, the definition of the relations between Islam and political authority remains at the heart of the debate opposing Islamists to the monarchy, a debate that has given shape to a differentiated set of political theologies.

CHAPTER 9

The Commander of the Faithful And His Religious Competitors

The monarchy seems to have made a wager that is hard to win: it opened the political sphere to relative pluralism in the second half of the 1990s, thereby permitting the establishment of a public space for deliberation. But the monarchy was at the same time determined to retain control of the definition of the rules of the game, creating the paradox of a state in possession of supreme authority working unceasingly to restore its legitimacy by trying halfheartedly to share power. The monarchy confronted a political society that was more open to competition but unable to play a role as counterforce. This contradiction, exacerbated from the 1990s on, triggered a reorganization of the relations between the monarchy and Islam.

The emergence of new opportunities for relative freedom of expression had consequences in the realm of religion: varied interpretations of Islam proliferated, circulated publicly, fragmented, and were appropriated by various individuals who became "religious authorities" because their public viewed them as such. They were a diverse group, including 'ulama seeking to free themselves from state control and religious authorities controlled by the monarchy, as well as the new "free" preachers, the men and women of the PJD, and Sheikh Yassine and his disciples. It should also be pointed out that in the 1990s, small political parties arose that adopted an Islamic basis, such as the Movement for the Umma and the Civilizational Alternative, two manifestations of the old Shabiba. The latter was the most original in that it developed a "progressive" Islamic discourse that brought it close to the left.

These new religious entrepreneurs formed a competitive sphere in which they shifted between alliance and opposition, and, as new authorities recognized by specific publics, they created a religious space in competition with the one the monarchy had patiently constructed around itself since independence. This space, which had long been institutionally fragmented, had become polyphonic, filled with increasingly discordant voices opposing or allying with one another according to circumstances. But this fragmentation, which Dale Eickelman and James Piscatori have pointed out as characteristic of Muslim societies in the late twentieth century, did not necessarily produce a fluid sphere of opposition forces.[1] The polyphony and diversity of proliferating religious authorities included at first only those the monarchy was willing to authorize, which imposed constraints on both their discourses and their action.[2] These authorities later took root, defined themselves in diverse ways, and were able to attain varying levels of visibility and centrality, depending on where they located themselves in the institutional structures mapped out by the history of relations between the monarchy and rival religious authorities.

The monarchy, the central religious authority from the 1960s to the late 1980s was thus called into question from all sides with respect to its religious basis, which was functioning with declining effectiveness. A religious sphere came into existence that partially threw off control by the monarchy and became autonomous to a degree. But those involved, like the opposition preachers who were members of the 'ulama councils or were sometimes certified by the Ministry of Religious Affairs, also adopted structures from the monarchy. Sometimes, as in the case of Abdessalam Yassine, who imitated the functioning of the institution of the monarchy, they adopted its logic and thereby created a minefield for the sacredness of the monarchy. The regime seemed not always certain what policy to adopt: control these rival religious authorities—a nearly impossible task—or allow them to speak—and lose its religious centrality. It often adopted one or the other strategy in reaction to the major crises that gave it the opportunity to intervene. In this back and forth between control and laxity, two major questions characterized the relations between the monarchy and its religious rivals: Who had the right to speak of Islam and interpret it? What were the principal categories that all those discussing Islam—including the monarchy—used to distinguish their religious repertoires from those of their rivals?

The Monarchy between Control and Laxity

Between Muhammad VI's ascension to the throne in 1999 and the suicide bombings in Casablanca on May 16, 2003, this sphere of religious authorities grew and diversified outside the control of the monarchy, which observed it with ambivalent feelings. The king himself seemed at times reluctant to intervene in the realm where religious ideas circulated: he did not answer the questions raised by political actors about the family code, even though these political actors adopted conflicting positions. In addition, virulent sermons were often delivered in mosques without causing trouble for their authors. Muhammad VI conducted himself as though, out of indifference, he were abandoning all discussion of religion to a sphere from which he was detached. He intervened infrequently, first by trying out a new way of regulating mosque activity in 2000, and then by appointing a new Minister of Religious Affairs in 2002, in order, according to press reports, to put an end to his predecessor's practice of co-opting Islamists tied to "Saudi" influences.

Whereas political liberalization remained limited, it seemed to be proceeding in religious matters between 2000 and 2003, with the monarchy withdrawing from center stage as though the king had agreed to loosen his ties with the religious sphere. Muhammad VI did not call into question the movement toward political opening his father had begun, just as, during the early months of his reign, he changed nothing in the details of the machinery controlling Moroccan Islam. Like Hassan II before him, Muhammad VI occupied the center of public and official religious displays, and during Ramadan in 1999, he inaugurated the celebrated religious lessons, repeating his father's role. But it soon became clear that the public religious dimension of the monarchy was becoming less significant than under Hassan II.

Contrary to the tradition that placed them in the front rank in the ceremony of the *bayʻa*, the ʻulama now signed the pact of allegiance after the political authorities of the kingdom. Lessons were less numerous, and the collections of Ramadan lessons less voluminous, while religious speech was circulating outside the Makhzen, and new religious authorities were speaking of politics in the mosques, during pilgrimages, and in organized political forums, legal or clandestine. Possibly the regime was waiting for the proper moment to intervene in the realm of Islam. The fact that it did not do so actively was perhaps simply a reflection of its latent conflict with the Minister of Religious Affairs, al-Mdaghri. Had it grasped the degree of importance of the religious factor? Or did it think that it could grant freedom to non-state religious authorities without running any risks? But in that case, did it understand that that freedom might call into question the monarchy's own religious legitimacy, and that opening up the political system could not go hand in hand with the sacredness of the monarchy?

A fundamental debate persisted beneath these questions, namely, the definition of the nation's religious identity and the status of the authors of that definition. The question of who might legitimately establish and appropriate that definition had repercussions for the content of the religious repertoires used by all participants—including the monarchy—who were competing to occupy that position. One of the elements at the center of the discursive repertoire used by the Islamists in this competition instituted a radical break between Islam and the West. Starting from the conflicts between colonized and colonizers that had arisen from colonial history and from the question of the acculturation of post-colonial Moroccan society, which reflected neo-colonialism and the wars of occupation going on in Palestine and elsewhere, the organization of the world and its conflicts were re-imagined following the lines of a religious map differentiating Islam from its enemies.

Between these two camps re-imagined in terms of religious lines of demarcation, the images of the self and the enemy were given reality by the actual mobilizations induced by those representations. The split grew even deeper after September 11, 2001. I turn now to the construction of these dichotomous categories, their use within and against religious institutions under the control of the monarchy, their circulation inside and outside of Morocco, and the representations of reality to which they gave rise, starting from a debate that developed after the attacks of September 11, 2001, which included official and opposition religious authorities. This debate shows how the religious rivals of the monarchy challenged the official response of the Minister of Religious Affairs to the attacks of September 11, 2001, and were temporarily reduced to silence. This challenge used the repertoire that opposed Islam to the West, recalling the image of the split between these two blocs invoked by the 'ulama since the 1970s and later by the PJD and the MUR. This critique also drew upon the history of the Moroccan 'ulama's opposition to colonization early in the century, in order to call into question the Makhzen's alliance with the United States and its desire to control the religious authorities.

I then turn to the networks for the training of these new religious entrepreneurs turned competitors to official religious authorities.

Changes in *Salafiyya* after September 11, 2001

The Fatwa of September 18, 2001

After the attacks in New York and Washington, the regime of Muhammad VI reaffirmed the alliance between Morocco and the United States. Public opinion, however, did not fall into step, reacting as it had to the First Gulf War of 1991. The extremely negative perception of American foreign policy (support of Israeli policies, alliance with the Gulf monarchies against Iraq, and more generally a judgment that the Americans had double standards) worsened further after September 11, the war in Afghanistan in the fall of 2001, and then the invasion and occupation of Iraq by the American coalition in March 2003.

At the same time, all political actors, including the Islamists, condemned the September 11 attacks, even though the criticism of American foreign policy was unanimous. September 11 initiated a new period in Morocco and the rest of the Muslim world: close attention by the United States—carefully counting its allies and enemies in its new "war on terror"—put pressure both on Islamists of all stripes who were worried about their future and on heads of state made anxious by the American drive to impose "democratization" on the Arab world at gunpoint. Muhammad VI thus had to walk a tightrope between public opinion that largely shared the view held on the other side of the Atlantic that a "clash of civilizations" was under way and the preservation of the alliance with the United States.

When he learned of the September 11 attacks, Muhammad VI cut short an official visit to Mauritania. The Palace and the government each published a communiqué condemning the attacks. On September 16, they jointly organized in the Cathédrale Saint-Pierre in Rabat an ecumenical ceremony in homage to the victims of the attacks. Attending were the prime minister and members of the government, including the Minister of Religious Affairs, 'Abd al-Kabir 'Alawi al-Mdaghri; the chairman of the Supreme Council of 'Ulama, Muhammad Yessef; the chief rabbi of Morocco, Aaron Monsonego; the head of the Casablanca International Protestant Church, Darrel W. Pack; the papal nuncio and church officials; party leaders, including the head of the PJD; and union leaders.[3] The king was not present, but his adviser 'Abbas al-Jirari read a royal communiqué in Arabic that denounced the attacks and extremist interpretations of Islam.[4] The ceremony served as an indication of the policy of both monarchy and government: opposition to terrorism, political solidarity with the United States, and religious tolerance.

But why had the regime chosen the cathedral of Rabat as the site to confirm its alliance with the United States, a site which had been constructed on the ruins of a mosque by the authorities of the French protectorate? This was the question raised by a fatwa on September 18, 2001, signed by sixteen "'ulama of Morocco," which cast the September 16 ceremony into the realm of impiety (*kufr*).[5] Along the same lines as the 1991 fatwa condemning the Islamic-Western alliance against Iraq, the context of the September 18 fatwa, the effects it produced, and its content all confirmed the increased presence of a new variety of religious authority seeking to occupy the public forum and to challenge specific state policies.

The fatwa at first went unnoticed. It was not until the French daily *Le Monde* published an article on October 7, 2001, that it came to public attention in Morocco and produced shock waves.[6] Its passage to the other side of the Mediterranean changed the fatwa's effects: its presence in foreign—in this case French—media provoked a reaction from the Makhzen, troubled by the export of a document that seemed too radical. Because the article in *Le Monde* did not specify the identity and status of the 'ulama responsible for the publication of the fatwa, and because the authors had identified themselves as "*the* 'ulama of Morocco," as if they represented official Islam, the Makhzen reacted vigorously to undermine them and render them ineffective within Morocco by specifying that they had no "official" status.[7] The circulation of the fatwa outside Morocco thus provoked the regime to distinguish authorized from unauthorized 'ulama, to stabilize the perception of an official "tolerant" Islam that was, in this particular case, in conformity with what countries north of the Mediterranean expected.

In an interview with a French magazine, the king explained himself without fear of contradiction:

> There is no more a fatwa than there are 'ulama in this affair. The individuals you mention can claim no authority, and they certainly don't have the legitimacy that would allow them to deliver a fatwa, which is the sole province of

the Supreme Council of 'Ulama, of which I am president. I don't need advice from anyone. Muslims don't need advice from anyone. Muslims have the Qur'an and God. There is no intermediary. The only judge is God. I will not allow anyone to set himself up as a conscience. That would be an insult to Muslims.[8]

Hesitating between two contradictory views, that of an Islam open to interpretation by all and that of an Islam controlled and interpreted by a single official body headed by the king, he clearly laid out, probably without wishing to, one of the greatest difficulties of his role as commander of the faithful: to represent Moroccan Islam without appearing to monopolize it.

The Al-Kattani Family's Tradition of Opposition

With two exceptions, the authors of the fatwa were not among the official representatives of Islam. Most of the sixteen signatories were free preachers who gathered disciples around themselves and taught Islam privately, in mosques or at home. "Official" Islam was represented by two 'ulama who were members of the Council of 'Ulama of Salé. But they backed down—along with a large majority of the signatories—as soon as the Ministry of Religious Affairs pressured them to do so. The third name that stands out is that of one of the principal figures behind the fatwa, Driss al-Kattani, who is not by any means an official representative of Islam in Morocco, but a man whose significant political and religious influence is derived from his family origins. The descendant of a family that has in the past opposed the 'Alawite dynasty, he is the son of Muhammad Ibn Ja'far al-Kattani (1858-1927), author of *Salwat al-anfas*, a biographical dictionary of the saints and scholars of Fez,[9] and of the celebrated "admonition to the people of Islam" (*Nasihat ahl al-islam*) published in 1908.[10]

The political postures of the various members of the Kattani family were not uniform. For example, on two occasions, Muhammad Ibn Ja'far al-Kattani, Driss's father, chose exile over direct confrontation with Sultans Mawlay 'Abd al-'Aziz and Mawlay 'Abd al-Hafiz, who had been unable to accomplish their obligation of jihad against the colonizer. Muhammad Ibn 'Abd al-Kabir al-Kattani (whom, as I have noted, Abdessalam Yassine took as a model), a first cousin of Muhammad Ibn Ja'far al-Kattani, adopted the position of martyr and died in the jails of Sultan 'Abd al-Hafiz. His junior, Muhammad Ibrahim al-Kattani (1907-90), an ally of 'Allal al-Fasi, chose to join the nationalist movement through *Salafiyya* and neutrality toward the monarchy. On the other hand, his cousin, Driss al-Kattani, chose a political option closer to opposition, while not directly or publicly criticizing the monarchy.

The fact remains that the Kattani family as a whole preserved the memory of a tradition of opposition, indeed of competition, in the face of the 'Alawite monarchy. Born in 1922, Driss al-Kattani followed a path that is difficult to characterize: he belonged to the Party of Democracy and Independence (PDI), headed by Muhammad Hasan al-Wazzani, and was one of the founders of the League of 'Ulama of Morocco in 1961. In 1980, he established the Association of the Circle of Islamic Thought, which later served him as a platform from which to propagate the ideas of Islamism. He has often opened it up to representatives of Moroccan Islamism, notably to the ideas of Abdessalam Yassine. He also writes frequently for the MUR daily, *Al-tajdid*. He has thus demonstrated a certain political independence and has remained rather eclectic in his political choices.

After a traditional education at the Qarawiyyin, he became a professor at the Faculty of Letters of Rabat. He has always been an advocate of the reform of education to favor Arabization and Islamization. This is the reason for his resignation in 1958 from the PDI—in opposition to its "drive to secularization"—and then in 1962 from his position as "co-director of Islamic and independent education" in the Ministry of Education.[11] His signing of the fatwa of September 2001 shows how a scholar educated in traditional institutions of religious learning, who defines himself via family heritage as holding a certain distance from the monarchy, can find himself, in building an alliance with 'ulama of a new kind, in a posture opposing the regime.

His nephew, Hasan al-Kattani, from a much younger and more impatient generation, was also a signatory of the fatwa. Unlike his uncle, he did not come out of the Moroccan religious educational system. His education was more secular, but he also received religious education in the Arab Gulf. Whereas his uncle wears a suit and tie, Hasan al-Kattani wears a long white robe and a white turban. He calls himself a "Salafist," "with no reference to any particular school of law," and believes that the signatories are among "the greatest 'ulama of Morocco."[12]

Against America, against Official Islam

The fatwa, which emphasizes the duty of the "community of 'ulama" "to command good and pursue evil," opens directly with the September 11 attacks. The authors anticipate a scenario similar to the one that took place during the first Gulf crisis: the sending of Moroccan, and more generally Muslim, troops to Muslim territories to defend American interests. The heart of the political argument is contained in the following: "Entering [into] an alliance with America would amount to asking for help from an infidel against a Muslim. Still more heinous, it would aid an infidel against a Muslim."

The text is based on a series of verses from the Qur'an, hadiths, and fatwas of Moroccan Maliki jurists. But none of these sources is placed in its historical context. The verses are not "interpreted" by means of commentary but are assumed to speak for themselves. Every assertion is illustrated and justified by one or more verses from the Qur'an, quoted one after the other, as in this example: "You who believe, do not establish protective relations with Jews or Christians. Let them do that among themselves. Whoever among you establishes ties with them will be one of them."[13] The prohibition is then applied to Morocco:

> Morocco is not permitted—as a people or a government—to join the alliance the United States of America has called for against terrorism, the particular meaning of which is tied to two criteria. No alliance with the purpose of oppos-

ing a Muslim community or a Muslim state is permitted. Entry into such an alliance is not only a great sin (*kabira*), but an apostasy (*ridda*) and an impiety (*kufr*), as the Qur'an, the Sunna, and the community of our 'ulama all say.

Later, the fatwa refers to the ceremony held in the cathedral in Rabat on September 16, 2001:

> We declare that every Muslim is forbidden to pray in a Christian church or a Jewish temple, according to Christian or Jewish religious rites, that that is among the greatest of mortal sins and an insult to the most important sacred beliefs of Morocco, which is an Islamic state by virtue of the text of the Constitution itself and by virtue of its actual history for more than thirteen centuries. We invite Moroccans and Muslims in general—governments and peoples—to be aware of the intentions of the colonizers against Islam and against Muslims.[14]

The fatwa thus opposes the statements made during the ecumenical ceremony, while offering condolences to the victims' families.[15]

The signatories were thereby expressing their desire for independence from the Islam institutionalized in the Ministry of Religious Affairs:

> We condemn and we disapprove the distortion practiced by the Ministry of Religious Affairs on religious texts as well as the falsification of the Friday political sermon, which preachers in the mosques of Morocco were forced to deliver on Friday, September 14, 2001, on the occasion of the events that took place in America. This is an operation that contradicts the freedom of imams and preachers in mosques and a transformation of the word of the omni-potent God and His Prophet, may God grant him His blessing.

Islam is thus represented as a religion and an identity under siege. The text juxtaposes two enemy lines: that of America and its allies conducting a war against Islam and that of the Ministry of Religious Affairs imposing a single "truncated" reading of the religion on those under its rule. This dual critique is not new for Driss al-Kattani who, during the First Gulf War, and along with other Moroccan 'ulama, had criticized in the same terms the Arab-American alliance against Iraq.[16]

Published ten years apart, the two texts set out the same notion of a clash of civilizations, replicating the lines opposing Islam and Judeo-Christian culture over the long term. Driss al-Kattani starts from the symbolic legacy of his father to establish the historical continuity of his anti-imperialist rhetoric. In particular, he echoes the admonition published by his father in 1908 in Madina, where he had gone into exile. Muhammad Ibn Ja'far al-Kattani, taking up the theme of the weakness of Morocco, where the foreign presence had begun to impose a sovereignty in competition with that of the sultan and more important in competition with Islam, there expressed his "personal distress" at considering again the question of the legitimacy of entering into relations with unbelievers.[17] In his view, "it [was] forbidden to be alone with them, to accompany them, to sit or travel with them, to visit them, to cultivate their friendship, to approve their way of life, to imitate them, to envy them, to admire them, to consult them, to appoint them to responsible positions."[18] For 'ulama such as Muhammad Ibn Ja'far al-Kattani at the time, the issue was to come back to divine law, to the *shar'* (norm) threatened from within and without, by using the language available to the men of his culture and his time.[19]

Nearly a century later, for Driss al-Kattani, one of the authors of the September 2001 fatwa, which quotes the 1908 *nasiha*, the enemy is defined as "crusaders and Zionists," not because they are Christians or Jews, but, he says, because their aim has always been to attack Islam, a view derived from some verses of the Qur'an. The current forms of the conflict are described as Israeli occupation of Palestinian territory and American presence in the Gulf since 1991. Similarly, moving from global to local conflict between Islam and its enemies, the ecumenical ceremony is seen as an element of the "anti-

Islamic" machinery put in place by the Ministry of Religious Affairs.

The enemy is thus localized and defined in terms of the defensive position of Islam: he is eternal, and his identity is crystallized in the religious status of the "other" in combination with the victimization of the self as a member of the suffering Islamic *umma*. The enemy is external (the non-Muslim West) and internal (the Ministry of Religious Affairs, which wants to impose its control on Islam, and the Westernized segments of Moroccan society). Distant suffering (of the Palestinians and the Iraqis, for example) is thus experienced indirectly, but it echoes the suffering of an Islam re-colonized by Western influence and state control. The religious construction of the world, divided between Islam and its enemies, lies at the root of external and internal political conflicts. Both Driss and Hasan al-Kattani, though using different terms, end up with a form of Salafism that is characterized by a feeling of xenophobia and an insistence on jihad in the context of a defensive war. The elements making up the dichotomy between self and other are not markedly novel and are not necessarily articulated from an opposition stance: in May 1970, *Da'wat al-haqq*, a journal published by the Ministry of Religious Affairs, printed an article by Driss al-Kattani entitled "The Islam of the Fourteenth Century [of the Hegira] Is the Islam of the First Century," in which he was already mentioning the threefold alliance of "colonization," "Zionism," and the "crusaders," against which Islam had to enter into battle.[20] The definition of the enemy had thus long been stored up, and in a semi-official manner, within state institutions.

The Domestication of the Religious Competition

The fatwa had thus not been published in direct opposition to the monarchy, but rather in a spirit of virulent opposition to official religious institutions. It was not so much the anti-American language—which became commonplace in the Arab world in the 1990s—that struck readers of the fatwa as it was the condemnation of the ecumenical ceremony and the attendance of the secretary-general of the Council of 'Ulama and the Minister of Religious Affairs. Driss al-

Kattani later clarified matters, qualifying his anti-American position: "We have always made a distinction between the requirements of conducting the public business and the strictly religious realm. Morocco must maintain good relations with the United States, particularly at a time when the Sahara affair is going through a crucial phase. The prime minister represents the government, and he can participate in the ceremony in that capacity. The problem is that he was not the only one who attended. Al-Mdaghri al-'Alawi compelled the chairman of the Council of 'Ulama to attend, and even worse, to speak in favor of the Americans. This is more than a heresy."[21] The text of the fatwa defines the Moroccan state itself as an "Islamic state." The repertoire of opposition to the West is the basis for the posture of opposition to the institutions of state control over the religious authorities, which Kattani's response is careful not to associate directly with the Council of 'Ulama and thus with the king.

The fatwa published by the 'ulama was thus both cautious in its stance toward the monarchy and very critical of the role of the Ministry of Religious Affairs and its monopoly of religious discourse by means of its control of Friday sermons. The use of the term *kufr*, a very serious accusation in Islamic jurisprudence, made the fatwa a potentially incendiary document. But the regime managed to extinguish it.[22] The government summoned and rebuked the signatories, who had to issue a retraction. At the same time it launched a campaign denying their legitimacy as 'ulama and initiated, perhaps unintentionally, a debate that became public on the definition of the status of the 'ulama. This strategy enabled it to increase the already significant fragmentation of the religious sphere by dividing the authors of the fatwa between those who agreed to withdraw their signature and those who refused to do so.

The task was relatively easy for the government because Islamists as a whole had not really agreed with the entire content of the fatwa. The criticism of the "double standard" of American foreign policy was generally shared by Islamists as well as most figures on the political scene. But the criticism of the ecumenical ceremony was not echoed along the entire spectrum of Islamist groups. A large number of them cautiously and discreetly criticized in particular the accusations of *kufr*. Justice and Benevolence published its own communiqué about the September 11 attacks, with no commentary on the September 16 ceremony, although it published the fatwa on its website. Sheikh Yassine, who spoke a week after September 11, condemned the attacks, but he also directly connected them to the Israeli-Palestinian conflict: "We are against violence from whatever source, and we recall the injustice of Israel to the Palestinian people. We have to reflect on the causes of this violence."[23] The PJD, whose leader 'Abd al-Karim Khatib chose to participate in the September 16 ecumenical ceremony, expressed an opinion very similar to that of Justice and Benevolence.[24] Moroccan Islamism as a whole thus put more emphasis on the principle of nonviolence than on the "mistakes" of American foreign policy, but it also pointed to the dangers of blind reprisal against Muslim countries.

While some 'ulama emerged onto the political stage in the winter of 2001, thanks to this crisis, they came out of it in a weakened condition. The regime's response had divided them, by muddying the definition of the status of the *'alim* and of his role as spiritual intermediary and interpreter in the public realm of religious texts. The political aspect of the confrontation defused the possibility of any public debate on ways of reading the sacred texts. Religious discourse served as the underlying basis for the political criticism of state practices, but at the same time, once the debate had become public, it was expressed in essentially political terms, at the expense of any theological content. Hence, discussion of religious texts was no longer a focus of attention: religious language was used as such, circulated, quoted by all sides, and entered into the political realm with no debate on its interpretations. The sacred texts were in fact used by all parties as a vehicle for political debate rather than being the subject of debate. At the same time, the monarchy's resolution of the conflict created and maintained a general consensus around condemnation of the September 11 attacks and an explicit and unanimous critique of American foreign policy. The monarchy itself did not respond on the issue the fatwa raised regarding the dichotomy opposing Islam to the

West. Rather than entering into theological and political debates on the question, which would have been troubling in view of its alliance with the United States, the monarchy dealt with the issue through institutional regulation, by denying any status to the authors of the fatwa.

The Emergence of a New Type of Religious Cleric

The makeup of the group of signatories also provides information about the emergence of a new type of religious cleric, those who lay claim to the status of 'ulama. Eleven of them were preachers, three were graduates of Dar al-Hadith, and two were members of 'ulama councils.[25] Individuals with varying allegiances, some had connections to the Makhzen, while others came from the diverse Moroccan networks of religious education that had links to institutions for Islamic education in the Middle East. Their association had always been headed for fragmentation, and they intervened according to the occasion. They could on the other hand serve as ideological transmission mechanisms for collectively organized political or religious networks.

These 'ulama have not all been educated in the same way, but they are not autodidacts in religion. While the establishment does not regard them as having the caliber of Kannun or Mukhtar al-Susi, they are nevertheless in constant contact with the sacred texts, which they use for preaching to the masses. They are the product of the Arabization of the elites, which by the 1970s had become the hasty and disorganized basis for training the younger generation.

But the new religious clerics are not defined solely by the fundamentalist ideology of the new *Salafiyya*, which, though very prominent because of press coverage, still holds sway among only a small active minority. It is possible also to detect the rise of a new generation of "professionals" of religion, which is not necessarily in step with this *Salafiyya*, but which presents itself as a corporate body that has its interests to defend and might sometimes enter discussions with political movements based on Islam. This appears, for example, in the demands of alumni of Dar al-Hadith al-Hassaniyya, some of whom follow the teachings of Sheikh Yassine and some of whom have joined the ranks of the PJD. A large number of them are now unemployed and in a state of latent conflict with the administration, which has led to clashes with the police.[26] Like other Moroccan graduates, they demonstrated in June 2002 outside the Parliament in Rabat to protest against the lack of employment opportunities for these new specialists in the Hadith.

Unemployment began to affect them in the mid-1990s, and the slogans they repeated in unison on the main artery in the center of the capital claimed that they would rather die than not get a job.[27] Those who had found work were, they said, "children of notables. . . . And yet the *Mudawwana* is still in conformity with Maliki law. We can certainly deal with that."[28] They also complained of not being able to freely exercise a profession of *da'wa*: "It's socialism," one of them told me, denouncing the neglect by the socialist government of religious education. Their demands are eclectic, but at the heart of the problem lies the pressing question of religious courses of study, a career path that has become increasingly proletarianized since the early years of independence.

Religious Education in Crisis

At the headquarters of the Office of Original Education in Rabat, whose shabby offices indicate the lack of resources provided for religious education at the primary and secondary levels, there are complaints about this lack of concern. The small number of students (17,900 in 1970,[29] shrinking to 17,400 in 1990[30] and 15,293 in 1998-99[31]) did not make it possible to really raise the level of instruction. There are about thirty schools in all Morocco; thus, not all of the sixty-eight provinces contain one. Students following traditional education have often been rejected by the modern public education system. Primary school students—often older than the norm—are small in number because of the lack of scholarships, which are provided only to secondary students. "That has had a negative influence," I was told at the head office for traditional education. "We are forced to lower standards. Even some officials in the Ministry of Education have contempt for traditional education or don't even know anything about it."[32]

Traditional education is thus facing numerous difficulties. Its legitimacy is not established, and it is lacking in material and intellectual resources. Moreover, the teachers, often badly trained, do not have enough textbooks. Secular subjects hold a secondary position within the curriculum. Teachers would like to reinforce secular subjects in combination with religious ones, in order to make this type of education more relevant to the modern world. They often take as a model the religious institutes of al-Azhar in Egypt, which have proliferated since the 1970s, offer hybrid courses of study combining secular and religious subjects, and have prepared students for study at the great religious university of al-Azhar.[33] They disregard all the faults of the Egyptian system, and by idealizing it they forget that Moroccan religious education faces the same problems as religious education in the rest of the Muslim world: whereas earlier in the century religious training was offered only to a small elite, the competition of "modern" institutions of learning, the opening of the doors of higher education to the wider population, and the increased demand for education have changed both its form and content.

In the late 1990s, more than one thousand diplomas were awarded each year by university departments of Islamic studies. Where were the graduates to be employed? What was to be done with this mass of religious specialists? Echoing many heads of religious institutes in Egypt, one of the representatives of traditional education in Rabat complains: "In the 1970s students were admitted who didn't know the Qur'an by heart!" And yet, 80 percent of early education, particularly in rural areas, was provided by the *msids*, the Qur'anic schools.[34] In the villages, many families tried to create their own system of Qur'anic education, but response to the demand was absent or very rudimentary, both in content and in material means.

The Qarawiyyin University also felt neglected. In the early 1970s, the Qarawiyyin faculties contained a little fewer than one thousand students. These numbers subsequently increased greatly: in the early 1980s there were about five thousand, and a little more than seven thousand ten years later. Twenty percent of them were female, a percentage that has also continued to increase over the years (women have been admitted to the Qarawiyyin since 1948, and classes are coeducational).[35] A decree in 1980 restored graduate education to the Qarawiyyin; in practice, it was not introduced into the Shari'a Faculty in Fez until the fall of 1987, and into the Faculty of Theology in Tetouan and the Faculty of Shari'a in Agadir until 1990. The largest number of students were in the Shari'a Faculty (about four thousand), and they were future magistrates, judges, and notaries. But fewer and fewer of the teachers were Qarawiyyin graduates, and more and more of them were former students from Dar al-Hadith, from departments of Islamic studies, or from faculties of law. Separated from other faculties, all of which had been geographically dispersed to avoid organized unrest—a "plot" in the view of some 'ulama—the Shari'a Faculty is situated a few kilometers from Fez, on the road to Sefrou, in an anonymous building, distant from the old city and from the ancient Qarawiyyin mosque, and difficult to reach by public transportation.

The new generations could no longer boast about a genealogy identified in the traditional way through family association with the Qarawiyyin. "The Qarawiyyin is now nothing but a name without much meaning," was the resigned comment of one teacher. The generation that graduated from the Qarawiyyin in the period around independence is now teaching there or elsewhere. Its members have become officials in the Education Ministry (inspectors, professors) and are close to retirement. They complain of the very modest backgrounds of their students in the Qarawiyyin, who are often from rural families: "They are no longer from Fez. They come from the south and the mountains."

"Books given out by the teachers are the same as they were fifty years ago . . . those in charge of religious education are too conservative," I was told by another 'alim educated at the Qarawiyyin in the 1950s and now an inspector for the Ministry of Education.[36]

> After independence, Islam ought to have become the very foundation of the country. But it came in second place. When independence came, personal interests took priority. The 'ulama therefore stepped back, and that period's generation was taken over by careerism. . . . Those who spoke French were the ones who got the best jobs. After independence [this teaching] went to sleep. The authorities thought it was dangerous. They therefore claimed they were "revitalizing" Islamic education. But all they did was create what we have now. . . . Among our students there are no longer any people from Fez. . . . Before, one went to the Qarawiyyin for religion, not for worldly interests. Today it's different, everyone wants to become a government employee. No one comes from the cities.[37]

The Qarawiyyin has thus become largely proletarian and rural: it has become a receptacle for rural students arriving in the city looking to higher education in religion as a path to social mobility. While this worked up to the 1960s, that path is now blocked, because it has long ceased being a place where the elite are trained. Modern faculties and, even better, study abroad have become the means for training and reproducing young elites, who may then attain positions of responsibility. For those who cannot follow that course, religious education is a way out. Dar al-Hadith was set up as a more prestigious training network, but it has not avoided the same pattern of unemployed graduates.

At the present time, Islamist ideologies are no longer necessarily transmitted by "*autodidacts* in religion," as they were earlier in their development, in the 1970s, but by agents who have institutionalized and legitimated themselves informally as "religious authorities," through official and state training networks. This training is then exploited in a public forum, whether by leaders of the PJD or by "free" preachers. As in Egypt, they may be called "peripheral 'ulama,"[38] and their authority may become important outside official Islam, even though they are sometimes connected to it.

Locations for the transmission of knowledge have thereby moved away from the control of political authorities, for whom it has become increasingly difficult to co-opt graduates in religion who might support an "official" Islam. The regime's fragmentation and neglect of networks of religious education have facilitated the proliferation of independent religious authorities. For many long years, the institution of the commander of the faithful had more or less accommodated itself to the situation; it had participated in a privileged way in these discussions by defining itself as the ultimate religious authority. For this reason, the commander of the faithful seemed to be protecting society from the violence that had stricken other Muslim countries, in particular neighboring Algeria. This is what changed suddenly on May 16, 2003.

CHAPTER 10

Redefining the Institution of the Commander of the Faithful

Around ten o'clock at night on May 16, 2003, in Casablanca, five suicide bomb attacks were launched simultaneously against a square in the old city, the Hotel Farah, the Casa d'España, a Jewish community center, and a restaurant. This event inflicted significant trauma on Moroccans: the carnage killed forty-five people and injured many more, most of them Moroccan citizens. The targets were not locations representing the state but rather foreign or non-Muslim Moroccan communities. Normally, Moroccans, foreign residents, and tourists would all frequent the Hotel Farah and the Casa d'España, where alcohol was served. The attackers intended to strike a symbol of Spain, at the time allied with the United States in the war in Iraq, and the small Moroccan Jewish community.

The May 16 attacks radically changed the political situation in Morocco. The kingdom lost its image as a haven of peace protected from Islamist violence by the existence of the institution of the commander of the faithful. This was the first time that terrorist attacks of such magnitude had struck the kingdom. Moreover, the utilization of suicide attacks and the absence of any demands or explanations by the perpetrators of the attacks made the event even more tragic and its reasons more obscure in Moroccan public opinion. A few months earlier, when the occupation of Iraq by American forces was in preparation, Osama bin Laden, in a statement broadcast on al-Jazeera on February 12, 2003, had described Morocco as one of the countries ready to be "liberated from the slavery of these ruling, apostate, unjust regimes who are enslaved by America."[1]

Had a movement organized under the authority of al-Qaeda carried out those instructions? Less than one year later, on March 11, 2004, three days before the Spanish legislative elections, another set of simultaneous bomb attacks struck morning commuter trains arriving in Madrid, killing 191 and wounding nearly 1,400. The ensuing elections brought to power a government that had promised to withdraw Spanish troops from Iraq. Attention turned again to the Moroccan trail. The press pointed out that Moroccan militants were overrepresented in the world of the jihadis: had Morocco become one of the rear bases of the al-Qaeda network? And why had Morocco itself become a target of armed jihad?

Three years later, in 2007, with the United States bogged down in the Iraq war and the American army the target of countless suicide attacks, new assaults were perpetrated in North Africa, particularly in Morocco. On March 11, 2007, a man blew himself up in an internet café in Casablanca. On April 10, 2007, in the Casablanca neighborhood of Hay al-Farah, two young men were flushed out and pursued by the police and blew themselves up. On April 14, 2007, more suicide attacks were carried out by two other young men not far from the American consulate and language center in Casablanca. In these latter incidents, the explosions missed their presumed targets, but seven people were killed, including the attackers, and several people were wounded. These new attacks echoed those that took place in Algeria in the spring of 2007—although those attacks had been directed against state institutions—and indicated that the ambitions of the radical Algerian network, the Salafist Group for Preaching and Combat (GSPC), had probably become regional: on September 11, 2006, the GSPC had officially become the representative of al-Qaeda in North Africa, an alliance announced in a videotaped message by

Ayman al-Zawahiri, second in command to bin Laden in al-Qaeda. The GSPC became "al-Qaeda in the Islamic Maghreb," bringing along in its wake the Moroccan Islamic Combat Group (GICM), with which, according to Moroccan police statements, it seems to have allied in the summer of 2006.[2]

Most of the information about these attacks has come from the security services and police forces of Morocco and Spain and of countries cooperating with them in the fight against terrorism, and it is therefore by definition difficult to verify. Waves of arrests in Morocco and Europe produced fragmentary and sometimes contradictory news reports on the identity of those involved and their backgrounds. This information cannot help reconstruct the personal motives of the perpetrators of the suicide attacks or offer a detailed map of the geopolitics of jihad in North Africa, two endeavors that are not the object of this chapter. I am interested, on the other hand, in the reactions of Moroccan public opinion as revealed in the media and in the language used by political actors. It is possible, on the basis of those sources, to understand how Moroccan public opinion and the political class represented and explained the attacks, in particular this new means of action, the suicide attack, which was used for the first time in independent Morocco on May 16, 2003. The language that the Moroccan media and political actors, including the state, used to describe the perpetrators of the attacks and to build an account of these events is crucial to understanding the transformation of the political and religious spheres after this traumatic moment of violence. Indeed, the explanations and hypotheses articulated about the causes of May 16, 2003, determined and legitimated in part the ways in which the state authorities reacted to the attacks.

Undoubtedly because the king suddenly became aware of the danger to his regime and also saw a new political opportunity, the May 16, 2003, attacks led to an immediate, though temporary, contraction of the sphere of circulation of religious ideas in the political realm. New oversight of the religious sphere by the Ministry of the Interior was accompanied by an attempt—difficult to implement, it should be pointed out, as long as the political sphere remained open to pluralism—to reassert control over the management of Islam by the monarchy through an appropriate bureaucratic mechanism. In the days following the attacks, Muhammad VI also attempted to solidify his status as commander of the faithful. For the monarchy, the question of methods of regulating Islam had become pressing: Who should be allowed to speak in the name of religion? How should religious speech be recognized and authorized? How should it be mobilized? How could religious voices who would speak up legitimately against violence be strengthened? Indeed, the media and a large segment of the political class perceived violence as having a direct religious basis: for them, it was engendered by an erroneous interpretation of Islam that was rooted in the convergence of foreign Islamist influences with the social and economic failing of Morocco. The Moroccan state did not have a great religious institution at its disposal, such as Egypt's al-Azhar, to counter this interpretation and play a mediating role between the state and the radical movements.[3] Neither did Morocco have an official mufti to whom the regime could offer a platform. Instead, it faced a sphere that had been fragmented by a long history of compromises, betrayals, and exploitation by both royal power and the 'ulama. For this reason—to remedy this fragmentation—the Palace's effort to resume monopolistic control over Islam under the aegis of the Ministry of Religious Affairs intensified after May 16, 2003. To confront a transnational radical Islamism and the violence that threatened the foundations of the nation as led by the commander of the faithful, the monarchy, which made use of a rhetoric of religious authenticity, also had to relocate and re-center Islam inside its national frontiers and within a strictly Moroccan Islamic tradition.

Explaining Jihadi Violence: The al-Qaeda Hypothesis

After the American intervention in Afghanistan in October 2001, al-Qaeda did in fact splinter into fragments that could at once claim adherence to the group while having no relationship with it. The pattern now ruling the constitution and development of jihadi terrorism is one of mobile transnational networks, which are more and more loosely connected and autonomous. They are made up of groups whose precise scale of action is not known, and who are not necessarily organized in a rigid way. These flexibly organized groups may follow orders from outside or be independent; they may easily change or develop apart from a command center like that of al-Qaeda, although remaining inspired by it and adopting its label.

The reaction of the Moroccan authorities to the attacks of May 16, 2003, was comparable to that of Western democracies in the face of terrorism: many analysts—including those in the political elite—used the label of al-Qaeda to identify the local perpetrators of the Casablanca attacks. On May 28, 2003, parliament passed a new anti-terrorist law increasing the length of detention for terrorist suspects, restricting access of the accused to lawyers during detention, and widening application of the death penalty. Photographs of suspects were displayed in public, and the press made hay out of the danger posed by radical Islamism. By the end of 2004, more than two thousand people had been apprehended, fifteen hundred of whom were officially arrested, some brought to trial, others held incommunicado.[4] Already by the end of 2003, several hundred people had been sentenced to terms ranging from a few months to thirty years in prison, and sixteen of the accused had been sentenced to death. The media in both Europe and Morocco seldom reported or discussed these repressive policies.

The Moroccan press mentioned several kinds of actors and linked them to one another in an effort to explain the attacks. There were first of all those who launched the attacks, the twelve young men from the Sidi Moumen slum, which spreads over ten square kilometers on the outskirts of Casablanca, where reporters from around the world ventured in search of information about the members of the suicide commando. There followed the transnational ramifications of the "Moroccan branch" of al-Qaeda: the Moroccan Islamic Combat Group (GICM) was said to have recruited locally the perpetrators of the suicide attacks. Then there were the scattered figures of "Salafi jihadi" Islamism who proclaimed themselves preachers and 'ulama, and who were also thought to be broadly influenced by "Wahhabi" ideologies, and in turn to have ideologically influenced the young men of Sidi Moumen. Socioeconomic factors such as economic poverty and social misery, as well as ideological factors, that is, radical Islam and foreign religious influences—bundled by the media and the public authorities under the labels of "*Salafiyya* jihadiyya" and "Wahhabism"—were the major factors marshaled to explain Islamist violence.

The Sidi Moumen Powder Keg: The Local Trail

After May 16, 2003, Moroccans discovered with stupefaction that twelve of their compatriots, aged around twenty, most of whom died in the bombings, had launched those bloody attacks and had left behind no explanation for their deed.[5] They also learned that these men almost all came from the slum neighborhoods of Sidi Moumen. No direct link with al-Qaeda, or a period of training in Afghanistan or Pakistan, could explicitly be established. Their level of education varied, but those who were not unemployed generally worked at low-level jobs—barbers, street sellers, sometimes factory workers—and some of them had thought of risking clandestine immigration to Spain. The press described their neighborhood environment at length: the area was densely populated, public services were nonexistent, streets were unpaved, there were no sewers, and huts built from pieces of scrap metal were stacked up in between open garbage dumps.[6] Running water in these improvised dwellings was rare, and public fountains were often dry. Children infrequently attended school. Overcrowding, drug trafficking, and criminality turned daily life into hell. The perpetrators of the May 16, 2003, suicide attacks thus came from the city outskirts, slums where social bonds had been stretched and the sense of community shattered.

The Moroccan media published many investigations and reports underlining that this socioeconomic context contributed to these young men's participation in sectarian groups and terrorist acts. For example, the tiny group "Straight Path" (*al-sirat al-mustaqim*) recruited its members around a leader and then launched a program of "purification" of public conduct through violence. Its members, articles in the press pointed out, combined surveillance and religious policing of neighborhoods with sordid crimes. The young Zakaria Miloudi, for example, was said to have stood at the head of Straight Path; born in 1970, the son of an itinerant peddler, he became a carpenter after dropping out of school at fifteen.[7] According to the press, having briefly been a member of the PJD, he was said to have later begun to hold radical views. He set himself up as a preacher, casting the Moroccan state and society as a whole into the realm of impiety. Creating a veritable sect that isolated itself from "impious" society, Miloudi prohibited his disciples from dealing with the state, not even allowing them to accept administrative documents delivered by the Makhzen authorities. It was reported that to these proscriptions was gradually added direct harassment and assassination of inhabitants of the slums who did not conform to Islamic morals as reinterpreted by the young Zakaria. Reports on this kind of sect proliferated in the press, but while they drew an implicit parallel between Islamist sectarian movements and the suicide attacks, they never explicitly established links between the two.

The Moroccan Islamic Combat Group: A Branch of al-Qaeda?

The Moroccan Islamic Combat Group (GICM) was accused of having organized the attacks. This group, which was set up in the late 1990s, was still known as the "Moroccan Afghans," because it was made up of militants who had returned from the Afghan jihad against the Soviet Union. Classified as a terrorist organization by the U.S. State Department in 2002, it was thought to be an al-Qaeda franchise. At first, the GICM regarded Morocco as a rear base for the activity of al-Qaeda and handled subsidiary tasks, such as logistical support for members of the "base" (al-Qaeda, in Arabic) passing through Morocco. But after September 11, 2001, and the confirmation of Morocco's cooperation with the United States, the GICM decided to strike in Casablanca to exact a price for this alliance.[8] The Palestinian Abu Qatada (now in jail in England) delivered a fatwa apparently to that effect.[9] From a mere rear base, Morocco, it was said, had become both a place to recruit radical militants to serve al-Qaeda on its various front lines and a target for armed jihad.[10]

Relying on the Factor of Saudi Influence

In the aftermath of the attacks, the press also expatiated copiously on Saudi influence in Moroccan religious representations, an influence backed up by the close alliance between the monarchy of Hassan II—whose envoys Ahmad Ibn Suda and 'Abd al-Hadi Bu Talib had been held in profound esteem in Saudi Arabia—and the Al-Sa'ud family. It was also pointed out that, since the 1970s, as in the rest of North Africa and the Muslim world, Wahhabism and its manifestations—thanks to the oil wealth accumulated and redistributed by the Saudi rulers—had spread rapidly. The Saudi monarchy, which had become a significant oil power after 1973, had supported the Moroccan monarchy in the war for Western Sahara and had started investing in Morocco's tourist infrastructure in the 1990s.

Many newspaper articles thus emphasized the "imported" source of the ideas used by Moroccan jihadism, noting that in the 1980s, Saudi princes in their Moroccan palaces could enjoy pleasures forbidden on the soil of the cradle of Islam, substituting Morocco as a vacation spot for Egypt (excluded from the Arab League after the Camp David accords) and war-torn Lebanon. The media also pointed out that starting in 1979, when Minister of Education 'Izz al-Din al-'Araki established departments of Islamic studies in place of departments of philosophy in Moroccan universities, they were staffed by Moroccans who had studied at Saudi universities, thereby giving official sanction to the indirect influence of Wahhabi doctrine.[11] These representations in the media sometimes turned into caricatures reifying the ancient and complex trail of Wahhabism in Morocco as one homogeneous ideology of puritanism and violence: they forgot that official Wahhabi ideology was certainly not in tune with the discourse of Salafi jihadis. On the contrary, it was the debates stirred up in Saudi Arabia by the most radical critiques of the Saudi monarchy that had in turn motivated some Moroccan Islamists to criticize their own monarchy.[12] But the way in which the media presented the facts is important because it reflected the strategies the monarchy used to counter Islamist violence: indiscriminate combat against "Wahhabi influences" and centralization of the definition of Islam around a purely national tradition.

The media as a whole also mentioned a third factor, which they had sometimes pointed to before the attacks but which the regime had not until then explicitly described as a danger: the militant and ideological circles of the *Salafiyya jihadiyya*. Well before May 16, 2003, two established press organs, the liberal newspaper *al-Sahifa* [*The Newspaper*] and particularly *al-Ahdath al-Maghribiyya* [*Moroccan Events*], linked to the socialist left, had presented critical accounts of their statements and actions. This loose network with no organizational unity was reified under the name of *Salafiyya jihadiyya* and often used indiscriminately by its adversaries to designate radical Islamist circles: for instance, the rudimentary ideology of a Zakaria Miloudi or that of a preacher such as Abu Hafs of Fez. It could also encompass the radical Islamist preachers claiming an intellectual genealogy and founding their legitimacy in Moroccan or foreign networks for religious education. Their ideologies—including those of Muhammad Fizazi,[13] Hasan al-Kattani, and ʿAbd al-Bari Zamzami— were represented by the press as the real source of violence.

The state elite and a large portion of the media thus explained the suicide attacks by focusing on three kinds of actors. First was the one dubbed al-Qaeda, the foreign actor at the source of the violence, who recruited local agents through its local franchise, the GICM. Second was the ideological intermediary–the *Salafiyya* and the *Salafiyya jihadiyya*—who linked al-Qaeda and the agents of violence by disseminating the repertoire of the religious war initiated by the "enemies of Islam." Some members of the press also included in this loose ideological grouping preachers connected to the Islamists of the PJD and the MUR, who had more or less implicitly constructed an ideology of victimization and confrontation by describing a radical split between Islam and the West. Third were the perpetrators of the attacks, young victims of underdevelopment and radical ideological influences, domestic or foreign. They articulated no political strategy or political discourse for the public. Through the act of violence and their own self-destruction, they kept their silence to the end, maintaining the mystery of their actions, especially because the ties officially linking the three forces remained obscure and difficult to demonstrate.

As for the monarchy, it reacted to the attacks with actions that called on a mixture of strongly asserted strategies and discourses: repression, the trial and imprisonment of many Salafists such as Muhammad Fizazi and Hasan al-Kattani, institutional changes in the apparatus for the control of Islam, and the reorganization of state-produced religious repertoires intended to respond to and prevent violence. The state fixed the definition of Islam against any domestic or foreign attempt to redefine it, and distinguished its content from the repertoires used by the Islamists, particularly by ignoring the question of Moroccan foreign policy and by developing a theology of political obedience to the sovereign.

Oversee, Liberate, or Reform Islam? The Monarchy's Religious Dilemma

The May 16, 2003, attacks deeply troubled all elements of the Moroccan political class, who condemned the attacks with one voice. Morocco was now confronted with one of the evils experienced by many countries, and the time had come to assess responsibilities. On May 25, the great march against terrorism in Casablanca, authorized by the government, did not include representatives of the PJD, whom the Makhzen did not allow to participate "for security reasons." Slogans did not hesitate to denounce the party of legitimist Islamists, even though this blurred distinctions: "Neither justice nor development, it is the Islam of butchers!" "Justice and development, a terrorist organization!" "Out with the brothers!"[14]

Immediately after the attacks, the PJD was, in fact, stigmatized from all sides: it was said to be "morally" responsible for the attacks through the "dual language" it had always spoken, an accusation based on the two-headed structure of the pair PJD and MUR. One minister proposed to dissolve the PJD, and the first assistant secretary of the Union Socialiste des Forces Populaires (USFP, the socialist party) requested on television that the party "present apologies to the Moroccan people." A few days after the attacks, King Muhammad VI himself announced the "end of the era of permissiveness," without referring to the PJD.[15] He tied this new strategy to the question of democratization: "The construction and consolidation of democracy can only be successfully carried out under the aegis of a state made strong by the supremacy of the law."[16]

In practice, apparent democracy, which had become one of Morocco's major assets on the international stage, would have to be preserved, while the regime would at the same time attempt to work on all fronts to stand up to Islamist radicalism: reform of education and the family code, restructuring of religious institutions, reform of political parties, new urban policies aimed at cleaning up the slums. His speech from the throne on July 30, 2003, pointed to the importance of these reforms and focused particularly on the foundations of Moroccan Islam: "attachment to the *one* commander of the faithful," "openness in matters of worship," "exclusivity of the Maliki rite." It emphasized the futility of importing "rites of worship foreign to [the] tradition [of Morocco]," implicitly referring to the influence of Wahhabism. It went on:

> The commander of the faithful being the *sole religious reference* for the Moroccan nation, no party or group can set itself up as spokesman or teacher of Islam. The religious function, in fact, depends on the supreme imamship of *amir al-mu'minin*, which has devolved on Us, assisted by the Supreme Council and the regional council of 'ulama, which We firmly intend to reorganize and revitalize, as We make their operations more dynamic.[17]

More specifically, political parties could not be established "on religious, ethnic, linguistic, or regional bases." The PJD was clearly targeted here. One year later, however, in the fall of 2004, the image of the party seemed to have been normalized. Saʿd al-Din al-ʿUthmani, who had become leader of the Islamist party, announced that the PJD was prepared to enter the government if the members of his party were given a major role. In the interval, the PJD had marginalized—at least formally—its militants who were least indulgent toward the regime.

The Monarchy Seeks to Reconquer Its Religious Territory

The monarchy found in the attacks of 2003 an opportunity to announce and initiate an authoritative process of monopolization of religious authority through a redefinition of the state's methods of religious regulation. The new methods reversed the process of fragmentation that the monarchy had set in motion after independence. Among Islamists, the left, and the rest of the political spectrum, there were calls for the freedom to issue fatwas and for the ability to freely debate interpretations of religious texts.[18] But the monarchy sought to restore and recentralize its religious authority: it clearly demonstrated its refusal to function as one religious enterprise among others, or even as an actor without religious authority, a possibility that had been considered by some political actors.[19] The monarchy then had to reinvent the forms of state regulation of Islam, by redistributing it between the king's personal religious authority and a state bureaucracy more centralized than before. The modalities of regulation of religion therefore now oscillate between these two principles: the personal authority of the sovereign deployed in moments of political crisis and exception, and the bureaucratic control and definition of Islam. The reform of family law is an example of the monarch's personal reassertion of control over religion in the aftermath of the 2003 attacks.

Contested Territory: The Status of Women

Beginning in the 1990s, one subject crystallized all political and cultural differences and at the same time initiated a debate on the place of Islam in Moroccan society: the legal status of women and the family.[20] In 1992, feminist associations began openly challenging the family code, which had long been the prerogative of the 'ulama. They launched a movement asking for a reform of the family code, which, they claimed, "maintains women in the status of minors for life, of inferiority [in relation to men, particularly husbands], places them under guardianship, and deprives them of control over their children."[21] This movement for the improvement in women's legal status was not necessarily always secular in inspiration and did not always speak against Islam, but rather against what it generally saw as an erroneous interpretation of it.

MARCH 2000: ISLAMISTS AGAINST REFORM OF THE FAMILY CODE

Although Hassan II was sensitive to these demands in the early 1990s, he was confronting many political forces that he wanted to involve in the transition to democracy, in addition to economic tensions that were difficult to resolve. He therefore did not respond to these demands for reform directly. To defuse the conflict that pitted conservative 'ulama and Islamists against advocates for a radical change in the legal status of women, the king resumed total control over the question while not resolving it, paternalistically advising "his dear daughters" to patiently rely on him:

> This is a matter that is under My jurisdiction. I am the one who bears responsibility for the *Mudawwana* and its application. Refer to Me. During the referendum campaign and the ensuing election campaigns, refrain from mixing what belongs to your religion with what belongs to the temporal realm of politics. . . . Moroccan woman, address yourself to Me, write to the royal cabinet. Feminist associations, send your observations, your criticisms, your complaints,

and what seems to you to harm women and their future to the king of Morocco, who as commander of the faithful has the competence to apply and interpret the last verse revealed to the Prophet, blessed be his name: "Today, I have made your religion perfect. I have made My grace on you complete." I know the constants of religion as I know where the effort of interpretation [*ijtihad*] may intervene in religion.[22]

Hassan II had thus closed the debate by bringing the question explicitly back to his personal monopoly over the interpretation of religious texts and to an individualized and paternal relationship, hence one of authority, which he wished to build with Moroccan women. But once Muhammad VI came to power, the debate resumed, especially because the young king was not insensitive to the problems posed by the condition of Moroccan women. The *bay'a* of 1999 contained the signature of a woman. He had, it was said, freed the women from his father's harem, who had long been cloistered in the palace. And in contrast to the portrait of his mother, the image of the king's young wife, Lella Selma, whom he married in July 2002, was in public circulation. With a change in election law, the 2002 legislative elections made it possible for thirty-five women to enter the previously all-male parliament.

Earlier in 1999, Zoulikha Nasri, appointed first woman adviser to the king, and Saïd Sadi, Secretary of State for Social Security, Children, and the Family, had drawn up a reform program that was intended to emancipate Moroccan women from their legal status as minors and was supported by the socialist government of Abderrahman Youssoufi. But in March 2000, Islamists of all varieties, notably militants of the PJD and Justice and Benevolence, demonstrated their strength with a large march organized in Casablanca. The march was impressive: men and women marched in their thousands in two separate files. They had no intention of placing themselves in the hands of the king and his religious authority. The march was designed to show the king the power of the Islamists to mobilize the masses. Many 'ulama had joined the movement, and the League of 'Ulama and the Minister of Religious Affairs published communiqués against the reform, which the PJD distributed.[23] Supporters of the reform also demonstrated in Rabat, but they were much smaller in number. The Islamist forces were thus not ready to leave the reform of the status of women in the hands of the regime and those that they considered its representatives, "minions of the secularized West," as well as their "foreign bosses," the IMF and the World Bank.

Supporters of the reform did not, however, define their proposal in opposition to Islam. But this abrupt polarization, arising less from a deep split in society than from an exacerbation of political postures that opposed "Islamists" to "anti-Islamists," drove the regime to abandon the plan. The country seemed to be split in two. But it was possible to detect nuances in the positions adopted by Islamists. For some of them, notably Nadia Yassine in the Justice and Benevolence movement, the *Mudawwana* is not a sacred text; it can be perfected. It can be changed, but within an Islamic framework and not by referring to Western feminism. In her view, the best way to improve the family code is to study the texts of the Qur'an and the Sunna for guidance. Strategies connected to the construction of political positions—crystallized in the dichotomy between "anti-Western Islamists" and "Westernized secularists"—triumphed over legal analysis and rigidified positions on religion that were in reality much more flexible and complex than they seemed to be.[24] Although Islamists of diverse tendencies came together to march in the spring of 2000, this was primarily to publicly demonstrate the strength of political Islam in all its varieties. Moreover, not everyone in the USFP was in favor of the proposal supported by the Prime Minister, Abderrahman Youssoufi. For example, Habib Furqani, a member of the political bureau and educated at the Ibn Yusif Institute in Marrakesh, had come out very clearly against the reform.

The regime's wait-and-see position and its silence following the Islamists' demonstration of strength in the spring of 2000 were radically challenged by the May 16, 2003, attacks, which publicly put Moroccan Islamists as a whole, and particularly the PJD, on the hot seat. The moment was particularly propitious for the king to resume control, both politically and religiously, of this territory that many religious actors had appropriated.

The Religious Authority of the Commander of the Faithful: The Unexpected Reform

At the opening of the new session of parliament on October 10, 2003, Muhammad VI surprised everyone by announcing a reform of the *Mudawwana*: "Who among you would accept having his family, his wife, and his children thrown into the street or seeing his daughter or his sister mistreated?" he asked the deputies.[25] The text of the reform had been put together by a commission made up of 'ulama, jurists, and members of feminist associations. Commission debates had been tense, but the commander of the faithful took pains to present the text to the Moroccan people himself and to emphasize the fact that the proposal was rooted in the interpretation of Qur'anic texts.

The new code was innovative on many points, some of which can be enumerated here: spouses now shared responsibility for the family, previously the husband's right and duty alone. The rule of the wife's obedience to her husband was abandoned and women no longer needed a guardian's consent to marry; the minimum age for marriage was raised from fifteen to eighteen. Divorce by Repudiation was limited by the requirement that a judge authorize it. A wife could ask for divorce, and custody of the children could go to either father or mother. The right to polygamy was restricted, although not entirely prohibited. In parliament, the king supported this restriction by quoting from the Qur'an: "The All-Powerful has accompanied the possibility of polygamy with a set of severe restrictions. *If you fear you may be unjust, marry only one woman*" (Qur'an IV, 3). "But the Most High has dismissed the hypothesis of perfect equity by saying, *You cannot treat all your wives with equality even if you want to*" (Qur'an IV, 129). The monarch was thus careful to set his desire for reform in the context of an interpretation of the revealed text, and he again took control—at least for a time—of a territory that had gradually been taken over and occupied by religious competitors of substance. But only the nonreligious provisions of the code were presented for parliamentary approval: "We considered it necessary and judicious that parliament be presented, for the first time, with the proposed family code, with respect to the civil provisions that it includes, it being understood that its provisions of a religious nature come exclusively under the authority of the *amir al-mu'minin*."[26]

Challenging the religious interpretations included in the proposed law would therefore amount to criticizing the religious prerogatives of the commander of the faithful, who here resumed his role as the "first *'alim* of Morocco." This reassertion of control by the king over religious interpretation, combined with the effects of May 16, 2003, prevented the Islamists from joining in opposition to the law, which was passed by parliament in January 2004, after having been discreetly debated by the Islamists in a parliamentary committee chaired by the Minister of Religious Affairs, Ahmad Tawfiq.[27] The PJD and Justice and Benevolence publicly accepted the text of the law. Basima Haqqawi, a PJD deputy, stated: "We disagreed with the left about the reform of the family code; we asked the king to arbitrate and, in return, we accept his decisions. . . . While the new *Mudawwana* is more influenced by the demands of secular feminists, the method is not the same and the texts are set in a Muslim framework."[28]

In reality, the real battle was not over the status of women, which almost everyone recognized was unjust in current practice, but over the question of cultural codes and identity markers which would form the framework for the rules governing that status. Now, because the text of the law referred principally to Islam and notably to the Maliki school, one of the most important demands of Moroccan Islamists had evaporated. Moroccan and Arab feminists and their supporters expressed pleasure at finally seeing a reform improve the legal status of women. But, they asked, will the law, even with its imperfect provisions, be implemented? The most radical of the Islamists, for their part, contested the king's assumption of control over the definition of women's legal status.[29] The monarchy was thus unable to completely close off debate or eliminate the risks of dissension. Nevertheless, this long series of conflicts, in which state and non-state actors had participated, led to a new law, defined within the framework of shari'a, that codified a consensus that had been negotiated at length and with great difficulty between 'ulama, Islamists, and feminists, under the control of the monarchy.

A widely circulated picture showed Muhammad VI surrounded by women who had worked for the reform. It idealizes and aestheticizes the result of these long negotiations. In the center, hand on his heart, dressed in a white and gold djellaba, the king smiles. The movement of the women surrounding him, dressed in white, some with veils, has been frozen by the photographer: we see them passionately addressing the monarch, who has succeeded in capturing in the picture his individualized relationship with the women who supported the law. On November 4, 2003, a woman presented before Muhammad VI a Ramadan lesson, recalling the moment in 1993 when Hassan II had surprised everyone by allowing a female poet to speak in public at the celebration of the anniversary of the Prophet's birth in the great mosque of Casablanca.[30] Like his father, the young king knew how to profit from moments of crisis by appropriating—for a time and on a particular subject—the power of interpreting religious texts, and in this case by physically gathering women around him who were the very subjects of this new law. The 2003 attacks provided him with the opportunity because they had, at least temporarily, weakened Islamists of all stripes. They also allowed him to explicitly relate the fight against terrorism to the improvement of women's rights, implicitly collapsing together mistreatment of women, the use of political violence, and Islamism.

In tandem with this kind of personal intervention, the opportunities for which occurred rarely, Muhammad VI revised the institutional forms for the regulation of Islam. Reforms in the monarchy's ways of regulating religion began well before the 2003 attacks, but the attacks accelerated the reforms and endowed them in some sense with new legitimacy in public opinion. After the spring of 2003, the reforms were presented as a veritable break with the past, but in practice they seemed to repeat the scenario dating from the 1980s of a limited but continual resumption of control over religious authorities by the monarchy.[31]

Resumption of Control over Religious Authorities: Feminization, Control, and "Modernization"

On November 7, 2002, Ahmad Tawfiq was appointed the new Minister of Religious Affairs. A professor of history who was born in 1943, he is a specialist in the history of Morocco and a novelist. He was assistant dean of the faculty of letters of Rabat between 1976 and 1978 and director of the general library between 1995 and 2002. He holds genuine legitimacy in university circles and has a profound knowledge of the religious history of Morocco. It must be pointed out that he is a member of the Budshishiyya brotherhood, which was the first organization to which Abdessalam Yassine belonged, and which today includes many Moroccan notables in its ranks. The new minister is not an *'alim* specialized in theology or in *fiqh*, but he represents a quietist Islam experienced through Sufi spirituality and practice and approached in historical and intellectual terms. His appointment has enabled the regime to emphasize the rehabilitation of popular and mystical Islam, and his style thus differs sharply from that of al-Mdaghri, a graduate of Dar al-Hadith who has been accused of collaboration with the Salafists. The profile of the new Minister of Religious Affairs has also provided impetus to a quietist Sufi repertoire, which directly counterbalances the messianic and mystical repertoires of the opposition figure Abdessalam Yassine by relying on the brotherhood with which Yassine had broken before launching his opposition to the monarchy.

In December 2003, Ahmad Tawfiq announced a revision of the internal organization of the Ministry of Religious Affairs that seemed to point in the direction of stricter supervision of religious actors and their education and to counter the fragmentation of the religious sphere which the monarchy wished to control.[32] Two new offices were established within the Ministry: the Direction of Mosques, which would strictly supervise the construction of and activities conducted in places of worship, and the Direction of Traditional Teaching, which would supervise traditional teaching not under the authority of the Ministry of Education and would work to "bring it up to standards." A program for the renovation of mosques —in particular the construction of large mosques in the poor neighborhoods on the outskirts of large cities—was launched in 2005. That same year, Dar al-Hadith came under the control of the Ministry of Religious Affairs,[33] and Ahmad Tawfiq announced its overhaul, deploring the state of "regression" of the institution.[34] With regard to the organization of studies, he introduced an undergraduate program. Dar al-Hadith thus became a site for the transmission of religious learning that covered the entirety of the period of apprenticeship in higher education. He introduced the study of comparative religion, history, philosophy, and ancient and modern languages. It was thus not just the structure of institutions of religious education that was revised but also the content of the knowledge transmitted, which had to be reformed from top to bottom, primarily by opening it up to "otherness," that is, to the plurality of other cultures and civilizations. This reform of the content of the curriculum was intended to contradict the representation of a dichotomy between Islam and the West.

The Ministry of Religious Affairs also considered the education of imams. An educational program was to be offered to them, and they would have to be accredited by the ministry after passing an exam. Women were included and given the title *murshidat*. They were to have primarily an educational role, but a short time later, in response to some objections about the integration of women, it was specified that they could not lead prayers. The ministry also began to publish a monthly bulletin providing general guidelines for imams.

Review of the role of the 'ulama councils began in April 2004.[35] They were given broader scope and more prerogatives. The reform that had been aborted in 2000 under al-Mdaghri was finally implemented: the regional councils came under the direct authority of the king and increased in number from nineteen to thirty, containing a total of 256 members. The introduction to the decree provided that women were to be included in the councils. The Supreme Council consisted of the Minister of Religious Affairs, renowned 'ulama chosen individually by the king (not to exceed one half the members of the Council), a general secretary appointed by the king, and the chairmen of the regional councils. The Supreme Council was to oversee the religious life of citizens and, it is important to emphasize, deliver fatwas through a commission established for that purpose.

This commission was to be the only institution entitled to deliver fatwas, which, according to article 7 of the April 2004 decree, were to be defined "in general terms." The absence of the official function of mufti in Morocco and the fact that many new informal religious authorities had adopted that function had in fact made it necessary for the regime to define the scope of these informal authorities.[36] Article 9 defined the process for the preparation of fatwas, now requiring a collective *ijtihad* leading to a majority vote by the members of the commission. Requests for fatwas addressed to the general secretary of the Supreme Council could come from the king himself or, theoretically, from any citizen.

The new provisions, in general, revealed a close interconnection between the Ministry of Religious Affairs and the 'ulama councils: the minister was to prepare an annual report to the king on the work of the councils. To more clearly indicate the relationship of religious institutions to the king and the religious function of the monarchy, the League of 'Ulama became *rabita muhammadiyya,* or Muhammadian League. But institutionally, the work of defining and regulating Islam was the responsibility of the Ministry of Religious Affairs, which made efforts to become more publicly visible and reach out to the public. Its new web site offered a rich variety of institutional, legal, professional, and interpretive information.[37] The minister also wished to integrate the "Moroccan religious field" into information technology, to equip mosques with internet access and with televisions. This policy was a way of going into the field and using adequate religious programs to counter Islamist preachers. The state thereby imitated methods of dissemination employed by major Moroccan and foreign preachers (for example, 'Amr Khalid and

Qaradawi, who were very successful with young audiences), hoping to recover a public that had long ago deserted it.

The king personally announced these new provisions in a speech on April 30, 2004. The councils were to "ally religious erudition and the opening to modernity," establish close relations with young people, and "protect their faith and their thinking from the deluded and the mystifiers." Like his father twenty years earlier, he invited the 'ulama of the League to "awaken from [their] lethargy." Muhammad VI again reminded his listeners of the predominance of the Maliki school of law, a "doctrinal unity that is akin to the territorial integrity and national unity of the fatherland," thereby restoring the national frontiers of Moroccan Islam. The monarchy defined national Islam in congruence with Moroccan territory and history in order to counter the effects of "Wahhabism" and of the transnational networks of religious and political mobilization and influence. It also replaced national Islam within the cultural heritage of the country, using emotion and aesthetics in contrast to the Salafist movements, which often defined Islam as disconnected from the manifestations of local and national history and culture.

It thus came about that in Casablanca, the "mosque of all Moroccans"—"throne of God on water," whose construction under Hassan II had been financed by a tax on all Moroccans—which had often been empty since it had been built, was filled in the month of Ramadan in 2004, because the Minister of Religious Affairs had appointed there as an imam 'Umar al-Kazabri, a young chanter of the Qur'an with an international reputation. People of all social classes crowded into the mosque, because, according to a report in a French-language magazine, "'Umar's voice makes people cry, and sometimes causes them to faint. It is strong. It is beautiful and it does one good."[38] The new minister used the collective emotion aroused by this young imam to draw the faithful to an expressive and emotional Islam that contrasted with the harangues of preachers on the subjects of good and evil and the confrontation of domestic and foreign enemies. But rather than allowing circumstances and the inclinations of each individual to define the content of sermons, the Ministry of Religious

Affairs in 2006 published a thick *Manual for Imams and Preachers* which, using the rhetoric of "authenticity," "reform," and "restoration of order," defined the *daʻwa* [call to Islam] conducted by religious specialists around three terms: the Ashʻari doctrine, the Maliki juridical school, and Sufism defined in accordance with the Sunna. These terms, authorized by the commander of the faithful, as the manual explained, were to define Moroccan Islam, circumscribed within its borders and intended to reach Moroccans abroad. "No religious discourse can succeed if it is not set under the aegis of the *bayʻa*."[39]

Hence, the state became the author of a theological discourse that described in lengthy detail the meaning of the three terms it had chosen to define the national Islam. The Ashʻari doctrine was the "choice of Moroccans," because it had summarized theological positions such as the question of the creation of the Qur'an and the question of human freedom, and had been able to find a balance between "reason" and "tradition."[40] The Maliki school was defined as a "civilizational legacy," a "social culture, and a religious identity."[41] In the manual, the religiosity and the culture of Moroccans were said to be delineated by this Maliki school, which had supplied them with a quasi-natural identity: "If . . . the preacher ignores that, then he deeply contradicts the civilizational uniqueness of Moroccan society, which has been shaped through the accumulation of deep historical strata. This is the ground for the failure of his religious discourse. He then creates pockets of pathology and closed-mindedness that lead to the tearing of the Moroccan social fabric," the manual asserted, directly referring to the 2003 attacks.[42] But there was no intention of presenting the Maliki juridical school as the direct basis for the definition and application of Moroccan law. The pages detailing its most important characteristics provide a historicized representation of the school, rather than a normative and legal description. The Maliki law school is presented as a historically flexible legal method that helps legal scholars search for the "common good" and is founded on consensus, rather than as a standard for the codifying of the law once and for all.[43] This flexible definition thus enabled the religious authority directly controlled by the monarchy to define for itself a religious repertoire broad enough to permit it to negotiate and formulate, whenever necessary, the definitions that would be useful, as it had been able to do when the new *Mudawwana* was formulated in 2004.

With regard to the Sufism the manual presented, it was set out under the banner of *mahabba* [mutual love of Sufis], the stations, and the different states of the heart at the approach to the divine. The text thus emphasized Islam as spirituality and a world of feeling. Contradicting this set of repertoires defined by the Ministry of Religious Affairs as the "tradition"—in an idealized and celebrated historical continuity—would be an attack on the identity of the nation and would lead to violence, perceived as the direct result of a deviation introduced into the reading of Islam by religious authorities outside this tradition.

The imams were to respect the unity of the nation and its leaders, and to avoid touching on delicate subjects that would provoke dissension. They were to demonstrate "open-mindedness" and to approach religious matter with "simplicity." Ritual practices were also delineated in detail. The text thus fixed the definition of Islam and the rules of collective and public worship, and it associated this definition not with a transnational *umma* but rather with the identity of the Moroccan nation, with its preservation, and with the status of the commander of the faithful as the representative and the leader of the nation.

Redefining the Institution of the Commander of the Faithful

The institution of the commander of the faithful was thereby reaffirmed: its political role in defining, authorizing, and regulating Islam was indivisible. In his speech from the throne on July 30, 2004, the king asserted:

> The reform of the religious sphere must not be approached solely with a view toward harmonization with the educational and cultural realms, it also calls for a reform of the political sphere, the quintessential arena for the democratic expression of differences of opinion. For this reason, a

clear separation must be made between religion and politics, in consideration of the sacredness of the dogma transmitted by religion, which must, because of that fact, be sheltered from any discord or dissension. From this arises the necessity to shield against any exploitation of religion for political ends. Indeed, under the Moroccan constitutional monarchy, religion and politics come together only in the person of the king, the commander of the faithful. We will therefore, in conformity with the sacred mission with which We are charged, see to it that the exercise of politics takes place within bodies, institutions, and spaces that are appropriate for that purpose. We will also ensure that religious questions are treated in councils of 'ulama and other authorized bodies, and that acts of worship take place in mosques and other appropriate places of worship, with complete respect for freedom of worship, of which We are the guarantor.[44]

While the monarch sought to regain control over the management and definition of Islam through the 'ulama meeting in councils, he combined this new demand with a necessary separation between politics and religion, introducing well defined secular spaces in which Islam should have no place. Only the monarchy could bring together Islam and politics, whereas the members of civil society would have to keep them separate. The commander of the faithful thus intended to wield monopolistic control over political and religious affairs, whereas political society had to become secular and religious groups operating outside political society had to become apolitical. In the king's language, a specific mode of secularism based on the separation of religion and politics thus came to define Moroccan society, except for the monarchy itself, which was the sole actor that could unite political and religious capacities. The monarchy wished to maintain a monopoly over politics *and* religion—while at the same time exhort political actors to separate themselves from religion—in a society that it claimed to want to open to democracy. The monarch's definition of the relations between politics, monarchy, and religion fundamentally contradicted the one many 'ulama, such as 'Allal al-Fasi, 'Abd Allah Kannun, and later Raysuni called for: in their view, the only role of the "commander of the faithful" was to be at the head of a pious society, and that was the basis for the legitimacy of his title as commander. Religious definitions should be the product of knowledge and the exegetical work carried out by 'ulama, and political institutions the product of the free choice of Muslim pious citizens. For these 'ulama, albeit in different ways, these two principles meant the possibility of a convergence between a religious society and free political choice.

Today, in a context of political pluralism, it is indeed paradoxical for the monarchy to make Islam one of the bases for its political power and to prohibit others from adopting religious repertoires for political purposes. The new bureaucracy supporting the intensive work of the Minister of Religious Affairs is intent on producing an anti-radical Islam that it describes as a "tolerant" and "authentic" Islam, but at the same time it is politicizing Islam simply by defining it authoritatively in the name of the monarchy.[45] The monarchy has never ceased connecting its political sacredness with Islam in a constant and difficult effort that has become increasingly arduous with the initiation of political liberalization. The monarch, who has seen himself as the first representative, the arbiter, and the center of a public Islam, has now become one of its segments, a religious authority of some weight who is surrounded by and competing with new religious authorities. Can he allow himself to enter into competition with religious figures such as Abdessalam Yassine, the Kattanis, or others? Such a relationship could only reduce the status of the commander of the faithful. Hence, the king often keeps silent in the face of his religious competitors, and it took the eruption of violence to provoke new interventions of the king in the religious domain. This is also the reason that the institutional form of the regulation of Islam is in the process of being profoundly changed by way of a new policy concentrating regulation and control of Islam in a bureaucracy with a more solid power base. This bureaucracy has explicitly and publicly given scriptural form to the definition of state Islam, in order to deploy it in schools and mosques. And this new type of control has shifted the definition of Islam toward a bureaucracy rather than focusing it on the person of the monarch, his public piety and his genealogy. This has not prevented the king from speaking out in religious matters when necessary and when that can be effective, especially in moments of crisis. While the monarchy is not losing its religious anchorage and continues to link its political authority to Islam, it is losing, despite all its efforts, a religious centrality that it had always had difficulty establishing definitively. Its political sacredness can only suffer from this loss, unless the monarchy decides to go against the political opening that it initiated itself.

EPILOGUE

The Disenchantments of Free Choice

Currently, the monarchy is maintaining its position as the arbiter of political life in Morocco by readjusting political and religious institutional arrangements. First, while the relative liberalization of the sphere of political competition through the presence of transparent elections transforms the monarchy's modes of authority, it does not lead to a more democratic regime. Rather, it allows the monarchy to continue controlling the government and hence to stabilize the political system into a competitive authoritarian regime. Second, the redefinition of the rules of political competition has several consequences for the ways in which religious language might be allowed into or be excluded from the political arena. The monarchy's characterization of the domain of electoral competition as areligious allows the regime to contain the integrated Islamist party and to divide the Islamist landscape. The legal Islamists have to adhere to the institutional constraints outlined by the monarchy, which coerce and orient their religious discourse. And as does the Moroccan state, they continue to characterize Islam as the normative framework organizing Moroccan society.

Engineering Free Choice in a Persistently Authoritarian System

In the 1990s, Hassan II, in an effort to ensure the survival of the monarchy, initiated the transformation of the political system by introducing more pluralism and transparency in the realm of political competition. In the new century, Muhammad VI has refined this system by crafting new mechanisms for ensuring that no political party will emerge as a majority in the parliament. Today the outcome of elections is determined by a combination of the *ex-ante* manipulation of the rules of the game and the free expression of the electors' preferences. In such a system, the monarchy no longer needs to rig the elections in order to control the electoral map. In 2002, surprised by the respectable outcome for the Islamist party, the monarchy had to negotiate the results of the election with opposition forces. To avoid repeating the 2002 scenario of *ex-post* bargaining, in 2007 the administration's authoritative engineering applied gerrymandering to the 2002 proportional list system. Gerrymandering prevented the victory of the PJD, the "undesirable" party, without tarnishing the image of Morocco as a "transitional democracy." The election results were published right after the counting of votes rather than four days later, as they were in 2002 due to the post-election negotiations. This absence of *ex-post* bargaining was engineered in order to demonstrate to the Moroccan public and the international community that the regime remained neutral and did not intervene to rig the elections, and that the electoral process was becoming increasingly transparent. And if undemocratic practices were revealed and complaints—denouncing vote buying, for instance—were filed during the elections, these imperfections were the political activists' responsibility; the administration could not take the blame. Transparency was therefore a means to show that the source of political corruption was not the state, but rather the parties' elites themselves.

This new transparency was hence exploited by the regime to weaken political parties in general and the PJD—perceived as the most threatening faction of the opposition—in particular. Indeed, the possibility of a significant Islamist victory was—rightly or wrongly—anticipated by all political actors: this contingency worried both the Palace and the incumbents, because the polls predicting a PJD victory were highly publicized by the media.[1] This is why the incumbent coalition accepted the reconfiguration of electoral constituencies, which the Ministry of Interior had presented as a way of guaranteeing no overwhelming victory for the PJD. Paradoxically, enhanced transparency allowed the monarchy to better predict and thus prevent a PJD victory. The modus operandi of the September 2007 election showed, on the one hand, that the king wished to preserve both the plurality of the partisan scene and the administration's neutrality during the elections, but, on the other hand, that he wanted to remain in control of the government. Through ad hoc institutional engineering, then, the monarchy held fair elections, thus exhibiting some of the features of a "democracy," but without the risk of diminishing its own power.

Although thirty-three political parties presented candidates in the September 2007 election, Moroccan electors did not go in throngs to the ballot box. The participation rate of only 37 percent troubled the political parties as well as the monarchy, which has explicitly expressed its disappointment. This participation rate—the lowest in the history of independent Morocco—sheds light on two crucial elements: first, it reflects a general disenchantment on the part of the electors, who do not believe that elections can have an impact on their daily lives. Second, it indicates the desire of the Palace to offer Moroccans more accurate data on their level of participation, which, before the mid 1990s, was regularly inflated.[2]

In the 2007 legislative elections, the Istiqlal Party came in first with 52 seats, followed closely by the PJD, which won 46 seats, despite its winning the majority of votes.[3] The PJD was profoundly disappointed by these results, although it thus became second in the electoral race and was able to add 4 seats to its representation in parliament. The PJD leaders had predicted a doubling of their number of seats, encouraged as they were by the American International Republican Institute's poll published in 2007 that had announced 47 percent of the votes going to the PJD. Also, contrary to the elections of 2002, the PJD did not censure itself and presented candidates in 94 constituencies out of 95.[4] It exhibited strength in the cities of Tangier, Rabat, Salé, and Casablanca but was absent from Marrakesh and its region, as well as from the rural regions of the Sahara and the Rif, where electors voted for families, tribes, or notables, and therefore for patronage rather than political ideologies. Dismayed by the results, the PJD's secretary-general accused the other parties of having bought votes, a practice that has been common in Morocco. However, the PJD's disappointing gain was also due to the gerrymandering of constituencies, which increased the number of seats in rural areas—where the PJD has a weak presence in contrast to that of Istiqlal—and decreased the number of seats in the urban constituencies, where the PJD had been previously successful. The unsatisfying result might also have been the sign of the normalization of the presence of the PJD on the electoral scene and the weakening of its appeal. Like other parties, the PJD will have to work harder to mobilize its electorate, demonstrating that political ideologies referring to religion might not be enough to mobilize citizens.

Respecting the results of the election, the king appointed 'Abbas al-Fasi, leader of the Istiqlal, as prime minister. Negotiations among the political parties to form the government proved so difficult that the king had to intervene and present his own list of ministers. The Istiqlal has reaffirmed its previous alliance with the incumbent coalition (Istiqlal, USFP, Party of Progress and Socialism, and the National Rally of Independents [RNI]), in order to form the new government, although the result for the USFP was its lowest (in 2007, it became the fifth party, with thirty-eight seats, compared with its being the first in 2002, with fifty seats). Hence, the Istiqlal, rather than forming a right-wing government by allying with the PJD and relegating the left to a role of opposition, has opted for the status quo. Therefore, the PJD has decided to remain in the opposition.[5]

Hence, although partisan life is thriving during electoral moments, it is also increasingly estranged from the sphere of government and policy making, where the same parties seem to rotate. This hybrid system of authoritarian government and free elections demonstrates that elections, even when relatively free and transparent, do not necessarily produce a more liberal and free political system. This is why several political parties and groups have decided to boycott the elections and why Justice and Benevolence has always criticized the electoral system and has asked its militants to abstain from voting.

The elections now serve as democracy in performance, but this electoral theater does not mean necessarily that elections are rigged and meaningless. Rather, it means that their main function is to regularly showcase for the Moroccan and international public what the monarchy calls the "democratic" or "transitional" nature of the regime, and to make these regular elections part of "normal" and "routine" political life. Campaigns are highly visible in the public square, on television, and more particularly in the press. They are also publicized in the European media and via Arab satellite television. Such an electoral authoritarian system, combining pluralism with the manipulative skills of the Palace, also offers both a temporary stability and a democratic window dressing with which American and European allies can easily compromise. As for the Moroccans, even under the constraints of an electoral system designed by the monarchy, they now have the opportunity to freely express their choices and political preferences. They have conferred on them, at least for the duration of the electoral mise-en-scène, the status of "citizens" rather than of "subjects." However, the contrast between the electoral process, which encourages high hopes in the opposition, and the reality of a government that remains under the tight control of the monarchy results in disappointment both for candidates and the electorate. Indeed, these electoral choices have no impact on government and, for these citizens, eventually lose their raison d'être.

However, for the monarchy, the elections serve a crucial function: it uses them as if they were regularly generated opinion polls providing information that can be used to manipulate the rules in local and national elections. They are also the means through which political resources—particularly positions within the government and the administration of the state—are regularly redistributed to the parties that are allowed to participate in the government and to share power —albeit unequally—with the monarchy.[6] Elections hence ensure the institutionalization of a regularly confirmed power sharing agreement between the "acceptable" parties and the monarchy. Moreover, they maintain and reproduce in ad hoc forms the division and fragmentation of the opposition within the parliament, rendering partisan coalitions and alliances more difficult and reinforcing the disagreements among political parties. Parties therefore invest in electoral competition rather than in opposition to the monarchy. Elections serve to pacify and domesticate political parties rather than to include them in political decision making when they win the vote.

Thus, the most pressing question for Moroccan public opinion is not how the legal Islamists will behave when they govern—as this possibility is not permitted by the monarchy—but rather how the partisan and non-partisan opposition will again negotiate the rules of political competition as defined in the constitution and the electoral code. Indeed, what is missing from this new configuration, compared with the election of 1997, is a negotiated consensus among all political actors over the rules of the game. In the 1990s, the opposition and the government negotiated the terms of the political pact. In 2007, these terms have been modified authoritatively by the monarchy without discussions inclusive of all political forces, including the PJD. The possibility of renegotiating the political pact depends on the desire of the monarchy to do so, as well as on the coalition strategies the partisan opposition will use—confronted as it is with the strong will of the monarch to monopolize the reins of government—to push the monarchy towards constitutional reforms.[7] Electors are disenchanted because the last government has not carried out the announced economic, educational, and judicial reforms. They have, in response, signaled their disappointment by not participating. On the other hand, the king remains largely popular and the ultimate power holder, especially after the attacks of 2003 and 2007. The eruption of violence since 2003 has helped him portray the monarchy, its function of commanding the faithful, and its arbitration over the political parties as the foundation that will shield the kingdom against terrorism.

Today, the monarchy also continues to employ the old strategy of dividing the structure of the opposition (excluding some political contenders as illegal while including others in the legal competition),[8] as shown by its continuous exclusion of Yassine's movement from the realm of legal competition. However, this strategy, which used to stabilize the political system in favor of the monarchy, is no longer sufficient. Today, in the face of the possibility of an overwhelming victory by the integrated Islamist party, political stabilization arises from the fragmentation of the parliamentary landscape, ensuring that there can emerge no parliamentary coalition that will force the monarchy into renegotiating the rules of political competition. The monarchy uses the possibility of the "undesirable" but legalized party's victory and participation in the government to tame the other parties into accepting the ex-ante manipulation of the electoral map. The "moderation" of the legalized Islamists legitimates their inclusion in the system and therefore confirms the pluralism of the system, but their potential "radicalization" allows the monarchy and their competitors to represent them as a "threat" and to keep them away from the government. The PJD's presence on the legal political scene suggests a political system in the process of liberalizing, but this opening can be reversed when the PJD is presented as a "threatening" force. Hence, the strategy of division of the opposition has been refined: to the exclusion of specific political groups from political society—which creates a dividing line between legal and illegal opposition—the monarchy has now added a new line of fragmentation, dividing between those legal political parties who are not accepted as possible participants in the government and those who might be integrated into it. The PJD, while having gained an important role in Moroccan politics, is hence condemned to remain in the parliamentary opposition in spite of its good electoral results, potentially triggering frustrations, internal divisions, and defections from the party, as well as a decline in its power of mobilization.

The Muslim State and Its Call for Secular Politics

How has this re-engineering of electoral institutions transformed Moroccan Islamism? This institutional transformation has reinforced the dividing up of the Islamist movements into those who wish to participate in the competition for seats in parliament and those who prefer to remain dissident, and it has helped the monarchy to weaken and contain organized political Islam. On the other hand, it has also allowed Islamists to demonstrate their exceptional powers of electoral mobilization and, within an undemocratic context, their ability to adopt the language of democracy—as the monarchy has done, but with a different content. At the same time, the PJD's participation in the electoral system and its integration into parliamentary politics have not necessarily "secularized" the Islamist party. During the electoral campaign, religious discourse and ideology generally played a minimal role. However, the PJD represented a notable exception: its platform did not shy away from strong religious vocabulary. In a thick programmatic document entitled "Let Us Build a Just Morocco Together," it detailed the socioeconomic woes of Morocco and proposed to solve the problems of poverty, corruption, and unemployment through reforms of education, justice, and health systems.[9] There were also religious aspects to this program, some with significant political repercussions, since it aimed for the Islamic shari'a to become the main source of legislation and wanted to reinforce the "Islamic civilization's identity" for Morocco. The PJD envisioned the inclusion of two 'ulama from the official councils in the constitutional council, which would ensure the constitutionality of laws and treaties as well as "guarantee their compatibility with the *shari'a islamiyya*."[10] But there was no precise explanation of what constitutes "shari'a islamiyya." Without mentioning the status of the commander of the faithful, the PJD's program thus envisioned a further integration of the 'ulama into the realm of the state's administration and the legislative and legal apparatus. And as in the Moroccan constitution, Islam was a significant element in the definition of the polity but did not acquire a specific content.

More particularly, the PJD's 2007 program proposed a governmental policy for regulating Islamic institutions. It converged with the reforms spearheaded by the Ministry of Religious Affairs since 2002. The PJD wanted to improve the work of *da'wa*, the creation of fatwas, the proximity of religious specialists and mosques to rural areas and poor neighborhoods, and the educational and social relevance of the Qarawiyyin and Dar al-Hadith. All these measures had, in fact, already been announced by the Ministry of Religious Affairs. The PJD's proposal in terms of religious policy was thus following the direction already taken by the monarchy, that is, the further bureaucratization of religious authority. The religious policies envisioned by the PJD did not question the religious institutional apparatus as established by the Moroccan state. Indeed, the PJD reproduced the existing model of the Moroccan state with regard to its regulation of Islam. However, in contrast, the PJD's program took the definition of religious authority clearly away from the person of the king, much more so than did the current state reforms of religious institutions. Hence, it contradicted the state's hybrid arrangement combining bureaucratic regulation of Islam and personal religious charisma, the latter being absent from the language of PJD's program.[11] Although they wanted Moroccans to continue to be able to freely articulate their own interpretations of Islam, they did not demand the autonomy of these institutions from state control. What they strove for was the further integration of the 'ulama into the political structure of the state administration so as to guarantee compatibility between Moroccan laws and shari'a. In other words, the 'ulama ought to remain at the service of the state, but they ought to actively participate in defining the principles on which the polity is based. While connecting Islam and the state was central to the program of the Islamist party, there was no mention of an "Islamic state." Rather, it produced a more historically palatable narrative of a democratic and ethical society regulated by the *shar'*, that is, legality. The implicit political theology sketched by this platform resonated with the paradigm of the *Salafiyya* as developed earlier by nationalist *'alim* 'Allal al-Fasi.

However, neither political parties nor the monarchy used religious vocabulary in order to legitimize the process of electoral competition. While Hassan II had in the past characterized the political system using Islamic political discourse,[12] Islam remained conspicuously absent from the description of the 2007 elections by those who participated in them. King Muhammad VI used the vocabulary of "democratic transition," "representative democracy," and "modernity." The Palace therefore abided by its own devised rule stating that the space of political competition had to remain free of religious language, as discussed in Chapter 10. This political space of competition thus operated as a stage for performing "democracy" as well as "politics without religion," in a context in which the monarchy described its own status as well as the identity of the state as "Muslim." These simultaneous and contradictory uses of political Islam—in other words, Islam's confinement to the state and exclusion from the sphere of political deliberation—show that the religious identity of the monarchy and the power of regulation of religious institutions it has appropriated for itself are at one and the same time a resource and a constraint for the king. If the monarchical state strives to appropriate, demarcate, and use Islamic language and institutions, it also works at circumscribing Islam to precisely delineated realms where religious narratives used by its political competitors cannot threaten the monarchy's control over the Moroccan state. As revealed in most of the literature on modern Morocco, the monarchy does mobilize religion and acts as a religious actor. However, this instrumental relationship between the monarchy and Islam is not always effective in enabling the monarchy to secure its own power. Indeed, non-state actors also build such a relationship and might compete with the monarchy on religious terms. This is why the monarchy painstakingly works at devising and redesigning the unstable boundaries between what can be allowed to be religious and what has to manifest itself as an activity in which religion does not intervene. For the commander of the faithful's monarchy, religion mixed with political competition is represented as a "dangerous" affair that can threaten the integrity of both the nation and the political process. Therefore, such a problematic mingling of political competition and religion has to be prevented, while the overlap of state and Islam is designated as legitimate. Hence, the Moroccan state is presenting itself and deploying its authority as a "Muslim state" while at the same time—without ever enunciating the word "secular"—establishing and imposing specific spaces of secularity.

The PJD abides by the same definitions and faces the same internal contradictions: it differentiates between political procedures and spaces of competition on the one hand and religion on the other hand. During the 2007 elections, the PJD leadership forbade its militants to campaign in mosques. Indeed, their legitimizing of the political system that includes them forces them to abide by the rules of the system. In the domain of electoral competition, they must marginalize their religious references so as not to be stigmatized by the rest of political society. However, this does not mean that they necessarily abandon their religious ideas. More particularly, they elaborate a discourse on how the state ought to characterize its relationship to Islam. In this regard, they agree with the monarchy that one of the functions of the state is to regulate religious institutions and to create an official Islam in a context in which the state is not necessarily the unique interpreter of religion. The PJD's case also fully demonstrates that legalized Islamist parties can support, commit to, and abide by the rules of transparent electoral competition without necessarily abandoning their religious claims and moral conservatism. In response to state-devised institutional constraints, the Islamist party has reconfigured the religious discourse it deploys in the electoral arena so that it echoes the religious policies of the monarchy. Hence, the legalized Islamists' programmatic discourse on the relationship between Islam and the state almost identically repeats the terms of the monarchy's relationship with religion and weakens their own oppositional stance. The monarchy, insofar as it has been able to prevent, through institutional manipulation, a significant electoral victory for the legalized Islamists, has also been successful in domesticating their religious discourse in the specific arena of electoral competition.

Thus, in this regard, state and legalized Islamist opposition resemble each other. In addition, the religious languages of the two actors are not necessarily opposed to one another but, rather, must be read in a relation of continuity, because state-controlled religious and political institutions orient and authorize the content of the Islamists' language. It must be added that a state constrained by and built in part on a religious legitimacy, as exemplified by the case of contemporary Morocco, might also use secularist policies—that is, policies that impose the preservation of specific domains of human activity as areligious—to weaken the mobilization efforts of religious oppositional movements. In this regard, a state that describes itself as anchored in religion is not that different from a state that anchors itself in the doctrine of secularism. While the idioms the former develops to represent itself might be radically different from those developed by a self-defined secular state, the state that describes itself as a religious actor and through religious language also imposes the existence of domains of political activity devoid of religious language and practices, and includes or excludes political actors based on the boundaries it authoritatively delineates between the religious and the secular.

NOTES

Introduction

1. A vast literature has developed since the 1990s to define different types of authoritarianism and to discuss the causes of processes of political liberalization and their evolution towards democracy as well as their reversals. More recent works about authoritarianism have abandoned the teleological paradigm of transition towards democracy and have engaged in discussions about the precise functioning of these regimes so as to clarify the role played by elections under authoritarian regimes. Exemplifying these works are Ellen Lust-Okar, *Structuring Conflict in the Arab World: Incumbents, Opponents, and Institutions* (Cambridge: Cambridge University Press, 2005); Andreas Schedler, *Electoral Authoritarianism: The Dynamics of Unfree Competition* (Boulder: Lynne Rienner Publishers, 2006); and Carles Boix and Milan Svolik, "Non-Tyrannical Autocracies" (unpublished manuscript, April 2007).
2. In the Moroccan constitution, the preamble states that the "Kingdom of Morocco is a Sovereign Muslim state." Article 6 states that Islam is "the religion of the state."
3. Following the independence of Morocco in 1956, the Sultan took the title of King (*malik*), a label used earlier by nationalist militants.
4. I draw this definition from Douglass North, *Institutions, Institutional Change and Economic Performance* (Cambridge: Cambridge University Press, 1990).
5. For recent studies of 'ulama in contemporary Muslim societies, see Malika Zeghal, *Gardiens de l'Islam. Les oulémas d'al-Azhar dans l'Egypte contemporaine* (Paris: Presses de Sciences Po, 1996); Muhammad Qasim Zaman, *The Ulama in Contemporary Islam: Custodians of Change* (Princeton N.J.: Princeton University Press, 2002); Robert W. Hefner and Muhammad Qasim Zaman, eds., *Schooling Islam: The Culture and Politics of Modern Muslim Education* (Princeton, N.J.: Princeton University Press, 2007).
6. The expression "religious institution" could also be replaced by the notion of church in the sense of an "organized religious body which claims com-

pulsory and universal membership," accepting José Casanova's definition, in José Casanova, *Public Religions in the Modern World* (Chicago: The University of Chicago Press, 1994), 175.

7. Religious professionals ('ulama) were recognizable as such, according to some scholars, as early as the second century of Islam, i.e., the eighth century. See Muhammad Qasim Zaman, *Religion and Politics under the Early 'Abbâsids: The Emergence of the Proto-Sunnî Elite* (Leiden, New York: E.J. Brill, 1997).

8. Democratic regimes, when dealing with religious institutions or when avoiding dealing with them, follow different rules from authoritarian regimes. However, they all have in common a tense or problematic relationship with religious institutions and organizations.

9. For examples of this perspective, see François Burgat, *L'islamisme en Face* (Paris: La Découverte, 1995), or some of the works published in Augustus Richard Norton, ed., *Civil Society in the Middle East*, vols. 1 and 2 (Leiden, New York, Köln: E.J. Brill, 1995). For the role of intermediate sites and actors, see Jean-François Bayart, "L'énonciation du politique," *Revue Française de Science Politique* 35, 3 (1985), 343-73.

10. For instance, Mounia Bennani-Chraïbi and Olivier Fillieule, eds., *Résistances et protestations dans les sociétés musulmanes* (Paris: Presses de Sciences Po, 2003) or Carrie Rosefsky Wickham, *Mobilizing Islam: Religion, Activism, and Political Change in Egypt* (New York: Columbia University Press, 2002).

11. I use the French adjective *frériste* in reference to the political name "Frères Musulmans" (Muslim Brothers).

12. Talal Asad, in particular, has shown that secularist states exclude religions or specific definitions of religion from the public sphere. Talal Asad, *Genealogies of Religion: Discipline and Reasons of Power in Christianity and Islam* (Baltimore: Johns Hopkins University Press, 1993).

13. Talal Asad defines a discursive tradition as "discourses that seek to instruct practitioners regarding the correct form and purpose of a given practice that, precisely because it is established, has a history. These discourses relate conceptually to a *past* (when the practice was instituted, and from which the knowledge of its point and proper performance has been transmitted) and a future (how the point of that practice can best be secured in the short or long term, or why it should be modified or abandoned), through a present (how it is linked to other practices, institutions and social conditions)." Talal Asad, *The Idea of an Anthropology of Islam* (Washington, D.C.: Center for Contemporary Arab Studies, Georgetown University, 1986).

14. Folklorists have commonly used the word *repertoire*, particularly in their

studies of music and oral literature. A repertoire is "the stock or inventory of songs or tales the folklorist knows the singer or narrator knows," as defined by Robert A. Georges, "The Concept of 'Repertoire' in Folkloristics," *Western Folklore* 53, 4 (Oct. 1994), 313-23, 315. I use the notion of repertoire to mean a stock of religious interpretations that can be mobilized.

15. This conceptual distinction is developed here for purposes of clarifying the exposition. In reality these two conceptions of authority might overlap and combine within specific historical interpretations and practices.

16. Abdellah Hammoudi, *Master and Disciple: The Cultural Foundations of Moroccan Authoritarianism* (Chicago: The University of Chicago Press, 1997).

17. Roxanne Euben uses the phrase "anti-hermeneutic" to describe the ideology of Sayyid Qutb, in *Enemy in the Mirror: Islamic Fundamentalism and the Limits of Modern Rationalism: A Work of Comparative Political Theory* (Princeton, N.J.: Princeton University Press, 1999).

18. Olivier Roy, "Les nouveaux intellectuels islamistes: Essai d'approche philosophique," in Gilles Kepel and Yann Richard, *Intellectuels et militants de l'islam contemporain* (Paris: Seuil, 1990), 261-83. An English version of these ideas is also developed in his *Failure of Political Islam* (Cambridge, MA: Harvard University Press, 1994). My thanks go to Deirdre DeBruyn and Claire Hoffman for their contributions to this translation of Olivier Roy's text.

19. Ibid., 266.

20. Ibid., 267.

21. Ibid., 267.

22. Olivier Roy writes: "Il y a un rapport très net entre la configuration du savoir du nouvel intellectuel et sa plasticité sociale." Roy, "Les nouveaux intellectuels," 266.

23. See Zeghal, *Gardiens de l'Islam*.

24. For a study of the interaction of religious doctrines—as flexible and malleable statements—with political institutions and actors, see, for instance, Stathis Kalyvas, "Religious Mobilization and Unsecular Politics," in Thomas Kselman and Joseph A. Buttigieg, eds., *European Christian Democracy: Historical Legacies and Comparative Perspectives* (Notre Dame: Notre Dame University Press, 2003), 107-35.

Introduction to Part I

1. See, for example, Roger Le Tourneau, *Évolution politique de l'Afrique du Nord* (Paris: Armand Colin, 1962). Clifford Geertz also emphasizes, rather

ambiguously, the central importance of the monarchy, in *Islam Observed* (New Haven: Yale University Press, 1968). The anthropologist who goes furthest in establishing parallels between the sacred, the religious, and the monarchy is Elaine Combs-Schilling, *Sacred Performances: Islam, Sexuality, and Sacrifice* (New York: Columbia University Press, 1989).

2. Henry Munson, *Religion and Power in Morocco* (New Haven: Yale University Press, 1993).
3. Le Tourneau, *Évolution politique de l'Afrique du Nord*, 265.
4. Rémy Leveau, *Le Fellah marocain, défenseur du Trône* (Paris: Presses de la Fondation nationale des sciences politiques, 1975); John Waterbury, *The Commander of the Faithful: The Moroccan Political Elite: A Study in Segmented Politics* (New York: Columbia University Press, 1970).
5. See Abdallah Laroui, *Les Origines sociales et culturelles du nationalisme marocain (1830-1912)*, 2d ed. (Casablanca: Centre culturel arabe, 1993), 92.

Chapter 1

1. This was all the more the case because the government was gradually becoming more secular in composition: seven members of the first government of independent Morocco had a traditional education; three of the second, in 1956; and practically none thereafter. 'Abd al-Hadi bu Talib, however, reappeared in the government from 1965 on. Pierre Vermeren, *École, élite et pouvoir au Maroc et en Tunisie au XXe siècle. Des nationalistes aux islamistes, 1920-2000* (Paris: La Découverte, 2003), 273.
2. Edmund Burke III, "The Moroccan 'ulama 1860-1912: An introduction," in Nikkie R. Keddie, ed., *Scholars, Saints, and Sufis: Muslim Religious Institutions in the Middle East since 1500* (Berkeley: University of California Press, 1972).
3. John Waterbury, *The Commander of the Faithful: The Moroccan Political Elite: A Study in Segmented Politics* (New York: Columbia University Press, 1970).
4. Burke, "The Moroccan 'ulama"; Abdallah Laroui, *Les Origines sociales et culturelles du nationalisme marocain (1830-1912)*, 2d ed. (Casablanca: Centre culturel arabe, 1993), 98.
5. Burke, "The Moroccan 'ulama," 94.
6. Roger Le Tourneau, *Fès avant le protectorat* (Casablanca: Atlantides, 1949), 214. Abdallah Laroui provides a slightly different description for the nineteenth century when there seemed to coexist some degree of independence due to the existence of pious foundations—the *habus*, which are still outside the Makhzen—and mechanisms for co-optation, along with a right of political oversight by the sultan: "They were . . . the only group with respect to

which the sultan considered himself obliged to justify his actions" (*Origines*, 100).
7. Laroui, *Origines*, 196.
8. M. A. Pérétié, "Les *madrasas* de Fès," *Archives marocaines* XVIII (1912), 314-15, 328-30.
9. Laroui, *Origines*, 375.
10. Bettina Dennerlein, "Asserting Religious Authority in Late 19th Century/ Early 20th Century Morocco: Muhammad b. Jaafar al-Kettani (d. 1927) and His *Kitab Salwat al-Anfas*," in Gudrun Krämer and Sabine Schmidtke, eds., *Speaking for Islam: Religious Authorities in Muslim Societies* (Leiden and Boston: Brill, 2006), 128-52.
11. Noureddine Sraïeb, "Université et société au Maghreb: La Qarawiyyine de Fès et la Zaytuna de Tunis," *Revue de l'Occident musulman et de la Méditerranée* 38 (1984), 63-74.
12. Abdelghani Maghnia, *Tradition et innovation à la Qarawiyyine*. Thèse de doctorat, Université de Paris VIII, 1996; Mohammed El Ayadi, *Religion, État et société dans le Maroc contemporain*. Doctorat d'État, Université Denis-Diderot-Paris VII, 1997.
13. On the competition between modern educational institutions and the Qarawiyyin in the early years of the protectorate, see Pierre Vermeren, "La mutation sociale de l'enseignement supérieur musulman sous le protectorat au Maroc," in Aïssa Kadri, ed., *Parcours d'intellectuels maghrébins* (Paris: Karthala, 2000).
14. This decree was intended to remove the Berber tribes from the supreme legal control of the sultan (religious in nature) and replace it with customary law. This policy of the protectorate provoked very vigorous reprobation in Muslim public opinion, which led the sultan to take on the leadership of the opposition movement against the notorious decree. The French authorities withdrew it in 1934.
15. Nationalist movement created in 1934 on the initiative of the "Jeunes Marocains," from bourgeois families and often educated in France.
16. The Ibn Yusif mosque was founded by the Almoravid Sultan 'Ali Ibn Yusif in 1120 or 1121.
17. Doctrine founded in Arabia by Muhammad Ibn 'Abd al-Wahhab (1703-92). The *'alim* Abu Bakr al-Qadiri dates the arrival of Wahhabism in Morocco to the period of Sultan Muhammad Ibn 'Abd Allah (1757-90) and more importantly to Sultan Mawlay Sulayman (1760-1822), who said that he followed the Maliki school in legal matters and the Hanbalite school doctrinally. Abu Bakr al-Qadiri, *Mudhakkarati fi'l-haraka al-wataniyya*

al-maghribiyya [*Memoirs of the Moroccan National Struggle*], vol. 1 (Casablanca: Matba'at al-najah al-jadida, 1992); Georges Drague, *Esquisse d'histoire religieuse du Maroc, confréries et zaouïas* (Paris: Peyronnet, 1951).

18. 'Allal al-Fasi, *Al-harakat al-istiqlaliyya fi'l-maghrib* [*The Independence Movements of North Africa*] (Cairo: Maktabat al-Risala, 1948).

19. See the chronicle of the 'Alawite dynasty of Morocco from 1631 to 1894 by Ahmad Ibn Khalid al-Nasiri, translated by Eugène Fumey, *Archives marocaines* 9 (1906). See also Muhammad Sa'ih, "The Arrival of the Book of the Hijaz Master, 'Abd Allah Ibn Sa'ud al-Wahhabi, in Fez, and What the 'ulama Said About It" (in Arabic) *Da'wat al-haqq* 12, 2 (Dec.-Jan. 1968-69), 38-39.

20. Jamal Abun-Nasr, *A History of the Maghrib in the Islamic Period* (Cambridge: Cambridge University Press, 1987), 246-47.

21. On relations between Mawlay Sulayman and the brotherhoods, see *History of the Maghrib*, 243-44.

22. 'Abd Allah al-Jirari, *Al-muhaddith Abu Shu'ayb al-Dukkali* [*The Traditionalist Abu Shu'ayb al-Dukkali*] (Casablanca: Dar al-thaqafa, 1979), 9-10. After 1910, the sultan appointed him as qadi of Fez. He died in 1937.

23. Laroui, *Origines*, 402.

24. Abun-Nasr, *History of the Maghrib*, 313.

25. Laroui, *Origines*, 402. See also Henri Laoust, according to whom the pre-1930s orthodox reformism of the *Salafiyya* "favored the cult of the Sunna." "Le réformisme orthodoxe de la *Salafiyya* et les caractères généraux de son orientation actuelle," *Revue des études islamiques* (Paris: Librairie orientaliste Geuthner, 1932), Cahier II, 175-224.

26. Al-Qadiri, *Memoirs*, 242.

27. Al-Qadiri, *Memoirs*, 243.

28. Al-Fasi, *Independence Movements*, 153.

29. There were many discussions and debates on the question. Al-Qadiri quotes Muhammad Makki al-Nasiri, *Idhar al-haqiqa*, as one of the works that had a good deal of influence on the subject. See also Sa'id Ibn Sa'id al-'Alawi, *Al-ijtihad wa'l-tahdith. Dirasa fi usul al-fikr al-salafi fi'l-maghrib* [*Ijtihad and Modernization: A Study of the Sources of Salafist Thought in Morocco*] (Malta: Islamic World Studies Center, 1992).

30. Al-Qadiri, *Memoirs*, 250. See also al-'Alawi, *Ijtihad*.

31. Using primarily the available secondary sources on Moroccan *Salafiyya*, I am setting out here the essential elements of the debate. Further research on the Salafi 'ulama of the time would be necessary to develop a fuller under-

standing of the history of this complex movement in the first half of the twentieth century.
32. Laroui, *Origines*, 220-21.
33. Laroui, *Origines*, 427-29.
34. Abun-Nasr, *History of the Maghrib*, 382.
35. See al-Qadiri, *Memoirs*, 490-95, as well as his account of the history of a free school in Salé, "The School of the Renaissance," in *Madrasat al-nahda* [*The School of the Renaissance*] (Casablanca: Matba'at al-najah al-jadida, 1984).
36. Article by Muhammad Ibrahim al-Kattani, *Al-'alam* (November 3, 1956), 2.
37. See Robert Rezette, *Les Partis politiques marocains* (Paris: Albin Michel, 1955), 23.
38. Clifford Geertz, *Islam Observed* (New Haven: Yale University Press, 1968), 88.
39. 'Allal al-Fasi, *Al-naqd al-dhati* [*Self-Criticism*] (Cairo: n.p., 1952).
40. Called the "sultan of the French," because he had been imposed by the colonial authorities following riots in Casablanca that had been violently repressed in December 1952; Muhammad V had been deposed and then deported on August 20, 1953, first to Corsica and then to Madagascar, leading one faction of the nationalist movement to engage in armed struggle against the colonizers.
41. *Nida al-Qahira* [*Appeal from Cairo*], Istiqlal leaflet, n.d., 56.
42. Muhammad Ibrahim al-Kattani, *Al-'alam* (November 19, 1956), 2.
43. The existence of this belief was confirmed to me by a former teacher at the Qarawiyyin, 'Abd al-Hadi Tazi, in a conversation in Rabat on June 19, 2002. See also the text of Muhammad Ibrahim al-Kattani, quoted in Maghnia, *Tradition et innovation*, 470.
44. Al-Kattani, *Al-'alam* (November 19, 1956), 2.
45. 'Allal al-Fasi, *Al-naqd al-dhati* [*Self-Criticism*], 3d ed. (Rabat: n.p., 1979), 156. In the same work, he wrote: "In any event, power belongs to the people" (118); and he proposed to give women the right to vote (158).
46. Quoted by Maati Monjib, *La Monarchie marocaine et la lutte pour le pouvoir. Hassan II face à l'opposition Nationale, de l'indépendance à l'état d'exception* (Paris: L'Harmattan, 1992). See the speech delivered by Muhammad V on November 12, 1956, at the opening of the first session of the "National Consultative Council."
47. It was only after the 1959 split, when Mehdi Ben Barka, one of the modernist leaders of Istiqlal, moved to the UNFP, that 'Allal al-Fasi became the

unchallenged political leader of the party. He had been isolated in exile in Gabon from 1939 to 1946; when Istiqlal was founded in 1944, Ahmad Balafrej was named secretary general. See Waterbury, *The Commander of the Faithful*, 175.

48. It was constructed through the myth of the martyr sultan, in Morocco as in the rest of the Muslim world. See, for example, the fatwa of the Association of Algerian 'ulama of 1953, which recognized Muhammad V as the imam of the Moroccans, and not Ben Arafa. Al-Qadiri, *Memoirs*, 265-69.

49. Quoted by Ahmed el-Kohen Lamghali, "'Allal El-Fasi," *Maghreb-Machrek* 58 (July-Aug. 1973), 8. An article by al-Fasi appeared in 1957 in one of the first issues of *Da'wat al-haqq* (the journal of the ministry of the Waqfs), under the name of *"za'im* 'Allal al-Fasi."

50. Monjib, *La Monarchie marocaine*, 31.

51. This was the first "government council," which lasted from December 7, 1955, to October 27, 1956. Eight of its nineteen members belonged to Istiqlal.

52. Born in 1900 in Ilgh in southern Morocco, Mukhtar al-Susi studied with the 'ulama of Sus and later entered the Yusufiyya of Marrakesh, where he took courses in particular with Abu Shu'ayb al-Dukkali, who influenced him in his teaching on the reform of Islam. He was especially interested in literature and in the intellectual and cultural aspects of Islam, rather than in questions of jurisprudence. He actively participated in the national struggle. He died in 1963.

53. Referred to hereafter, as Moroccans in general do, variously as the Ministry of *Habus*, of Religious Affairs, or of Waqfs.

54. Al-Fasi, *Self-Criticism*, 175.

55. After Hassan II was crowned in 1961, Rédha Guédira, a liberal, became director general of the royal cabinet, a position he held from 1961 to November 1963. He was simultaneously Minister of the Interior and of Agriculture. He thus had very extensive powers, which he exercised in the shadow of Hassan II. Speaking of the early 1960s, John Waterbury calls him a "grand vizier" (*The Commander of the Faithful*, 255).

56. Quoted by Monjib, *La Monarchie marocaine*, 253.

57. Istiqlal was not in government for the first time after the May 1963 legislative elections.

58. Muhammad al-'Alami, *'Allal al-Fasi, ra'id al-haraka al-wataniyya al-maghribiyya* [*'Allal al-Fasi, Patriarch of Moroccan Nationalism*] (Rabat: Arrisala, 1972), 145-46: "The following account . . . represents solely . . . the personal version of the president of Istiqlal."

59. Al-'Alami, *'Allal al-Fasi*, 149.

Chapter 2

1. See the decree of November 22, 1957.
2. Joseph Lucioni, *Les fondations pieuses "Habous" au Maroc* (Rabat: Imprimerie royale, n.d. [probably 1982]).
3. This Ministry is sometimes known as the Ministry of Habus and Religious Affairs, or of Waqfs and Religious Affairs. For the sake of simplicity, I will use "Ministry of Religious Affairs."
4. Al-Makki al-Marruni, *Islah al-taʿlim fiʾl-maghrib* [*The Reform of Education in Morocco*] (Rabat: Publications of the Faculty of Letters and Human Sciences, 1996), 23.
5. The *collège* Moulay-Idriss, like the *collège* Moulay-Youssef in Rabat, was one of the Muslim *collèges* established under the protectorate to train the Moroccan elite. It offered courses taught in Arabic and in French. See al-Makki al-Marruni, *Le Collège musulman de Fès (1914 à 1956)*. Thèse de la Faculté des Sciences de l'Éducation, Université de Montréal, 1983.
6. Of the same generation as ʿAllal al-Fasi (he was born in 1908), Muhammad al-Fasi was likewise educated in the Qarawiyyin, but he also had a modern education. He was one of the first students to enter the *collège* Moulay-Idriss; he later received a *licence de lettres* from the Sorbonne and the diploma of the Institut des Langues Orientales. Like his cousin, he was molded by the nationalist struggle and belonged to Istiqlal. He was Minister of Education again from October 1956 to March 1958.
7. See, for example, "The Reform of Religious Institutes" [in Arabic], *Al-ʿalam* (September 25, 1956), 2. In this article the Istiqlal organ accuses the colonizer of having worked to keep the Qarawiyyin from reforming and thus traditional. But this certainly needs to be qualified: the more conservative ʿulama fiercely resisted any modernizing reforms.
8. See the document that proposed complete equivalence, with free transfers, between the "Islamic lycées" of the Qarawiyyin and university faculties. "Islamic Higher Education. Report on Higher Education Inspired by Islam" [in Arabic] (National Documentation Center, 1959), microfiche 51599-59-RA. Another document shows that there were discussions between ʿulama and the Ministry of Education: "Summary of Transcripts Concerning the Reform of Higher Education Related to Islam" [in Arabic], microfiche 5197-60-RA.
9. Built around the *Institut des Hautes Études* of Rabat (Decree of July 21, 1959).
10. ʿAbd al-Hadi Tazi, *Jamiʿ al-Qarawiyyin* [*The Qarawiyyin Mosque*], vol. 3 (Beirut: Dar al-kitab al-lubnani, 1972).
11. *Al-ʿalam* (January 28, 1956), 4.

12. "Is Teaching Done in Stages in the Qarawiyyin?" *Al-'alam* (December 14, 1956), 3. The article criticizes the lack of continuity between the subjects taught in the primary and secondary stages of education at the Qarawiyyin, which requires students to move directly from studying summaries to reading complete works by writers.
13. *Al-'alam* (January 18, 1957), 6.
14. *Al-'alam* (January 25, 1957), 4. Students at the Qarawiyyin were increasingly from the countryside and of modest origins. c Allah 'Anan, who visited the Qarawiyyin in Fez during the winter of 1956, noted that students were old. *Al-'alam* (December 26, 1956), 2. The article mentions that the scientific council of Qarawiyyin University had just accepted the enrollment of two thousand students, most of whom were at least thirty years old.
15. Clifford Geertz, *Islam Observed* (New Haven: Yale University Press, 1968), 53.
16. Transcript in *Al-'alam* (July 14, 1956), 1-2.
17. *Al-'alam* (December 14, 1956), 4.
18. Letter of December 12, 1956, published in *Al-'alam* (December 17, 1956), 1-2.
19. Mehdi Ben Barka, *Écrits politiques, 1957-1965* (Paris: Syllepses, 1999), 62-64. Lecture delivered in August 1957 at the Benedictine seminary in Tioumliline (near Azrou), to an audience including the *fqih* Muhammad Ibn al-'Arbi al-'Alawi, the Minister of Justice 'Abd al-Karim Ibn Jallun, Louis Massignon, and other Moroccan and foreign dignitaries.
20. Ibid., 64-65.
21. See 'Umar al-Sahili, *Al-ma'had al-islami bi-tarudant*, [*The Islamic Institute of Tarudant*] vol. 1 (Casablanca: Dar annachr al-maghribiyya, 1985), 63. This association was set up in April 1953. Closely tied to Sheikh Mukhtar al-Susi, it is described at length by al-Sahili, who relates the fidelity of the association to the monarchy. The association became official in 1956, and it made its internal rules public, the first article of which declares the association's loyalty to King Muhammad V.
22. *Al-'alam* (May 12, 1957), 4.
23. 'Abd Al-Hadi Tazi, *Jami' al-Qarawiyyin*.
24. Sheikh Kannun was being ironic: the term "Moroccan university" was indeed frequently used in reference to Muhammad V University, disregarding the Qarawiyyin.
25. *Da'wat al-haqq* III, 3 (December 1959). Graduates who had been awarded the *'alimiyya* could not become shari'a magistrates or teach in primary school.

26. Published in Tetouan, undated.
27. *Project*, 3.
28. Ibid., 9.
29. Quoted in *L'Annuaire de l'Afrique du Nord* (1962), 781.
30. Until 1962, the king might be any male member of the 'Alawite family who fulfilled the necessary conditions for becoming a sultan. See Paul Chambergeat, "Le référendum constitutionnel du 7 décembre 1962 au Maroc," *Annuaire de l'Afrique du Nord* (1962), 182-83; John Waterbury, *The Commander of the Faithful: The Moroccan Political Elite: A Study in Segmented Politics* (New York: Columbia University Press, 1970), 259; and the hagiographic book by Abderrahim Ouardighi, *Un cheikh militant, Mohamed Belarbi al-Alaoui* (Rabat: Éditions du Littoral, 1985).
31. See, in particular, an article by 'Allal al-Fasi in *Al-'alam* (November 28, 1962), written under the pseudonym of "Salafi."
32. *Dahir* 1-62-249.
33. See Malika Zeghal, "État et marché des biens religieux. Les voies égyptienne et tunisienne," *Critique internationale* 5 (October 1999).
34. See Malika Zeghal, *Gardiens de l'islam. Les oulémas d'al-Azhar dans l'Égypte contemporaine* (Paris: Presses de Sciences Po, 1996).
35. Several 'ulama who were students at the Qarawiyyin around 1963, conversations with author, May 1999.
36. Zeghal, "État et marché des biens religieux."
37. It was in fact the one thousand one hundredth anniversary.
38. 'Allal al-Fasi, "The Message of the Qarawiyyin in the Past, the Present, and the Future," *Al-iman* 7 (November 4, 1967), 15.
39. Ibid., 15.
40. Ibid., 15. [my italics]
41. 'Allal al-Fasi, "*Da'iman ma'a al-sha'b*," [Always with the people] speech delivered at the Istiqlal congress of November 24-26, 1967.
42. Ibid., 170.
43. Ibid., 165, 169.
44. In 1972, al-Fasi again compared the Qarawiyyin to al-Azhar; the former had only 500 students in 1968, compared with the 10,000 of al-Azhar. Ibid., 161.
45. Ibid., 173.
46. Mohamed Tozy, *Monarchie et islam politique au Maroc* (Paris: Presses de Sciences Po, 1999).
47. According to Muhammad Dharif, *Al-islamiyyun al-maghariba* [*Moroccan*

Islamists] (Casablanca: Matba'at al-najah al-jadida, 1999), 18.
48. "The Reform of Religious Institutes," *Al-'alam* (September 25, 1956), 2.
49. Al-Marruni, *Islah*.
50. Pierre Vermeren, *École, élite et pouvoir au Maroc et en Tunisie au XXe siècle* (2002; Paris: La Découverte, 2003), 270-71.
51. Gilbert Grandguillaume, *Arabisation et politique linguistique au Maghreb* (Paris: Maisonneuve et Larose, 1983), 72.
52. Vermeren, *École, élite et pouvoir*, 314.
53. Al-Marruni, *Islah*, 207.
54. Vermeren, *École, élite et pouvoir*, 315.
55. Lucette Valensi, *Fables de la mémoire. La glorieuse bataille des trois rois* (Paris: Seuil, 1992), 244-50; Lucette Valensi, "Le roi chronophage. La construction d'une conscience historique dans le Maroc postcolonial," *Cahiers d'études africaines* XXX, 3-4 (1990), 279-98.
56. *Da'wat al-haqq* XII, 1 (November 1968), 14-15.
57. Ibid., 15.
58. The Mission Universitaire et Culturelle Française (MUCF) in Morocco, established by a Franco-Moroccan convention in October 1957, initially ran seven secondary schools and dozens of primary schools for the children of French families living in Morocco. As time went by and French aid workers left, the proportion of Moroccan students in the French Mission, all from well-to-do families, became preponderant—reaching two thirds in 2000. See Pierre Vermeren, *Le Maroc en transition* (Paris: La Découverte, 2001), 150.
59. "Manifesto of the Intellectuals of Morocco on the Educational Policy of Morocco" [in Arabic], *Al-furqan* 35 (1995).
60. *Msid*, contraction of the word *masjid* (mosque), is one of the terms used in Morocco to designate a Qur'anic school.
61. 'Abd al-Salam Harras, "Toward an Islamic Education" [in Arabic], *Da'wat al-haqq* III, 7 (June 1960), 7.
62. Ibid., 8. Harras went on to emphasize the need to organize an Islamic conference that would bring together the great men of Islam: "Islam is the best way for us to bring our personality forward. Although we are weak and underdeveloped from the material point of view, Islamic thought places us among the major movements of the world. It puts in the hands of this nation what can save the world from the grave spiritual problems in which it is mired."
63. *Da'wat al-haqq* XIV, 6-7 (June-July 1971), 202.
64. *Al-ihya* [magazine published by the League of 'Ulama of Morocco] 14 (1992), 209.

65. Vermeren, *École, élite et pouvoir*, 433.
66. See, for example, the memoirs of Ahmad Ibn Suda, adviser to the king, in *Al-msid*, journal of the *kuttabs*.
67. *Daʻwat al-haqq* XII, 2 (December 1968-January 1969), 4.
68. ʻAbdullah Yusuf ʻAli, *The Meaning of the Holy Qurʼan* (Beltsville, Maryland: Amana Publications, 1997), 1080-1081.
69. *Al-ihya* 14 (1992), 207.
70. *Daʻwat al-haqq* XII, 2 (December 1968-January 1969), 15-18.
71. The next-to-last sultan of the *tolbas*, who played the role in 1967, conversation with author, June 16, 2002. In the Moroccan dialect, *tolbas* is the plural of *taleb* (student).
72. Abdelghani Maghnia, *Tradition et innovation à la Qarawiyyine*. Thèse de doctorat, Université de Paris VIII, 1996, 227.
73. Pierre de Cenival, "La légende du Juif Ibn Mechʼal et la fête du sultan des tolbas à Fès," *Hespéris* V (1925), 137-218.

Chapter 3

1. *Daʻwat al-haqq* I, 2 (August 1957), 21-22, 30 (my italics). It is also noteworthy that he refers to the letter King Saʻud sent to Sultan Mawlay Sulayman in 1811.
2. Reinhard Schulze, *A Modern History of the Islamic World* (New York: New York University Press, 2000), 172.
3. See "The Waqfs in Morocco" [in Arabic], *Daʻwat al-haqq* XXII, 1 (March 1981), 140-45.
4. See, for example, "They Want Atheism and We Want Islam" [in Arabic], *Daʻwat al-haqq* XX, 10 (September 1979), 1-4.
5. *Daʻwat al-haqq* XIX, 4 (April 1978), 1.
6. *Daʻwat al-haqq* XX, 6-7 (June-July 1979), 51.
7. See, for example, *Daʻwat al-haqq* XIX, 2-3 (February-March 1978), 15, 19.
8. Mohamed Tozy, *Monarchie et islam politique au Maroc* (Paris: Presses de l'Institut des Études Politiques, 1999).
9. *Daʻwat al-haqq* XXII, 1 (March 1981), 37.
10. *Daʻwat al-haqq* XX, 6-7 (June-July 1979), 42.
11. The same issue of *Daʻwat al-haqq* describes the Iranian revolution as an "exemplary revolution in the history of liberation movements and in the history of Islam" (48).
12. *Daʻwat al-haqq* XX, 6-7 (June-July 1979), 68-77.

13. Ibid., 68. This denunciation of political and economic neocolonialism recurs in another article by 'Abd Allah Kannun, "Subordination Must End," *Da'wat al-haqq* XXII, 2 (April 1981), 11-13.
14. *Da'wat al-haqq* XX, 6-7 (June-July 1979), 69.
15. See particularly the homage from the 'ulama and the Ministry of Waqfs to Mawdudi after his death, *Da'wat al-haqq* XX, 10 (September 1979).
16. Clifford Geertz, *Islam Observed* (New Haven: Yale University Press, 1968).
17. Olivier Carré, *Mystique et Politique. Le Coran des islamistes. Lecture du Coran par Sayyid Qutb Frère musulman radical (1906-1966)* (Paris: Cerf, 2004).
18. Lecture delivered on May 11, 1973, at Dar al-Hadith al-Hassaniyya.
19. 'Allal al-Fasi, *Difa' 'an al-shari'a* [*Defense of Shari'a*] (Rabat: Maktabat al-Risala, 1966), 300.
20. Ibid., 125.
21. Mohamed Dharif, *Al-islamiyyun al-maghariba* [*The Moroccan Islamists*] (Casablanca: Matba'at al-najah al-jadida, 1999), 20, n. 34.
22. Letter of October 16, 1972, to King Hassan II, in the Istiqlal publication *Taqyim al-wadh' al-siyasi* (November 1972), 13.
23. Ibid., 120. Al-Fasi devoted an entire chapter to the cause of the peasants: he proposed actions for improving land, limitations on the size of agricultural holdings, and the nationalization of colonial lands. Even though the Tunisian experiment in the field had just failed, he proposed to set up cooperatives.
24. Ibid., 61. He also mentioned, on pages 103 and 130, the tribe of the Khalifa, whose lands had been seized.

Introduction to Part II

1. *Nasiha* may also designate a section of a treatise on other subjects or a direct written or oral exhortation to the ruler.
2. Jacques Berque, *Ulémas, fondateurs, insurgés du Maghreb, XVIIe siècle* (1982; Paris: Sindbad, 1998), 76. On the figure of the Mahdi, see also Halima Ferhat, *Le Maghreb aux XIIe et XIIIe siècles: Les siècles de la foi* (Casablanca: Wallada, 1993).
3. Berque, *Ulémas*, 242.
4. Abdessalam Yassine, *Islamiser la modernité* (Rabat: al-Ofok, 1998).
5. Berque, *Ulémas*, 73.
6. John Waterbury, *The Commander of the Faithful* (New York: Columbia University Press, 1970), 304-15.

7. Mounia Bennani-Chraïbi, *Soumis et rebelles: Les jeunes au Maroc* (Paris: Éditions du CNRS, 1994).
8. For an analysis of the distortions of the labor market in Morocco, see Pierre-Richard Agénor and Karim El-Aynaoui, "Labor Market and Unemployment in Morocco: A Quantitative Analysis" (Washington, D.C.: The World Bank, October 26, 2003).

Chapter 4

1. In *Al-islam ghadan* [*Islam Tomorrow*] (Casablanca: Éditions Matba'at al-najah al-jadida, 1973), Yassine explicates certain Arabic terms with French translations, because he is using terms from the social sciences: *awham* for utopia (9), *tajmi'* for totalization *(*45), and *shumuliyya* for totality (45).
2. The Idrissid dynasty was founded in A.D. 789 (year 172 of the Hegira) by Idriss I, a descendant of the Prophet through 'Ali Ibn Abi Talib. It disappeared in 985. The first Muslim dynasty in Morocco, it thus established the political legitimacy of the sharif on the basis of his descent from the Prophet. With the end of the dynasty, the principle of sharifism as a political foundation did not come back to life in Morocco until the sixteenth century with the Sa'dis, followed in the seventeenth by the 'Alawites. The birth of the Idrissid dynasty coincided with the birth of the Moroccan nation: Idriss I received the first *bay'a* in Morocco. The *mawsim* (religious festival) of Mawlay-Idriss is one in which the 'Alawite monarchy participates: Hassan II attended in person along with thousands of pilgrims. Muhammad VI now does the same. Linking itself with the Idrissid dynasty in this way enables the 'Alawite monarchy to give itself a basis in an extended history through sharifism and the cult of saints. Describing Moroccan political iconography in the 1990s, Lucette Valensi calls Idriss I an "additional link between the Prophet and his descendant . . . Hassan II." Lucette Valensi, *Fables de la mémoire* (Paris: Seuil, 1992), 243-48.
3. Nadia Yassine, Abdessalam's daughter and unofficial spokesperson of the *al-'adl wa'l-Ihsan* movement. Conversation with author, December 12, 2001.
4. See www.yassine,net/bio (accessed November 9, 2004).
5. Mukhtar al-Susi (1900-63) founded this institute in the context of the nationalist fight against the colonial education system.
6. Gaston Deverdun, *Marrakech des origines à 1912* (Rabat: Éditions techniques nord-africaines, 1959). See Muhammad Ibn 'Uthman, *Al-jami'a al-yusufiyya fi Marrakush* [*The Yusufiyya University in Marrakesh*] (Cairo: Economical Press, 1935); Dale F. Eickelman, *Knowledge and Power in Morocco: The Education of a Twentieth-Century Notable* (Princeton, N.J.: Princeton University Press, 1985); 'Allal al-Fasi, *Al-harakat al-istiqlaliyya*

fi-l maghrib al-'arabi (Cairo: Maktabat al-Risala, 1948).
7. Conversation with François Burgat, reprinted in *L'Islamisme au Maghreb* (Paris: Karthala, 1988).
8. Thami al-Glawi, pasha of Marrakesh who collaborated with the authorities of the French protectorate.
9. For instance, he sent his daughter Nadia, now the unofficial spokesperson of the movement led by her father, to the French lycée in Rabat.
10. Nadia Yassine, conversation with author, December 12, 2001.
11. Abdessalam Yassine, *Al-islam aw al-tufan* [Islam or the Deluge] (Marrakesh: n.p., 1974). A version of this document is also accessible on Yassine's website www.jspublishing.net/chrif/toufane/Islam_ou_deluge.htm. It will be cited hereafter as *Deluge*, and page numbers will be given for both the pamphlet and the text published on the website.
12. Quoted in Burgat, *L'Islamisme au Maghreb*, 21.
13. Dale F. Eickelman notes that the reform of the Yusufiyya in 1939 was modeled on that of the Qarawiyyin in the early 1930s: teachers became civil servants and thus fell under government control. They thereby lost prestige and were deprived of some of the resources that their relations with patrons in the political and economic elite had provided. Many left the Yusufiyya after 1939 and took up teaching in smaller mosques. See his *Knowledge and Power in Morocco*, 163.
14. This is the interpretation of Mohamed Tozy, *Monarchie et islam politique au Maroc* (Paris: Presses de Sciences Po, 1999).
15. Ahmad al-Ghazali, *Musahama fi'l-bahth 'an zawaya bani yaznasin, al-qadiriyya al-budshishiyya namudhajan* [Contribution to the Research on the Zawiya-s of Bani Yaznasin. The Case of the Qadiriyya Budshishiyya] (Fez: n.p., 1998), 90.
16. Karim Ben Driss, *Sidi Hamza al Qaâdiri Boudchich: Le renouveau du soufisme au Maroc* (Beirut and Milan: al-Bouraq/Arché, 2002), 123 and 139.
17. Ibid., 119-20.
18. Letter from Sidi al-Haj al-'Abbas in which he speaks of his investiture by Bu Madyan, quoted ibid., 120.
19. Ibid., 139.
20. Ibid., 143-44.
21. Nadia Yassine, conversation with author, December 12, 2001.
22. *Deluge,* 8 (5).
23. Of Haj 'Abbas he has said: "He was not illiterate, but he had only a traditional rural education. And yet I, who was then full of self-importance—I

was someone in the Education Ministry—I became his disciple, and I understood what Islam was, what God was." Quoted by Burgat, *L'Islamisme au Maghreb*, 22.
24. *Deluge*, 68 (31), 5 (8).
25. *Deluge*, 69 (31).
26. Nadia Yassine, conversation with author, December 12, 2001. "He criticized their withdrawal from politics. It was time for him to go beyond the image of the Sufi who is concerned only with his spiritual development. He had to rediscover the life of the community."
27. Ibid.
28. Hassan El-Boudrari, "Quand les saints font les villes: Lecture anthropologique de la pratique sociale d'un saint marocain au XVIIe siècle," *Annales ESC* 40 (1985), 489-508; Abdellah Hammoudi, *Master and Disciple: The Cultural Foundations of Moroccan Authoritarianism* (Chicago: University of Chicago Press, 1997).
29. *Al-islam bayna al-da'wa wa'l-dawla* [*Islam between Preaching and State*] (Casablanca: Éditions Matba'at al-najah al-jadida, 1972); *Al-islam ghadan* [*Islam Tomorrow*] (Casablanca: Éditions Matba'at al-najah al-jadida, 1973).

Chapter 5

1. *Al-islam bayna al-da'wa wa'l-dawla* [hereafter *Islam between Preaching and State*] (Casablanca: Éditions Matba'at al-najah al-jadida, 1972), 27.
2. *Islam between Preaching and State*, 143.
3. Mohamed Tozy, *Monarchie et Islam politique au Maroc* (Paris: Presses de Sciences Po, 1999).
4. This recalls Jacques Berque's description of the way the chastiser Hasan al-Yusi (b. 1631) presented his origins: "The rural heritage, which obscurely dominated so many careers of scholars and even courtiers . . . he did not conceal. He broadcast it. . . . He brought it forth from an examination of his own genealogy, which everything indicates was shrewd and sincere." Jacques Berque, *Al-Yousi. Problèmes de la culture marocaine au XVIIe siècle* (Paris and The Hague: Mouton, 1958), 10.
5. He was jailed again on December 27, 1983, and sentenced to two years in prison in May 1984.
6. *Deluge*, 1 (7-8).
7. *Deluge*, 4-5 (8).
8. *Deluge*, 8-9 (9).
9. *Deluge*, 10 (9).

10. Yassine gives himself a contradictory genealogy: is it possible to be both Berber through his father and a descendant of the Arab Idrissid lineage?
11. *Deluge*, 9 (9).
12. *Deluge*, 9 (9).
13. *Mémoire à S. M. le Roi*, letter that was never published. Written in French while Yassine was interned in the psychiatric hospital, it is accessible at www.yassine.net/letters/french-memoire.htm. This *mémoire* is a French version of the 1974 letter, although it is not a literal translation.
14. *Deluge*, 23 (14).
15. *Deluge*, 23 (14).
16. *Deluge*, 40 (20).
17. *Deluge*, 46 (22).
18. *Deluge*, 10 (9).
19. *Deluge*, 21 (13).
20. *Deluge*, 12 (10).
21. *Deluge*, 34 (18).
22. *Deluge*, 44 (22). Yassine "reports" in his letter the admonition delivered by Ziyad Ibn Abi Ziyad to the king at the king's request: "'Oh, commander of the faithful, tell me what is the condition of a man who has an implacable enemy?'
"'Umar said: 'He is in a very bad state.'
"Ibn Abi Ziyad said: 'What if he has two implacable enemies?'
"'Umar said: 'That is even worse.'
'And three?'
'He cannot live peacefully.'
'By Allah, commander of the faithful, there is not a person in the *umma* of Muhammad who is not your enemy!' 'Umar wept so much that Ziyad came to believe that he should not have spoken to him like that."
23. Message from Hassan II to the nation, July 11, 1971, quoted in "Le putsch du 10 juillet 1971 au Maroc," *Maghreb* 47 (July-Aug. 1971), 12.
24. "Le putsch," 15.
25. Houari Touati, "Approche sémiologique et historique d'un document hagiographique algérien," *Annales ESC* 5 (Sept.-Oct. 1989), 1224.
26. *Deluge*, 19-20 (13).
27. *Deluge*, 21 (13).
28. *Deluge*, 24 (15).
29. *Deluge*, 16-17 (12).

30. *Deluge*, 10 (10).
31. *Deluge*, 23 (14).
32. *Deluge*, 31 (17).
33. *Deluge*, 32 (18).
34. *Mémoire à S. M. le Roi*, 42.
35. *Deluge*, 16 (12).
36. *Deluge*, 16 (12).
37. *Deluge*, 20 (13).
38. *Deluge*, 66 (30).
39. *Deluge*, 46 (22-23).
40. *Deluge*, 39 (20). "Make your repentance a pact between you and Allah, and a *mubaya'a* between you and the *umma*."
41. *Deluge*, 109 (45).
42. *Deluge*, 42 (21). 'Umar Ibn 'Abd al-'Aziz, often called in Muslim tradition, particularly in Maliki literature, the "fifth rightly guided caliph," is for the same tradition a model of virtue: he is often described as a reformer (*mujaddid*) and a Mahdi, who reigned in the hundredth year of the hegira, which makes it possible to link this model of moral and political virtue to messianic expectations.
43. Abdellah Hammoudi, *Master and Disciple* (Chicago: University of Chicago Press, 1997).
44. *Deluge*, 1 (8).
45. *Deluge*, 4 (8).
46. *Deluge*, 24 (14).
47. *Qawma*, uprising, in contrast to *thawra*, revolution as conceptualized by Marx. But *qawma* also means "stand up together," from the verb *qama*, in contrast to the attitude of submission, and, by allusion here, to the elite that bows before the king.
48. For example: "You must know that the madness of this world and the total disorder that you see are only signs from all-powerful Allah announcing the destruction of the civilization of the *jahiliyya* (pre-Islamic period of ignorance) and also announcing . . . the renaissance of Islam and of the caliphate according to the path of the Prophet." *Al-jama'a* 5 (1980), 52. On earlier figures of messianism and millenarianism in Islam, see Mercedes Garcia-Arenal, ed., *Mahdisme et millénarisme en Islam, Revue des mondes musulmans et de la Méditerranée*, 91-94 (Aix-en-Provence: Édisud, 2000).
49. *Deluge*, 39 (20).

50. *Deluge*, 56 (26).
51. *Deluge*, 25 (15).
52. *Deluge*, 31 (17).
53. *Deluge*, 37 (19).
54. *Deluge*, 39 (20).
55. See Richard P. Mitchell, *The Society of the Muslim Brothers* (Oxford: Oxford University Press, 1969); Olivier Carré, *Les Frères musulmans: Égypte et Syrie (1928-1982)* (Paris: Gallimard, 1983); Olivier Carré, *Mysticism and Politics: A Critical Reading of Fizilâl al Qur'ân by Sayyid Qutb (1906-1966)* (Leiden: Brill, 2003); Gilles Kepel, *Le Prophète et Pharaon* (1984; Paris: Seuil, 1993).
56. *Deluge*, 22 (14).
57. See Mohamed Chekroun, "Islamisme, messianisme et utopie au Maghreb," *Archives des sciences sociales des religions* 75 (July-Sept. 1991), 127-52.
58. Mohamed Tozy, *Monarchie et islam politique au Maroc*, 63ff.
59. European penetration (notably by Spain, France, and England) into Morocco was carried out by force, but also by trade. The Madrid Conference of 1880 broadly extended rights of protection to European citizens.
60. Abdallah Laroui, *Les Origines sociales et culturelles du nationalisme marocain (1830-1912)* (Casablanca: Centre Culturel Arabe, 1993), 375.
61. Édouard Michaux-Bellaire, "Une tentative de restauration idrisside à Fès," *Revue du monde musulman* V, 7 (July 1908), 424-35.
62. Mohamed El-Ayadi, "Abdessalam Yassine, ou le poids des paradigmes dans le parcours d'un nouveau clerc," in Aïssa Kadri, ed., *Parcours d'intellectuels maghrébins* (Paris: Karthala, 1999), 129-64.
63. The Sharifian dynasty of the Sa'dis reigned from 1548 to 1641.
64. Jacques Berque, *Al-Yousi: Problèmes de la culture marocaine au XVIIe siècle*, 85. Berque speaks of an era of "founding heroes" (86).
65. Jacques Berque, *Ulémas, fondateurs, insurgés du Maghreb* (Paris: Sindbad, 1982), 241.
66. Passage translated by Eugène Fumey, "Chronique de la dynastie alaouite du Maroc, 1631 à 1894," part 4, *Archives marocaines* 9 (1906), 111; see also Abdelfatah Kilito, "Speaking to Princes: al-Yousi and Mawlay Isma'il," in Rahma Bourqia and Susan Gilson Miller, eds., *In the Shadow of the Sultan: Culture, Power and Politics in Morocco* (Cambridge, MA: Harvard University Press, 1999), 30-46.
67. Ahmad Ibn Khalid al-Nasiri al-Slawi, *Kitab al-istiqsa li-akhbar duwal al-maghrib al-aqsa*, trans. In Fumey, "Chronique," 112.

68. Hasan al-Yusi, *Muhadharat*, vol. 2 (Beirut, 1982), 398-401.
69. Hasan al-Yusi, *Rasa'il*, vol. 1 (Casablanca: Éditions al-Qabli, 1981), 192-93.
70. Berque, *Ulémas*, 242.
71. Ibid., 243-44.
72. Reported by Henry Munson, *Religion and Power in Morocco* (New Haven: Yale University Press, 1993), 171.
73. Yassine uses the verb *iqtabasa*, which means "draw from" and "imitate" or "borrow." There is simultaneous imitation of the master out of submission and appropriation of a quality.
74. *Islam between Preaching and State*, 313-14.
75. Quoted by François-André Isambert, *Le Sens du sacré: Fête et religion populaire* (Paris: Minuit 1982), 215-245.

Chapter 6

1. On January 13, 1990, the members of the advisory board of Justice and Benevolence were arrested outside Yassine's home, along with other members of the association, including Nadia Yassine's husband, 'Abd Allah Shibani. On May 8, 1990, disciples assembled outside the court of appeals in Rabat, near the Parliament, at the opening of the trial of the members of the advisory board. This assembly took place on the same day that the government announced the establishment of a "Council for Human Rights." After Friday prayers at the Ibn Sa'id mosque on August 3, 1990, Yassine announced the opening of a new front against the government through the practice of invocations and abstinence for a month. The advisory board members and 'Abd Allah Shibani were released on January 21, 1992.
2. *Al-minhaj al-nabawi* [hereafter *Way*] (N.p.: n.p., 2d ed., 1989), 5.
3. *Way*, 5. It also presents the notion of *ghazw* (invasion) (10); and on page 2: "Free the land of Muslims from the Zionist enemy that is crushing the part of our country that is most precious to us beneath all its dead weight."
4. *Way*, 14.
5. *Way*, 16 (on the same page, Yassine speaks of an "educational, organizational, public (*maydani*), financial, war, and political jihad").
6. *Way*, 11.
7. *Way*, 15.
8. *Way*, 13.
9. *Way*, 8 (on the notion of *'ubudiyya*) and 4 (on *hakimiyya*).
10. *Way*, 2.

11. *Way*, 6.
12. *Way*, 43.
13. *Way*, 4: "God's knowledge of the ranks in which his creatures should be placed is a mystery. But we place each of God's soldiers at a rank fitting with what we can see of their capacity for jihad and what they can offer jihad. We leave aside what is between God and his creature."
14. *Way*, 4.
15. *Way*, 25.
16. *Way*, 11 (see also the reference to Hasan al-Banna on p. 15).
17. *Way*, 9.
18. *Way*, 9.
19. *Way*, 17.
20. *Way*, 35.
21. *Way*, 59.
22. *Way*, 115.
23. Yassine quotes the following hadith: "Faith is made up of seventy-odd branches (*shu'bas*). The highest among them is to recite *la ilah illa allah* [There is no God but Allah], and the lowest is the unveiling of evil on the way." From this he directly infers the seventy-seven branches of the organization, which he classifies—a "classification in which not a word deviates from the book of Allah and the Sunna of the Prophet" (*Way*, 36). He organizes them into ten *khisal* (merits), which include companionship and community (*suhba wa jama'a*) and culminate in the tenth, jihad (this classification was sketched in the 1974 letter). Yassine attributes a very strong meaning to the classification of individuals according to the quality of their faith, their relationship to the divine, which will determine their hierarchical position in the movement. He thus multiplies the master-disciple relationship throughout the structure of his movement.
24. *Way*, 53 and 90.
25. *Way*, 92.
26. The Yassine case was brought up in parliamentary debates during the decade, notably on January 12, 1994, and December 27, 1995.
27. Conversation with author, June 29, 2003.
28. *Assahifa* 22 (Feb. 5-11, 1999), 4. The magazine *Maghrib al-yawm*, 111 (Mar. 14-28, 1998), mentions a "war of cassettes" between Yassine and Bashiri; in one of these video cassettes, in which the sheikh is speaking principally to students, he makes accusations against Bashiri without naming him: "Correct yourself; if you do not, the group will have to separate itself from

you, for you have entered into diabolical tyranny and you have given up what brings you close to God, you have made yourself into a pharaoh and a devil."
29. *Maghrib al-yawm*, 107 (Feb. 14-20, 1998), 9-10.
30. *Al-majalla al-maghribiyya*, 66.
31. Abdessalam Yassine, *Al-'adl* [*Justice*] (Casablanca: Dar al-afaq, 2000), 432.
32. This has led some of his fiercest critics to say that Yassine is a hidden Shiite. See Sa'id Lakhal, *Shaykh 'Abd al-Salam Yasin min al-darwasha ila'l-qawma* (N.p.: Al-ahdath al-maghribiyya, 2003); in Arabic.
33. *Al-bayane*, June 5, 1966.
34. When Muhammad V died on February 26, 1961, the army occupied strategic points in the capital. The king's death was kept secret. It was not until he had had a council of 'ulama sign the act of the *bay'a* that Hassan II had the radio announce the death of his father. Maati Monjib, *La Monarchie marocaine et la lutte pour le pouvoir* (Paris: L'Harmattan, 1992), 233.
35. Abderrahim Lamchichi, "De véritables défis pour le jeune roi Mohamed VI," *Confluences Méditerranée* 31 (Fall 1999), 9-23.
36. Abdessalam Yassine, *Mémorandum à qui de droit* [hereafter *Memorandum*] www.aljamaareview.com/chrif/memorandum.htm.
37. Nadia Yassine, conversation with author, December 12, 2001.
38. *Memorandum*.
39. The secret prison where, starting in the 1970s, Hassan II had incarcerated, in frightful conditions, many opposition figures. See Ahmed Marzouki, *Tazamart, cellule 10* (Paris: Paris-Méditerranée, 2001).
40. *Memorandum*.
41. *Assahifa* 11 (Nov. 20-26, 1998), 7.
42. Jacques Berque, *Ulémas, fondateurs, insurgés du Maghreb, XVIIe siècle* (1982; Paris: Sindbad, 1998), 266. [my italics]

Introduction to Part III

1. Most of these movements have been described, notably by Mohamed Dharif and Mohamed Tozy, but these writers have not related their presence in the public sphere to institutional Islam and have not studied the effects on these movements' strategies and ideologies of the political liberalization initiated by Hassan II. Mohamed Tozy, *Monarchie et islam politique au Maroc* (Paris: Presses de Sciences Po, 1999); Mohamed Dharif, *Al-islamiyyun al-maghariba* (Casablanca: Matba'at al-najah al-jadida, 1999).
2. Ghassan Salamé, ed., *Democracy Without Democrats* (New York: St. Martin's Press, 1994); Rex Brynen, Bahgat Korany, and Paul Noble, *Politi-*

cal Liberalization in the Arab World. 2 vols. (Boulder and London: Lynne Rienner, 1995 and 1998); John Waterbury, "Fortuitous By-Products," *Comparative Politics* 29, 3 (April 1997), 383-402; Abdo Baaklini, Guilain Denoeux, and Robert Springborg, *Legislative Politics in the Arab World: The Resurgence of Democratic Institutions* (Boulder and London: Lynne Rienner, 1999).

3. Guillermo O'Donnell and Philippe Schmitter, *Transitions from Authoritarian Rule: Tentative Conclusions about Uncertain Democracies* (Baltimore: Johns Hopkins University Press, 1986).

4. Steven Levitsky and Lucan A. Way "The Rise of Competitive Authoritarianism," *Journal of Democracy* 13, 2 (April 2002).

5. Indeed, in recently published accounts, Morocco is among the Muslim countries whose citizens most strongly support democratic norms and institutions. See Moataz A. Fattah, *Democratic Values in the Muslim World* (Boulder and London: Lynne Rienner, 2006), 103.

6. Dankwart Rustow, "Transitions to Democracy," *Comparative Politics* 2, 3 (April 1970), 337-63. See also, for the notion of pact, Otto Kircheimer, "Changes in the Structure of Political Compromise," in Frederic S. Burin and Kurt L. Shell, eds., *Politics, Law, and Social Exchange* (New York: Columbia University Press, 1969), 131-59. Beginning in the late 1980s, innovative work has examined the question of democratic transition but very rarely focusing on the Middle East and the Muslim world. See Guillermo O'Donnell and Philippe Schmitter, *Transitions from Authoritarian Rule: Tentative Conclusions about Uncertain Democracies* (Baltimore: Johns Hopkins University Press, 1986); Juan J. Linz and Alfred Stepan, *Problems of Democratic Transition and Consolidation: Southern Europe, South America, and Post-Communist Europe* (Baltimore: Johns Hopkins University Press, 1995). For more recent work dealing with the Arab world, see note 2.

7. Rustow, "Transitions to Democracy," 344-45.

8. Ibid., 358.

9. Ibid., 358.

10. Olivier Roy, *L'islam mondialisé* (Paris: Seuil, 2002), 36. Roy also writes: "This means not necessarily secularization of society but rather the redefinition of the relationships between religion and politics as two quite autonomous spheres," in Olivier Roy, *Globalized Islam. The Search for a New Ummah* (New York: Columbia University Press, 2004), 81.

11. See, for example, John Waterbury, "Democracy Without Democrats? The Potential for Political Liberalization in the Middle East," in Ghassan Salamé, ed., *Democracy Without Democrats;* the conclusion of Gilles Kepel, *Jihad: The Trail of Political Islam* (Cambridge, MA: Harvard University

Press, 2002); Patrick Haenni, *L'islam de marché: L'autre révolution conservatrice* (Paris: Seuil, 2005). There are exceptions to this tendency, for example, Charles Butterworth, "State and Authority in Arab Political Thought," in Ghassan Salamé, ed., *The Foundations of the Arab State* (London: Croom Helm, 1990); Jean Leca, "Opposition in the Middle East and North Africa," *Government and Opposition* 32, 4 (1997), 557-77; Gudrun Krämer, "Islamist Notions of Democracy," *Middle East Report* 183 (July 1993), 2-8. In a different way, Carrie Rosefsky Wickham studies mechanisms of persuasion in her analysis of Egyptian Islamist movements in *Mobilizing Islam: Religion, Activism, and Political Change in Egypt* (New York: Columbia University Press, 2002). Rustow himself recognizes that conflicts linked to religion have often been problematic for nascent democracies (Rustow, "Transitions to Democracy," 359).

12. In this regard, Olivier Roy is correct when he writes that the major Islamist movements "have abandoned transnational militant solidarity and are centered on national politics, with an agenda based on three main points: a call to replace corrupt ruling elites, a conservative sociocultural agenda, and robust nationalism." Olivier Roy, *Globalized Islam*, 58.

13. Linz and Stepan, *Problems of Democratic Transition and Consolidation*, 8.

14. Ibid. Linz and Stepan enumerate the institutions of political society as follows: "political parties, elections, electoral rules, political leadership, interparty alliances, and legislatures—by which society constitutes itself politically to select and monitor democratic government." One might, however, speak of political society even if it does not necessarily intervene to censure a democratically elected government.

15. The case of legalist Moroccan Islamism is thus close to the notion of "ethical civil society" proposed by Linz and Stepan for Poland in *Problems of Democratic Transition and Consolidation*, 270-71. But whereas Polish civil society did not compromise itself with the authoritarian regime of the 1980s and engaged in informal methods of action, the PJD, in contrast, is integrated into the political society controlled by the monarchy.

16. There is no doubt that these two areas of study are not the only ones possible. The public sphere and civil society have often been studied as the site of the political activity of Islamists in the Middle East and North Africa. For a recent example, see Armando Salvatore and Mark Le Vine, *Religion, Social Practices and Contested Hegemonies: Reconstructing the Public Sphere in Muslim Majority Societies* (New York: Palgrave Macmillan, 2005).

17. I borrow the idea of a "proliferation" of religious authorities from Gudrun Krämer and Sabine Schmidtke, eds., *Speaking for Islam: Religious Authorities in Muslim Societies* (Leiden, Boston: Brill, 2006).

18. John Waterbury, "Democracy Without Democrats?" 40.

Chapter 7

1. Decree of November 15, 1958.
2. Jean-Claude Santucci, *Les Partis politiques marocains à l'épreuve du pouvoir*, (Rabat: Publications du REMALD, 2001), 38. [my italics]
3. For a detailed description of the new Moroccan Constitution of 1993 and its later developments, see Abdo Baaklini et al., *Legislative Politics in the Arab World* (Boulder, CO: Lynne Rienner, 1999).
4. International Republican Institute poll, unpublished but leaked to the press. See Roula Khalaf, "Morocco Sees the Rise of 'Acceptable' Islamist Party," *Financial Times* (May 23, 2006). In this poll, the USFP is credited with 16.41 percent of voting intentions and Istiqlal with 10.76 percent.
5. Ellen Lust-Okar has generalized this model on the basis of a comparison of several examples of authoritarian regimes in the Middle East, explaining that the division of the opposition stabilizes the process of political liberalization. Ellen Lust-Okar, *Structuring Conflict in the Arab World: Incumbents, Opponents, and Institutions* (Cambridge: Cambridge University Press, 2005).
6. My analysis contradicts the hypothesis of Ellen Lust-Okar, who considers the case of Morocco in the mid-1990s and does not analyze the effect of the electoral success of the party included in the sphere of legal competition. At the time, the electoral success of the PJD was still very modest, and it might in fact have seemed that the monarchy's strategy of division had remained effective.
7. The lack of complete information thus has to be taken into account in analyzing the processes of political opening, in contrast to the hypothesis of complete information formulated by Ellen Lust-Okar.
8. Abdelsamad Dialmy, "L'islamisme marocain entre révolution et intégration," *Archives des sciences sociales des religions* 110 (April-June 2000), 5-27. See also Mohamed Dharif, *Al-islam al-siyasi fi-'l-maghrib* [*Political Islam in Morocco*] (Casablanca: Éditions Al-majalla al-maghribiyya li 'ilm al-ijtima' al-siyasi, 1992), 226-50.
9. Abdessalam Yassine, *La révolution à l'heure de l'islam* (N.p.: n.p., 1980).
10. Quoted by Rémy Leveau, "Aperçu de l'évolution du système politique marocain," *Maghreb-Machrek* 106 (Oct.-Dec. 1984), 21.
11. Quoted in "Chronique marocaine de l'année 1980," *Annuaire de l'Afrique du Nord* (1980), 698.
12. Speech delivered in Marrakesh, February 1, 1980, quoted in *Le Matin du Sahara*, 3015 (February 3, 1980).
13. See Runda Siddiq, *Thalathin 'am min hayat rabitat 'ulama al-maghrib* [*Thirty*

Years of the Life of the League of 'Ulama of Morocco]. Publications of the General Secretariat of the League of 'Ulama (Casablanca: Matba'at al-anba, 1991), 97.

14. My italics.
15. *Le Matin du Sahara*, February 3, 1980, quoted by Mohamed Tozy, "Monopolisation de la production symbolique au Maroc," *Annuaire de l'Afrique du Nord* (1979), 226.
16. Siddiq, *Thirty Years*, 98.
17. Decree of April 8, 1981. It also provided for the establishment of a training institute for preachers.
18. Rémy Leveau, "Aperçu de l'évolution du système politique marocain," *Maghreb-Machrek* 106 (Oct.-Dec. 1984), 21.
19. Dharif, *Political Islam in Morocco*, 119.
20. Conversation with the author, Casablanca, May 20, 1999.
21. Conversation with the author, Casablanca, May 21, 1999.
22. In the late 1970s, Mohamed Tozy and Bruno Étienne found twenty Islamic associations in Casablanca. Mohamed Tozy and Bruno Étienne, "Obligations islamiques et associations à Casablanca," *Annuaire de l'Afrique du Nord* (1979), 246.
23. Ben Kirane, conversation with the author, Rabat, June 24, 2003.
24. On *Jama'at al-tabligh* in Morocco, see Mohamed Tozy, *Monarchie et Islam politique au Maroc* (Paris: Presses de Sciences Po, 1999).
25. Mounia Bennani-Chraïbi, *Soumis et rebelles. Les jeunes au Maroc* (Paris: Éditions du CNRS, 1994).
26. Driss al-Kattani, *Harb al-Khalij, Nihayat al-Suqut al-'Arabi* [*The Gulf War: The End of the Arab Decline*] (Rabat: Maktabat Badr, 1992).
27. Ibid., 164-65.
28. Decree no. 1-84-150. A construction permit for mosques was required (it was granted by the provincial governor); mosques could not be private property: they were defined as pious endowments and their management and operation assigned to the ministry.
29. For a detailed investigation of these studies in the mosque, see Geoffrey David Porter, "At the Pillar's Base: Islam, Morocco and Education in the Qarawiyyin Mosque, 1912-2000." Ph.D. dissertation, New York University, 2002.
30. 'Abd al-Kabir 'Alawi al-Mdaghri, *Dhill Allah* [*The Shadow of Allah*] (N.p.: n.p., 2003). The polemics over this lesson are reprinted there.
31. *Al-'alam*, April 6, 1990.

32. Quoted by Dharif, *Political Islam in Morocco*, 274.
33. Ibid., 275.
34. *Tel Quel* 150 (November 13-19, 2004), 32.
35. Quoted by Michel Rousset, "Maroc 1972-1992. Une Constitution immuable ou changeante?" *Monde arabe, Maghreb-Machrek* 137 (July-September 1992), 15, 20.
36. The change of name was announced in *Al-raya* on February 10, 1992.
37. *Mithaq [Charter]* of the association, published by Dharif, *Political Islam in Morocco*, 278-88.
38. See Mohamed Dharif, *Al-islamiyyun al-maghariba [The Moroccan Islamists]* (Casablanca: Matba'at al-najah al-jadida, 1999), 172-73.
39. Ben Kirane, conversation with the author, Rabat, June 24, 2003.
40. See Tozy, *Monarchie et Islam politique au Maroc*, 143.
41. 'Abd al-Salam Harras, conversation with the author, Fez, 1999.
42. Tozy, *Monarchie et Islam politique au Maroc*, 252-53.
43. Ibid., 253; see also Santucci, *Les Partis politiques marocains à l'épreuve du pouvoir*.
44. Parliamentary Group of the PJD, *Hasilat al-sanawat al-khams. Iltizam wa 'ata (1997-2002) [Results of the Parliament for the Five Years 1997-2002]* (Rabat: Manshurat hizb al-'adala wa'l-tanmiya, 2002), 4.
45. Party of Justice and Development, *Ashghal al-majlis al-watani [Proceedings of the National Council]* (Rabat: Manshurat hizb al-'adala wa'l-tanmiya, 3-4 October 1998), 6.
46. Ibid., 7. Khatib went on to say that the political crisis had grown to unprecedented dimensions, in both socioeconomic and moral terms.
47. The MPDC received 364,324 votes, or 4.14% of those cast. The party complained about irregularities in the balloting, but, despite them, was pleased with the nine seats it won. See *Results of the Parliament*, 4-5.
48. Ibid., 9-10.
49. Ibid., 19-20.
50. Interview with Abdellilah Ben Kirane, in *Al-sahifa* 75 (July 19-25, 2002), 10.
51. Abdellilah Ben Kirane, conversation with the author, Rabat, June 24, 2003.
52. According to article 51, financial questions, if they commit too much of the state budget, can be excluded from discussion by the government. The Youssoufi government made frequent use of this article to reject proposals for Islamic finances and an Islamic economy offered by the PJD.
53. *Results of the Parliament*, 22. During the summer of 2002, the government

press and the leftist press conducted a campaign against the Islamists.
54. Despite certain qualifications: 48 percent of registered voters did not go to the polls, and 15 percent of the ballots were invalidated. It should also be recalled that 61 percent of the electorate was illiterate, and that the number of rural districts had increased in relation to urban districts. The government had promised to lower the voting age to eighteen, but it had not done so, thereby preventing 1.5 million young people from voting, which also provided a breeding ground for the Islamists. The two million Moroccans living abroad did not have the right to vote. Those without party affiliation could be candidates only if they had five hundred signatures, which made it possible to avoid having organizations banned by the regime use this label to present candidates.
55. Sa'd al-Din 'Uthmani, conversation with the author, PJD headquarters, Rabat, June 26, 2003.
56. See Tozy, *Monarchie et Islam politique au Maroc*.
57. Noureddine Ben Malek, "One Eye on the Government and the Other on the Municipal Councils" [in Arabic], *Al-sahifa* 83 (October 17-23, 2002), 9.
58. Mohamed Chikir, "Between Partisan Alliances and Technocracy" [in Arabic], *Al-sahifa* 83 (October 17-23, 2002). See also the declarations of Abdellilah Ben Kirane in *Al-sahifa* 81 (October 3-9, 2002), 8.
59. Chikir, "Between Partisan Alliances and Technocracy."
60. Ben Malek, "One Eye on the Government and the Other on the Municipal Councils," 9.
61. That is, filled by the royal palace without regard to election results, as was already the case for the Ministries of the Interior, Foreign Affairs, Justice, and Religious Affairs.
62. Omar Aharchane, "An Unacceptable Solution for an Unacceptable Situation" [in Arabic], *Al-sahifa* 83 (October 17-23, 2002).
63. Ben Malek, "One Eye on the Government and the Other on the Municipal Councils," 9.
64. The term *government* is used in the sense of the "executive," that is, the body whose members administer the state.
65. 'Abd al-Karim Khatib, conversation of Dr. Khatib with the author, Rabat, June 24, 2003.

Chapter 8

1. Ahmad Raysuni, *Nadhariyyat al-maqasid 'inda'l-imam al-shatibi* [*The Doctrine of the Intentions of Shari'a in Imam al-Shatibi*] (Rabat: Dar al-aman, 1990).

2. Muhammad Khalid Masud, *Islamic Legal Philosophy. A Study of Abu Ishaq al-Shatibi's Life and Thought* (Islamabad: Islamic Research Institute, 1977), 193-95.
3. Raysuni, *Nadhariyyat*, 325.
4. Ahmad Raysuni, *Al-fikr al-maqasidi* [*The Thought of the Intention of Shari'a*] (Rabat: Manshurat al-zaman, 1999), 46.
5. Ibid., 46.
6. Ibid., 48-49.
7. Ibid., 132-33.
8. Ibid., 131.
9. Ibid., 132-33.
10. Ibid., 133.
11. Ahmad Raysuni, *Al-haraka al-islamiyya. Su'ud am uful?* [*The Islamic Movement:. Ascent or Collapse?*] (Casablanca: Manshurat alwan maghribiyya, 2004), 52.
12. Ibid., 50-51.
13. Ibid., 50.
14. Ibid., 54-55.
15. Ibid., 45.
16. Ahmad Raysuni, *Al-umma hiyya al-asl* [*The Nation Is the Foundation*] (Meknès: Manshurat 'uyun al-nadawat, 2000), 12-14.
17. Raysuni, *Al-haraka*, 61.
18. Raysuni, *Al-umma hiyya al-asl*, 22.
19. Raysuni, *Al-haraka*, 32.
20. Ibid., 84.
21. Ibid., 82-83.
22. Ibid., 19.
23. Ibid.
24. Ibid., 22-23.
25. Papers published by the MUR include *Al-islah* between 1987 and 1989, *Al-raya* between 1990 and 1998, and *Al-tajdid* since 1999.
26. Movement of Unity and Reform, *Mithaq* [*Charter*] (Rabat: n.p., 2d ed., 1999), 35. In support, there is a quotation from verse 29 of the "Surat of the cave": "Say: truth emanates from our Lord. May those who will, believe, and those who will not, be unbelievers."
27. Movement of Unity and Reform, *Al-Ru'ya al-siyasiyya* [*Political Vision*] (Rabat: n.p., 1998).

28. Ibid., 36.
29. Ibid., 36-37.
30. Ibid., 49.
31. Ibid., 49.
32. Ibid., 49-50.
33. Ahmad Raysuni, "In Support of the *Bay'a* That Was Performed in Accord with the Book of Allah and the Sunna of His Prophet, as Well as in Obedience to the Good," *Al-tajdid* 27 (July 28, 1999), 1.
34. Movement of Unity and Reform, *Political Vision*, 47.
35. Ibid.
36. Ibid.
37. Ibid., 49.
38. Ibid., 44-45.
39. Ibid., 47.
40. Ibid., 32.
41. Ibid., 35.
42. Ibid., 37.
43. Ibid., 38.
44. Ibid., 46.
45. Ibid.
46. A MUR leader, conversation with author, June 2003.
47. Abu Hafs, "Our Islamists in Parliament and Their White Robes," *Al-sahifa* 83 (October 17-23, 2002), 15.
48. Party of Justice and Development, Parliamentary Group of the PJD, *Hasilat al-sanawat al-khams. Iltizam wa 'ata (1997-2002)* [*Results of the Parliament for the Five Years 1997-2002*] (Rabat, August 2002), 31-32. The PJD asked that Muslims be prohibited from selling and consuming wine, with the provision of severe penalties and restriction of sales to tourist zones.
49. Ibid., 37.
50. Ibid.
51. See the interview with Abdellilah Ben Kirane, in *Al-sahifa* 81 (October 3-9, 2002).
52. Interview with Sa'd al-Din 'Uthmani, in *Al-sahifa* 80 (September 28-October 3, 2002), 19.
53. *Al-sahifa* 81 (October 3-9, 2002), 8.

54. Ibid.
55. MUR, *Al-Barnamij al-tamhidi* [*Preparatory Program*] (Rabat: n.p., 2d ed., 2000).
56. Sa'd al-Din 'Uthmani, "The PJD Is Not a Lamb, It Will Be Difficult to Dismember," *Le Journal Hebdomadaire* (May 31-June 6, 2003), 13.
57. I have adopted the term "ethical civil society" from Juan J. Linz and Alfred Stepan, *Problems of Democratic Transition and Consolidation: Southern Europe, South America, and Post-Communist Europe* (Baltimore: Johns Hopkins University Press, 1996), 170-72, who use it for Poland. Islam—in its contemporary legitimating interpretations—is an important element that has made it possible to establish a rapprochement between the legalist Islamist opposition—which has abandoned its past great political utopia—and the monarchy. In this sense, the PJD has succeeded where 'Allal al-Fasi had failed for Istiqlal.
58. *Al-sahifa* 155 (April 10-16, 2004).
59. *Aujourd'hui le Maroc* (May 12, 2003).
60. Interview with Abdellilah Ben Kirane, in *Al-sahifa* 75 (July 19-25, 2002).
61. Sa'd al-Din 'Uthmani, conversation with author, June 26, 2003.
62. *La Tribune*, August 25, 2004.

Chapter 9

1. Dale Eickelman and James Piscatori, *Muslim Politics* (Princeton: Princeton University Press, 1997).
2. The idea of the proliferation of religious authorities was introduced by Gudrun Krämer. Gudrun Krämer and Sabine Schmidtke, eds., *Speaking for Islam: Religious Authorities in Muslim Societies* (Leiden and Boston: Brill, 2006).
3. *Le Matin du Sahara* (September 17, 2001).
4. *Le Matin du Sahara* (September 16, 2001).
5. The fatwa was published in *Al-Sahifa* 34 (October 5-11, 2001).
6. Jean-Pierre Tuquoi, "Les oulémas marocains accusent le gouvernement d'avoir 'péché' par œcuménisme," *Le Monde*, October 7, 2001.
7. Two signatories of the fatwa, Driss and Hasan al-Kattani, conversation with author, Rabat, December 15, 2001. Driss and Hasan al-Kattani made no retraction. They accused the Ministry of Religious Affairs of having threatened them. Hasan al-Kattani and two other signatories who had refused to back down were barred by the ministry from preaching. Hasan al-Kattani explained his refusal by emphasizing his role as *'alim*: "I am not

an official in the Ministry of Religious Affairs. But I am an *'alim* who tells people of what I have learned from Allah. That is my duty." Quoted in *Al-Sahifa* 36 (October 19-25, 2001).

8. Interview with King Muhammad VI by Anne Sinclair, in *Paris-Match* (October 31, 2001).

9. See Évariste Levi-Provençal, *Les Historiens des chorfas. Essai sur la littérature historique et biographique au Maroc du XVIe siècle au XXe siècle* (Paris: Larose, 1922); Abdallah Laroui, *Les Origines sociales et culturelles du nationalisme marocain (1830-1912)*, 2d ed. (Casablanca: Centre Culturel Arabe, 1993), 328-33.

10. First published in Fez in 1908, it was reprinted in 1989 with an introduction by Muhammad Ibrahim al-Kattani and a commentary by Driss al-Kattani himself: Muhammad Ibn Ja'far al-Kattani, *Nasihat ahl al-islam* (Rabat: Maktabat Badr, 1989). See Bettina Dennerlein, "Asserting Religious Authority in Late 19th/Early 20th Century Morocco: Muhammad b. Ja'far al-Kattani and His *Kitab Salwat al-Anfas*," in Krämer and Schmidtke, eds., *Speaking for Islam*.

11. Driss al-Kattani, conversation with author, Rabat, December 15, 2001.

12. Hasan al-Kattani, conversation with author, Rabat, December 15, 2001.

13. In *al-Ma'ida* 51. The fatwa also quoted verses *al-'Umran* 28 and 149 and *al-Nisa* 141.

14. The text then quotes the Surat *al-Baqara* 120: "Never will the Jews or the Christians be satisfied with thee unless thou follow their form of religion"; and *al-'Umran* 118: "They only desire your ruin: rank hatred has already appeared from their mouths: what their hearts conceal is far worse. We have made plain to you the Signs, if ye have wisdom."

15. Three of the signatories, 'Abd al-'Aziz Barrak (a preacher in Tangiers), 'Umar Ibn Mas'ud Ibn 'Umar al-Hudush, and Bashir Ibn Muhammad 'Isam, however, refused to join in this final clause of the document.

16. Driss al-Kattani, *Harb al-khalij, nihayat al-suqut al-'Arabi* [The Gulf War. The End of the Arab Collapse] (Rabat: Maktabat Badr, 1992).

17. Laroui, *Les Origines,* 327.

18. Ibid., 328. Driss al-Kattani rejects Laroui's interpretation of his father's *nasiha*. Laroui's Marxist-leaning analysis is invalid according to Kattani, who wants to return to a simple repetition of the religious terms used by his father to interpret present-day relations between Islam and the West. See the introduction by Driss al-Kattani to Muhammad Ibn Ja'far al-Kattani, *Nasihat ahl al-islam*, 23.

19. Laroui, *Les Origines,* 416.

20. *Da'wat al-haqq* XIII, 5-6 (May 1970), 111-13.
21. *Maroc-Hebdo International* 483 (October 31, 2001), 15.
22. The notion of impiety is used to characterize those who would enter into an alliance with the United States against a Muslim country. The accusation can only collapse once Morocco has chosen not to join a military alliance. Participation in the ecumenical ceremony is, on the other hand, described as a sin, not as impiety.
23. Declaration made one week after September 11, 2001, according to "La fatwa du cheikh Yassine," *Maroc-Hebdo International* 479 (September 28-October 4, 2001), 15.
24. See ibid. The PJD sent an open letter to the President of the United States expressing its compassion but warning America: "The Islamic nation, leaders, 'ulama, political parties, and organizations all together, who have condemned this odious act and expressed their solidarity with the American people, will not allow an innocent people to be punished for the crime committed by an isolated organization or a regime in power."
25. On the denunciation by some of the signatories, see *Al-sahifa* 35 (October 15-18, 2001).
26. As in the intervention of anti-riot police against demonstrators from Dar al-Hadith outside their school on the night of July 31, 2002.
27. Students from Dar al-Hadith, conversation with author, Rabat, June 2002.
28. Ibid.
29. *Maghreb* 37 (January-February 1970).
30. *Al-ihya* 1 (1992), 209.
31. Figure given by the Office of Original Education in 1999 in Rabat. In 1998-99, the great majority of students in this kind of school were at the secondary level (10,732 students).
32. Conversation with author, May 18, 1999.
33. See Malika Zeghal, *Gardiens de l'islam. Les oulémas d'al-Azhar dans l'Égypte contemporaine* (Paris: Presses de Sciences Po, 1996).
34. In 2002-03, early education covered 684,783 students (figures from the Ministry of Education). Dale F. Eickelman estimated the number of *msids* in Morocco in 1980 at 70,000. Dale F. Eickelman, "Traditional Forms of Education within a Diversified Educational Field: The Case of Quranic Schools," International Institute of Educational Planning, Paris (December 10-12, 1984).
35. Ri'asat jami'at al-qarawiyyin, *Dalil jami'at al-qarawiyyin* [Guide to Qarawiyyin University] (N.p.: n p., 1990).

36. Conversation with author, Qarawiyyin University, Fez, May 14, 1999.
37. A Qarawiyyin teacher, conversation with author, Fez, May 12, 1999.
38. Malika Zeghal, *Gardiens de l'islam*.

Chapter 10

1. Quoted in "Tape Ascribed to bin Laden Urges Muslims to Stand with Iraq," *New York Times* (February 12, 2003), A18.
2. "North Africa Feared as Staging Ground for Terror," *New York Times* (February 20, 2007), A1.
3. On al-Azhar's role in this regard, see Malika Zeghal, *Gardiens de l'islam. Les oulémas d'al-Azhar dans l'Egypte contemporaine* (Paris: Presses de Sciences Po, 1996).
4. Human Rights Watch, *Morocco: Human Rights at a Crossroads* (October 2004), 2.
5. On this tragedy, the reader can learn a good deal from the DEA memoire by Abdellah Tourabi, *Les Attentats du 16 mai 2003 au Maroc. Anatomie d'un suicide collectif* (Paris: Institut d'Études Politiques, 2003). I draw part of the description of the Sidi Moumen group from this memoire.
6. See Ahmed Benchemsi and Driss Ksikes, "Le ghetto de Sidi-Moumen: Une poudrière," *Cahiers de l'Orient* 74 (2004), 93-103.
7. See especially *Al-sahifa* 100 (February 14-20, 2003) and "L'archange de la mort," *Maroc-Hebdo International* (May 22-29, 2003).
8. Interview with Mohamed Dharif by Samy Ghorbal, "Ces Marocains qui sèment la mort en Europe," *Jeune Afrique L'intelligent* 2258 (April 18, 2004), 38.
9. See Gilles Kepel, *The War for Muslim Minds: Islam and the West*, trans. Pascale Gazaleh (Cambridge, MA: Harvard University Press, 2004), 142.
10. Interview with Mohamed Dharif by Samy Ghorbal, "Ces Marocains qui sèment la mort en Europe," *Jeune Afrique L'intelligent* 2258 (April 18, 2004), 38.
11. See Karim Boukhari and Khalid Tritki, "Nos amis les Saoudiens," *Tel Quel* 135 (July 2004), 10-16; Muhammad Dharif, "Le Wahhabisme face aux islamistes," *La Gazette du Maroc* (August 17, 2003); Abdellatif al-'Azizi, "Le procès de la Salafia," *Maroc-Hebdo International* 569 (August 1- September 5, 2003).
12. For lack of space, and in the absence of sufficiently solid data for the moment, I have not included an analysis of Moroccan jihadi Salafism. On the complex and recent debates surrounding the definition of Saudi Wahhabism, see Madawi al-Rasheed, *Contesting the Saudi State:. Islamic*

Voices from a New Generation (Cambridge: Cambridge University Press, 2007).

13. After the May 16, 2003, attacks, Muhammad Fizazi was sentenced to thirty years in prison for his ideological influence on those responsible for the attacks. *Maroc-Hebdo International*, close to the security services, called him in the aftermath of the attacks the "prince of the Salafists of Morocco." *Maroc-Hebdo International* 561 (June 5-12, 2003). Zakaria Miloudi and the suicide bombers of Sidi Moumen were said to be among his followers. But the Makhzen was reluctant to accuse him of direct responsibility for the attacks, because it had been trying to show that they had been planned from outside the country.

14. Translations of, respectively, *La 'adala, la tanmiya, islam lgzara. Al-'adala wattanmiya, munaddhama irhabiyya. Likhwanjiyya barra.*

15. Speech by Muhammad VI in Casablanca, May 29, 2003.

16. Ibid.

17. Speech from the throne on July 30, 2003, in Tangiers. [my italics]

18. See, for example, 'Abd al-Hayy al-'Amrani, "The Minister of Religious Affairs Wants to Monopolize the Legal Fatwa and Make it an Emanation of the Makhzen," *al-Ahdath al-Maghribiyya* (November 30, 2001), 13. This author delivers an acid critique of the Ramadan lessons and the uncritical discussions organized by the Minister of Religious Affairs.

19. See the declaration of Ahmad Raysuni concerning the institution of the commander of the faithful in *Aujourd'hui le Maroc* (May 12, 2003).

20. This debate actually began in the 1970s: plans for reform emerged out of a rereading of Islam, in proposals offered by the jurist 'Abd al-Raziq Mawlay Rashid. For a detailed history of these proposals and criticisms of them, see Mustafa al-Ahnaf, "Maroc. Le code du statut personnel," *Maghreb-Machrek* 145 (July-September 1994), 3-21. On the family law and its codification in early postcolonial Morocco, see Mounira Charrad, *States and Women's Rights: The Making of Postcolonial Tunisia, Algeria, and Morocco* (Berkeley: University of California Press, 2001).

21. Open letter of the Union for Feminine Action to Parliament, *Le 8 mars* 57 (March 1992).

22. Quoted by al-Ahnaf, "Maroc. Le code du statut personnel," and in a slightly different version by Zakya Daoud, *Féminisme et politique au Maghreb* (Paris: Maisonneuve et Larose, 1993), 19.

23. *Al-tajdid* 5 (January 12, 2000).

24. For further details, see Khadija Mohsen-Finan and Malika Zeghal, "Le Maroc entre maintien de l'ouverture et fin du laxisme," *Afrique du Nord-*

Moyen-Orient. Édition 2004-2005 (Paris: La Documentation française, 2004), 119-33.
25. *Le Matin du Sahara* (October 11, 2003).
26. Speech on October 10, 2003.
27. Law no. 70-30 reforming the family code. See also Alain Roussillon, "Réformer la Moudawana," *Maghreb-Machrek* 179 (Spring 2004), 79-99.
28. *Le Monde* (December 18, 2003).
29. See the pamphlet by Muhammad Fizazi ("Dossier Muhammad Fizazi"), on the web site <Alsunnah.info>, where one can also find texts attributed to the al-Qaeda leaders Ayman al-Zawahiri and Osama bin Laden (accessed November 15, 2004).
30. Elaine Combs-Schilling, "Casablanca 1993: Negotiating Gender and Nation in Performative Space," *Journal of Ritual Studies* 10, 1 (Summer 1996), 1-35.
31. In June 2000, the Ministry of Religious Affairs distributed four memoranda outlining new religious orientations: the regional councils of 'ulama came under the king's supervision and would be responsible for Islamic training and the choice and education of officials in charge of mosques. The mosques would be open all day (abrogating the decree of 1984 restricting access outside times of prayer) and would offer courses in literacy in which women could train other women. But at the time, these new provisions remained a dead letter. *Al-sahifa* 40 (November 16-22, 2001).
32. Decree no. 1.03.193 of December 4, 2003.
33. Decree no. 1.05.159 of August 24, 2005.
34. "Dar al-Hadith al-Hassaniyya. Ce qui va changer," *Sezame Magazine* (March 16, 2007; www.sezamemag.net, accessed March 30, 2007).
35. Decree no. 300.03.1, published May 6, 2004 in the *Journal Officiel du Royaume du Maroc,* abrogating Decree no. 270.80.1, published April 8, 1981.
36. Part IV of Decree no. 300.03.1.
37. www.islam-maroc.ma.
38. *Tel Quel* 153 (December 4, 2004).
39. Ministry of Religious Affairs, *Dalil al-imam wa'l-Khatib wa'l wa'idh* [*Manual for Imams and Preachers*] (2006), 35.
40. Ibid., 17.
41. Ibid., 18.
42. Ibid., 19.

43. Ibid., 20-26.
44. Speech from the throne on July 30, 2004.
45. See the vocabulary used in Decree no. 1.03.193 of December 4, 2003.

Epilogue

1. The American International Republican Institute poll predicting 47% for the PJD party was published in Morocco by *Le Journal Hebdomadaire* (18-24 March 2006).
2. Participation was as high as 58% in the 1997 elections and 51% in the 2002 elections.
3. The PJD won 503,396 votes (10.9%), while the Istiqlal Party won 494,256 votes (10.7%). Following are the results of the 2007 legislative election, in terms of the number of seats for the most important parties: Istiqlal, 52; PJD, 46; Mouvement populaire, 41; Rassemblement National des Indépendants, 39; USFP, 38; Union Consitutionnelle, 27; Parti du Progrès et du Socialisme, 17; other parties and independent candidates, 65.
4. The PJD had presented candidates in 56 constituencies in 2002. However, the fact that it almost doubled this number in 2007 could not guarantee a doubling of its number of seats, since the constituencies chosen in 2002 were the ones where it was most popular.
5. The Mouvement populaire has also decided to be part of the opposition.
6. Carles Boix and Milan Svolik call this type of regime "non-tyrannical or electoral autocracies," in which the polity is "governed by an unelected executive that shares power with an elected legislature." The authors show that in this type of regime "the legislature allows the notables to monitor whether the leader honors their agreement to share power. . . . On the other hand, elections allow the leader to monitor the local influence of local notables and thus ensure that he maintains a coalition that is capable of defeating any threat by a challenger or a revolutionary action." Carles Boix and Milan Svolik, "Non-Tyrannical Autocracies" (unpublished manuscript, April 2007).
7. Choices made by opposition elites to form strategic coalitions are shown to be a crucial factor in the existence of liberalizing electoral outcomes. See Marc Morgé Howard and Philip G. Roessler, "Liberalizing Electoral Outcomes in Competitive Authoritarian Regimes," *American Journal of Political Science* 50, 2 (April 2006), 365-81.
8. Ellen Lust-Okar, *Structuring Contestation in the Arab World: Incumbents, Opponents, and Institutions* (New York: Cambridge University Press, 2005).
9. PJD, *Al-Barnamij al-'intikhabi. Jami'an nabni maghrib al-'adala* [Electoral

Program: Let Us Build Together a Morocco of Justice] (N.p.: n.p., 7 Sept. 2007).
10. *Al-Barnamij*, 38.
11. Personal power and charisma were also criticized in the PJD's program through the critique of clientelism.
12. See Part I of this book.

GLOSSARY

'Alawite: dynasty of a line of sharifs that has ruled Morocco since 1635.

Almoravid: Berber dynasty (1056-1147) that established an empire in North Africa and Andalusia.

Bay'a: allegiance.

Bid'a: blameworthy innovation.

Bismillah: invocation of Allah ("in the name of God the kind and merciful").

Brotherhood (*tariqa*): group of disciples who devote themselves to mystical practices under the direction of a master. The brotherhood is generally named after its founder, who establishes its rules.

Caliph: leader of the Muslim community.

Dhikr: recitation of the names of God.

Faqih: specialist in Muslim jurisprudence. In Morocco, may be the equivalent of a Qur'anic teacher and is pronounced *fqih*.

Fatwa: religious legal opinion.

Fiqh: Muslim jurisprudence.

Habus: pious foundations, religious endowments.

Hadith: the prophet's activities or sayings as reported by his companions.

Hanbali: refers to one of the four main schools of law in Sunni Islam—the three others are the Shafi'i, Maliki, and Hanafi schools—and was founded by Ahmad Ibn Hanbal (780-855). Wahhabi theology was in part grafted onto this school of law in 18th-century Arabia.

Hegira: literally emigration, but more specifically the emigration of the Prophet Muhammad from his city of Mecca to Madina in 622.

Hisba: designates the obligation the law imposes on every Muslim to "command good and pursue evil." In the history of Islam, it gave rise to the office of *muhtasib*, an agent who ensures respect for the rules of Muslim conduct and respect for legal rules in markets and trade associations.

Idrissid: Moroccan dynasty (789-974), descended from a line of sharifs through 'Ali and Hasan, which established a regime independent from the 'Abbasid caliphate.

Islah: reform.

Jahiliyya: ignorance; pre-Islamic period.

Jihad: striving or struggling for a goal; holy war.

Khatib: author of a *khutba* or sermon.

Madrasa: religious school.

Mahdi: messiah, envoy of God.

Mahdism: messianism.

Makhzen: term from the Middle Ages designating the "storehouse" of the state treasury and, by extension, the administration in charge of that treasury. In Morocco today, the term designates the government and the system of power associated with it.

Maliki: one of the schools of law of Islam, founded by Malik Ibn Anas (711-96); the official school of law of Morocco.

Minbar: pulpit in a mosque from which the preacher delivers his sermon.

Mudawwana: until 2004, Moroccan family code, officially based on a codification of Maliki jurisprudence.

Mufti: author of a fatwa.

Qadi: judge.

Qarawiyyin: mosque and Moroccan religious university, known as the "mosque of the Kairouanis," built in 857.

Salafiyya: Islamic reform movement based on the return to the *salafs* ("pious ancestors"), who lived during the first three generations of Islam.

Shari'a: body of rules of Islam relating to religious, political, social, and private life.

Sharif: descendant of the prophet.

Sharifism: principle of descent from the Prophet.

Sheikh: describes 'ulama or any person known for his wisdom and piety.

Shirk: the process through which one associates people, objects, or other deities with Allah, or polytheism. The opposite of *tawhid*, which recognizes the uniqueness of God.

Sunna: custom of the Prophet, his words and deeds. They are recorded and transmitted through hadith.

Tahdith: modernization.

Tariqa: see *Brotherhood*.

'Ulama: plural of *'alim*, a term designating those learned in religious law and Muslim theologians.

Umma: the entire Muslim community; nation.

Waqfs: pious foundations, religious endowments.

Wirds: litanies made up of Qur'anic texts organized in a certain order by the sheikh of a brotherhood.

Zawiya: small mosque, small space set aside for prayer, or residence of the sheikh of a Sufi brotherhood. By extension, it also designates the brotherhood.

BIBLIOGRAPHY

Abun-Nasr, Jamal. *A History of the Maghrib in the Islamic Period.* Cambridge: Cambridge University Press, 1987.
Agénor, Pierre-Richard, and Karim El-Aynaoui. "Labor Market and Unemployment in Morocco: A Quantitative Analysis." *The World Bank* (October 26, 2003).
al-Ahnaf, Mustafa. "Maroc. Le code du statut personnel." *Maghreb-Machrek* 145 (July- September 1994): 3-21.
al-'Alami, Muhammad. *'Allal al-Fasi ra'id al-haraka al-wataniyya al-maghribiyya.* Rabat: Arrisala, 1972.
al-'Alawi, Sa'id Ibn Sa'id. *Al-ijtihad wa'l-tahdith.* Malta: Islamic World Studies Center, 1992.
'Ali, 'Abdullah Yusuf. *The Meaning of the Holy Quran.* Beltsville, MD: Amana Publications, 1997.
Anderson, Lisa. *The State and Social Transformation in Tunisia and Libya, 1830-1980.* Princeton, NJ: Princeton University Press, 1986.
_____, ed. *Transitions to Democracy.* New York: Columbia University Press, 1999.
Asad, Talal. *The Idea of an Anthropology of Islam.* Washington, D.C.: Center for Contemporary Arab Studies, Georgetown University, 1986.
_____. *Genealogies of Religion: Discipline and Reasons of Power in Christianity and Islam.* Baltimore, MD: Johns Hopkins University Press, 1993.
Ashford, Douglas Elliott. *Political Change in Morocco.* Princeton, NJ: Princeton University Press, 1961.
El-Ayadi, Mohamed. "Religion, État et société dans le Maroc contemporain." Doctorat d'État diss., Université Denis Diderot-Paris-7, 1997.
_____. "Abdessalam Yassine ou le poids des paradigmes dans le parcours d'un nouveau clerc." In *Parcours d'intellectuels maghrébins*, ed. Aïssa Kadri. Paris: Karthala, 1999, 129-164.
Baaklini, Abdo, Guilain Denoeux, and Robert Springborg. *Legislative Politics in the Arab World.* Boulder, CO: Lynne Rienner, 1999.
Bayart, Jean-François. "L'énonciation du politique." *Revue Française de Science Politique* 35, no. 3 (1985): 343-373.
Beck, Herman. *L'image d'Idriss II, ses descendants de Fas et la politique sharifi-*

enne des sultans marinides, 656-869/1258-1465. Leiden, New York: E. J. Brill, 1989.
Ben Barka, Mehdi. *Écrits politiques, 1957-1965.* Paris: Syllepses, 1999.
Ben Driss, Karim. *Sidi Hamza al-Qâdiri Boudchich. Le Renouveau du soufisme au Maroc.* Beirut, Milan: al-Bouraq-Arché, 2002.
Benchemsi, Ahmed, and Driss Ksikes. "Le ghetto de Sidi-Moumen: une poudrière." *Cahiers de l'Orient* 74 (2nd trimester 2004): 93-103.
Bennani-Chraïbi, Mounia. *Soumis et rebelles. Les jeunes au Maroc.* Paris: CNRS Éditions, 1994.
Bennani-Chraïbi, Mounia, and Olivier Fillieule, eds. *Résistances et protestations dans les sociétés musulmanes.* Paris: Presses de Sciences Po, 2003.
Bennani-Chraïbi, Mounia, et al., eds. *Scènes et coulisses des élections au Maroc. Les législatives de 2002.* Paris: Karthala, 2004.
Berque, Jacques. *Al-Yousi. Problèmes de la culture marocaine au xviie siècle.* Paris, Le Haye: Mouton, 1958.
———. *Maghreb: Histoire et Sociétés.* Paris, Alger: Duculot-SNED, 1974.
———. *L'Intérieur du Maghreb.* Paris: Gallimard, 1978.
———. *Le Maghreb entre les deux guerres.* 2d ed. Paris: Seuil, 1979.
———. *Ulémas, fondateurs, insurgés du Maghreb.* Paris: Sindbad, 1982.
Bezzaz, Sahar. "Challenging Power and Authority in Pre-Protectorate Morocco: Shaykh Muhammad al-Kattani and the Tariqa Kattaniyya." Ph.D. diss., Harvard University, 2002.
Boix, Carles, and Milan Svolik. "Non-Tyrannical Autocracies." Unpublished manuscript, April 2007.
Bonte, Pierre, et al. *Emirs et présidents. Figures de la parenté et du politique dans le monde arabe.* Paris: CNRS Éditions, 2001.
El-Boudrari, Hassan. "Quand les saints font les villes. Lecture anthropologique de la pratique sociale d'un saint marocain du xviie siècle." *Annales ESC* 40, no. 3 (1985): 489-508.
———. "Transmission du charisme et institutionnalisation: le cas de la zaouïa d'Ouezzane Maroc, xviième-xixème siècles." *Al-Qantara* 12, no. 2 (1991): 523-536.
Bourqia, Rahma, and Susan Gilson Miller, eds. *In the Shadow of the Sultan: Culture, Power and Politics in Morocco.* Cambridge, MA: Harvard University Press, 1999.
Brown, Nathan J. *Constitutions in a Nonconstitutional World.* Albany: State University of New York Press, 2002.
Brownlee, Jason. *Authoritarianism in an Age of Democratization.* Cambridge: Cambridge University Press, 2007.
Brumberg, Daniel. "Democratization in the Arab World? The Trap of Liberalized Autocracy." *Journal of Democracy* 13, no. 4 (2002): 56-68.
Brynen, Rex, Bahgat Korany, and Paul Noble. *Political Liberalization in the Arab World.* 2 vols. London, Boulder, CO: Lynne Rienner, 1995, 1998.
Burgat, François. *L'Islamisme au Maghreb.* Paris: Karthala, 1988.

_____. *L'Islamisme en face*. Paris: La Découverte, 1995.
Burke III, Edmond. "The Moroccan Ulama, 1860-1912: An Introduction." In *Scholars, Saints, and Sufis: Muslim Religious Institutions in the Middle East since 1500*, ed. Nikkie R. Keddie. Berkeley: University of California Press, 1972, 93-125.
Butterworth, Charles. "State and Authority in Arab Political Thought." In *The Foundations of the Arab State*, ed. Ghassan Salamé. London: Croom Helm, 1990.
Camau, Michel. *Pouvoirs et Institutions au Maghreb*. Tunis: Ceres Productions, 1978.
_____. "La transitologie à l'épreuve du Moyen-Orient et de l'Afrique du Nord." *Annuaire de l'Afrique du Nord* 38 (1999): 3-9.
Camau, Michel, and Vincent Geisser. *Le Syndrome autoritaire. Politique en Tunisie de Bourguiba à Ben Ali*. Paris: Presses de Sciences Po, 2003.
Carothers, Thomas. "The End of the Transition Paradigm." *Journal of Democracy* 13, no. 1 (January 2002): 5-21.
Carré, Olivier. *Les Frères musulmans: Égypte et Syrie*. Paris: Gallimard, 1983.
_____. *Mysticism and Politics: A Critical Reading* of *Fi zilal al-Qur'an by Sayyid Qutb*. Leiden: Brill, 2000.
_____. *Mystique et Politique. Le Coran des islamistes. Lecture du Coran par Sayyid Qutb Frère musulman radical (1906-1966)*. Paris: Cerf, 2004.
Casanova, José. *Public Religions in the Modern World*. Chicago: The University of Chicago Press, 1994.
Cavatorta, Francesco. "Neither Participation Nor Revolution: The Strategy of the Moroccan Jamiat al-Adl wal-Ihsan." *Mediterranean Politics* 12, no. 3 (2007): 381-397.
de Cenival, Pierre. "La légende du Juif Ibn Mech'al et la fête du sultan des tolbas à Fès." *Hespéris* 5 (1925): 137-218.
Chambergeat, Paul. "Le référendum constitutionnel du 7 décembre 1962 au Maroc." *Annuaire de l'Afrique du Nord* (1962): 182-183.
Charrad, Mounira. *States and Women's Rights. The Making of Postcolonial Tunisia, Algeria, and Morocco*. Berkeley: University of California Press, 2001.
Chekroun, Mohamed. "Islamisme, messianisme et utopie au Maghreb." *Archives des sciences sociales des religions* 75 (July-September 1991): 127-152.
Cleveland, William L. *Islam against the West. Shakib Arslan and the Campaign for Islamic Nationalism*. Austin: University of Texas Press, 1985.
Combs-Schilling, Elaine. *Sacred Performances: Islam, Sexuality, and Sacrifice*. New York: Columbia University Press, 1989.
_____. "Casablanca 1993: Negotiating Gender and Nation in Performative Space." *Journal of Ritual Studies* 10, no. 1 (1996): 1-35.
Cubertafond, Bernard. *Le système politique marocain*. Paris: L'Harmattan, 1997.
Dahl, Robert. *Polyarchy: Participation and Opposition*. New Haven, CT: Yale University Press, 1971.

Dakhlia, Jocelyne. *Le Divan des rois. Le politique et le religieux en Islam.* Paris: Aubier, 1998.

Daoud, Zakya. *Féminisme et politique au Maghreb.* Paris: Maisonneuve et Larose, 1993.

Dennerlein, Bettina. "Asserting Religious Authority in Late 19th Century/Early 20th Century Morocco: Muhammad b. Ja'far al-Kattani (d. 1927) and His *Kitab Salwat al-Anfas.*" In *Speaking for Islam: Religious Authorities in Muslim Societies,* ed. Gudrun Kramer and Sabine Schmidtke. Leiden, Boston: Brill, 2006, 128-152.

Denoeux, Guilain P., and Helen R. Desfosses. "Rethinking the Moroccan Parliament: The Kingdom's Legislative Development Imperative." *The Journal of North African Studies* 12, no. 1 (2007): 79-108.

Deverdun, Gaston. *Marrakech des origines à 1912.* Rabat: Éditions techniques nord- africaines, 1959.

Dharif, Mohamed. *Al-islam al-siyasi fi'l-maghrib.* Casablanca: Al-majalla al-maghribiyya li 'ilm al-ijtima' al-siyasi, 1992.

_____. *Al-islamiyyun al-maghariba.* Casablanca: Matba'at al-najah al-jadida, 1999.

Dialmy, Abdelsamad. "L'islamisme marocain entre révolution et intégration." *Archives de sciences sociales des religions* 110 (2000).

Diamond, Larry. "Elections without Democracy: Thinking about Hybrid Regimes." *Journal of Democracy* 13, no. 2 (April 2002): 21-35.

Diamond, Larry, Marc F. Plattner, and Daniel Brumberg. *Islam and Democracy in the Middle East.* Baltimore, MD: Johns Hopkins University Press, 2003.

Drague, Georges. *Esquisse d'histoire religieuse du Maroc, confréries et zaouïas.* Paris: Peyronnet et Cie, 1951.

Droz-Vincent, Philippe. *Moyen-Orient: pouvoirs autoritaires, sociétés bloquées.* Paris: Presses universitaires de France, 2004.

Eickelman, Dale F. *Moroccan Islam: Tradition and Society in a Pilgrimage Center.* Austin: University of Texas Press, 1976.

_____.*Traditional Forms of Education within a Diversified Educational Field: The Case of Quranic Schools.* Paris: International Institute of Educational Planning (December 10-14, 1984).

_____. *Knowledge and Power in Morocco: The Education of a Twentieth-Century Notable.* Princeton, NJ: Princeton University Press, 1985.

_____. "Madrasas in Morocco. Their Vanishing Public Role." In *Schooling Islam: The Culture and Politics of Modern Muslim Education.* ed. Robert W. Hefner and Muhammad Qasim Zaman. Princeton, NJ: Princeton University Press, 2007, 131-148.

Eickelman, Dale F., and James Piscatori. *Muslim Politics.* Princeton, NJ: Princeton University Press, 1997.

Entelis, John P. *Comparative Politics of North Africa: Algeria, Morocco and Tunisia.* Syracuse, NY: Syracuse University Press, 1980.

_____. *Culture and Counterculture in Moroccan Politics.* Boulder, CO: Westview Press, 1989.

———. "Un courant populaire mis à l'écart." *Le Monde Diplomatique* 589 (2002): 20- 21.
Entelis, John P., ed. *Islam, Democracy, and the State in North Africa.* Bloomington, IN: Indiana University Press, 1997.
Esslaoui, Ahmed Ben Khaled Ennasiri. "Kitab al-istiqsa li-akhbar duwal al-maghrib al- aqsa," trans. Eugène Fumey. *Archives marocaines* 9, 4th part (1906).
Étienne, Bruno, and Mohamed Tozy. "Obligations islamiques et associations à Casablanca." *Annuaire de l'Afrique du Nord* (1979): 235-259.
Euben, Roxane. *Enemy in the Mirror: Islamic Fundamentalism and the Limits of Modern Rationalism: A Work of Comparative Political Theory.* Princeton, NJ: Princeton University Press, 1999.
al-Fasi, 'Allal. *Al-Harakat al-istiqlaliyya fi'l-maghrib.* Cairo: Maktabat al-Risala, 1948.
———. *Al-naqd al-dhati.* Cairo: n.p., 1952.
———. *Nida al-Qahira.* Istiqlal leaflet, n.d.
———. *Difaʻ 'an al-shariʻa.* Rabat: Maktabat al-Risala, 1966.
———. "Risalat al-Qarawiyyin fi'l-madhi, al-hadhir wa'l-mustaqbal." *Al-iman* 7 (November 4, 1967): 15.
———. *Taqyim al-wadhʻ al-siyasi.* Istiqlal Party's Publications (November 1972).
Fattah, Moataz A. *Democratic Values in the Muslim World.* London, Boulder, CO: Lynne Rienner, 2006.
Ferhat, Halima. *Le Maghreb aux xiième et xiiième siècles: les siècles de la foi.* Casablanca: Wallada, 1993.
Ferrié, Jean-Noël. *La Religion de la vie quotidienne. Rites, règles et routine chez les Marocains musulmans.* Paris: Karthala, 2004.
Ferrié, Jean-Noël, and Jean-Claude Santucci, eds. *Dispositifs de démocratisation et dispositifs autoritaires en Afrique du Nord.* Paris: CNRS Éditions, 2006.
Garcia-Arenal, Mercedes. "Sainteté et pouvoir dynastique au Maroc: la résistance de Fès aux Saʻdiens." *Annales ESC* 45, no. 4 (1990): 1019-1052.
———. "Imposture et transmission généalogique: une contestation du sharifisme?" In *Émirs et présidents. Figures de la parenté et du politique dans le monde arabe,* ed. Pierre Bonte. Paris: CNRS Éditions, 2001, 111-136.
Garcia-Arenal, Mercedes, ed. "Mahdisme et millénarisme en Islam." *Revue des mondes musulmans et de la Méditerranée.* Vols. 91-94. Aix-en-Provence: Édisud, 2000.
García-Rivero, and Carlos and Hennie Kotzé. "Electoral Support for Islamic Parties in the Middle East and North Africa." *Party Politics* 13, no. 5 (2007): 611-636.
Gaudio, Atilio. *Allal al-Fassi, ou l'histoire de l'Istiqlal.* Paris: Alain Moreau, 1972.
Geertz, Clifford. *Islam Observed.* New Haven, CT: Yale University Press, 1968.
———. *Savoir local, savoir global. Les lieux du savoir.* Paris: PUF, 1986.
Geertz, Clifford, et al. *Meaning and Order in Moroccan Society: Three Essays in*

Cultural Analysis. Cambridge: Cambridge University Press, 1979.
Gellner, Ernest. *Saints of the Atlas*. Chicago: University of Chicago Press, 1969.
——. "Pouvoir politique et fonctions religieuses dans l'islam marocain." *Annales ESC* 25, no. 3 (1970): 699-713.
——. *Muslim Society*. Cambridge: Cambridge University Press, 1981.
Georges, Robert A. "The Concept of 'Repertoire' in Folkloristics." *Western Folklore* 53, no. 4 (October 1994): 313-323.
al-Ghazali, Ahmad. *Musahama fi'l-bahth 'an zawaya Bani yaznasin. Al-qadiriyya al- Budshishiyya namudhajan*. Fez: n.p., 1998.
Göle, Nilüfer. *Interpénétrations. L'islam et l'Europe*. Paris: Galaade Editions, 2005.
Grandguillaume, Gilbert. *Arabisation et politique linguistique au Maghreb*. Paris: Maisonneuve et Larose, 1983.
Haenni, Patrick. *L'islam de marché: L'autre révolution conservatrice*. Paris: Seuil, 2005.
Halstead, John P. "The Changing Character of Moroccan Reformism, 1921-1934." *The Journal of African History* 5, no. 3 (1964): 435-447.
Hammoudi, Abdellah. "Segmentarité, stratification sociale, pouvoir politique et sainteté. Réflexions sur les thèses de Ernest Gellner." *Hesperis-Tamuda* 15 (1974): 147-179.
——. *La Victime et ses masques*. Paris: Seuil, 1988.
——. *Master and Disciple: The Cultural Foundations of Moroccan Authoritarianism*. Chicago: University of Chicago Press, 1997.
——, and Rémy Leveau, eds. *Monarchies arabes. Transitions et dérives dynastiques*. Paris: Études de La Documentation française, 2002.
Hassan II. *La Mémoire d'un roi. Entretiens avec Éric Laurent*. Paris: Plon, 1993.
Hefner, Robert W., and Muhammad Qasim Zaman, eds. *Schooling Islam: The Culture and Politics of Modern Muslim Education*. Princeton, NJ: Princeton University Press, 2007.
Hermet, Guy. *Sociologie de la construction démocratique*. Paris: Economica, 1986.
——. *Les Désenchantements de la liberté. La sortie des dictatures dans les années 90*. Paris: Fayard, 1993.
——. *Passage à la démocratie*. Paris: Presses de Sciences Po, 1996.
Hervieu-Léger, Danièle. *Le Pèlerin et le converti*. Paris: Flammarion, 1999.
Huntington, Samuel. *The Third Wave: Democratization in the Late Twentieth Century*. Norman and London: University of Oklahoma Press, 1991.
Ibn 'Uthman al-Marrakshi, Muhammad. *Al-Jami'a al-yusufiyya bi marrakish fi tis'a mi'atin sana*. Cairo: Economical Press, 1935.
Isambert, François-André. *Le Sens du sacré. Fête et religion populaire*. Paris: Minuit, 1982.
Jamous, Raymond. *Honneur et Baraka. Les structures sociales traditionnelles dans le Rif*. Paris: Maison des sciences de l'homme, 1981.
al-Jirari, 'Abd Allah. *Al-muhaddith Abu Shu'ayb al-Dukkali*. Casablanca: Dar al-tháqafa, 1979.

Julien, Charles-André. *Le Maroc face aux impérialismes*. Paris: Jeune Afrique, 1978.
Kably, Mohammed. "Société, pouvoir et religion au Maroc des Mérinides aux Wattasides (xive-xve siècles)." Doctorat d'État diss., Université Paris-I, 1986.
Kalyvas, Stathis. *The Rise of Christian Democracy in Europe*. Ithaca, NY, and London: Cornell University Press, 1996.
_____. "Commitment Problems in Emerging Democracies: The Case of Religious Parties." *Comparative Politics* 32, no. 4 (July 2000): 379-399.
_____. "Religious Mobilization and Unsecular Politics." In *European Christian Democracy: Historical Legacies and Comparative Perspectives*, ed. Thomas Kselman and Joseph A. Buttigieg. Notre Dame: Notre Dame University Press, 2003, 107-135.
al-Kattani, Driss. *Harb al-khalij. Nihayat al-suqut al-'arabi*. Rabat: Maktabat Badr,1992.
al-Kattani, Muhammad Ibn Ja'far. *Nasihat ahl al-islam*. Rabat: Maktabat Badr, 1989.
Kedourie, Elie. *Democracy and Political Culture*. Washington D.C.: Washington Institute for Near East Policy, 1992.
Kepel, Gilles. *Le Prophète et Pharaon. Les mouvements islamiques dans l'Égypte contemporaine*. Paris: La Découverte, 1984 (rev. ed. Paris: Seuil, 1993).
_____. *Jihad: The Trail of Political Islam*. Cambridge, MA: Harvard University Press, 2002.
_____. *The War for Muslim Minds: Islam and the West*. Cambridge, MA: Harvard University Press, 2004.
_____, and Yann Richard. *Intellectuels et militants de l'Islam contemporain*. Paris: Seuil, 1990.
Khosrokhavar, Farhad. *Les Nouveaux Martyrs d'Allâh*. Paris: Flammarion, 2002.
Kilito, Abdelfatah. "Speaking to Princes: Al-Yusi and Mawlay Isma'il." In *In the Shadow of the Sultan: Culture, Power and Politics in Morocco*, ed. Rahma Bourqia and Susan Gilson Miller. Cambridge, MA: Harvard University Press, 1999, 30-46.
Kircheimer, Otto. "Changes in the Structure of Political Compromise." In *Politics, Law, and Social Exchange*, ed. Frederic S. Burin and Kurt L. Shell. New York: Columbia University Press, 1969.
Kostiner, Joseph, ed. *Middle East Monarchies: The Challenge of Modernity*. Boulder, CO: Lynne Rienner Publishers, 2000.
Krämer, Gudrun. "Islamist Notions of Democracy." *Middle East Report* 183 (July 1993): 2-8.
Krämer, Gudrun, and Sabine Schmidtke, eds. *Speaking for Islam: Religious Authorities in Muslim Societies*. Leiden, Boston: Brill, 2006.
Lakhal, Sa'id. *Al-Shaykh 'Abd al-Salam Yasin*. 3 vols. N.p.: Al-ahdath al-maghribiyya, 2003.

Lamchichi, Abderrahim. "De véritables défis pour le jeune roi Mohamed VI." *Confluences Méditerranée* 31 (Autumn 1999): 9-23.
Laoust, Henri. "Le réformisme orthodoxe de la *Salafiyya* et les caractères généraux de son orientation actuelle." *Revue des études islamiques* Cahier II (1932): 175-224.
Laroui, Abdallah. "Tradition et traditionalisation, le cas du Maroc." In *Renaissance du monde arabe,* ed. Anouar Abdelmalek, Abdelaziz Belal, and Hassan Hanafi. Paris: Duculot, 1972, 265-276.
_____. *La Crise des intellectuels arabes. Traditionalisme et historicisme*. Paris: Maspero, 1974.
_____. *Islam et modernité*. Paris: La Découverte, 1986.
_____. *Les Origines sociales et culturelles du nationalisme marocain (1830-1912)*. 2d ed. Casablanca: Centre culturel arabe, 1993.
Lauzière, Henri. "Post-Islamism and the Religious Discourse of 'Abd al-Salam Yasin." *International Journal of Middle East Studies* 37 (2005): 241-261.
Le Tourneau, Roger. *Fès avant le protectorat*. Casablanca: Atlantides, 1949.
_____. *Évolution politique de l'Afrique du Nord*. Paris: Armand Colin, 1962.
Leca, Jean. "Opposition in the Middle East and North Africa." *Government and Opposition* 32, no. 4 (1997): 557-577.
Leveau, Rémy. *Le Fellah marocain, défenseur du trône*. Paris: Presses de la Fondation nationale des sciences politiques, 1975.
_____. "Aperçu de l'évolution du système politique marocain." *Maghreb-Machrek* 106 (October-November-December 1984): 7-36.
_____. *Le Sabre et le Turban. L'avenir du Maghreb*. Paris: François Bourin, 1993.
_____. "Morocco at the Crossroads." *Mediterranean Politics* 2, no. 2 (1997): 95-113.
Lévi-Provençal, Évariste. *Les Historiens des chorfas. Essai sur la littérature historique et biographique au Maroc du xvième siècle au xxème siècle*. Paris: Larose, 1922.
Lévi-Strauss, Claude. *The Savage Mind*. Chicago: The University of Chicago Press, 1966.
Levitsky, Steven, and Lucan A. Way. "The Rise of Competitive Authoritarianism." *Journal of Democracy* 13, no. 2 (April 2002): 51-65.
Lewis, Bernard. *The Political Language of Islam*. Chicago: The University of Chicago Press, 1988.
Linz, Juan J., and Alfred Stepan. *Problems of Democratic Transition and Consolidation: Southern Europe, South America, and Post-Communist Europe*. Baltimore, MD: Johns Hopkins University Press, 1996.
Lucioni, Joseph. *Les Fondations pieuses "Habous" au Maroc*. Rabat: Imprimerie royale, n.d. (~ 1982).
Lust-Okar, Ellen. "Divided They Rule: The Management and Manipulation of Political Opposition." *Comparative Politics* 36, no. 2 (January 2004): 159-179.

_____. *Structuring Conflict in the Arab World: Incumbents, Opponents, and Institutions*. Cambridge: Cambridge University Press, 2005.
_____."Elections under Authoritarianism: Preliminary Lessons from Jordan." *Democratization* 13, no. 3 (June 2006): 456-471.
Lust-Okar, Ellen, and Amaney Jamal. "Rulers and Rules: Reassessing Electoral Laws and Political Liberalization in the Middle East." *Comparative Political Studies* 35, no. 3 (2002): 337-370.
Maghnia, Abdelghani. "Tradition et innovation à la Qarawiyyine." Doctorat d'État diss., Université Paris-8, 1996.
Maghraoui, Abdeslam M. "Monarchy and Political Reform in Morocco." *Journal of Democracy* 12, no. 1 (January 2001): 73-86.
_____. "Depoliticization in Morocco." *Journal of Democracy* 13, no. 4 (2002): 24-32.
Malka, Haim, and Jon B. Alterman. *Arab Reform and Foreign Aid: Lessons from Morocco*. Washington D.C.: The Center for Strategic and International Studies Press, 2006.
Al-Marruni, Makki. "Le Collège musulman de Fès (1914 à 1956)." Thèse de la Faculté des Sciences de l'Éducation, Université de Montréal, 1983.
_____. *Islah al-ta'lim fi'l-maghrib, 1956-1994*. Rabat: Manshurat kulliyat al–adab wa'l-'ulum al-ijtima'iyya, 1996.
Marzouki, Ahmed. *Tazmamart, cellule 10*. Paris: Paris-Méditerranée, 2001.
Masud, Muhammad Khalid. *Islamic Legal Philosophy: A Study of Abu Ishaq al-Shatibi's Life and Thought*. Islamabad: Islamic Research Institute, 1977.
Mayeur-Jaouen, Catherine, ed. *Saints et héros du Moyen-Orient contemporain*. Paris: Maisonneuve et Larose, 2002.
Mdaghri, 'Abd al-Kabir 'Alawi. *Dhill Allah*. N.p.: n.p., 2003.
Mervin, Sabrina. *Un réformisme chiite: ulémas et lettrés du Gabal 'Amil, actuel Liban- Sud, de la fin de l'Empire ottoman à l'indépendance du Liban*. Paris: Karthala, 2000.
Michaux-Bellaire, Édouard. "Une tentative de restauration idrisside à Fès." *Revue du monde musulman* 5, no. 7 (July 1908): 424-435.
Ministry of Religious Affairs. *Dalil al-imam w'al-khatib wa'l wa'idh*. Rabat: Ministry of Religious Affairs Publications, 2006.
Mitchell, Richard P. *The Society of the Muslim Brothers*. Oxford: Oxford University Press, 1969.
Mohsen-Finan, Khadija. *Sahara occidental. Les enjeux d'un conflit régional*. Paris: CNRS Éditions, 1997.
Molina, Fernàndez Irene. *Le PJD et la politique étrangère du Maroc. Entre idéologie et pragmatisme*. Documentos CIDOB Mediterràneo, no 7. Barcelona: Edicions Bellatera (mayo 2007).
Monjib, Maâti. *La Monarchie marocaine et la lutte pour le pouvoir. Hassan II face à l'opposition nationale de l'indépendance à l'état d'exception*. Paris: L'Harmattan, 1992.
Montagne, Robert. *Les Berbères et le Makhzen dans le Sud marocain. Essai sur*

les transformations politiques des Berbères sédentaires. Paris: L'Année sociologique, 1930.

———. *Révolution au Maroc.* Paris: France-Empire, 1953.

Morgé Howard, Marc, and Philip G. Roessler. "Liberalizing Electoral Outcomes in Competitive Authoritarian Regimes." *American Journal of Political Science* 50, no. 2 (April 2006): 365-81.

Movement of Unity and Reform. *Al-Ru'ya al-siyasiyya.* Rabat: n.p., 1998.

———. *Al-Mithaq.* 2d ed. Rabat: n.p., 1999.

———. *Al-Barnamij al-tamhidi.* 2d ed. Rabat: n.p., 2000.

———. *Al-Ru'ya al-tarbawiyya.* Rabat: n.p., 2000.

Munson, Henry. "Morocco's Fundamentalists." *Government and Opposition* 26, no. 3 (1991): 331-344.

———. *Religion and Power in Morocco.* New Haven, CT: Yale University Press, 1993.

Al-Nasiri, Ahmad Ibn Khalid. *Kitab al-istiqsa li-akhbar duwal al-maghrib al-aqsa.* Casablanca: Manshurat Wizarat al-Thaqafa wa'l-Ittisal, 2000-2005.

North, Douglass. *Institutions, Institutional Change and Economic Performance.* Cambridge: Cambridge University Press, 1990.

O'Donnell, Guillermo, and Philippe Schmitter. *Transitions from Authoritarian Rule: Tentative Conclusions about Uncertain Democracies.* Baltimore, MD: Johns Hopkins University Press, 1986.

Ossman, Susan. *Picturing Casablanca: Portraits of Power in a Modern City.* Berkeley: University of California Press, 1994.

Ouardighi, Abderrahim. *Un cheikh militant, Mohamed Belarbi al-Alaoui.* Rabat: Éditions du Littoral, 1985.

Party of Justice and Development. *Ashghal al-majlis al-watani.* Rabat: Manshurat hizb al-'adala wa'l-tanmiya (October 3-4, 1998).

———. *Hasilat al-sanawat al-khams. Iltizam wa 'ata (1997-2002).* Rabat: Manshurat hizb al-'adala wa'l-tanmiya, 2002.

———. *Al-Barnamij al-'intikhabi. Jami'an nabni maghrib al-'adala.* Rabat: n.p., September 7, 2007.

Pérétié, M. A. "Les madrasas de Fès." *Archives marocaines* 18 (1912).

Porter, Geoffrey David. "At the Pillar's Base: Islam, Morocco and Education in the Qarawiyyin Mosque, 1912-2000." Ph.D. diss., New York University, 2002.

al-Qadiri, Abu Bakr. *Madrasat al-nahdha.* Casablanca: Matba'at al-najah al-jadida, 1984.

———. *Mudhakkarati fi'l-haraka al-wataniyya al-maghribiyya.* Casablanca: Matba'at al-najah al-jadida, 1992.

Quandt, William B. *Between Ballots and Bullets: Algeria's Transition from Authoritarianism.* Washington, D.C.: Brookings Institution Press, 1998.

Rachik, Hassan. *Le Sultan des autres. Rituel et politique dans le Haut Atlas.* Casablanca: Afrique-Orient, 1992.

al-Rasheed, Madawi. *Contesting the Saudi State: Islamic Voices from a New*

Generation. Cambridge: Cambridge University Press, 2007.
Raysuni, Ahmad. *Nadhariyyat al-maqasid 'inda'l- imam al-shatibi*. Rabat: Dar al-aman, 1990.
_____. *Al-fikr al-maqasidi*. Rabat: Manshurat al-zaman, 1999.
_____. *Al-umma hiyya al-asl*. Meknès: Manshurat 'uyun al-nadawat, 2000.
_____. *Al-haraka al-islamiyya. Su'ud am uful?* Casablanca: Manshurat alwan maghribiyya, 2004.
Rézette, Robert. *Les Partis politiques marocains*. Paris: Albin Michel, 1955.
Ri'asat jami'at al-qarawiyyin. *Dalil jami'at al-qarawiyyin*. N.p.: n.p.,1990.
Rosefsky Wickham, Carrie. *Mobilizing Islam: Religion, Activism, and Political Change in Egypt*. New York: Columbia University Press, 2002.
Rosen, Lawrence. *The Anthropology of Justice: Law as Culture in Islamic Society*. New York: Cambridge University Press, 1989.
_____. *The Culture of Islam: Changing Aspects of Contemporary Muslim Life*. Chicago: The University of Chicago Press, 2002.
Rousset, Michel. "Maroc 1972-1992. Une Constitution immuable ou changeante?" *Maghreb-Machrek: Monde arabe* 137 (July-September 1992): 15-25.
Roussillon, Alain. "Réformer la Moudawana: statut et conditions des Marocaines." *Maghreb-Machrek* 179 (Spring 2004): 79-99.
Roy, Olivier. "Les nouveaux intellectuels islamistes: essai d'approche philosophique." In *Intellectuels et militants de l'Islam contemporain*, ed. Gilles Kepel and Yann Richard. Paris: Seuil, 1990.
_____. *The Failure of Political Islam*. Cambridge, MA: Harvard University Press, 1994.
_____. *L'Islam mondialisé*. Paris: Seuil, 2002.
_____. *Globalized Islam: The Search for a New Ummah*. New York: Columbia University Press, 2004.
Rustow, Dankwart. "Transitions to Democracy." *Comparative Politics* 2, no. 3 (April 1970): 337-363.
al-Sahili, 'Umar. *Al-ma'had al-islami bi tarudant*. Casablanca: Dar al-nashr al-maghribiyya, 1985.
Salamé, Ghassan, ed. *Democracy without Democrats*. New York: Saint Martin's Press, 1994.
Salvatore, Armando, and Mark Le Vine. *Religion, Social Practices and Contested Hegemonies: Reconstructing the Public Sphere in Muslim Majority Societies*. New York: Palgrave Macmillan, 2005.
Santucci, Jean-Claude, ed. *Le Maroc actuel. Une modernisation au miroir de la tradition?* Paris: CNRS Éditions, 1992.
_____. *Les Partis politiques marocains à l'épreuve du pouvoir*. Rabat: Publications du REMALD, 2001.
Schedler, Andreas. "The Menu of Manipulation." *Journal of Democracy* 13, no. 2 (April 2002): 36-50.
_____. *Electoral Authoritarianism: The Dynamics of Unfree Competition*.

Boulder, CO: Lynne Rienner Publishers, 2006.
Schulze, Reinhard. *A Modern History of the Islamic World.* New York: New York University Press, 2000.
Sharabi, Hisham. *Neo-Patriarchy: A Theory of Distorted Change in Arab Society.* Oxford: Oxford University Press, 1988.
Sharabi, Hisham. ed., *Electoral Authoritarianism: The Dynamics of Unfree Competition.* Boulder, CO: Lynne Rienner Publishers, 2006.
Siddiq, Runda. *Thalathun 'aman min hayat rabitat 'ulama al-maghrib.* Casablanca: Manshurat al-amana al-'amma li rabitat 'ulama al-maghrib, Matba'at al-anba, 1991.
Sraïeb, Nourredine. "Université et société au Maghreb: la Qarawiyyine de Fès et la Zaytuna de Tunis." *Revue de l'Occident musulman et de la Méditerranée* 38 (1984): 63-74.
Tazi, 'Abd al-Hadi. *Jami' al-Qarawiyyin,* 3 vols. Beirut: Dar al-kitab al-lubnani, 1972.
Touati, Houari. "Approche sémiologique et historique d'un document hagiographique algérien." *Annales ESC* 44, no. 5 (September-October 1989): 1205-1228.
———. *Entre Dieu et les hommes. Lettrés, saints et sorciers au Maghreb (xviième `siècle).* Paris: Éditions de l'École des hautes études en sciences sociales, 1994.
Tourabi, Abdellah. *Les Attentats du 16 mai 2003 au Maroc. Anatomie d'un suicide collectif.* Paris: Institut d'études politiques, 2003.
Tozy, Mohamed. "Monopolisation de la production symbolique au Maroc." *Annuaire de l'Afrique du Nord* (1979): 226.
———. *Monarchie et Islam politique au Maroc.* Paris: Presses de Sciences Po, 1999.
Tuquoi, Jean-Pierre. *Le dernier roi. Crépuscule d'une dynastie.* Paris: Grasset, 2001.
Valensi, Lucette. "Le roi chronophage. La construction d'une conscience historique dans le Maroc post-colonial." *Cahiers d'études africaines* 119-120, 30-3/4 (1990): 279-298.
———. *Fables de la mémoire.* Paris: Seuil, 1992.
Vermeren, Pierre. "La mutation sociale de l'enseignement supérieur musulman sous le protectorat au Maroc." In *Parcours d'intellectuels maghrébins,* ed. Aïssa Kadri. Paris: Karthala, 2000.
———. *Le Maroc en transition.* Paris: La Découverte, 2001.
———. *École, élite et pouvoir au Maroc et en Tunisie au xxe siècle. Des nationalistes aux islamistes.* Rabat: Alizés, 2002; and Paris: La Découverte, 2003.
Volpi, Frédéric. *Islam and Democracy: The Failure of Dialogue in Algeria.* London, Sterling, VA: Pluto Press, 2003.
Waltz, Susan E. *Human Rights and Reform: Changing the Face of North African Politics.* Berkeley: University of California Press, 1995.
Waterbury, John. *The Commander of the Faithful: The Moroccan Political Elite*

—*A Study in Segmented Politics*. New York: Columbia University Press, 1970.

———. "Democracy Without Democrats? The Potential for Political Liberalization in the Middle East." In *Democracy without Democrats*, ed. Ghassan Salamé. New York: Saint Martin's Press, 1994, 23-47.

———. "Fortuitous By-Products." *Comparative Politics* 29, no. 3 (April 1997): 383-402.

Wiktorowicz, Quentin. *Islamic Activism: A Social Movement Theory Approach*. Bloomington: Indiana University Press, 2004.

Willis, Michael. "Morocco's Islamists and the Legislative Elections of 2002: The Strange Case of the Party That Did Not Want to Win." *Mediterranean Politics* 9, no. 1 (2004): 53-81.

———. "Containing Radicalism through the Political Process in North Africa." *Mediterranean Politics* 11, no. 2 (2006): 137-50.

Yassine, Abdessalam. *Al-islam bayna al-daʻwa waʼl-dawla*. Casablanca: Matbaʻat al- najah al-jadida, 1972.

———. *Al-islam ghadan*. Casablanca: Matbaʻat al-najah al-jadida, 1973.

———. *Al-islam aw al-tufan*. Marrakech: n.p., 1974.

———. *L'Islam à l'heure de la révolution*. N.p.: n.p., 1980.

———. *Al-minhaj al-nabawi*. 2d ed. N.p.: n.p., 1989.

———. *Hiwar maʻa al-fudhala al-dimuqratiyyin*. Casablanca: Matbuʻat al-ufuq, 1994.

———. *Al-ʻadl*. Casablanca: Dar al-afaq, 2000.

———. *Mémorandum à qui de droit*. <www.aljamaareview.com/chrif/memorandum.htm>, 2000.

Yassine, Nadia. *Toutes voiles dehors*. Casablanca: Le Fennec, 2003.

Al-Yusi, Hasan. *Muhadharat 2*. Beirut: n.p., 1982.

———. "*Rasa'il*." Casablanca: Éditions al-Qabli, 1981.

Zaman, Muhammad Qasim. *Religion and Politics under the Early 'Abbasids: The Emergence of the Proto-Sunni Elite*. Leiden, New York: Brill, 1997.

———. *The Ulama in Contemporary Islam: Custodians of Change*. Princeton, NJ: Princeton University Press, 2002.

Zartman, William. *The Political Economy of Morocco*. New York: Praeger, 1987.

Zeghal, Malika. *Gardiens de l'islam. Les oulémas d'al-Azhar dans l'Égypte contemporaine*. Paris: Presses de Sciences Po, 1996.

———. "État et marché des biens religieux. Les voies égyptienne et tunisienne." *Critique internationale* 5 (October 1999): 75-95.

———. "S'éloigner, se rapprocher: la gestion et le contrôle de l'islam dans la république de Bourguiba et la monarchie de Hassan II." In *Monarchies arabes. Transitions et dérives dynastiques*, ed. Abdellah Hammoudi and Rémy Leveau. Paris: Les études de La Documentation française, 2002, 59-79.

———. "Les enjeux autour d'une fatwa marocaine." In *Le Maghreb après le 11 septembre*, ed. Rémy Leveau et Khadija Mohsen-Finan. Paris: Publication de l'Institut Français des Relations Internationales 44 (2002): 51-65.

———. "Islam, Islamistes et ouvertures politiques dans le monde arabe. Quelques jalons pour approche non culturaliste." In *La démocratie est-elle soluble dans l'islam?* ed. Abdellah Hammoudi, Denis Bauchart, and Rémy Leveau. Paris: CNRS Éditions, 2007, 93-110.

———. "The Recentering of Religious Discourse and Knowledge: The Case of al-Azhar in 20th Century Egypt." In *Schooling Islam: The Culture and Politics of Modern Muslim Education*, ed. Robert W. Hefner and Muhammad Qasim Zaman. Princeton, NJ: Princeton University Press, 2007, 107-130.

Zeghal, Malika, and Marc Gaborieau, eds. *Autorités religieuses en Islam. Archives des sciences sociales des religions* 125 (January-March 2004).

Zeghal, Malika, and Khadija Mohsen-Finan. "Le Maroc entre maintien de l'ouverture et fin du laxisme." *Afrique du Nord-Moyen-Orient, Édition 2004-2005*. Paris: La Documentation française, 2004, 119-133.

Zeghal, Malika, and Khadija Mohsen-Finan. "Les islamistes dans la compétition politique. Le cas du Parti de la Justice et du Développement au Maroc." *Revue Française de Sciences Politique* 56, no. 1 (February 2006): 79-119.

INDEX

'Abd al-'Aziz, Mawlay (Sultan) 12-13, 24, 106, 108, 112, 116, 171, 217, 289, 303
'Abd al-Hafiz, Mawlay (Sultan) 17-18, 24, 112, 217
'Abduh, Muhammad 17, 19, 188
Abu Hafs 200, 239, 302
Abu Hazm 105
al-'adl wa'l-ihsan (see also Justice and Benevolence) 120, 285
Admonition (see also *Nasiha*) 79-80, 82, 91, 93-95, 97-99, 101, 103, 105-107, 109, 111-117, 126, 132-133, 135, 216, 220, 288
al-'Alawi, Ibn al-'Arbi 14, 19, 20, 22, 33, 44
'Alawite 4, 16, 18, 43, 70, 84, 113, 131, 141, 152, 169, 196, 216-217, 276, 281, 285, 311
Algeria 17, 33, 63-64, 74, 170, 229, 232, 307, 317-318, 324, 326
'Alimiyya 22, 45, 280
ALM (Moroccan Army of Liberation) 23
Arabization 36, 45, 50-57, 61, 65, 74, 95, 164, 198, 217, 224
al-'Araki, 'Izz al-Din 56, 238
Asad, Talal xxii, 272, 315
Ash'ari doctrine 253
Association of Algerian 'Ulama 19, 278
Association of the Circle of Islamic Thought 217
Association of the Islamic Group 167, 171, 175
Association of 'Ulama of Morocco 38, 42
Association of 'Ulama of Sus 41
Authoritarianism xi, xxiii, 4, 109, 131, 145, 147, 153, 155, 157, 160, 165, 193, 271, 273, 287, 294, 316, 320, 322-326
Awrid, Hasan 134

Al-'Aynayn, Ma 112, 172
al-Azhar, University of 226

Baha'i 28, 44
Balafrej, Ahmad 278
al-Banna, Hasan 72, 111, 191, 292
Bargaining: 148, 180, 200, 260
  ex-post 260
  ex-ante 260, 265
Bashiri, Muhammad 129
Basri, Driss 131, 134, 182
Basri, Fqih 14, 87
Bay'a ix, 4-5, 23, 57, 68, 75, 112, 114, 127, 131-133, 195-196, 212, 244, 253, 285, 293, 301, 311
Ben Barka, Mehdi 14, 39-40, 277, 280, 316
Ben Driss, Karim 89, 286, 316
Ben Kirane, Abdellilah 167, 172, 175, 181, 298-299, 302-303
Bennani-Chraïbi, Mounia 272, 285, 297, 316
Berque, Jacques 113, 116, 140, 284, 287, 290, 293, 316
Bin Laden, Osama 232, 307
al-Bishri, Tariq 172
Boumediene 63
Bourguiba, Habib 32, 45-46, 63, 317, 327
Bricolage (bricoleur) xxvii
Bu Madyan, Sidi 88
Budshishiyya 87-90, 92-93, 119, 249, 286
Burgat, François 272, 286, 316
Burke, Edmund 10-11, 274
Bu Talib, 'Abd al-Hadi 51-52, 58, 238, 274
Al-Buti, Sa'id Ramadan 172

Carré, Olivier 284, 290, 317
Citizen Forces 206
Civilizational Alternative 210
Combs-Schilling, Elaine 274, 307, 317

Comité d'Action Marocaine 14
Commander of the faithful xiv, xxvi, 3, 23, 28, 44-45, 60, 74, 79, 96, 128, 132, 171, 173, 178, 195, 199, 204-205, 207, 209, 216, 229, 231, 233-235, 237, 239, 241, 243-247, 249, 251, 253-257, 266, 268, 274, 278, 281, 284, 288, 307, 326
Companionship (*suhba*) 89, 91, 117, 292
Competitive authoritarianism 147, 294, 322
Councils of 'Ulama 65, 140, 165, 170-171, 210, 224, 250, 255, 308

Dahir, Berber 14, 85
Daoud, Zakya 307, 318
Dar al-Hadith (Dar al-Hadith al-Hassaniyya) xxix, 49-50, 56, 59, 71, 169, 171, 224-225, 227-228, 249-250, 267, 284, 305, 308
Darqawiyya 17, 21
Democracy xx, xxvi, 25, 29, 72, 74-75, 147, 149, 155-156, 173, 183, 187-188, 190-191, 193-195, 197, 207, 217, 241, 243, 255, 260-261, 263, 266, 268, 271, 273, 293-295, 315-319, 321-323, 325-327
Deverdun, Gaston 85, 285, 318
Dharif, Muhammad 281, 306
Dialmy, Abdelsamad 296, 318
Didat, Ahmad 172
Drague, Georges 276, 318
al-Dukkali, Abu Shu'ayb 22, 41, 85, 276, 278, 320

Education, Ministry of 35, 37-38, 42-43, 46, 48-49, 51, 54, 72, 161, 217, 226-227, 250, 279, 305
Egypt xix, 11, 13-16, 19, 29, 33, 36, 38, 46, 48, 50, 63, 156, 161, 193, 226, 228, 234, 238, 272, 295, 325, 328
Eickelman, Dale 210, 285-286, 303, 305, 318
El-Ayadi, Mohamed 290, 315
El-Aynaoui, Karim 285, 315
Election: xxi, 73, 135, 148, 150, 153, 155, 157-160, 172-175, 180, 182-185, 191, 200, 202, 232, 244, 259-264, 268-269, 271, 278, 295, 308-309, 316, 318, 323, 327
 election of 1997 180-181, 264
 election of 2002 182-186
 election of 2007 259-269
 municipal election 160, 179
Etienne, Bruno 297, 319

Family Law 57, 198, 242, 307
Fanon, Frantz 67
Faqih (see also *Fqih*) 20, 311
al-Fasi, 'Abbas 262
al-Fasi, 'Abd al-Qadir 114
al-Fasi, 'Abd al-Wahid 22
al-Fasi, 'Allal 6, 16, 19-23, 25-30, 33, 35, 44-48, 57, 63, 69-75, 85, 87, 102, 188, 192-193, 217, 256, 267, 276-279, 281, 284-285, 302, 315, 319
al-Fasi, Muhammad 20, 30, 35, 278-279, 315
Fatwa 12, 169, 213, 215-224, 238, 278, 303-304, 307, 311-312, 327
FDIC (Front for the Defense of Constitutional Institutions) 29
Ferhat, Halima 284, 319
Fez vii, xxix, 12-13, 17, 21-22, 34, 36-37, 41, 45, 47-49, 55, 60, 66, 85-87, 112, 114, 116, 139, 171, 177, 180, 188, 216, 227-228, 239, 276, 280, 286, 298, 303, 305, 320
Fiqh 18-20, 71, 86, 249, 311
Fizazi, Muhammad 239-240, 306-307
Fqih (see also *Faqih*) ix, 14, 53-54, 87, 169, 280, 311
Furqani, Habib 245

Gad al-Haqq, Gad al-Haqq 'Ali 169
Geertz, Clifford 22, 273, 277, 280, 284, 319
Genealogy xxvi, 17, 52, 83-84, 93, 227, 239, 257, 287-288
Ghannushi, Rashid 172
al-Ghazali, Ahmad 286, 320
GICM (Groupe Islamique Combattant Marocain) 233, 235, 237, 239
Gilson Miller, Susan 321
Green March 64, 156

INDEX

GSPC (Salafist Group for Preaching and Combat) 232-233
Guédira, Rédha 28, 278

Habus 27, 34, 274, 278-279, 311
hadith 18-19, 49, 59, 88, 225, 292, 311-312
Hammoudi, Abdellah xxiv, 109, 273, 287, 289, 320, 327-328
Haqqawi, Bassima 247
Harras, 'Abd al-Salam 55, 177, 282, 298
Hasan, Mawlay (Sultan) 17
Hassan II, King xi, 97, 129, 131, 284
Hassanian lessons 57

Ibn 'Abd al-'Abbas, Yusif 14, 39-40, 51, 85-87, 98, 245
Ibn 'Abd al-'Aziz, 'Umar (Caliph) 106, 108, 116, 289
Ibn 'Abd al-Malik, Sulayman 105
Ibn 'Abd al-Wahhab, Muhammad 275
Ibn Abi Mahalli 80
Ibn Abi Ziyad, Ziyad 102, 288
Ibn 'Arafa, Muhammad (Sultan) 23
Ibn 'Ashur, al-Tahar 188
Ibn Baz 169
Ibn Hima, Muhammad 51
Ibn Ishaq, Khalil 19
Ibn Jallun, Majid 30
Ibn Jallun, 'Umar 162
Ibn Sa'id al-'Alawi, Sa'id 276
Ibn Sa'ud, 'Abd al-'Aziz 24, 276
Ibn Siddiq, 'Abd Allah Muhammad 169
Ibn Siddiq, 'Abd al-'Aziz 169, 171
Ibn Suda, Ahmad 58, 165, 238, 283
Ibn Taymiyya 19, 24
Ibn 'Uthman, Muhammad 87, 285, 320
Ibn Yusif Institute (see also Yusufiyya) 85, 245
Idriss, Mawlay (Sultan) 53
Ijtihad 244, 251, 276
Institutions: xi-xiii, xvi-xviii, xxii-xxiii, xxv-xxviii, xxx, 6, 9-10, 13-14, 29, 32, 34-36, 56, 58, 73-74, 86-87, 94, 107, 145, 149-151, 170, 173, 176, 181, 193-194, 196-197, 203, 213, 217, 221-222, 224, 226, 232, 241, 250-251, 255-256, 266-275, 294-296, 309, 317, 323-324
  political xi, 73, 107, 109, 149-150, 155-169, 176, 196, 256, 270, 273
  liberalization of xix, xxix, 25, 147-150, 152, 155-169, 256, 259, 271, 293, 296
  redefinition of 131, 194
  religious xi, xiii, xvi-xviii, xxiii, xxv-xxvii, xxx, 9-10, 32, 35, 58, 74, 94, 151, 181, 193, 213, 221, 241, 251, 267, 268-269, 272, 274, 317
  design of xi, xvi-xviii, 9-14, 31-41, 43-47, 52-60, 249-257, 267
  fragmentation of xviii, xxv, 31-38, 48-52, 57, 65, 151, 188, 210, 222, 224, 229, 234, 242, 249
Isambert, François-André 291, 320
Islamic Association of Ksar al-Kabir 188
Islamic Salvation Front 170
Islamic State xvi, xix-xxi, 94, 96, 123, 151, 167, 187, 191-192, 197, 219, 222, 267, 306, 324
Islamism viii, xii-xvi, xviii-xx, xxii, xxiv, xxvi, xxviii, xxx-xxxii, 4-6, 10, 12, 14, 16, 18, 20, 22, 24, 26, 28, 30, 32, 34, 36, 38, 40, 42, 44, 46, 48, 50, 52-54, 56, 58, 60, 62, 64-66, 68, 70, 72, 74-76, 80, 82, 84, 86-88, 90, 92-94, 96, 98, 100, 102, 104, 106, 108, 110-112, 114, 116, 118, 120, 122, 124, 126, 128, 130, 132, 134, 136-138, 140, 142, 145-146, 148-150, 152-154, 156-162, 164-170, 172-178, 180-182, 184, 186, 188-190, 192-194, 196, 198, 200, 202-204, 206, 210, 212, 214, 216-218, 220, 222-224, 226, 228, 232, 234-236, 238, 240, 242, 244, 246, 248, 250, 252, 254, 256, 260, 262, 264, 266, 268, 270, 295, 312, 316, 318, 320, 322, 324, 326, 328, 330-331
Isma'il, Mawlay (Sultan) 113-114, 116, 131, 290, 321
Istiqlal, party of 10, 70, 262

Jettou, Driss 185
Jihad 13, 38, 95, 122-123, 125-126, 217, 221, 232-233, 237-238, 291-292, 294, 312, 321
Al-Jirari, 'Abbas 214
Jordan xix, 147, 323
Justice and Benevolence (see also *al-'adl wa'l-ihsan*) xxix, 81, 119-121, 123, 125, 127-129, 131, 133-135, 137-139, 141, 146, 159, 167, 170, 172, 174, 194, 223, 244-245, 247, 263, 291

Kamal, Mustafa 33
Kannun, 'Abd Allah 42, 58, 66-67, 119, 165, 256, 284
al-Kattani, 'Abd al-Hayy 31
al-Kattani, 'Abd al-Kabir (Muhammad ibn 'Abd al-Kabir) 13, 80, 94, 111, 217
al-Kattani, Driss 169, 194, 216-217, 220-221, 297, 303-304, 321
al-Kattani, Hasan 218, 221, 239-240, 303-304
al-Kattani, Muhammad ibn Ja'far 216-217, 220, 303-304, 321
al-Kattani, Muhammad Ibrahim 20, 23, 217, 277, 303
Kattani (family) 14, 216-217
Kattaniyya 112, 316
Al-Kazabri, 'Umar 252
Khalid, 'Amr 251
Al-Khatib, 'Abd al-Karim 28
Khomeini 130, 162
Kuttab (see also *msid*; Qur'anic schools) 54

Laroui, Abdallah 17, 20, 274, 290, 303, 322
Le Tourneau, Roger 3, 12, 273-274, 322
League of 'Ulama of Morocco 42, 56, 217, 282, 297
Leveau, Rémy 274, 296-297, 320, 322, 327-328
Lévi-Strauss, Claude 322
Liberalization xix, xxix, 25, 58, 147, 149-150, 152, 159, 211, 256, 259, 271, 293-294, 296, 316, 323, 327
Linz, Juan J. 294, 302, 322
Lust-Okar, Ellen 271, 296, 309, 322-323

Mahdi 80, 110, 284, 289, 312
Maliki (school of law) 18-19, 33, 178, 188, 218, 225, 241, 247, 252-253, 275, 289, 311-312
Mallakh, Ahmad 97-98
Al-Mannuni, Muhammad 169
Maqasid 188, 190, 197
Maraghi, Mustafa 38
Maslaha 188-189, 197
Mauss, Marcel 118
Al-Mawdudi, Abu al-'Ala 68
Al-Mdaghri, 'Abd al-Kabir al-'Alawi 169-172, 194, 212, 214, 222, 249-250, 297
Messianism 79, 81, 110, 112, 122, 145, 289, 312
Miloudi, Zakaria 237, 239, 306
Miswak, Dr. 102
Monjib, Maati 26, 277, 293, 323
Monsonego, Aaron 214
Moulay-Idriss, Collège 86, 279
Moulay-Youssef, Collège 86, 279
Movement for the Umma 210
MPDC (Popular and Democratic Constitutional Movement) 74, 177-180, 298
Al-Mrabit, 'Ali 205
Msid (see also kuttab, Qur'anic schools) 59, 282
Mudawwana 34, 128, 181, 197, 225, 243, 245-247, 254, 312
Muhammad V, King 23-24, 37, 280
Muhammad VI, King 133-134, 181, 205, 241, 268, 303
Munson, Henry 3, 274, 291, 324
MUR (Movement of Unity and Reform) xxx, 177-181, 187-188, 191, 194-200, 203, 205, 207, 213, 217, 239, 241, 301-302, 324
Muslim Brotherhood 50, 72, 96, 111, 172
Al-Mutawakkil, 'Abd al-Wahid 134
Muti', 'Abd al-Karim 161, 167

Mysticism 70, 80-81, 87, 90-91, 93, 110, 145, 290, 317

Nabhan, Faruq 50
Nahnah, Mahfuz 172
Nasiha (see also admonition) 98, 101, 105, 110, 116, 126, 133, 220, 284, 304
Al-Nasiri, Ahmad ibn Khalid 114, 276, 290, 324
Nasiri, Makki 165, 172
Nasiriyya 17
Nasri, Zoulikha 244
Nasser (Jamal 'Abd al-Nasir) ix, 33, 46, 64, 72, 156
National Assembly of Independents 183-184
Nationalism xxvi, 3, 5-6, 15-16, 20-23, 49, 61, 63, 65-67, 69, 71, 73, 75, 85, 87, 278, 295, 317

OIC (Organization of the Islamic Conference) 63-64
Original Education (*ta'lim asli, ta'lim asil*) xxix, 35, 43, 52, 56, 199, 203, 225, 305

Pack, Darrel W. 214
Pact (transition through pacts) xx, 5, 108, 127, 131-132, 146-147, 158, 168, 178, 196, 212, 264, 289, 294
Party of Progress and Socialism 262
PDI (Parti Démocratique d'Indépendance) 14, 217
Pious Foundations (see also Habus) 33, 57, 274, 311, 313
Piscatori, James 210, 303, 318
PJD (Party of Justice and Development) xix-xx, xxii, xxv, xxx, 142, 145-146, 149-151, 153, 157, 159, 167, 172-175, 178-188, 191, 194-195, 198-207, 210, 213-214, 223, 225, 228, 237, 239-242, 244-245, 247, 260-262, 264-267, 269, 295-296, 298-299, 302, 304, 308-309, 323-324
Political society xx, 150-153, 159, 186, 201, 206-207, 209, 255-256, 265, 269, 295

PSM (Association of Muslim Participation and Spirituality) 137-138

Public Islam xii, xviii, xxi, 73, 140, 165, 256

qadi 12, 276, 312
al-Qadiri, Abu Bakr 18, 275, 324
al-Qadiri, Sidi 'Ali 88
al-Qadiri, Sidi Hamza 316
Qadiriyya 88, 286
al-Qaeda 232-239, 307
Qaradawi, Yusuf 252
Qarawiyyin, University of 36, 42, 51, 280
Qatada, Abu 238
Al-Quds Committee 64, 163
Qur'anic Schools (see also kuttab; *msid*) 53-54, 226
Qutb, Sayyid 70, 72, 74, 111, 122, 161, 273, 284, 290, 317

Ramid, Mustafa 185, 202, 205
Ramzi, Ahmad 66
Rashid, Mawlay (Sultan) 60, 307
Raysuni, Ahmad 169, 177, 181, 187-188, 196, 299-301, 307, 325
Reform and Renewal (*Islah wa tajdid*) 175-177
Reforms of religious education (modernization of education) 10, 14, 35
Religious Affairs, Ministry of xv, xxx, 29, 35, 42, 49, 58-59, 62, 64, 66-68, 72, 103, 119, 128, 140, 152, 166, 170-172, 204, 210, 216, 219-222, 234, 249-251, 254, 267, 279, 303, 308, 323
Repertoires 149-153, 187, 207, 211-212, 240, 249, 254, 256
Rida, Rashid 19, 24
Roy, Olivier xxvi, 149, 273, 294-295, 325
Royal Academy 58
Rustow, Dankwart 148, 294, 325

Sacred xiv-xv, xxix, 10, 12, 19, 21, 44,

60, 69, 76, 82, 93, 100, 116-118, 142, 145, 171, 195-196, 205, 219, 223-224, 245, 255, 274, 317
Sadi, Saïd 244
Sadiki, Collège 13
al-Sahili, 'Umar 280, 325
al-Sa'ih, Hasan 62
Sainthood (saint, saintly cult) xxiii-xxiv, xxix, 80, 83-84, 93, 104-105, 107, 109, 129-130, 287, 316, 325, 327
Salafism (*Salafiyya*) xxiii-xxvi, xxix, 6, 15-16, 17-24, 27, 44, 61-62, 112, 189, 213, 217, 224, 236, 239, 267, 276, 306, 312, 322
Salamé, Ghassan 293-295, 317, 325, 327
al-Sannusi, 'Abd Allah 17
Secularism (secular) xii-xiii, xix, xxi-xxii, 4, 10, 14, 33-34, 42, 47, 54, 57-58, 61, 124, 133, 135-136, 151, 153, 163, 165, 184, 196, 201-202, 207, 218, 226, 243, 247, 255, 266, 269-270, 274
Shabiba Islamiyya 161, 175, 197
Shari'a 27, 39, 48, 56, 63, 70-72, 75, 92, 94, 166, 188-190, 195-198, 200-202, 227, 248, 266-267, 280, 284, 299-300, 312
Sharifism xxiv, 4-5, 75, 84, 285, 312
Sharqawiyya 17
Al-Shatibi, Abu Ishaq 188, 300, 323
Shibani, 'Abd Allah 134, 291
Shraybi, 'Abd al-Hadi 14
Sidi Moumen 235-236, 306
Stepan, Alfred 294, 302, 322
Sufi brotherhoods xxiv, 15, 17, 20
Sufism xxiii-xxiv, xxvi, xxix, 17, 27, 89-90, 138, 253-254
Sulayman, Mawlay (Sultan) 17, 275-276, 283
Al-Sulaymani, Muhammad al-'Alawi 97-98
Sunna xxiv, 15, 18-20, 71, 110, 195, 219, 245, 253, 276, 292, 301, 312
Supreme Council of 'Ulama 165, 214, 216

al-Susi, Mukhtar 27, 33, 41, 85, 87, 224, 278, 280, 285

Tawfiq, Ahmad 247, 249-250
Tayyibiyya 17
Tazi, 'Abd al-Hadi 36, 58, 277, 279-280, 326
Tijaniyya 17-18
Touati, Houari 104, 288, 326
Tozy, Mohamed 97, 112, 281, 283, 286-287, 290, 293, 297, 319, 326
Transition 147, 149-150, 153, 158, 207, 243, 268, 271, 282, 294-295, 302, 317, 322, 324, 326
Tunisia 11, 13-14, 33, 45-46, 63, 156, 307, 315, 317-318

Ugati, Ben 'Abd Allah 177
'Ulama ix, xxii-xvii, xix-xx, xxiv-xxx, 1, 4, 6-7, 9-25, 27-43, 45-46, 49-67, 69-70, 72, 75, 85, 87, 91, 93-96, 102, 105-107, 111-114, 118, 121, 131, 133, 140, 153, 163-166, 168-172, 178, 184, 192-194, 198, 203, 209-210, 212-224, 227-228, 234, 236, 241, 243, 245-246, 248, 250-252, 255-256, 266-267, 271-272, 274, 276, 278-279, 281-282, 284, 293, 296-297, 304, 308, 312-313, 317, 326-327
UNEM (National Union of Moroccan Students) 162, 170
UNFP (National Union of Popular Forces) 14, 25, 44-45, 161-162, 277
UOIF (Union of Islamic Organizations of France) 138
USFP (Socialist Union of Popular Forces) 174, 180-184, 241, 245, 262, 296, 309
'Uthmani, Sa'd al-Din 178, 184, 203, 206, 299, 302-303

Wahhabism 15, 18, 236, 238, 241, 252, 275, 306
Waterbury, John 10, 80, 156, 274, 278, 281, 284, 294-295, 326
al-Wazzani, Muhammad Hasan 14, 217
World Muslim League 63

Yassine, Abdessalam ix, xix, xxix, 56, 67, 75, 77, 79-80, 82, 84-85, 87, 97, 129, 145, 159, 162, 172, 189, 210, 217, 249, 256, 284-286, 290, 293, 296, 315, 327
Yassine, Nadia xxix, 127, 129, 134-135, 137, 245, 285-287, 291, 293, 327
Yessef, Muhammad 214
Youssoufi, Abderrahman 157, 180, 244-245
al-Yusi, Hasan 80, 113, 116, 287, 291, 327
Yusif, Mawlay (Sultan) 18
Yusufiyya 85-87, 278, 285-286

Zaman, Muhammad Qasim xxviii, 271-272, 318, 320, 327-328
Zamzami, 'Abd al-Bari 239
Al-Zawahiri, Ayman 233, 307
zawiya 18, 21, 88, 93, 116, 119, 126, 130, 137, 313
Zaytuna, University of 13, 45-46, 275, 326

ABOUT THE AUTHOR AND TRANSLATOR

Malika Zeghal is Associate Professor of the Anthropology and Sociology of Religion at the University of Chicago's Divinity School. She is a political scientist who studies religion through the lens of Islam and power. She is particularly interested in the institutionalization of Islam in the Muslim world, focusing principally on Egypt and North Africa in the postcolonial period and on the Muslim diaspora in North America and Western Europe. Her more general interests encompass the circulation and role of religious ideologies in situations of conflict and/or dialogue.

Professor Zeghal has published a study of central religious institutions in Egypt (*Gardiens de l'islam. Les oulémas d'al-Azhar dans l'Egypte contemporaine* (Paris: Presses de Sciences Po, 1996); a special issue of the French review *Archives des Sciences Sociales des Religions*: *Autorités religieuses en Islam* (125, 2004); and a special issue of the *Revue des Mondes Musulmans et de la Méditerranée*: *Intellectuels de l'islam contemporain, Nouvelles générations, nouveaux débats* (123, 2008). She is now working on a book about the state and Islam in the contemporary Arab world, forthcoming from Princeton University Press.

George Holoch has translated more than twenty books: works of philosophy, history, biography, and current affairs, including books by Bernard-Henri Lévy and Jean Lacouture. His most recent translations are of *Secularism Confronts Islam* by Olivier Roy and *Notes on the Occupation: Palestinian Lives* by Eric Hazan. He lives in Hinesburg, Vermont.